Aikido in Japan

and The Way Less Traveled

Aikido in Japan and the Way Less Traveled

W. T. Gillespie

© Copyright 2014 Budoka Books

San Mateo, California

Contact books@budokabooks.com

See www.aikidoinjapan.com

First Edition

ISBN: 978-0-615-95014-3

Printed in the United States of America

Aikido in Japan

and The Way Less Traveled

by W. T. Gillespie

Published by Budoka Books

2014 California

Dedication

To my father and mother, who were my first teachers, and to all the other good teachers, martial arts or otherwise, who have pointed the way. Most of all, to my loving and cherished wife, Angela, whose spirit shines with a spark that brightens all around her.

Special Gratitude

Thank you to all the amazing people I met and friends I made in Japan and elsewhere in Asia, who have made and continue to make my life adventure so rewarding. God bless and Godspeed on your own journeys.

Many thanks to the team of initial editors: Angela Im, Ryo Takagi and Jim Christensen, plus part of the Tokyo Canadian mafia: Ben Peacock, Stuart Ablett and Wesley Peasely. Each one really helped improve the manuscript in meaningful ways. And deep appreciation to Steve Earle, a student in my dojo in Beijing, who lived sixteen years in Japan and had his first aikido class in 1970, but still took the time to read my manuscript and provide feedback despite his busy schedule as the head of a Japanese company in China.

And to my professional publishing team: patient copy editor Valerie Valentine in Wisconsin, my rescue book designer at Unauthorized Media in Los Angles and the creative team at Whale Shark in Serbia (of all places) who brought my cover concept to life.

And praise on high for all those Americanos at Costa Coffee and Starbucks in Wangjing (Korea Town of Beijing) and Gail's and Café Mio in London. Java makes a great Muse.

Contents

Prologue 序章 (*Joshou*)

Winter 冬 (*Fuyu*)

Spring 春 (*Haru*)

Summer 夏 (*Natsu*)

Autumn 秋 (*Aki*)

Epilogue 跋 (*Batsu*)

Prologue

"Security is mostly a superstition. It does not exist in nature,
nor do the children of men as a whole experience it.
Avoiding danger is no safer in the long run than outright exposure.

Life is either a daring adventure, or nothing."

—*Helen Keller (1880 - 1968)*
Author, political activist, and lecturer.
First deaf and blind person to earn a Bachelor of Arts degree

The Way Less Traveled

兵法 は 術 に 非ず, して道 なり
(Heihou wa jutsu ni arazu, shite michi nari)
—*Martial arts is a Way, not a technique*

By the start of 1997, I had resigned from a developing professional career as a trial attorney in Los Angeles, leaving too my position as a *deshi* (弟子, でし, disciple) and assistant instructor in my home *dojo* (道場, どうじょう, training place), had given-up a nice car, new motorcycle, good home and all the enviable benefits and considerable comforts of life in Southern California.[1] My worldly possessions, such as they were, sat in: the storage space I had rented in L.A., the hold of a ship crossing the Pacific, or in the baggage compartment of the 747 I was seated in jetting to Japan. I was actually living a dream that I'd had for many years. I was moving to Tokyo for a year of intensive study of aikido at the Aikikai World Head-quarters.[2]

Japanese I met later while living in Tokyo were baffled that I had left sunny Santa Monica to study *budo* (武道, ぶどう, martial arts or ways) in Japan. "You left where for what? *Hen na gaijin!*"[3] I'll admit that I've got to be one of the few people (dumb enough or smart enough, you choose) to trade about 250,000 USD a year in 1997 and the California beach for a Japanese flat (single six-mat *tatami* room, sliding paper doors, small kitchen and tiny bathroom/tub/shower) and a hard year of daily aikido training, six days a week, three, four, and even five times a day. What started off

---

1   Except for commonly known words, proper and place names, Japanese words in the book are *italicized* and I've often included both *kanji* and *hiragana* or *katakana* for them. The names of Japanese people are printed family name and then personal name in the style used in Japan and some other East Asian countries.

2   It seems these days that saying "I practice aikido" is akin to saying "I'm a Muslim" or "I'm a Christian" or "I'm a Jew." There's an ill-informed, unfair stereotype and then there's the truth. In each case, the statement could have as many meanings as there are actual human living expressions of the particular word. For me, aikido is *budo*, a martial way, first and foremost.

3   *Hen na gaijin* (変な外人; へんな がいじん) translates as "strange foreigner," an expression you may hear once or twice (whispered behind your back or to your face) if you live in Japan.

as a year sabbatical to study intensively, while living simply and essentially, turned into eight fantastic years in Japan and a sixteen-year-long life-changing, enriching adventure in East Asia that is still unfolding.

This book is intended to encourage other *aikidoka* to visit Japan and train at the Aikikai World Headquarters ("*Hombu Dojo*", 本部道場、ほんぶどうじょう, headquarters dojo) in Wakamatsu-cho.[4] I would say, "the" Aikido World Headquarters, but some might find that upsetting. Indeed, there are many sub or splinter groups or so-called "styles" of aikido. However, the Aikikai Hombu Dojo is what it is: the largest center of aikido in the world, created under the auspices of the founder of aikido, Ueshiba Morihei, and under the direction of his son, Ueshiba Kishomaru, and now by his grandson, the current Doshu, Ueshiba Moriteru.[5][6] If you disagree, feel free to write your own book. As the old bad joke goes, "How many *aikidoka* does it take to replace a light bulb? One, and all the rest to tell you how O-Sensei did it."

There are many excellent aikido teachers around the world—both Japanese and non-Japanese. However, aikido, its techniques, philosophy and traditional method of instruction and training originate from Japan. Obviously. In my view, as part of an effort to understand the art more deeply and better develop themselves physically, mentally and spiritually, serious *aikidoka* should live in Japan and train at Hombu Dojo, particularly if you aspire to become an instructor. I am convinced of this for a number of reasons, some of which this book endeavors to touch upon. However, my fundamental intention is to convey my perceptions and experiences of what it was like to be a student there, particularly that first year in 1997 when (by design) I had no job and was focused singularly on training multiple times a day, each and every day, for an entire year.[7]

The book follows the Hombu Dojo calendar year, its annual events, and the four seasons in the order and way that I experienced them after arriving in Japan in

---

[4] See www.aikikai.or.jp.

[5] *Dōshu* (道主, どうしゆ), means leader or master of the way.

[6] In 1940, second Doshu Kisshomaru Ueshiba, the son of O-Sensei Morihei Ueshiba established The Aikikai Foundation (財団法人合気会, *Zaidan Hōjin Aikikai*). The headquarters of the organization is located in the Aikikai Hombu Dojo (合気会本部道場) in Wakamatsu-cho area of Shinjuku-ward, Tokyo. Built in 1967, it replaced the original wooden structure of the dōjō founded by O-Sensei in 1931 under the name *Kobukan* (皇武館, imperial war-skills hall).

[7] Actually, it lasted longer than one year in the end.

winter: *Fuyu, Haru, Natsu, Aki*.[8] However, by no means is it a complete portrayal of Hombu Dojo, or my adventure in Japan. It only gives flickering glimpses, like the view from the window of a speeding bullet train. And, I claim no special expertise in aikido, Hombu Dojo or Japanese language, history, or culture. My fundamental intention isn't to advise you about what you should or shouldn't do or how you should or shouldn't do it (with a few exceptions) if you go to Hombu Dojo.[9] So be forewarned that this book is *not* a travel guide about how to go to Japan to train at Hombu Dojo or what to do when you get there. Unlike 1997 and before, you all have the Internet now as a plentiful resource, and there are useful blogs and other websites covering the topic. A guidebook would become increasingly obsolete from the day it was finished. Plus, to me, a website isn't the right medium to convey a cohesive narrative. A hardcopy or e-book, you can carry with you. This book aims to speak to "why to" rather than "how to" go to Japan, though inescapably there's a bit of what you might do and how you might do it.

Oh; and it's heavily footnoted because some folks like minute details and supporting references. Plus I didn't want to break the flow, whenever I included something oblique but which might be interesting, amusing, or instructive to some readers. My intention is that you don't have to read the "footies" to enjoy the book. So if you find them tedious, skip 'em![10] Likewise, my thought is that each chapter may be enjoyed independent of the linking storyline. Pick it up and put it down as you like.

It's also not the kind of book that endlessly regales the training experience at Hombu Dojo. How can you convey that in words sufficiently? "How was training?" "Really hard. My partner was so tough." It's experiential not conceptual. Go try it! And, the book is not limited to aikido, my experiences on the mats or otherwise at the dojo, but recounts many of the warm, wonderful and wacky aspects of life in Japan, which may affect your life training there, plus a few tales of my travels in East Asia since I had to leave Japan periodically to renew my visa.

---

8 Winter 冬, spring 春, summer 夏, fall 秋. The four seasons (or six if you include the two "rainy seasons") significantly affect life in Tokyo and training at the dojo. In Japanese, four seasons is *Shiki* (四季, しき) or *Shyunkashyuutou* (春夏秋冬, しゅんかしゅうとう).

9 It's not a technical book either. To the extent I've learned anything in going on thirty years studying aikido, I'll keep it to myself, maybe discuss with teachers, a few friends or share with some students. I'm disinclined to get on YouTube and say, in effect, "Gee, look what I know (or don't)." My advice is, steal what you can from whoever you can. Find your own way.

10 But if you read them, you might discover some gems.

Most of all, it's about pursuing your dream. Life is short; make it an adventure. My hope is to inspire you to "seize the day" and visit Hombu Dojo or even move to Japan to study aikido, or to pursue whatever other dream you may have in life. "Whatever you can do or dream you can, begin it. Boldness has genius, power and magic in it!"[11] Hopefully, this simple book will ignite some small spark towards helping you make that decision and, once made, will help prepare you in some modest way for your own adventure, or at least entertain you before you get there. As the Japanese proverb goes, "*suru no ha shippai nani mo shinai no ha daishippai*" (するのは失敗何もしないのは大失敗 doing is a mistake, not doing is a big mistake).

Many people could have and probably should have written this book instead of me.[12] Certainly, many are more qualified, but I have chosen to do so, out of respect and regard for Aikikai Hombu Dojo and for all foreign students of aikido who, as I did, desire to go to Japan to train. And, I did not want to forget my adventure! All of this really happened. Years ago now, I chose "the [Way] less traveled by" and indeed it has made all the difference.[13] Not only in my aikido but in my life.

---

[11] So read the quotation in the note sent to me by an extraordinary and now lost acquaintance, Ira Goldberg, a 6'-8" tall African-American adopted by Jewish Americans (yes only in America), while I was deliberating whether or not to go to Japan. The popular quote attributed to the German novelist, poet, playwright and scientist Johann Wolfgang von Goethe is actually a misquotation of a passage from Goethe's *Faust*. It's apparently attributable to the Scottish mountaineer W. H. Murray who may have been borrowing from "a very free translation" of Goethe's work. See http://german.about.com/library/blgermyth12.htm.

[12] As they read this, all my friends from Hombu Dojo (both of them) are nodding their heads in agreement.

[13] "... Two roads diverged in a wood, and I – I took the one less traveled by, And that has made all the difference." Frost's classic poem *The Road Not Taken* remains so memorable because of its simplicity, imagery and wisdom. Robert Frost's (1874–1963) *Mountain Interval*, 1920.

River 2.0

My Hombu Dojo,
Your Hombu Dojo

We've all heard the expression, "You cannot step in the same river twice." Flowing, flooding, receding, it's never really the same from moment to moment. So it is with Hombu Dojo.

The Hombu Dojo that I trained in no longer exists. Sure, the building is there, though it was retrofitted years later to comply with new building code, bringing modest heat/air in the men's locker room and other "improvements." (Thankfully it still only has cold showers.) Much of the dojo remains the same, but much of it has fundamentally changed and will continue to change. Greek philosopher Heraclitus of Ephesus was right when he wrote, "You could not step twice into the same river; for other waters are ever flowing on to you."[14]

I moved to Japan in the winter of 1997. As it had been since its founding in 1955, the Liberal Democratic Party (自由民主党, *Jiyū-Minshutō*) was in power. Ryūtarō Hashimoto was serving as the 83rd Prime Minister of Japan. William Jefferson Clinton was the 42nd President of the United States. The People's Republic of China (PRC) was waiting for Britain to relinquish rule of Hong Kong. Al-Qaeda and Osama Bin Laden were not yet household names. Scottish scientists had just cloned the first mammal, "Dolly" the sheep. The Internet was in its infancy, commercially. My new Toshiba Satellite Pro laptop seemed technologically slick but it was nearly as thick and heavy as two bricks duct-taped

---

[14] Author of the intentionally cryptic 5th century BC cosmological, political and theological work *On Nature*, Heraclitus "the Riddler" or "the Obscure" was born circa 500 BC in the great Ionian Greek city of Ephesus (Ἔφεσος) on the west coast of of Asia Minor (present-day Turkey). Heraclitus believed in a single element—fire—and in eternal change—'everything flows'—describing his doctrine of flux in terms of a flowing river ever renewing its waters. Somewhat similar to yin and yang, Heraclitus saw unity in opposites. There could be no day without night, no good without evil, no hot without cold. "It is wise to agree that all things are one. In differing it agrees with itself, a backward-turning connection, like that of a bow and a lyre. The path up and down is one the same." www.trincoll.edu/depts/phil/philo/phils/heraclitus.html

together. Globalization was barely underway and would not become a main-stream topic in Japan until about 1999 when Citibank arrived like a "black ship," bringing twenty-four-hour banking and a host of other innovations to custom-ers.[15] Before that fleet arrived, you could not use a foreign bank card in a Japanese bank's automated teller machine (still can't in many cases) and there were no foreign bank ATMs. When I wanted cash, I had to go down to the local Visa Card shop at the south exit of Shinjuku station and get a cash ad-vance—in front of a gaggle of giggling pink-suited office ladies—to fund each month's rent and activities. By 2000, the "Internet Tsunami" would make ven-ture capital mainstream in Japan. [16] Japanese cellphones were a fraction of the size of their foreign counterparts and had cameras! Oooooh.

In 1997, Ueshiba Kisshomaru sensei was *doshu*. Current *doshu*, Ueshiba Moriteru, would conduct the warm-up for most morning classes and then Kisshomaru sensei would teach it. Tada sensei, Arikawa sensei, Ichihashi sensei, Watanabe sensei and Endo sensei were all still on the weekly teaching schedule. Current core teachers at the dojo were "young" teachers then and were often training in the same classes with us. There was a genuine opportunity to prac-tice with them, which was daunting. Many of the current younger teachers were either *deshi* in 1997 or had just moved out of the dojo. You could train with them weekly, if not daily.

Given the continuous inflow and outflow of foreign students, the stu-dent body of Hombu Dojo is understandably not the same now. The students I trained with are obviously older; many have returned home. One Japanese friend had started aikido when he was eight (he's forty-nine now) and Koichi Tohei was his children's class teacher at Hombu Dojo. A close disciple of Arikawa sensei, he has started his own *budo ryu-ha*.[17] The global Mixed Martial Arts movement was in its infancy and had yet to instigate its notable talent drain (for worse, in my view) on traditional martial arts, including aikido. When I moved to Japan, there were still a lot of athletic people studying aikido. One close friend was rumored to have played First Division rugby in his homeland and trained to box pro-fessionally before taking up aikido. He remains the single strongest fellow

---

15 See *Commodore Perry and the Opening of Japan*. U.S. Navy Museum   www.his-tory.navy.mil/branches/teach/ends/opening.htm

16 A suitable metaphor in 2000 rendered inappropriate by the 2011 tsunami tragedy.

17 *Ryūha* (流派, りゅうは) means systems or school.

student I have encountered on the mat—both in physique and technique. Aikido is no different than any other undertaking. There is no substitute for talent, assuming the talented work just as hard as the less talented. This guy had worked at it.

However, the Hombu Dojo my *senpai* experienced was not the same as the one I came to in 1997, nor the one I had visited in 1994 nor in 1992. As Heraclitus liked to point out some 500 years before Christ, and as Japanese culture accepts if not celebrates, transience is the inescapable nature of life, *mujo*, (無常, むじょう, impermanence); nothing is complete, nothing in this world is perfect and nothing lasts. Of course, people are ever prone to say that about anything: "It's not like back in the day!" My father, a former U.S. Marine Corps rifleman, joked: America, 10 November 1775, a soldier carrying a rifle steps onto the deck of a Continental Navy ship and the Captain asks him, "Who are you?" "I am a U.S. Marine, sir!" "What's a Marine?" asks the Captain. "The fighting man of the Navy, sir!" "Alright, permission to come aboard; stand over there, Marine," replies the Captain. Five minutes later, a second guy with a rifle steps on deck. Same questions; same answers. "Alright ... over there" (with the first Marine). As he joins the first Marine, the first looks at the second and says, "You should've been in the old Corps."

Look closely enough and you will see strong connecting threads through the years, the emphasis on *kihon waza* being at the core of Hombu Dojo practice. Basics, basics, basics.

> In these teachings listen most
> To the rhythm of the strike and thrust
> To train in the basics (*omote*)
> Is to practice the very secrets of the art.
> —Ueshiba Morihei[18]

This is preached daily, starting with the *Doshu's asageiko* – The Morning Class. However, in many ways the Hombu Dojo you experience when

---

[18]   To the extent, I may quote translations of words attributed to O-Sensei, his *Doka*, I am aware that people may have differences of opinion as to the source of these sayings. Of course, O-Sensei's words were not often recorded and, by all reports, he often spoke obliquely about Aiki. The verifiable evidentiary sources may be few and perhaps even disputed. Still, I believe many of the sayings (regardless of source) have great wisdom. It's notable too that while I didn't go about tape recording or transcribing my first teacher, I can recall verbatim a number of the things he said over the years.

you visit will not be the same one I did. It cannot possibly be the same. This is true for me, too, whenever I return. Since I left Japan, I have continued to visit Tokyo regularly—anywhere from two to five times a year—but the dojo is ever changing and so am I. Hopefully, you will realize and appreciate that you will experience Hombu Dojo in your own way and enjoy it for what it is for you at the time of your particular visit—stepping "into the river" at that moment.[19]

---

[19] In visiting for a few days, a week, even a month, you cannot possible understand or evaluate Hombu Dojo. Your experience will depend on who is teaching, who is there when you are there, who you train with and so on. And, some people just don't like new experiences. They cling to the familiar for a sense of security, ignoring the inescapable reality that life is imperma-nent.

Hombu Dojo Facts

You may know it as the "Aikikai Foundation" but in 1940, under the direction of his father, Doshu Kisshomaru Ueshiba founded the *Zaidan Hojin Aikikai* (財団法人合気会, ざいだんほうじんあいきかい) as an organization to promote and otherwise administer the art of aikido.[20] In 1967 the Aikikai Foundation built (next door to the Ueshiba family residence) a new headquarters and the present Hombu Dojo on the site of the dojo that O-Sensei established in 1931, which Doshu had overseen since O-Sensei relocated from war-ravaged Tokyo to the Iwama country-side in 1942.

Located on a narrow quiet residential street adjacent to the *Nuke Ben-ten* shrine in Wakamatsu-cho, a far larger five-story concrete building has replaced the previous wooden one. It houses the foundation's offices and three dojos with a total of 220 tatami mats and is colloquially referred to as the Hombu Dojo.[21] The second floor dojo (floors by American, rather than British reckoning) has seventy-two tatami (112 square meters) and is used principally for beginners and children's classes but holds some weekly special classes for women or particular shihan, e.g., Yokota sensei's. The main dojo is on the third floor, has 105 tatami (about 162 square meters) and holds the daily "open" classes, plus university and other classes. The fourth floor dojo has forty-two tatami (approx. sixty-five square meters) and is used for the Aikido Academy, personal practice by teachers and other special or private classes.[22] According to the Aikikai website,

---

[20] For any legal-geeks reading, a *zaidan houjin* (財団法人, ざいだんほうじん) is an incorporated foundation and has juristic personage under Japanese law. It has rights and remedies at law like a natural
person or other juristic persons, e.g., *kabushiki-kaisha* (large stock company) etc. Establishing one is
not an easy task (as is the case for most legal entities under Japanese law) nowadays let alone back in
1940. The fact that the Ueshiba family chose to do so shows long term vision and reveals the power
of the family and its supporters. (It's not just a matter of filling out the paperwork.) While Japanese
law pre-Meiji was influenced by Chinese and Korean law, that tradition (along with other Japanese
expressions of "Chinese learning") was overwritten when the country opted to join the "modern"
world. The source of inspiration for Japanese law became French and German law. A common joke
among Western lawyers about Japanese law was that it's German law translated into Japanese by a
Frenchman. In fairness, Japanese law is deeply grounded in the Civil Law tradition (European style
codes) but more recently has been influenced by the Common Law tradition (e.g., Britain and the U.S.)
in some respects, e.g., the recent establishment of U.S. style law schools.

[21] Each tatami is made of straw and covered with a canvas cloth that is stitched to it tightly.

[22] Sneaking up there once to do some *suburi* (there's a massive suburito), I was caught by a shihan, as I
was finishing and leaving, who was coming up (blade in hand) to practice *iaido*.

the teaching staff, including Doshu and his son, consists of thirty-two instructors locally and twenty-one instructors overseas.

Training Tips
- The Seven Simple Ones -

"I train every day of my life as they have never trained a day in theirs."
—*Aleksander Karelin, Russian super-heavyweight Greco-Roman wrestling*
Olympian and World Champion, who went undefeated in international competition
from 1987 to 2000, the last six years of which he never gave up a point.

So you are in Japan and you want to maximize your training experience? Here are a few suggestions. If you are an experienced visitor, you will already know your own way.

1. Buy traveler's health insurance before you leave, if you don't have it already. If you get seriously injured or very ill, you want OUT of Japan ASAP. While aspects of care are good and access to care is laudable, you absolutely do not want to go to the hospital in Japan (unless you are coming from an undeveloped country) in complex emergency circumstances. In such cases, Japanese hospitals can be dangerous in my personal experience, particularly since dealing with foreigners adds another level of complexity.

2. If you are not particularly fit and experienced, be extra careful how much you train at the start of your visit.

    •   Flying dehydrates you, so does drinking alcohol, and the winter in Japan is very dry and the summer is hot, humid and enervating. A friend flying the other way for a U.S. summer camp one year nearly died of kidney failure. He had flown, boozed, slept little, failed to rehydrate and then practiced a lot. Be smart. Be safe.
    •   For all but a few visitors, the pace of practice will be faster than you are accustomed to back home, for various reasons, including that the surroundings are unfamiliar to you.
    •   The tatami mats are very hard and canvas covered, which

will no doubt test your knees and otherwise inflict various burns, bumps and bruises when you arrive. Tough it out and your body will grow accustomed to it, but be sensible to avoid having your knees swell up like melons and ruin your stay.

- Bring supplies with you that may be useful for addressing common injuries: analgesics, athletic tape, antibiotic cream, powder for heat rash, etc. You won't know where or what to buy in Japan (though it's easier these days).

- If you are ill or injured, do not come or, if it happens after you arrive, do not practice. One "American Idiot" came with a huge group on a tour led by a well-known teacher. Apparently, the student suffered from an undetermined condition, which would periodically render him very sick, e.g., fevers, vomiting, etc. It had flared up shortly be-fore he left California but he told no one about it because he really wanted to come to Japan. He arrived in Japan, became gravely ill, was hospitalized and then my Hombu-mates and I watched over him in the hospital in Tokyo so the rest of the visiting group could complete their tour. The guy was terrified of the Japanese hospital and the doctors seemed clueless as to what was wrong. They put him on an IV-drip while he rested and slowly recovered. Thankfully, He was lucky to make it home alive. Don't be dumb. If you are sick, don't come. Wait until you are healthy.

3. Go to "morning class" at 06:30. Doshu's class. It's part of your forging experience. Pay your respects.

4. If you are a beginner or unsure of your *ukemi*, start with class on the second floor at 07:00.[23]

5. Sample a variety of classes and teachers. Open your mind. Are you so skilled and knowledgeable that you cannot learn something from every one of the teachers at Hombu Dojo?

---

[23] Many of you know, *ukemi* (受身, うけみ) is the art of receiving the technique safely. (Rolling or falling when thrown or safely stretching the joints on joint locks.) Actually, the word has several meanings, but in aikido it is used this way.

6. On the third floor, a good rule of thumb for finding a partner used to be that at the start of class, the "serious minded" or perhaps more vigorous students tended to sit on the right-hand side of the back of the dojo (by the schedule and locker-key board near the back window). For example, this is where the *deshi* sat when attending class. Why? So the teacher knows where they can find one if they need one, and they are near the entry/exit doors. If you sat in that area back in the day, your odds of getting crunched by someone increased substantially. Perhaps it's changed. That said, there are many *very* experienced people who sit on the left but they are perhaps more "rounded" and complete as *aikidoka* and not interested in pounding someone into dust.

7. If you are living there and want to train often, find a flat that is near the dojo and set up a work schedule so that you can actually train. I have met many people who moved to Tokyo "for aikido" but then they hardly ever showed up at the dojo. They either lived too far away, were working too much, or both.

Mr. Japan

ミスター ジャパン

In writing this book, I make no claim of expertise regarding Japan, aikido or Hombu Dojo. I am merely recounting my personal experiences and observations during my "sabbatical year" in Tokyo, and since.[24] I have now lived, worked and traveled in East Asia for over seventeen years, but if there is anything that I know for certain about East Asian culture, history and sociology, it's that I know very little about it—a drop in a fathomless pool.[25]

A friend of mine from Australia (a longtime Tokyo resident) used to deride foreigners we met in Tokyo who thought they knew it all about Japan. Typically, they just couldn't wait to show (and tell) you what they knew. "Mr. Japan" he dubbed them in his Queensland Aussie accent. A Mr. Japan always seemed to share his knowledge a little bit too early and too freely, plus their Japanese was almost too good or more likely too affected, e.g., *"eh; ma, so desu ne"* (yes; um, yes it is), aping vernacular speech—complete with practiced local facial expressions and hand gestures—that they had picked up while eavesdropping on the conversations of inebriated salarymen. Particularly comical ones sounded like exaggerated imitations of characters in the annual NHK samurai drama, complete with grunting, guttural gruff speech or stiffly crossing their arms and sucking air through their teeth in disapproval of something they have just heard.[26]

---

[24] The concept of a sabbatical is biblical (see, e.g., the creation story of Genesis or Leviticus 25 and the commandment to stop in the seventh year). The word is derived from Latin *sabbaticus*, which is from the Greek *sabbatikos*, which is from the Hebrew *shabbat*, akin to Sabbath, literally, a "ceasing." It's come to describe a lengthy cessation of work or career (particularly in academia) in order to pursue a course of study, writing, research and the like. Progressive Western companies have instituted career break policies whereby employees can take a periodic extended break on reduced pay.

[25] Eight years in Japan, seven in China and I've probably been to Korea 50-60 times to see the in-laws or my wife when she was a student at Ewha Womans University. www.ewha.ac.kr/kor/index.jsp

[26] You can't help but pick up some local mannerisms in order to communicate effectively. For example, an American when referring to himself in conversation will use a hand and a thumb

It was always "Mr. Japan," because we never met a Miss, Ms. or Mrs. Japan (though we all probably dreamed of meeting "Miss Japan"). Perhaps men are more inclined to be braggarts? Maybe it's because, being a foreigner in Japan, one can become deluded into considering oneself as "special" due to the attention bestowed on foreigners (some good, some not). There was a satirical comic in one of the local magazines that was titled "Charisma Man." In it, the main character, Charisma Man, was depicted as a big blond stud whenever a Japanese girl was present. However, when his arch enemy Gaijin Woman appeared, he would lose his superpowers and be revealed for what he really was ... a weedy little spotty-faced white guy.[27]

No doubt the linguistic skills of a Mr. Japan often were remarkably good, ペラペラ (*pera pera*) as the locals say, but (apparently having missed the cultural lesson on modesty and humility) their showiness was ベラベラ (*bera bera*). What in the name of Zeus' butt and all Olympus is that, you ask? Well, one of the amusing and highly expressive things about Japanese language are the many onomatopoeic (sound symbolic) or mimetic words: *giseigo* (擬声語, ぎせいご), *giongo* (擬音語, ぎおんご), *gitaigo* (擬態語, ぎたいご) and *gijogo* (擬情語, ぎじょうご) that are used in daily speech. English and most other languages have such words, but sound symbolic words occur more frequently in Japanese, being used in both formal and ordinary speech.[28] According to the wordsmiths, *giseigo* and *giongo* are phonomime or onomatopoeia. They mimic actual sounds, like "bang," "whoosh," "zip," and "zoom" in English. *Giseigo* concern sounds made by living things, like the sound people make when they skip 6:30 a.m. practice ぐうぐう (guu guu, fast asleep and snoring). *Giongo* concern sounds made by inanimate objects, like the sound of thunder during a lightning storm in rainy season ざわざわ (*zawa zawa*, rumbling). *Gitaigo* are phenomime: mimetic words concerning the senses other than hearing, like your skin itching from heat rash following three practices in

---

to point towards his own chest. "You talking to me?" A Japanese will use his index finger to point towards his own nose. "Me?"

27   "Charisma Man first appeared in the February 1998 issue of the 'The Alien' magazine, and immediately catapulted into legendary-status among readers in Japan's expat/Gaijin world." See www.charismaman.com.

28   I've often heard *shihan* using them to describe things.

August in 38.5C heat and 85% humidity, むずむず (*muzu muzu*, small itches like tiny bugs crawling on your skin). *Gijōgo* are psychomime, which are apparently mimetic words concerning bodily feelings or psychological states, like your knees first getting used to the hard tatami mats at Hombu ひりひり (*hiri hiri*, smarting). These words are highly expressive and can be great fun.[29] *Pera pera* means to do something smoothy and skilfully, particularly speaking a language. In other words, their Japanese is really good. *Bera bera* can mean to talk, talk, talk ... too much ... nonstop. In other words, they cannot stop showing you how good their Japanese is.

Perhaps the American aikido-specific counterpart to the "Mr. Japan" is what an old acquaintance (and *budo-otaku* or "martial arts geek," aikido, judo, kendo, etc.) had called the "Sammy Samurai." In other words, people doing aikido (or whatever Japanese martial art) and thinking they are the embodiment of *Bushido*. Don't get me wrong, the "warrior's way" is highly admirable, but taken to some of the extremes one sees, it's akin to Japanese people dressing up as Cowboys and Indians ... "Yokamoto U.S. Marsharr." Me hav'em heap-big Aiki-powwow.

Funny thing is that after living in East Asia for so long and speaking bits of various languages at various levels of proficiency (including English), my English can easily slip into sounding like a stereotype of a Native American in a bad Western, dropping articles all the way. "Night-time, we go bar, drink beer, look girls, have fun, okay?"

Anyway, I digress and drone. Oh shit. I'm a Mr. Japan!!!

---

[29] Online resources include: http://home.alc.co.jp/db/owa/s_kaydic?ctg_in=4&char_in=adic-tionary or www.nihongoresources.com/dictionaries/onomatopoeia.html

Some Sound Vocab for Aikidoka

どんどん, *don don*, drumming (noise) or (doing something) rapidly, steadily, e.g., two atemi in quick succession from say ... Miyamoto sensei.

ゴロゴロ, *goro goro*, summer thunder or your stomach grumbling after practicing 06:30 and 08:00. Or the sound of something large and heavy starting to roll, like my 130 kilo pal on *kokyu-nage*.

よぼよぼ, *yobo yobo*, your unsteady, tottering legs after five hours of practice, too many years on the planet (old age or infirmity), or both.

ぼちぼち, *bochi bochi*, how you improve in aikido: little by little, gradually; or how you should feel about your aikido in order to keep improving: not bad; passable; so-so.

ばらばら, *bara bara*, your technique if you break it into "steps:" disconnected; bits and pieces.

うつらうつら, *utsura utsura*, your consciousness in Morning Class if you are out on the town the night before, drifting between sleep and wakefulness.

びっしょり, *bisshori*, everything you do or own during rainy season: soaked.

あっぷあっぷ, *appu appu*, struggling speaking Japanese (or doing anything) upon arrival.

うずうず, *uzu uzu*, itching (aching) to do your first practice at Hombu Dojo.

おろおろ, *oro oro*, your first few months in Japan, confused, flustered and not knowing what to do.

かちかち, *kachi kachi*, the sound of two stiff *aikidoka* colliding, someone or something rigid in mentality or physicality. Tense.

がぶがぶ, *gabu gabu,* that first frosty draft beer after Friday night practice, gulp-gulp, glug-glug.

くたくた, *kuta kuta,* your body after practice in July, 90+ degrees and 90+ humidity, exhausted, withered.

ころころ, *koro koro,* the sound of my diminutive *deshi* pal taking *ukemi,* rolling like a spider (any small light object).

さむざむ, *samu zamu,* the 05:30 walk to Morning Class in February: cold, bleak, wintery.

すらすら, *sura sura,* a Hombu shihan doing aikido, smoothly, effortlessly.

うろうろ, *uro uro,* you underground in Shinjuku station searching for the way you came in, wandering about (or hanging around).

ぬくぬく, *nuku nuku,* climbing back into your futon after 06:30 and 08:00 classes: snug, cozy.

めきめき, *meki meki,* your aikido with Morning Class as the foundation: rapid progress.

ひやひや, *hiya hiya,* taking *ukemi* for Arikawa sensei: scared, terrified.

Your Worst
Foot Forward

土足のまま上がる
(*Dosoku no mama agaru*)

One of the most common cultural gaffes by foreigners unfamiliar with Japanese culture is wearing their shoes into tatami rooms. One enters sock-footed, of course. This blunder is right up at the top of the list with failing to rinse off the soap before getting into the *onsen* (hot spring bath), but it happens often enough that the phrase "entering with your shoes on" (土足のまま上がる, *dosoku no mama agaru*) has taken on a broader cultural meaning and is used to describe all sorts of screw-ups in business and other interactions between foreigners and Japanese that occur largely due to a lack of effort or mindfulness to understand Japanese ways. Being aware of it, try to put your best foot forward rather than your worst when you visit Hombu Dojo. If not, you may still leave an impression but could end up being remembered for all the wrong reasons.

Many years ago, shortly after I began aikido in Los Angeles' Little Tokyo, a fellow student with a particularly warped sense of humor confessed that during his first Buddhist memorial service at the dojo, he feared he would walk up to the *tokonoma* (床の間, とこのま), bow in respect, reach for the pinch of incense offered for the deceased, trip, fall forward into the altar onto the candles and set himself ablaze. He could picture the report on the lead-in to the nightly TV news: "This just in. Human Torch at memorial service; film at 11:00." He would forever be remembered as "that guy." "Hey, remember *that guy* who set himself on fire?" "At the memorial service?" "Yeah; whatever happened to *that guy*?"

On occasion "that guy" visits Hombu Dojo, i.e., students who come to the dojo and make a name for themselves, though perhaps not the name they were hoping for. Behaving foolishly, they become part of the lore of strange foreigners. While I was there, we had the likes of:

"Baby Huey" – nicknamed after an annoying cartoon character, this massive Australian black belt asked loudly in the locker room (after his first practice) why foreigners (read "him") can't teach at Hombu.[30] He proclaimed his keen desire for "hard training," but could barely finish a class without collapsing in near cardiac arrest. He disappeared within months—*mikka bōzu*—out with a whimper, not a bang.[31]

"Dumb and Dumber" – a young Canadian lad lands in Tokyo and after "Hello," starts in with how he is here to become an aikido sensei ... blah, blah, blah-ditty-blah. Heard it all before. That's what he *says*. What he *does* is become best mates with a likable but sometimes thick American kid from my old dojo, and the two of them spend hours in Roppongi (entertainment area known for its *gaijin* bars) boozing and chasing Japanese girls and minutes on the mats at Hombu.[32] (Everyone has to have a hobby.) Surprise; surprise. In perhaps the most expensive city in the world, these two geniuses manage to burn through all their money and are out of Japan within three or four months. One of the more memorable quotes attributed to one of them is, "Where is the train that takes you up Mt. Fuji?" Perhaps their bright shining moment was the night "*Los Dos Geniuses del Shinjuku*" bought a bottle of cheap *shochu* (sorgum vodka) to save on the drinks later in Roppongi and drank it on the subway on the way to their lads-night-out only to get so pissed they passed out and woke up well after midnight, still in the subway car, but at the end of the line—and having missed the last

---

[30] See the big dumb duck (not the soul singer of the same name) at www.toonar-ific.com/show.php?show_id=354 and www.youtube.com/watch?v=VkkTbOs6pmA&feature=related.

[31] *Mikka bōzu* (三日坊主、みっかぼうず) means literally: a monk for (just) three days. Someone who gives up at the first sign of difficulty.

[32] You can get an idea of the dynamic duo (or dumb-dumbs) at www.imdb.com/title/tt0109686/quotes or www.youtube.com/watch?v=ZgBnkexAbRU.

train. Hopefully, instead of an eye-poppingly expensive
taxi ride, they were able to catch the "train from Mt. Fuji"
back to their flat. *Baka wa shinanakya naoranai!* (You can't
fix stupid.)[33]

"Swami de Espana" – this Spanish self-styled "yogi"
claimed to have just come from an ashram in India where
he (no doubt) had achieved rapturous enlightenment. He
had changed his name to something gloriously Indian but
ridiculous for a Westerner. Swami was caught napping in
the fourth floor dojo during the "morning classes" that he
was supposed to be taking daily to fulfill the requirements
of his "cultural visa." Eat, Pray, Snooze. He vanished
without a trace; left for a higher spiritual plane, no doubt.
Unsan musho![34]

This phenomenon of the foreign fool is apparently not a generational thing, as my
first teacher recalled a German guy in 1969 who *never* washed his uniform. Ne! Ver!
Surprise, surprise; it became green, slick and reeked of ammonia. Bio-slime. Yum!
Clearly, the list of *"hen na gaijin"* (変な外人, へんな がいじん, strange foreigners) characters that visit Hombu Dojo is long and distinguished.

So when you go to Hombu Dojo, try your best to avoid being remembered as "that guy" or "gal," er, woman. Remember at all times that you
are a guest and behave accordingly. A good rule of thumb might be to
behave like you would want someone to behave if they were a visitor in
your home and on their best behavior. Remember too that sincerity
counts a lot with Japanese people, at least from all I have read and in my
limited personal experience. So if you do manage to make a fool of yourself, a sincere apology and contrition go a long way towards smoothing
things out. Don't offer excuses. Put your hand up and "accept responsibility."

I penned an unofficial list of do's and don'ts for newcomers but

---

[33] *Baka wa shinanakya naorana* (馬鹿は死ななきゃ治らない, ばかはしななきゃなおらない)
meaning literally "unless an idiot dies, he cannot be cured." Once a fool, always a fool.

[34] *Unsan musho* (雲散霧消, うんさんむしょう) means disappearing like clouds or fog, like
mist.

scrapped it as tediously pedantic, recalling an expression coined by an old family friend: "K-So" (kay-so) which is her acronym for Keen Sense of the Obvious. Newbies can figure it out for themselves, starting by reading the official dojo website, then grabbing one of the handouts at the front desk of the dojo when they arrive and asking seniors if they still have questions.[35] But, as Albert Einstein reportedly said, "Only two things are infinite: the universe and human stupidity, and I am not sure about the universe." So, with apologies to you all, greet people. Be polite and considerate of others.[36] Be punctual (very important in Japan). Be quiet. Be alert and careful.[37] Be helpful.[38] Pay your dues on time.[39] Bring exact change.[40] Bring 100 yen for your locker. Bring a clean uniform.[41] Bring documentation of your dojo, teacher and rank in aikido, on the day you arrive.[42] And so on. K-So.

Your training begins as you come up the street to the dojo (if not

---

[35] These days most of the front desk staff speaks some English, if you don't speak Japanese. FYI, speaking your home language *louder* at them won't improve their comprehension. "HOW MUCH ARE THE DUES?!!!" They're not deaf. You can always take the handout and point at things in it relating to your questions. Japanese people often read English quite well, even if they may be reserved about speaking it.

[36] Don't use your mobile phone in the dojo. Don't eat or drink in the dojo. Don't leave a class if a different teacher steps onto the mat to teach than the teacher you had expected. Don't ever act angrily towards staff. This rarely if ever works in solving problems in Japan. Locals just think you are a jerk or crazy or both.

[37] The third-floor dojo is often very crowded, so you may need to alter your usual *ukemi* for the lack of space, e.g., don't break fall (*tobu ukemi*) or execute complete backrolls in crowded classes and risk injuring others.

[38] Participate in cleanup after class. Grab a broom when students bring them out to sweep. Grab a wet towel from the bucket they will bring out to wipe down the wood floor. Some may think otherwise, but I think it's best not to clean the *tokanoma* unless you are a long-standing and sufficiently high-ranking Hombu student.

[39] ALWAYS pay on time at the beginning of each month or earlier. One idiot American who claimed to be a student of a famous teacher—but was reportedly unknown at that dojo—left Japan without paying his dues, and before he left said in gist "How cool; they are not hassling me at all about my late dues." They don't hassle you about the fees because it is probably unthinkable to them that someone would practice without paying. Paying on time is *atarimae*! (当 たり前, あたりまえ, (1) natural; reasonable; obvious; (2) usual; common; ordinary).

[40] It's a dojo, not a bank.

[41] Don't ask the front-desk staff for spare belts or uniforms. If you forget yours, suffer the consequences and do not practice.

[42] If there is some issue about your rank, don't argue with them. Find someone who speaks Japanese and your native tongue to try to work it out. Things usually get done in Japan with an indirect approach rather than a confrontational one, and it usually takes more time than you might be accustomed to back home. If you practice there long enough and sincerely enough, people will get to know you and then maybe someone will help you with your problem. Maybe.

sooner). Don't disturb the neighbors and don't litter. If you are riding a bicycle or even more so if it's a motorbike or you're driving a car, *do not* speed up the street. One student from Israel used to dangerously race up the street on his Honda, revving it loudly, until some of us told him to knock it off. How much trouble would you cause the dojo (and us foreigners) if in your selfish haste to rush to class you run down an old lady, child or pet of someone who lives on that street? A friend in Tokyo recently asked me for a referral to a lawyer because his mate, while riding his bicycle, had "frightened" a Japanese lady on her bicycle causing (in her mind) her to fall and injure herself. She had filed charges and was pursuing claims against him, even though from the sound of it the ol' gal had come shooting out of a side street without looking, nearly struck him, lost her balance and fell. He's the foreigner, so he's (more likely than not) at fault.

Remember; everything you do reflects on you, your teacher back home, your home country and the local perception of foreigners. Remember, too, that my comments are absolutely not dojo official policy. They are my own opinions based on personal experience and common sense. And, before you conclude from this chapter that I lack humility and condemn me, believe me when I confess that I have been the poster child for screw-ups more times than I can remember. I've "walked in with my shoes on" so many times the tatami have a permanent impression of my size-twelve shoe. Experience is indeed the best teacher.

Winter

虎穴に入らずんば虎子を得ず。

(Koketsu ni irazunba koji wo ezu)

If you do not enter the tiger's cave, you will not catch its cub.

Breaking the Mirror

鏡開き

(Kagami biraki)

I left sunny L.A. for Tokyo in early February. I'd given sixty days notice of my resignation, so that I could smoothly distribute my case load to other lawyers at the firm and finish: selling my car, packing and shipping my belongings and moving the rest of my things into storage or giving them away to friends or charities. There was no looking back. I'd taken Chinese master strategist Sun Tzu's sage advice and "burned my boats and bridges," though I never could find his plan for moving to a land an ocean away.[43] Boarding the United jumbo jet at LAX for the ten-hour flight across the Pacific, stowing my carry-on, sliding into my seat and buckling up, I breathed a stereotypical sigh of relief. "All the tasks done." Piece of advice? Plan. Make lists. Accept help offered by friends. Don't be so bound to a plan that you're inflexible or unbalanced when things don't go according to plan. Snug in my seat in coach, sipping the warm beer in my plastic cup, my sense of relief was followed by peace of mind and satisfaction. Excitement overwhelmed both. I'd really done it. I was embarking on my adventure. Flying into the headwinds of the jet stream, the nose trimmed up slightly, meant for a gentle flight. Somehow, I managed a little sleep.

Waking with about forty minutes to go, I took an immigration card from the stewardess and spent the next twenty minutes filling it out, trying to reckon whether I was "Embarking" or "Disembarking" so I that would tick the right box. Landing smoothly at Narita airport, disembarking and clearing immigration with equal ease, bags in hand, I looked for the Limousine Bus ticket counter. Despite two prior visits to Japan, I still didn't know the difference between a bus and a "Limousine Bus."[44] It's part of

---

[43] "When your army has crossed the border, you should burn your boats and bridges, in order to make it clear to everybody that you have no hankering after home." Sun Tzu, *Art of War*, "11. The Nine Situations."

[44] You can see a Limousine Bus at www.limousinebus.co.jp/en/.

the magic of language. "You're not a garbage-man; you're an industrial refuse engineer." I suppose saying, "I took the Limousine Bus from the airport" versus "I took the bus from the airport" sounds special? Those clever marketers. Finding the counter, I busted out my novice Japanese, asking for a ticket on the next bus from Narita to the Tokyo City Air Terminal, T-CAT, a transport depot in central Tokyo that was very convenient for pre-airport check-in on certain airlines and bus service to and from Narita.[45] The charming, consummately polite young saleswoman, smartly attired in her orange-and-white uniform (everybody's got a uniform in Japan) complete with a hat and white gloves, suppressed a giggle, took my 3000 yen and handed me a ticket. Speaking to me quickly in Japanese, she smiled and pointed outside to the bus stops in front of the terminal. Responding initially with that slight tilt of the head look of confusion that my childhood dog would give me when I was admonishing her, "blah, blah, blah, Tessa," I recovered, bowed awkwardly and hustled outside. Buses whipped in and out with precision timing that would make the Swiss envious. "TEE-CA-TO NO BASU!" "Huh? Ticket? No pass? What? Oh, the bus to T-CAT; right," I blurted in English to the attendant, for no reason other than habit. Minutes after boarding, I was snoozing in my reclining seat as my "limousine" rumbled down the *Higashi-Kantō* Expressway for the eighty to one hundred minutes to Tokyo.

A friend I'd made during practice on my visit to Hombu Dojo in 1994 was waiting at T-CAT. He'd very kindly offered me a spare room at his home until I could find my own flat. Foreign students at Hombu Dojo are often very willing to help newcomers, so don't be reluctant to ask or accept if help's offered. There's a shared sense of community in being a foreigner in Japan, and even more, a fellow Hombu Dojo student.

Pulling into the arrival driveway for T-CAT, a gentle female voice announced over the intercom that our journey was complete. The familiar gush of air-brakes releasing as the bus shuddered to a stop confirmed it. Peering through the foggy bus window into the wintery cold, I could see my friend sitting on a metal bench inside the terminal. Though seats inside were scarce, no one was sitting on either side of him. Ahhhh: the "yikes; it's a *gaijin!*" effect we visitors have on the locals. Stumbling off

---

[45] High fees for the airlines and 9-11 were the one-two knockout blow to early check-in service. See www.tcat-hakozaki.co.jp/eng/top.html.

the bus, picking up my black duffel bag and slinging it over my shoulder, we exchanged pleasantries.

> "Welcome to Japan!"
> "Good to be here; thanks for picking me up and
> letting me stay."
> "No problem; how was the flight?"
> "Uneventful, like I like 'em."

We were quickly back inside the terminal, riding escalators down into the Hanzomon-line subway station beneath T-CAT. He tossed a few coins into the wall-mounted machine; it spat out two small tickets. Tickets into the turnstile, through it and soon we were in a subway car rolling along to his home clear across Tokyo.

Practice would start for me at 06:30 the next day, as he never missed a morning practice. I don't usually sleep much on planes, so I was tired, it was dead cold (compared to Southern California) and, though I'd twice before been to Tokyo for training, things were still new and a bit bewildering. Sure; I'd previously experienced signs I couldn't read, announcements I couldn't understand and the zen-like quiet of a Japanese subway car, but none of it was yet familiar. As a foreigner, early days in Tokyo, you spend an inordinate amount of energy striving to overcome befuddlement and, if you've studied little or no Japanese, to catch any useful bits of the language. Coping, until overcoming with study, depends on how well you react to the unfamiliar. Like *ukemi*, if you just "go with it," you'll have a much better experience.

So, it's a chilly February night in 1997. I'm in Japan; safe and (reasonably) sound; off to my friend's house to offer his wife the swag I'd brought to say thanks for their extreme kindness in having me as a guest, especially when they had a one-year-old baby boy. Back then, simple things like good coffee, Parmesan cheese, olive oil and all sorts of other food stuffs that we take for granted in the West weren't available in Japan, unless you were willing to pay a small fortune. She put the goods to use immediately. One amazing meal by his gracious Japanese wife, a wee dram of the eighteen-year-old single malt scotch I'd brought him, and soon I was in bed trying to sleep before *asageiko*. Nineteen hours after leaving L.A., "I'm living in Japan!?!"

Following the seasons, this book tracks a year in the life of Hombu Dojo. No surprise then that the dojo's story started a month earlier in January when it reopened after New Year. Happy New Year! *[Shinnen] Akemashite ometedou gozaimasu, Kotoshi mo yoroshiku onegai shimasu!* So goes one of the acceptable Japanese greetings for New Year or, rather, *O-sho-gatsu* (お正月, literally "precise month"). Don't forget the sincere standing bow when saying it. Naturally there are longer versions of the salutation. It's Japan, so there are ever additional ways to be more polite, but this one means something like: "Congratulations on the [new year] opening; please continue your goodwill towards me this year."

In Japan, *O-shogatsu* is celebrated on the first of January because in 1873, following the Meiji Restoration, Japan adopted the Gregorian calendar used in the West. Prior to that, the Chinese lunar calendar determined the new year, as it still does in China. *O-shogatsu* is the biggest holiday celebration in Japan (ahead of Golden Week in May and *O-bon* in August)—something which combines the national focus and festivity of Christmas in the West and the food and family of an American (or Canadian) Thanksgiving with the "auld lang syne" remembrance and renewal of a New Year celebration.[46] It is an extremely busy time of year, starting with schools in recess (typically from December 24th), then workers on leave, followed by closures of attractions, businesses and government facilities as the big day draws near. Braving planes, trains and automobiles, the entire nation goes on holiday, returning home to family and traditional roots. Domestic travel spikes from December 29 to December 31 when the urbanites migrate from the metropolitan centers to their hometowns and spikes once again from January 2 to January 4 when they all journey back to the big cities.

Leading up to the big day, homes are cleaned thoroughly. Clean the home, cleanse the mind of the year's toils and troubles and start the New Year with serenity. Once cleaned, homes are traditionally decorated (after taking down any Christmas decorations) with items of simple clean design of Shinto or folk spiritual origins, but rich with symbolism, intended to

---

[46] *Auld lang syne* is Lowland Scots for "for old times' sake" made famous in the poem of Robert Burns sung at Hogmany (New Year) celebrations worldwide, to which all but a few know any lyrics but the first two stanzas.

ward off or welcome *kami* (gods). Standing sentry at the front door may be a pair of *Kadomatsu* (門松, かどまつ) an upright floral decoration of three diagonally cut stalks of bamboo (earth, woman, man) in a vase of wood, hemp or straw and accompanied by pine branches, plum blossoms or other flora, and other touches of bows, fans or calligraphy. Gates, doors and even the front grills of autos may be festooned with a *shimeka-zari* (しめ飾り, しめかざり) comprised of a twisted straw rope, fern leaves, a *daidai* (bitter orange) and other items of power or auspicious augury.[47] As with many things in Japan, there are regional differences, so one man's *Kadomatsu* or *Shimekezari* is not another's.

Decorating complete, activity moves to the kitchen to prepare traditional foods, like *Osechi-ryori* (お節料理, おせちりょうり). It's a mix of dishes of varying sweetness or saltiness, each symbolic in composition, color or presentation of prosperity, health, happiness, longevity or the like. It features local seasonal ingredients, all packed punctiliously, exquisitely and purposefully, with a precise balance of color and flavor, into beautiful lacquer trays. Each tray has several compartments; each compartment contains a different dish. When finished, each tray is stacked snugly on top of another like a lunch box built by Lego. Dishes may include *daikon*, lotus root or black beans and other vegetables, brightly colored pink and white fish cakes and salads, fish roe and seaweeds and grilled fish like *tai* (sea bream) and *buri* (yellowtail). If you're not a fan of Japanese food, *ganbare!*[48] The functional genius is that it can be prepared (laboriously) in advance of *O-shogatsu* and, because the techniques involve curing with salt or vinegar or simmering with soy sauce or sake, it can, if covered, be stored in a cool place without spoiling. Eaten at room temperature, it requires no additional preparation on New Year's Day. It's a practical, beautiful and festive way for families to cope with shopping closures during *O-shogatsu* – a functional problem solved with an elegant solution. Of course, these days you can do "take-away" by purchasing them well in advance at department stores, supermarkets or even online.

Before or in the midst of all this preparation at home, people will have

---

[47]   The Japanese bitter orange or "*daidai*" is written 橙 but is considered auspicious because the *kanji* 代々 sounds the same and can be translated as "from generation to generation."

[48]   See www.bento.com/fexp-osechi.html.

mailed umpteen *nengajou* (年賀状, ねんがじょう)—small, simple post-cards—sending New Year's greetings to their extended family, friends, business colleagues and customers. Post offices around the country hold them until New Year's Day, delivering them all at once. Every household, all the people, all together; go!

So why drone on and on about all of these detailed holiday preparations? Such minutiae? Precisely! Understanding how much thorough thought and minute preparation goes into a cultural celebration like *O-shogatsu* offers glimpses into the Japanese mind. Becoming familiar with the broader cultural context of Japan helped me understand why Japanese martial arts are so polished, yet so practical.[49] (And yes, aikido—practiced correctly—is very practical.) Armed with such cultural knowledge, of course I had a healthy ROFLMAO when someone told me that Brazilians had put "leverage" and "softness" into the brutish techniques of "Japanese jiujitsu" to create "Brazilian Jiujitsu" or "BJJ." Uh-huh. Right. What the hell did he think the character 柔 means?[50] Japanese culture is all about the details, the subtleties, perpetual refinements, finding the most efficient but effective and flawless way of doing anything—the end product of this process usually has an intrinsic beauty. Brazilians? Fall in love with their Japanese teacher's all-comers match-fighting *Kodokan Judo*?[51] Yes! Train very very hard? Yep! Create a highly successful sporting culture focused on *newaza*? No doubt! Become highly and impressively skilled? Absolutely! Hold aloft the "lamp of *newaza*," giving light to all, rather than hiding it under a bushel? Amen! But when I look at video of someone like judo legend Oda Tsunetane (as one example), my gut reaction is <u>B</u>asically <u>J</u>apanese <u>J</u>udo.[52] Nothing wrong with that.[53] Subtlety

---

[49] It also helped me understand the locals at the dojo.

[50] The *Onyomi* (Japanese pronunciation of the Mandarin word) of 柔 is *jiu*, ジュウ meaning tenderness; weakness; gentleness; softness.

[51] The father of "Brazilian" Jiujutsu, Maeda Mitsuyo was a *Kodokan judoka* and in all probability that's what he taught. The evidence is that he had no teaching license in any *koryu jiujutsu*. Would love to see credible evidence to support the apocryphal tale that's been passed round the internet umpteen times of a link to an obscure, later, *jiujutsu ryu-ha*, *Fusen-ryu*, but when you watch *Fusen-ryu* it's obviously not a *newaza*-focused system.

[52] See Oda sensei at play at www.youtube.com/watch?v=Y1pZkv1trEI.

[53] Brazilians didn't invent football either, the English did; but how many World Cups have England won?

and simplicity in resolving complexity and perpetual refinement are hall-marks of Japanese culture. Leverage and softness are fundamental principles of all *jiujutsu,* and *jiujutsu* comes from Japan.[54] Japanese martial arts are all about finding that one extra bit that will make the difference, other things being equal.

Certainly the celebration of New Year's Eve (*Ōmisoka,* 大晦日, おおみそか) is universal rather than indigenous and it is celebrated enthusiastically in Japan, although typically much more quietly with family rather than at big parties with countdowns, champagne popping and hats and horns, though that's available these days. Special dishes are eaten on New Year's Eve like *Toshikoshi-soba* (年越しそば, Year-End Noodles), a bowl of hot thin buckwheat noodles in a simple broth with a few slices of veg, maybe a fish cake or an egg. There's no set recipe. *Soba* is a homophone for a Japanese word for being in close proximity or near (側, そば) so "Year End is Near!"[55] People stay up till midnight to hear the *Joya-no-kane* (除夜の鐘, じょやのかね) of a local temple bell or watch the TV broadcast of it at the famous Chion-in temple, Kyoto, seventeen monks tolling the nearly 400-year-old, seventy-four-ton bell 108 times, once for each of the 108 earthly temptations that the Buddha taught followers to extinguish.[56] The bell chimes symbolically ring away the sins of the past year. Diehards may stay up all night for a glimpse of the year's first sunrise or *hatsu-hinode* (初日の出, はつひので), a most auspicious way to welcome the New Year in the Land of the Rising Sun.

New Year's Day, families rest and feast. Lift the lids! It's *O-sechi-ryori* time. *O-Zoni* (大雑煮, おおぞうに), a clear soup of *mochi* and vegetables, purportedly of battlefield origin, is another staple of the New Year's menu. And, for those of age, you can wash it all down with longevity-inducing cups of the spiced sake *O-toso* (大屠蘇, おおとそ), a Japanese take on a

---

[54] Apologies to my friends of Han Chinese descent, but I'm not buying the jingoistic myth that football comes from China, either. Certainly the wheel came from China (or more likely Korea) to Japan at some point, but the Lexus came from Japan.

[55] One Japanese friend claims noodles are used because noodles are long, and you want to be with those you are dining with a long time.

[56] See www.chion-in.or.jp/e/ and hear at www.youtube.com/watch?v=adRiZzh_SH0&feature=related.

supposed concoction of a late Han dynasty Chinese physician. Historically, traditional games like *hanetsuki* (Japanese badminton), *takoage* (kite
flying) and others were part of New Year's Day, but I wonder if such
traditions have been waylaid by Nintendo Wii, Playstation and the like.
Children in particular enjoy *O-shogatsu* because they receive *O-toshidama*,
special little envelopes of money, from their parents and extended relatives.[57]   Just like Christmas when Santa Claus is coming to town, Japanese
parents and relatives "know if you've been bad or good, so be good for
goodness sake!" if you want a thick *O-toshidama*.   When stores reopen,
there's a run of wee shoppers on Tokyo's Kiddy Land in Omotesando
and other toy shops, each kiddy flush with New Year's cash.

Later, or on another day, some Japanese dress in *hakama* or *kimono* for
Hatsumode (初詣で、はつもうで), which is a visit to a Shinto shrine or
Buddhist temple to ring bells, give offerings, say prayers of "thanks" and
receive blessings for a prosperous year.   Tokyo's *Meiji Jingu* and other well-
known shrines or temples can be overrun by several million people during
this period, so there's plenty of time to formulate your prayers in the epic
line for the main prayer hall.   Prayers sent aloft, you can enjoy the festive
atmosphere wandering through the colorful booths and shops on the
grounds or just outside the gates that offer new good-luck charms and
souvenirs, food, candy, balloons and toys. (So not everybody has the day
off.)   If you see people during *O-shogatsu* carrying arrows, it's not an archery convention; they've been to a temple or shrine for *Hatsumode* and
purchased a *hamaya* (evil-repelling arrows) as a good-fortune charm for
the coming year.   You can even get a set that includes a *hamayayumi* (evil-
repelling bow).

On the second of January, the Emperor makes a series of short public
appearances at the Imperial Palace in Tokyo.   Only on this day and his
birthday, the 23rd of December, are the inner grounds of the palace ever
opened publicly to any extent.   Between 10:00 and 14:30, at regimented
times, the Emperor and royal family members step out onto a low, broad
balcony (shielded by ballistic-proof glass) to wave and speak briefly to the
flag waving, cheering crowds. *"Tennouheika Banzai"* (天皇陛下万歳)[58]

---

[57]   *O-toshidama*. 御年玉、おとしだま. Honorable Year Jewel.
[58]   See www.youtube.com/watch?v=ZIBTB-chN0o&feature=related or
       www.youtube.com/watch?v=EOLspaJXh00.

So if you visit Japan during the New Year period, expect restaurants, shops and tourist attractions (museums, castles, gardens, parks, etc.) to be closed at some point between December 26 and January 4, which may limit your sightseeing, shopping and dining choices. There's no nationwide pattern, apart from January first, though temples and shrines naturally are not closed. More recently "modern" shopping districts or malls in bigger cities may be open, and of course the ubiquitous fast food chains are serving.[59] You have the Internet now, so checking closures is light years easier than in the past. Hombu Dojo is closed following the last practice on December 25th until New Year's Eve practice on December 31st and thereafter until the first practice of the year, which in 2012 was the 6th of January. Always check the dojo website before visiting, because the dojo is usually closed for public holidays. You can also see if teachers will be traveling, etc.

So with all the closures and local travel should you visit this time of year? Taking a contrary view, yes! Absolutely, especially if you have about three or four weeks to stay. Come the week before the dojo closes and train vigorously. If you celebrate it, celebrate Christmas in Tokyo. Help with the dojo cleaning. Do *O-misoka* practice or go to a temple for the midnight bells. See the New Year's first sunrise in Japan. Find somewhere to enjoy *O-shogatsu* festivities: go to a shrine; buy an arrow to keep the demons away, see and hear the Emperor. Do the year's first practice. Attend the final event of the New Year, *Kagami biraki* and stay another week to train. What an extraordinary experience for any *aikidoka*![60]

Kagami biraki (鏡開き, かがみびらき), which literally means "Mirror Opening," marks the end of the New Year's holiday season. What probably started as an agrarian folk Shinto observance was taken up by the samurai class some time in the fifteenth or sixteenth century and is still observed today by many Japanese. Back in the day, along with other tasks of military preparedness and religious observance, weapons and armor were polished, blessed and displayed. Mirror? A mirror, which reflects what is placed before it, was a powerful symbol of Japanese mythology

---

[59] Skip McDonald's and give Freshness Burger a try. www.freshnessburger.co.jp
[60] If you have still more time, you can go on Hombu Dojo's annual pilgrimage to Tanabe, the birthplace of O-Sensei.

with links to the Sun Goddess (天照, *Amaterasu*).[61] It was also considered emblematic of the virtues of fairness and justice and a vessel of the soul or conscience. "Mirror opening?" There are various explanations, with most claiming the mirror refers to the breaking and eating of baked-hard round mirror-shaped rice cakes *kagami-mochi* (鏡餅), as a symbol of breaking from the old year and bringing in the new one. *Kagami-mochi* served as a religious offering to *Amaterasu-sama* and the deity of the New Year (年神, *Toshi-Gami*) plus the spirits of ancestors as the living embarked on the new year. Check with your favorite Mr. Japan, but some people apparently believed that by eating *kagami-mochi* they were absorbing the vital energy of the gods in renewal and readiness for the new year.

Given its samurai connection, *kagami biraki* is celebrated in many martial arts dojo in Japan (typically the second weekend of the new year) as a ceremonial reminder for teachers and students to renew and rededicate their efforts. Perhaps you celebrate it in your home dojo. As the year ends, just like the homes, the dojo is cleaned and repaired; everything is straightened up and squared away. Obviously martial arts are rooted in soldiering traditions, particularly in Japan, so this regimen of keen preparedness is hardly surprising. We polish our dojo, we polish ourselves, we "polish the mirror" that reflects our true selves, not our imaginings of ourselves. There may be Shinto purification ceremonies or blessings of some kind as part of the event. Likewise, all manner of foods and ornaments of symbolic meaning are prepared, in addition to *kagami-mochi,* and displayed, such as *kudomatsu,* at the front entrance. Again, certain colors are considered auspicious, particularly red and white in combination (紅白, *kouhaku*): white symbolizing purity and red the sun.

At Hombu Dojo, *kagami biraki* starts with an early morning *mochitsuki* (餅搗き) or a traditional *mochi*-pounding ceremony. The rice is cooked out in front of the dojo. When ready, it is placed in a large wooden mortar (*usu,* 臼, うす, I've seen a hollowed-out tree stump used at other events). Wielding a massive wooden mallet (杵, *kine*) like a *suburi-to,* sensei and *deshi* (弟子, trainees at the

---

[61] In Japanese mythology, a mirror was used to lure the sun goddess from a cave. Glimpsing her radiant countenance, in a mirror hung on a tree just outside, she left the grotto, restoring light and order to the world.

dojo) and some students take turns bashing the big ball of rice dough (糯粉, *mochiko*, basically glutinous rice flour and water). Thaaauummmp! Steady wet hands dash in, repositioning the rice dough and swiftly retreat. Thaaauummmp! And so it goes, over and over, rather energetically, until the dough is ready to be formed into the small round "mirror-shaped" cakes, which will be given later to guests at the celebration at the dojo. After drying out, they can be broken and eaten.

At the afternoon ceremony, there is a brief aikido demonstration by *Doshu*, some speeches (in Japanese), *dan* promotion certificates are presented by *Doshu* to students who are present to receive them and then worldwide *dan* promotions are revealed. A banner spans the back wall of the dojo up high near the ceiling. Two cords are pulled, removing the paper covering the banner and revealing the promotions.

Rows of long narrow short tables (for sitting on the floor) are set up, and all the teachers and students gather around to sit. Bottles of *sake* are opened and people pour for one another, smiling and exchanging New Year's greetings. It is a very warm and spirited (yet reserved, unlike some Japanese festivals that seem completely mental to foreigners) way to commemorate the year past and the year ahead as we will work together to forge our minds, bodies and spirits through the practice of aikido.

Some foreign students at Hombu Dojo seem to tire of these group events on the dojo's annual calendar: *Kagami biraki, Kanchugeiko, Shinobukai, Aiki Jinjya Taisai, Zen Nihon Aikido Embutaikai, Shochugeiko* and so on. However, I believe it's vital to respect and observe these traditions. And having just arrived, it was all new to me. They were enjoyable events for many reasons, like realizing connections between present-day Japan and its ancient past and feeling linked to the students who passed through Hombu Dojo before commemorating these very same events. Indeed, "what's past is prologue."[62] At the very least, such events were a chance

---

62   In 1676, Sir Isaac Newton, English physicist, mathematician, astronomer, natural philosopher, and theologian, one of the greatest scientific minds in human history, penned a letter to his rival Robert Hooke stating, "What Descartes did was a good step. You have added much several ways ... If I have seen a little further it is by standing on the shoulders of Giants." However, it seems that in 1159, another Englishman, John of Salisbury, a theologian and author, used something similar in a treatise on logic called *Metalogicon*. Written in Latin, the gist of what Salisbury said is: "We are like dwarves sitting on the shoulders of giants. We see more, and things that are more distant, than they did, not because our sight is superior or because we are taller than they, but because they raise us up, and by their great stature add to ours."

to see all the teachers, *deshi* and fellow students at a single gathering and to collectively acknowledge and recommit to our shared path, aikido. *Akemashite ometedou gozaimasu; Kotoshi mo yoroshiku onegai itashimasu!*

Who knows; maybe John of Salisbury borrowed it from a predecessor. As to aikido and Hombu Dojo, we owe everything to our predecessors as well. Each time I stepped into the third-floor dojo, I was mindful that today's students are "standing on the shoulders of giants," our aikido ancestors, so to speak, though I doubt seriously that we see anywhere near as far, let alone farther.

The Morning Class

朝稽古
(*Asageiko*)

"Sons of Scotland!!! I am William Wallace!!!"

"William Wallace is seven feet tall!"

"Aye and if he were here, he'd consume the English with fireballs from his eyes and bolts of lightning from his arse. [laughter] I AM William Wallace and I am here in defiance of tyranny!"

So bellows Mel Gibson to the army of Scots in his role as thirteenth-century Scottish freedom fighter William Wallace in the Oscar-winning film *Braveheart,* but this time his voice is coming from my laptop. I had rigged my laptop's alarm clock to launch the stirring "Sons of Scotland" speech every morning at 5:30 AM to ensure that I got out of bed for "the morning class." Monday to Friday.

"Will you fight?!!"

"No, we will run; and, we will live."

"Fight, and you may die. Run, and you'll live … at least awhile. But lying in your beds, many years from now, would you trade all the days from this day to that for one chance, just one chance to tell our enemies that they may take our lives but they'll NEVER take our Freedom!!!!! *Alba gu brath*!!! (Scots' Gaelic for "Scotland forever!")

Being half Scottish, if that exhortation didn't stir me out of bed in the morning, there's little if anything that would.   Get up, roll up the futon, shower, shave, two glasses of water, cup of green tea and then make the 500-600 meter walk (I wasn't clever enough to buy a bike year one) up the street from my flat to the dojo … in the cold, the heat, the rain, the dark, the snow, whatever.   Arriving in early February, it was plenty cold and dark in the early morning, which was a stark change from sunny Santa Monica, and added another challenge to my new life in Japan. By March first, I had my own flat, about 500 meters from Hombu Dojo. The first several months, just the excitement of being there made it easy to attend;

but it's not just beginning but persisting to the end that makes the difference in life. Many people do the morning class their entire aikido lives. It's the only class they can attend due to work or other obligations. It's just a normal part of their day, like brushing their teeth.

The morning class or "*asageiko*" is the 6:30 a.m. class led each day by *Doshu*. When I moved to Japan, *Doshu* meant Ueshiba Kisshomaru sensei and then in turn Ueshiba Moriteru sensei. Someday it will be Ueshiba Mitsuteru sensei. Attending this class is particularly important for visiting *aikidoka*, in my view. First, doing so shows respect for *Doshu*. Attending regularly improves the likelihood that he and other staff will remember you. You may even get to take some *ukemi* for him if you attend consistently and long enough. Second, *asageiko* is a rite of passage of sorts, or at least it used to be. It was also the one class that all the *deshi* must attend, each day, for the three years (typically) that they are living in the dojo. Sometimes other Hombu teachers attend as well. Teachers and students visiting from abroad often attend. University students do too. Of course, this gives you the opportunity to train with them all, which may improve your technique and present opportunities to build lifelong relationships.

In Japan, I wanted to follow a training path that copied the *deshi* (in ways available to me) and that meant being certain to attend the morning class, rain or shine, good or poor health, come what may. It was very challenging at times. Of course, my new *aiki*-friends helped me out. Early days, while in a particularly helpful mood, after we had been eating and drinking into the wee hours of the next day, they had me join in their drunken oath that we were NOT going to miss class that morning. As the newbie, I showed up like a rube for class on three hours of sleep and the final fumes of alcohol, while my party-mates were home soundly sleeping it off. The joke was on me, apparently. I just held my breath (so as not to poison my partner) and made it through somehow.

More typically, I would do the morning class and then go down to the second floor and join the remaining half-hour of the beginners' class (wait at the door to be waved in) so that I could observe the teacher's technique at a slower pace. Then I would go back up to the third floor to do the 8:00 class. That way I could start the day with two and a half hours of aikido and then get in a good meal and a nap before 3:00 p.m. practice or racing off to teach aikido in the afternoon at the British school or American Club or such before coming back for evening classes.[63]

Third, *asageiko* helps ensure that you cover core basics each week, because the curriculum and structure is methodically predictable. It's the structural carpentry of your aikido.[64] Each day focuses on basic techniques from a particular "attack," Monday through Saturday. Monday may be *katate-tori gyaku hanmi*. *Irimi-nage* is customarily the first technique, and at 6:30 a.m., that's a stiff cup of espresso. BAM! Then *ikkyo*, *omote* and *ura*. *Nikko*, s*hihonage*, *sankyo*, *kotegaeshi*. Tuesday *ushiro ryote tori*. Wednesday *shomenuchi*. Thursday *suwari waza kata-tori*. Friday, *yokomenuchi*. Saturday *tsuki*.[65] Basics, basics, basics.[66] That's what it is. Training. Repetition to imprint muscle memory. Not entertainment.

In the study of any martial art (or anything), seek to distinguish between teachers who are entertaining you (so you come back and pay more money) and those who are actually teaching you. The former may feel more "fun," but the latter develops you. I've attended a *newaza* (寝技, ねわざ, ground grappling) class in another martial art where one instructor's hour-long class tends to be a ten-minute warm-up, thirty-five to forty minutes of him showing four or five, maybe even six, "magic tricks," meaning he wows the class with a series of techniques that you don't know and can't possibly know after one class of drilling each one a few times. Then there is ten to fifteen minutes of "play" (*randori* or "rolling"). The students in this class "feel" good! They feel like they are learning because they saw lots of technique. They feel like they are doing the art when they roll, but in reality (for years) *randori* is mostly one student trying to muscle his way to victory over the other student, while both make the same mistakes that they've been making for the past six to twelve months, since they are seldom if ever corrected. They feel happy because the teacher

---

[63] During my sabbatical year, I volunteered to help a friend two or three days a week with his teaching aikido in various places in Tokyo, principally at schools and to adults at the American Club.

[64] Attending the other teachers' classes, you complete the build.

[65] I've intentionally not told you the exact order, wishing only to convey the concept; go experience it yourself.

[66] The class structure hasn't changed a bit from second Doshu to third Doshu. Of course, when he started, third Doshu didn't have the gravitas of his father, but how could he? Half the people in the class had watched him grow up from boyhood. His demeanor had to be different but would change as he grew into the role.

places few demands on them. I guess the teaching method is, if they are happy, they come back. If they learn slowly, they pay more money over time. To learn a martial art you have to drill, perpetually. *Randori* is important, too, but you have to drill to develop something other than physical power and natural ability to use while doing it.

Each day of *asageiko*, as the class heads into the final ten to fifteen minutes, *morote-tori gyaku-hanmi tenkan kokyu-ho*. Having to cope with two hands grabbing your arm, after you are tired from practice, is perhaps one teaching objective—muscles are tired so you are less able to muscle technique. Next, Doshu tells students to sit, and then one by one, seniors begin practicing *jiyuuwaza* (自由技, じゆうわざ, free practice), which in my view should involve the techniques that have been taught in that session, until everyone has rejoined the training enthusiastically. Finally Doshu calls for the last technique, shows *suwari kokyu-ho,* and then the class will soon end. It is thorough, brisk, clean and clear. Aikido just as it is—a daily demonstration of the form of the Way.

Aikido gu brath!

In the Bleak Midwinter

寒中稽古
(*Kanchugeiko*)

In the bleak midwinter, frosty wind made moan,
Earth stood hard as iron, water like a stone;
Snow had fallen, snow on snow, snow on snow,
In the bleak midwinter, long ago ...
—*Christina Rossetti, 1872*

American humorist and author Samuel Clemens (Mark Twain) wrote, "The coldest winter I ever spent was a summer in San Francisco." Apparently, Ol' Sam had never been to Tokyo in February. It's not that the temperatures are particularly severe. Though global temperatures are in flux these days, the annual average for Tokyo in January is about 4°C, February maybe 5°C and March 7°C. [67] It's that, in 1997 at least, much of Tokyo seemed ill constructed for cold-weather living. Poorly insulated housing and no central heating means drafty, cold flats, at least the one I could afford. The Japanese answer to staying warm indoors seemed to consist of a *kotatsu* (炬燵, こたつ), an *o-furo* (お風呂, おふろ, deep bathtub for soaking yourself) and bundling up in warm clothes. [68] Some Canadians visiting from Montreal confessed that they had never been colder than in Tokyo: "At least at home, we're prepared for it."

Somewhere else on the planet, I might have reflexively attributed it to shoddy workmanship, poor planning or other human error or vice, but not in Japan. Was the apparent lack of concern over insulation intentional? Perhaps so. In his book *Japan's Cultural Code Words: 233 key terms that explain the attitudes and behavior of the Japanese,* "Asia hand" Boye Lafayette De Mente remarks on the hardy attitude of the Japanese towards the cold,

---

[67] See www.climatetemp.info/japan.
[68] A *kotatsu* is a low table—floor seating—with a heater in the middle and heavy cloth hanging off the sides to keep the heat under the table, where you legs and feet are when sitting cross-legged.

e.g., elementary school children in shorts in the dead of winter, company workers robustly exercising outside in snow or shine, attributing it to:

> "the ancient *Shinto* concept that enduring the cold of winter was one of the fastest and most efficient ways to develop extraordinary mental control and intellectual and spiritual awareness—all of which were essential to mastering martial arts and other skills."[69]

Noted scholar of Japanese and East Asian history and culture Edwin Oldfather Reischauer (what a sublime middle name), who was born and raised in Tokyo and served as U.S. Ambassador to Japan in the '60s, offers a simpler explanation in his indispensable book *The Japanese Today*.[70] Winter in most of Japan was seldom severe enough, often enough, or long enough for pre-industrial Japanese to develop or adopt better heating solutions. The Shinto explanation is certainly more romantic and inspiring than the environmental determinist view.[71] Hopefully, the answer to this and other unsolved mysteries would be revealed during my adventure.

Planned over many years, my move to Tokyo was originally conceived as a six-month to one-year sabbatical to study aikido intensively. I would stay eight years. Once the pieces were in place, I resigned from the law firm, signed on as a consultant lawyer with its Tokyo office, organized my affairs, said my goodbyes and boarded the plane for Japan.

Of those lawyers at the firm who cared, half of them thought I was crazy—those who fundamentally define themselves by the accomplishment of becoming a lawyer. "Why would someone ever leave?" The other half thought I was a genius – those who are proud of their achievements in law but more open to new challenges. "Why would someone ever stay?"

I simply followed my heart's desire and sought a new adventure. If I needed or wanted to work, I could do so on a project basis at the firm,

---

[69]   *Japan's Cultural Code Words: 233 key terms that explain the attitudes and behavior of the Japanese*, Boye Lafayette De Mente, Tuttle Publishing, 2004, p. 52.

[70]   *The Japanese Today—Change and Continuity*. Edwin O. Reischauer, Charles E. Tuttle Company, 1988, pp. 12-13.

[71]   Notably the Japanese do have a word for visiting a shrine naked in winter, *hadakamairi* (裸参り, はだかまいり) so perhaps ol' E.O. Reischauer is only half-right.

but I'd saved a lot of money and strongly preferred not to work. I'd know what to do after I landed and did a bit of recon. Work would only get in the way, as it does for many *aikidoka* who come to train but spend the majority of their time teaching English. The objective was to be singularly focused on studying aikido and to enjoy a once-in-a-lifetime break in one of the world's truly extraordinary cities, in a country I had dreamed of living in for many years. After all the structure of law school, work at the law firm and my duties in my home dojo, it was tremendously exciting and liberating.

Having put my "money where my mouth is" by resigning, I had to put my mind and body there, too.[72] February in Tokyo was c-o-l-d that year. I had moved from Los Angeles, so it was an adjustment, even if my ancestors hail from cold northern climes and I tend to thrive in frosty weather. Unfortunately, there was no time to recover from jet lag and ease into it. Cold plunge. Rising early every frigid windy morning that month, exceptionally early at the beginning when I was staying with my friend and his family in their home on the outskirts of Tokyo, taking the subway to Akebonobashi station on the Tohei Shinjuku line, trudging up the hill to the dojo, I made the daily trek to Wakamatsu-cho for daily training, starting with *asageiko*. Sunday was a day of rest.

The tatami in Hombu Dojo are genuine straw mats covered in canvas. They are very hard, which I prefer, frankly, and rather abrasive. They can prove a shock and adjustment for newcomers, all the more so in cold weather. They become quite slick in dry Tokyo winters, too, which I came to view as good for developing balanced footing. A former *kenshusei* (研修生, けんしゅうせい, trainee) told me they used to keep a slightly damp towel at the back center post of the third-floor dojo that could quickly be stepped on (wetting their feet slightly for better traction) before walking up to bow and then take ukemi for Kisshomaru *Doshu*. The last thing anyone wanted to be remembered for was slipping and falling on *Doshu*.

My first practice was tough. I'd left my home dojo in October because my teacher was displeased with my decision to leave for Japan. To stay fit,

---

[72] I gave up annual compensation of about $200,000 in 1996, with a present value of nearly $300,000 in 2012.

I continued my soft-sand beach runs and open-water and pool swims. I joined Rickson Gracie's old Brazilian Jiujitsu Academy near Pico and Sepulveda in Los Angeles and visited other aikido dojos in L.A., but my aikido fitness had dipped before I arrived in Japan. Add in jet lag, and my first practice was exhausting. I nearly got into a fight with a *deshi* (who would became a dear friend). I was completely gassed by the end, but happy beyond words. I was a Hombu Dojo student. In another of my first week's practices, I was introduced to Miyamoto sensei. He grinned (we had actually met in '94) and held out his hand for me to grab. *Katate-dori, gyaku-hanmi.* Whaaaaaaaaam. *Katate-tori shihonage.* "I have to do that again?" was my first thought, once I stopped bouncing. I stood up and grabbed again. Whammmmm! "I left what, for where, to do what, with who?" That was my second thought, or maybe it was, after "I'm not quite dead." I can't remember exactly; concussions do that, apparently. I would say it was a baptism by fire, but it was too frigid for anything to burn. Windows were open and there was no heat; it could have been much colder on the mat but for sixty to eighty people whirring about. Steam was soon rising off the students' *dougi* (道着, どうぎ, uniform). I would later learn that class in the second-floor dojo with the beginners was another matter (ちょこちょこ, *choko-choko*, toddling); bodies moved less swiftly and surely down there.

Each winter or perhaps rather "in the bleak midwinter" as the Christmas hymn goes, Hombu Dojo holds *kanchugeiko* or "mid-cold-season practice" a sort of midyear intensive to chase off "seasonal affective disorder" (or "the blues" if you prefer). It lasts for ten days in February, right in the middle of *Daikan* (大寒) which is the "Big Chill" from January 20 to February 20. The objective is to do *asageiko* for a week in the coldest time of the year.[73] Do so and in recognition you will receive a commemorative *tenugui* (手拭い, てぬぐい, hand towel). Doesn't sound like much, but it's useful during practice and will remind you of your forging experience midwinter. After all, O-Sensei is quoted as saying:

"Iron is full of impurities that weaken it; through forging,
 by exposure to heat, cold and hammering, the impurities

---

[73] Technically you can do practice any time of day, but if you do, "wimp."

are forced out and the iron is transformed into razor-
sharp steel. Human beings develop in the same fashion."
—Morihei *Ueshiba*

After completing my first *kanchugeiko* at Hombu Dojo, having been
exposed to the cold and the hammering, I couldn't wait for the summer
heat to continue forcing out my impurities and completing the transformation from Iron Man to Razor-sharp Steel Man.

Like so many things in Japan, whatever the endeavor, the spirit and
commitment with which you do it matters a great deal. Even common
tasks are seen as a means or "way" to forge a strong spirit. You may have
seen Japanese men at *matsuri* (festivals) dressed in *happi* coats and *tabi*
(socks) straining together to carry *omikoshi* (お神輿, portable *shinto*
shrines) through the streets as they relentlessly chant: "*wasshoi, wasshoi,
wasshoi!!*" (perhaps 和背負い, harmony on our backs).[74] Whether this
gusto comes from centuries of villagers' collective labor-intensive small-
plot rice farming (as some scholars contend), Japan's warrior traditions,
its indigenous religion or something else, I don't know, but in my experience, Japanese do tend to perform tasks with great enthusiasm and commitment regardless of the tasks' appeal, importance or difficulty.

In 1904, author Lafcadio Hearn, perhaps the first Mr. Japan, wrote:

> "For this national type of moral character was invented the
> name *Yamato-damashii* (or *Yamato-gokoro*), —the Soul of
> *Yamato* (or Heart of *Yamato*), —the appellation of the old
> province of *Yamato*, seat of the early emperors, being figura-
> tively used for the entire country. We might correctly, though
> less literally, interpret the expression *Yamato-damashii* as 'The
> Soul of Old Japan.'"[75]

Yamato (大和, great harmony) was indeed the original Japanese name for
the country, and if you have spent any time around Japanese culture, particularly martial arts, you will have heard of *Yamato damashii* (大和魂, or

---

[74] A happi coat (法被, はっぴ) is a short cotton robe closed with a belt.
[75] *Japan: An Attempt at Interpretation*, Lafcadio Hearn, Chapter IX, The Rule of the Dead.

Yamato kokoro, 大和心). Perhaps it escapes precise definition, but it has been used to define the intrinsic nature of being Japanese and lies at the core of Japan's cultural uniqueness.

Regrettably, but understandably, the expression carries negative connotations for many non-Japanese (and some locals), due to the militarism of the 1930s and '40s and the persistence of *nihonjinron* (日本人論, にほんじんろん, dubious expository writings on Japanese racial or cultural "specialness"). Even today, many Japanese may believe that *Yamato damashii* is fundamentally inaccessible to non-Japanese, because any understanding must start with linguistic fluency and, in particular, clear understanding of original Japanese words (大和言葉, やまとことば, *Yamato kotoba*) rather than words borrowed into Japanese from Chinese and other foreign languages (外来語, がいらいご, *gairaigo*). Some might even contend that without physically being Japanese, one cannot fully understand. Hmmmmm. Does this differ materially from my African-American friends saying a person cannot understand their discrimination without being black? Maybe. Perhaps sharing certain physical attributes affects how we experience or interpret our environment. I don't know; I am neither a geneticist, neurologist, sociologist nor philosopher. I can, however, affirmatively choose to believe that "people are people," emphasizing our commonality rather than our differences—only the food, clothes and some customs really change much in my experience on three continents. I can also refuse to allow raving ultra-nationalists, racists or ethnocentrists (of any race, nation or creed) to co-opt admirable aspects of this Japanese or any other worthy human ideal.

The Encyclopedia of Shinto defines *Yamato damashii* as:

> Literally, "Japanese spirit"; *Yamato damashii* is also written 大和魂. This term is often contrasted with "Chinese Learning" (*karasae*), that is, knowledge and scholarship imported into Japan from China. *Yamato damashii* refers to an inherent faculty of common-sense wisdom, resourcefulness, and prudent judgment that is characteristic of, and unique to, the Japanese people. It also refers to a practical, "real life" ability and intelligence that is in contrast with scholarship and knowledge acquired through formal education. It is a term

used to express such ideas as the essential purity and resolute spirit of the Japanese people, the wish for the peace and security of the nation, and the possession of a strong spirit and emotion that will meet any challenge, even at the expense of one's own life. *Yamato damashii* is synonymous with *Yamato gokoro* (lit. "Japanese heart").[76]

Written sources are sparse, but about a thousand years ago or so, the Japanese conceived of *Yamato gokoro* (大和心) or *wakon* (和魂)—a kind of Japanese native spiritual essence—in contradiction to "Chinese learning" (knowledge from the Chinese classics). *Wakon* was viewed as a kind of "real world" wisdom or intelligence that complimented the "book smarts" of Chinese learning (漢才, *kansai*). The expression *wakon-kansai* was created (和魂漢才)—"Japanese spirit and Chinese scholarship." Simplistically, think common sense verses intellectualism. As a working-class friend describes some scholastic types, "smart in school but dumb on the bus."

Recognizing this tension between good sense and good books is not particularly unique in human thought. Hindu Prince Gautama Siddhartha, the founder of Buddhism (563-483 B.C.), is quoted as saying "Believe nothing, no matter where you read it, or who said it, no matter if I have said it, unless it agrees with your own reason and your own common sense." On January 10, 1776, Englishman Thomas Paine published his explosive revolutionary pamphlet, *Common Sense*, arguing in plain language (rather than Latin or flowery English prose) for freedom from the British crown in support of the American Revolution. In the eighteenth and nineteenth century, great Scots, including philosophers David Hume, Dugald Stewart, Thomas Reid and William Hamilton, established the Scottish School of Common Sense, which was highly influential on the European continent but particularly so in America. To this day, Americans (like many other peoples) highly value common sense. As the American poet Ralph Waldo Emerson (1803-1882) put it, "Common sense is genius dressed in its working clothes."

If you study martial arts, you should recognize this truth. You can talk about martial arts and be book smart all you like, but in the end you have to do it. Martial arts are experiential, not conceptual. Words don't

---

[76] See http://eos.kokugakuin.ac.jp/modules/xwords.

always connect so neatly and cannot convey the depth of experience or complete understanding. And a word may connect differently in one person's mind than in another's. Gaps appear between words and the things they are meant to represent when explaining something that's a matter of feel and physicality—you have to do it to "get it." Of course, every culture has its own "common sense" and it would be foolish to equate Scots-Anglo notions of common sense with those of the Japanese, or Japanese of one era with Japanese of another. To a Japanese, "common sense" may be as simple as doing what he or she thinks every other Japanese would do in that instance.

Cultural geography studies, among other things, the impact of nature on humans and the physical environment's ability to shape the culture. Environmental determinism may have fallen out of favor but if indeed the physical environment materially shapes culture, then the Japanese have had their ample share of shaping forces. An island nation of limited space, limited resources and limited contact with other peoples historically, Japan continues to be routinely subjected to avalanches (it's over 70 percent mountains), earthquakes, tsunami, typhoons, volcanoes, etc. Think how this must have affected the Japanese psyche or *Yamato damashii*, if you prefer, over the centuries. Faced with this kind of environment, one would expect a person or a people to do one of two things: fold up or fight back.

Perhaps then, in response to borrowing many of the wonderful—but foreign—creations of ancient Chinese (and Koreans and Indians) intellectuals in philosophy, writing, art, medicine and so on, the Japanese sought to protect their national identity by saying to themselves in effect "this is all very good, but we have something innately beneficial in our own culture." Having lived in both Japan and China (the P.R.C.), I can confirm that although there are threads of similarities, they are very different peoples, cultures and languages.[77]

In 1853, when Japan was forced to open up by the United States, at battleship gunpoint, and in response began modernizing and adopting Western technology and learning, once again they sought to affirm their

---

[77] The Human Genome project has confirmed the physical aspects of my observation. See www.genome.gov.

individual identity, coining the the phrase *wakon-yōsai* (和魂洋才)—"Japanese spirit and Western learning." Change, especially rapid change, is uncomfortable for most individuals and perhaps for peoples or nations as well. People seek security in life by grasping onto things like race, ethnicity, culture, language … all very transitory in fact … as if they are immutable. It is a common, if not fundamental, human delusion. The shoe is on the other foot now, and China finds itself borrowing every sort of Western (and Japanese and Korean) learning and technology—its own "Meiji modernization" in the late twentieth and twenty-first centuries—and what do we hear from Beijing? We have a market economy "with Chinese characteristics." This isn't a criticism but rather a confirming revelation of human nature.

Of course *Yamato damashii* came to be linked closely to what would later be termed *Bushidō* (武士道), "Way of the Warrior." Rectitude (義, *gi*), Courage (勇, *yū*), Benevolence (仁, *jin*), Respect (礼, *rei*), Honesty (誠, *makoto*), Honor (名誉, *meiyo*), Loyalty (忠義, *chūgi*) were the core virtues of Bushido that should be exhibited in the Japanese spirit. Japanese history is filled with examples of bold acts of heroism by larger-than-life characters like Minamoto no Yoshitsune (源 義経) or Tokugawa Ieyasu (徳川 家康). For example, at the historically pivotal Battle of Sekigahara (關ヶ原の戰ひ, *Sekigahara no Tatakai*), *Ieyasu* ordered his troops to fire on his own ally who had been dithering on whether or not to enter the fray as pledged. Fired upon, woken up, the ally charged in, Tokugawa's forces prevailed and he became Shogun. Sadly, these days Japanese men seem more likely to be portrayed by the local and foreign media as docile salarymen or herbivores. Maybe journalists aren't looking at the *budo* community or foolishly dismiss it as somehow cliché or reactionary.

While unquestionably conceived as being unique to Japanese, *Yamato damashii* was a matter of spirit, heart or soul (*seishin*, 精神,せいしん), subjective and could be cultivated. Awhile ago, I read a fascinating essay by a famous aikido *shihan* where he quoted the writings of *Kamiizumi Ise-no-kami Fujiwara-no-Nobutsuna* (上泉伊勢守藤原信綱, *1508–15?*), the founder of *Shinkage-Ryu* sword school: "The way he handles a sword may look unskillful and awkward, however, should he attain the immovable spirit, even if he is crushed under tons of rocks, he is a master." To me, that is so very "Japanese," and yet part of a larger human context as well. Many cultures admire heroes and respect a spirit of honor, commitment and unyielding perseverance. As Americans often say, "winners never quit and quitters never win." Maybe Winston Churchill would've made a good samurai? "Never give in—never, never, never, never, in nothing great or small, large or petty, never give in except to convictions of honour and good sense. Never yield to force; never yield to the apparently over-whelming might of the enemy."

So broadly stated, *Yamato damashii* is common sense balancing intellect, valorous and virtuous and developing your spirit? Like many others, I found this cultural quality deeply attractive, and it has profoundly affected my attitude towards work and daily life. Doing something with enthusi-asm helps dull the edge of otherwise tedious tasks and enhances other more enjoyable ones. Be brave and bold in the face of life's challenges large or small—never give up. Strive daily to polish your spirit and im-prove yourself. These were some of the things that attracted me to Japa-nese martial arts and aikido in the first place.

Is there something inherently wrong then with this, so far? It's prob-ably understandable and relatively harmless that nations or peoples seek to maintain their sense of identity, unless and until they start ascribing aspects of culture to be intrinsically racial or ethnic in some regard—in-nate (*koyu*, 固有) as opposed to learned abilities (*noryoku*, 能力). The notion that every individual of a particular race, ethnicity or nationality shares a particular spiritual or moral character, inherent merely by being born of that "tribe," is a gross generalization if not overtly racist. *Yamato damashii* was created as an adulation of the Japanese, being somewhat akin to Pioneer Spirit, Yankee Ingenuity, Chosen People, Middle (Center) Kingdom, but if the affirmation requires negation (of all others outside the group) then it carries the nauseating stench of racism or ethnocen-trism.

Stay long enough in Japan and you will encounter both (beyond the occasional "No Gaijin" signs), just as perhaps Japanese might if visiting your home country. Alas, racism, ethnocentrism and tribalism are all part of the human condition. One of the regrettable "us versus them" dramas played out unceasingly across human history. If you have never experi-enced it before, it will be a good lesson for you. I looked ten years younger than I was when I moved to Japan and, if dressed, say, in jeans, a flannel shirt, my black Vans skater-shoes and my old UCLA baseball cap, I would be followed around stores by Japanese shopkeepers who just KNEW I was stealing something – *furyo gaijin* (不良, ふりょう, bad foreigner). Being seated at a restaurant was often amusing, as the hostess would walk back and back and back through the tables to the farthest reaches of the premises and proudly present us with our seating. "*Ahhhh Gaijin Koh-nah*" (foreigner corner), I would say with a wink and a smile, as they lowered their head in shame. One night towards the end of my time in Japan, I was asked by a young *shihan* to join him and his group later for a drink. I did. One of his students, an ever friendly little Japanese woman in her late thirties who I knew fairly well from many practices together in Dosh-u's Friday evening class, was there and a bit drunk and consequently uncharacteristically chatty. What a revelation. She turned out to be shockingly ethnocentric and anti-foreign. I thought, "What a racist" and "How amazing she'd hidden her true face for years." Disgust and admiration in one thought.

One thing common to my experiences in Japan and China (and Korea) is that "dumb foreigner look" locals will give you when you say or do something that is unusual (you already look unusual) in their view (or tedious, in the case of P.R.C. Chinese who, like most people, are far less patient and polite than Japanese). Given East Asians' love of Western things: telephones, radio, television, cars, computers, shoes, clothes, etc. etc. (basically the entire modern world), whenever I face such racism or ethnocentrism I cannot help but think of John Cleese, who played a Jewish revolutionary (among other characters) in the provocative Monty Python film comedy *The Life of Brian*, set in ancient Palestine at the time of Christ: "Okay … apart from the sanitation, the medicine, education, wine, public order, irrigation, roads, the fresh water system <u>and</u> public health, what have the bloody Romans ever done for us?"[78] It's like when people look at you in amazement because you can read a few *kanji*. "Oh right; somehow foreigners managed satellites, semi-conductors, the telephone, flight, space travel, syringes, antibiotics, antiseptics, computers, particle-physics

---

[78] I remain ever mindful of the eras and ways in which East Asian cultures have been comparatively advanced as well.

and the like, but these lines and squiggles are absolutely baffling!" I recall recently staring at the hopelessly rude cashier in the shopping market behind our home in Beijing—an exact copy of a U.S. supermarket— when she got cranky because I momentarily forgot the Mandarin word for "bag" (包, bāo), my Id declaring silently. "Lady, be thankful they aren't binding feet anymore." Living abroad can bring out the "best" in us all. Bring a bucketful of patience with you, because no doubt you will need it and will test the patience of others, too. Not very long ago, the world was a much bigger place, and we are all still growing accustomed to one another.

In his book, *The Fracture of Meaning: Japan's Synthesis of China from the Eighth through the Eighteenth Centuries*, American university professor David Pollack predicts the eventual extinction of *Yamato damashii*.

> "Synthesis comes to an end only when antithesis ceases to appear. For many centuries Japan found its most significant antithesis in China. During the last century and a half the West has been the antithetical term in the dialectic, and as always it has been in that 'other' that Japan has sought its own image, peering anxiously for signs of its own identity into the mirror of the rest of the world. After the challenge of Western technology has been successfully met, one wonders what will be left that is 'alien,' besides the very fact that the historically necessary 'other' is lacking. In that case, 'Japanese spirit' (*Yamato-damashii*) will find itself face to face with the most frightening "other" of all – its lack – at which point opposition must cease or else feed upon itself."[79]

But I think (and I hope) Dr. Pollack's got it half wrong. Perhaps his book smarts impair his common sense? The notion that *Yamato damashii* is somehow innate only to Japanese and incomprehensible and unattainable for foreigners that may and should disappear in time. Hopefully, what will be left will be the admirable aspiration and means for anyone to forge a strong, loyal, valorous and otherwise honorable spirit – through hard training – what a wonderful gift that would be from Japan to the world. Wasn't

[79] *The Fracture of Meaning: Japan's Synthesis of China from the Eighth through the Eighteenth Centuries* pages 52-53, David Pollack, Princeton University Press, 1986.

this part of O-Sensei's vision? Fifty years ago, in February of 1961, O-Sensei made his only visit to the United States and stated that his visit to Hawaii was to "build a 'silver bridge' between Hawaii and Japan ... I want to link East and West through aikido. Aikido's role is to link the world together through harmony and love."

Nihongo wo Tabemasen

I don't eat Japanese (language)

When I left the U.S. for aikido in Japan, I was intent on keeping an open mind in my training and attending as many different teachers' classes as possible. After all, I was there to learn as much as possible, so I would "steal" what I could, when I could, from whoever I could. I was also reluctant to get too close to any one teacher. My decision to depart Los Angeles had been unpopular with my teacher—yeah; and the Grand Canyon is a big hole in the ground—but that disappointment had lessons in it, including how to manage expectations, consider other views and give "face" to people sometimes. A polite excuse would have been more considerate. "Ah, sensei, my law firm has offered me a job in Japan." True; spin, but true. Then again, I was in the U.S., not Japan, and my culture, as an American (and the son of Scots and Germanic *volk*) respects you if you say it straight.[80] Now, having lived in East Asia for sixteen years, my feeling is that the right balance is for people everywhere to develop thicker skins while equally being more considerate to others—the right balance of frankness and face. In the end, it worked out well for us both. He didn't have to take responsibility for me in Japan, and I could make a fresh unencumbered start. I truly became (and remain) "a Hombu Dojo student." Nevertheless, I certainly valued and deeply appreciated his teaching. Without it, I would never taken the extraordinary path to Japan.

Though I had studied conversational Japanese for about a year before I left California for Tokyo, I couldn't speak very much very well when I landed. Japanese lessons had been a perk at work. However, as a trial lawyer at a large multinational firm, not a corporate lawyer doing transactional work for Japanese clients, and as an associate, not a partner, I had to lobby management hard to get into the class. It took years, but I finally was admitted. The new beginners class consisted of lowly me, about

---

80 "Sensei, I want to live in Japan and train at Hombu Dojo; I've decided I need to go." Perhaps I could have invented a polite excuse; "Oh, my job is transferring me to Tokyo." Perhaps, but live and learn and besides cultural respect cuts both ways.

seven firm partners and a Japanese sensei who was a skilled teacher and lovely person in her fifties. The student attrition was fascinating. In Japanese class, one's stature was unrelated to the firm's hierarchy. Senior partner, junior partner and associate were equals. This made most people noticeably uncomfortable, because we all had to take turns speaking in front of each other. This may come as a complete surprise, but lawyers are a highly competitive bunch.

One by one, they dropped out, until there was only me and one partner. She was a cherub-faced, highly intelligent and very pleasant person, but I can remember her murdering the Japanese language with abandon, e.g., "Watta-KOOshee-wah for *watakushi ha* (a personal pronoun for "I" and a subject particle, written *ha* in romaji (your ABC's) but pronounced *wa*). In fairness, while I was no genius or particularly disciplined student, my maternal grandfather was Swiss and spoke seven languages without accent (if my Oma is to be believed) and German was a second language in our home. Mimicking sounds comes easy to me. Like a parrot, I could hear and repeat the words well, but did I really know what I was saying? In the end, even the last partner quit. You see the same thing in the dojo with students who come into aikido having a sense of self importance from elsewhere in their lives. They find being a beginner uncomfortable. I recall a very wealthy middle-aged Asian-American socialite who came into the L.A. dojo for her first class, completed it and then asked if she could join but just throw people and not fall.

A Canadian friend in Japan had a genuine gift for intentionally speaking Japanese atrociously. "Soomee-maysun de'sheetah" for *sumimasen deshita* (excuse me). He'd do it loudly entering his seating row in a cinema, and the high school girls sitting in front of him would spit their cola out through their noses from laughing so hard. "I had this friend" who, when the NHK rep (national broadcast station, think BBC in Britain or PBS in the U.S.) paid a visit to collect the NHK fee for having a TV and the privilege of tuning in to NHK (the programming of which this "friend" could not yet understand more than a few words), just grinned and kept repeating very sincerely and enthusiastically, like he was so pleased he could speak some Japanese, "*Nihongo wo tabemasen!*"[81] "Cable guy" stared,

---

[81] 日本語を食べません! *Nihongo wo tabemasen*! I don't eat Japanese (language) as opposed to

pointed at the form on his clipboard, said in Japanese (in gist), "You gotta pay the tax." "*Nihongo wo tabemasen*!" replied the foreigner, smiling even bigger and nodding his head affirmatively. Cable guy gave up, lacking the heart to correct him. This ruse was at least one healthy step short of the Aussie who, after the NHK rep visited him relentlessly to catch him with his television on (no TV in the home, you don't pay), finally answered the door stark naked. "*Konichawa!!! Irrashaimasse!!*" (Hiya, come on in!) The rep collected his dropped jaw and sprinted off—a uniformed streak down the street. Some guys will do anything to escape picking up the check.

In the end, the Japanese class at the law firm was canceled a few months before my departure when the sole surviving student in the class above mine (a Japanese-American who was also a solo student) complained to management, asking if we could change teachers. Stupid. Stupid with stupid sauce and a side order of stupid. With the Eye of Sauron, um, I mean firm management firmly focused on the classes—now consisting of only two associates—"Frodo and Sam" were doomed. Of course! Hadn't my fellow associate lawyer read Sir Isaac, "An object in motion tends to remain in motion," especially in a big institution. Not even I was that clueless about organizational behavior.

Japan, and living abroad in general, would change and expand my understanding and views of many different things, great and small, including Japanese and aikido words like s*ensei* (先生), teacher or master, literally "previous (or old) life" in Japanese. It turned out that as an attorney I was a sensei; so were physicians, so were school teachers and professors and clergy and politicians and so on. Of course, whether or not someone used the term in referring to me was based on context and relationship. I certainly didn't expect my *aikido-otaku* friends to call me Gillespie Sensei ... unless they came to me for legal advice and hoped for a break on the bill! (Kidding.) *Gomasuri* (胡麻磨り) "grinding sesame" (on someone's rice) or as the Chinese say "pāi mǎ pì" (拍马屁(股), patting the horse's rump or "ass kissing" (the graphic U.S. English equivalent) is an important skill anywhere in the world, particularly in East Asia. Regrettably, despite plenty of opportunity and ample intent, I lack the gift but marvel at those who do. "That's a lovely housecoat you're wearing, Mrs. Cleaver." It's a rather useful skill for obtaining all kinds of favor in life.

日本語が話せん! *Nihongo ga hanasemasen*! I can't speak Japanese.

It was interesting to discover that teachers at Hombu Dojo, who we always addressed as sensei, quite often did not refer to each other in that regard unless age, position or context dictated it.[82]   Like their aikido, they effortlessly recognized the right timing leaving most, if not all, of the rest of us wondering. It was sort of like my ongoing effort to comprehend the mystery of exactly what time of day *O-haiyo gozaimasu* (おはようございます) became *konichiwa* (今日は, こんにちは) and later became *konbanwa* (今晩は, こんばんは). (Good morning, good day, good evening.) Obviously, *Doshu* was always referred to as *Doshu* by everyone. (Same as at the law firm; the head guy and elder statesman of the firm was always Sensei to everyone.) Junior teachers, in speaking to teachers who were closer to them in age but still most definitely senior, typically used the warmer term *sempai* – particularly in a more relaxed social setting.[83] Though surprised when I first heard it, after being in Japan a bit longer, it made sense. I learned that honorifics in Japanese, like *san* (さん), *sama* (様), *dono* (殿), *kyou* (卿) *shi* (氏), *kun* (君), *chan* (ちゃん), *chama* (ちゃま), sensei (先生) , *senshu* (選手), *sempai* (先輩) *and kōhai* (後輩) ... to name a few ... not only conveyed levels of respect but depth of relationship as well, and their use was situational and emotional, not logical and predictable.   To complicate matters for me, correct use of titles is considered very important in Japan. Calling somebody merely by their name, without adding a title, is called *yobisute* (呼び捨て, よびすて) and is ordinarily very bad manners, if not an intended insult.

Since returning to the West, part-time at least, I have tried to use titles in aikido in a more natural, i.e., Japanese, way. For example, I consider it rather odd to refer to most aikido "teachers" I meet outside of Japan as so-and-so "sensei" unless they are on the mat teaching or the context otherwise makes it appropriate, e.g., introducing them to a junior third party in some aikido-related situation. Off the mat (outside of Japan) in a social context, am I really going to call someone who teaches aikido (who is not

---

[82] I suspect that usage is inconsistent among Japanese.

[83] Calling somebody merely by their name is acceptable in three basic situations: when a boss or teacher refers to his underling/student to a third party, between two people of equal rank such as classmates, or when addressing someone of lower rank (like sempai and *kōhai*). Actually, being called by name to take *ukemi*, rather than just being pointed at, was very polite. "ウィリアム!"

my teacher), "sensei"? Highly unlikely, with perhaps a few exceptions. I am inclined to call them by their first name, or if they are senior to me and older than me I may call them *sempai*, particularly in front of their students or if I hold them in particular regard or affection. It all depends on context. It's situational and emotional, not logical and predictable.

You haven't learned much about Japanese culture if you haven't learned about *sempai* and *kōhai*: seniors and juniors. The terms became more meaningful for me in Japan than they had been in the U.S. Of course, I had heard of them in the dojo in California, but usage was limited to a transplanted martial arts sub-culture whereas in Japan they were an intrinsic part of society, being derived from the broader concept of *giri* (義理, ぎり, duty; honor; debt of gratitude; social obligation) at the heart of Japanese society. In Japan, I learned that the terms *sempai* and *kōhai* were both straightforward and more nuanced. For example, someone I didn't know at all, like another older graduate of UCLA, would be my *sempai* based on age, experience or both. It just meant she was senior. On the other hand, if we were in a particular organization together and were materially interacting, regularly, then our *sempai* and *kōhai* relationship might become a genuine mentoring relationship. *Kōhai* is expected to respect and listen to *sempai*, and *sempai* in turn must guide, protect, and teach *kōhai* as she is able. Being a real *sempai* is a great deal of responsibility and not simply a license to pull rank and "crap" on your junior. A real *sempai* will take responsibility for you and help guide you through problems and challenges, even if you caused or contributed to the particular situation. That takes a person of remarkable maturity, character and self awareness, which so many of us are lacking in some regard.

As a Westerner, I found the idea of seniors guiding juniors and juniors respecting seniors rather appealing, seeking wisdom from those who have "gone before you" and looking after those who follow you on a path. In the U.S., at least, there seems to be an ever increasing disconnect between generations. Among other things, there is scarce opportunity for interaction other than in the workplace, and even then the age range is fairly narrow. In Japan, doing aikido, there were often three generations of people on the mat, maybe four, and when we went out for drinks/dinner after class, the ages might range from eighteen to sixty or even seventy. This seemed very healthy for a society.

Like the locals, I took to using the terms liberally, referring to some of my seniors as *sempai* and actually considering some of them my *sempai*. Here's what I mean. It's not like you walk about calling everyone who is your senior at the dojo *sempai* instead of using their name, especially if you don't really know them. And not everyone who happens to be your *sempai* in years is your mentor whose guidance you follow. For me to regularly call someone in aikido "*sempai*" instead of by name, particularly outside of Japan, meant there had to be some relationship beyond mere seniority. Sometimes they were senior students who I was learning from regularly at the dojo. Other times, it may have been someone I really respected. There were two Frenchmen, for example, with over thirty years each in Japan. The story on one was that he had driven his Volkswagen all the way to the right-edge of the Asian continent, got out of it and boarded a ship to Japan. Both studied *kyuudo* (弓道, きゅうどう) as well, which made their grip incredibly strong in aikido. We weren't particularly close, but we practiced or drank together on occasion and I deeply respected their years and experience in Japan and in martial arts, so I usually called them *sempai* when speaking with them to convey my feeling of esteem.

Most of my *sempai* who became real mentors were foreigners, but not all. Some proved to be good mentors in many ways. Some proved to be big disappointments, after initially seeming sincere in wanting to help me develop in aikido or as a foreigner living in Japan. Some were more interested in having their asses kissed or bossing people around than really being a mentor. Maybe their situation outside of aikido was not so stable, successful or satisfying so their status as *sempai* salved their self esteem. From time to time, I have wondered whether aikido, particularly because of its philosophy and the lack of open competition, is filled with people who, having failed at more mainstream pursuits in life, stumbled upon this rather esoteric activity where they then try to compete for the same things they failed to achieve in the mainstream. Even so, I never resented any of them. On the contrary, when foreigners try to adopt Japanese cultural behaviors (many of which are admirable and worthy of imitation in whole or in part) they can be rather clumsy in expressing them, so even if a sempai and I had disagreements from time to time, I remained grateful for the help I had received.

Right or wrong, for better or worse, I'm stubborn to the strands of my DNA and reflexively resisted any and all attempts by anyone who insisted that I do exactly as he or she said just because of his or her personal experience—*sempai* or not: you HAVE to go to this teacher's or that teacher's class; you HAVE to study Japanese here: nobody does that; anyone with any brains does this; etc. Right or wrong, my decisions and my experience in Japan would be my own. In the end, all the advice in the world is just that—you have to live and learn for yourself, just like on the mat.

One risk in blindly following others is that their choices may prove completely wrong for you, like when I accepted advice lock-step from a new friend in Tokyo about where to study Japanese. Soon after landing, I enrolled in the same Japanese school that he was attending. Finding "fault" is often pointless, but the fault was mine because I didn't do my homework. The school was fine for him—his determinants were price and location and it was adjacent to Shin-Okubo station—and he meant well with his advice, but for me it was 100 percent wrong. It was too small, obscure and I arrived midterm, so no class fit well. Placed in a class that was too advanced, I soon quit, thinking I wouldn't be in Japan more than six months anyway. Dumb; full of dumb; *koshinage* ("hip-throw") me and the dumb would've fallen out.

Had I done my homework, I would have learned that *Nichibei Kaiwa Gakuin*, one of the best schools in Tokyo, was just down the hill (and then up) from my flat in Yotsuya.[84] It's a bit expensive, but the teachers are skilled and it is great resume material, which in my case, as a lawyer, is important. Eventually, I realized my initial errors, studied privately and at *Nichibei* and slowly progressed, but, early days in my adventure, I had lost valuable study time.

Thankfully, for you, the Internet is a complete game-changer. Now, if you want them, you can have millions of "e-*sempai*." There are countless consumer, traveler and review sites plus personal blogs, vlogs and tweets from which to draw advice about Japan: where to stay, where to study, what to see, where to eat, etc. etc. None or next to none of this was available in 1997. I say use the tech, but ask your *sempai* at home and around the dojo too after you arrive. Sometimes old-school ways are still the best ways.

---

[84] You can find it here. www.nichibei.ac.jp/jli/

I don't have many regrets about my adventure in Japan, but now, blessed with the clear perceptions of hindsight, the temptation is to think that completing a six-month course at *Nichibei* maybe six months after my arrival might have been smart. Better if I'd done it after completing the first year of aikido-only study. If you plan to focus on aikido, focus on aikido. Blessed with hindsight, my advice is to study Japanese at home before you leave. After you land, get a private teacher and take lessons once or twice a week. Find a "language-exchange partner," too. You can probably use the Internet and arrange both before your departure. Once in-country, bust out your lingo-skills. Sing Loud, Sing Proud! All of To-kyo is your classroom. Listening and speaking (and making mistakes) is how you learn.

I must have had the same conversation in a taxi in Beijing twenty times a week, but I am improving each and every time. Of course, I have a bad Beijing-hua accent, too—qu Sanlitua(n)rrrrr—but they understand me when I say "Shīfu, Wangjing, Big Atlantic Place and don't spare the horses." You will make some hilarious mistakes, like when I used *uwaki* instead of *iiwake* with a partner at the law firm.

- *iiwake* – (言い訳、いいわけ) (1) excuse; (2) explanation

- *uwaki* – (浮気、うわき) (1) extramarital sex; affair; fooling around

"Yes, William Sensei, by all means let's review the law and find the client a valid extramarital affair." I thought I would have to phone paramedics, as he pounded his fists on his desk while pissing himself laughing. "The talking horse screwed up! The talking horse screwed up!" I exaggerate; a little. While Japanese grammar is light-years more difficult than Mandarin, and word (mis)usage can cause some funny moments, in speaking Japanese, it is less likely that small slips of the tongue will produce monstrous gaffs. In Mandarin, how-ever, you are one wrong tone away from "I really want to ride your horse" be-coming "I really want to ride your mom."

- 我非要骑你的马, wǒ fēiyào qí nǐ de mǎ.

- 我非要骑你的妈, wǒ fēiyào qí nǐ de mā.[85]

If you are going to stay in Tokyo longer than six months, enroll in a school at some point— the Confucian work ethic rubbed off on me, so more education is good education. If you plan to stay longer and will work professionally or in business, then go to a notable school and take one of the national language proficiency tests:

- Japanese Language Proficiency Test (日本語能力試験, *Nihongo Nōryoku Shiken or JLPT)* www.jlpt.jp

- Business Japanese Proficiency Test (BJT, ビジネス日本語能力テスト) www.kanken.or.jp/bjt/english/index.html

- J-Test – Practical Japanese (http://j-test.jp)

So as your *sempai* ... hold on a minute while I put down my scrimshaw and light up my pipe and tell you a whale of a tale ... I strongly encourage you to study Japanese, before you go to Japan and while there. Speaking at least some Japanese will deepen your experience at Hombu Dojo. I have seen good Japanese speakers—who aren't particularly skilled *aikidoka*, frankly—receive a lot of attention from teachers. Of course! They can communicate! Well beyond "*Nihongo wo tabemasen!*"

---

[85]   People always ask me, what's more difficult, Chinese, Japanese or Korean? Korean. Hands down. It combines Japanese grammar and polite speech with challenging sounds as in Chinese (though it's not a tonal language or in anyway related to Mandarin). Frankly, there just can't be that many ways to say "eu."

On the Town

ちょっと一杯
(*Chotto Ippai*)

Chotto ippai yarimasho! "Let's have a drink!" Or, "Let's have a little full one [glass]." There is a long tradition in Japanese culture of socializing after hours in a more relaxed atmosphere where (with the "help" of alcohol) people can shed the shackles of formal etiquette that bind so tightly in the daily workplace. The Japanese have the expression *hame wo hazusu* (馬銜を外す，はみをはずす) or "remove the horse's bit [from its mouth]". Informal instances of "nomini-cation," *nomi* (to drink) + communication, can be more important than those on the job. Aikido in Japan is no different. A memorable and enjoyable part of being in Japan and studying aikido was going out with a teacher and fellow students after practice. For all their apparent reserve, Japanese do know how to have fun.

Indeed, those nights out were a time for relaxing together and strengthening relationships and friendships. It was a significantly less formal atmosphere than I had been accustomed to in the U.S. in regards to aikido. At home, I had been out in the evening with teachers, but people tended to sit around the table like a bunch of wooden Indians, which, looking back, was a bit bizarre.[86] People outside of Japan just don't seem to get the balance quite right. In an effort, albeit sincere, to imitate Japanese manners, we become awkward. Don't misunderstand. I'm not advocating behaving as you please when out with your teacher; a (real) teacher is not one of your pals. However, should lives be so controlled that they become some kind of rehearsed *Noh* play?[87] Real life has vitality, spontaneity, liveliness! It doesn't imitate it. It is it. Of course, etiquette

---

[86] One-on-one or the teacher with the other assistant instructors was a different and more real interaction.

[87] See, e.g., www.the-noh.com

and other forms of personal restraint serve to contain, concentrate and focus the spark, but it's got to have that glow at the core to be truly alive.

Tokyo nights had "it." More boisterous but more genuine. You were expected to join in, relax and have fun too—whether or not you drink and can carry the tune of "Danny Boy" in a solo *karaoke* performance. I knew my life had been "globalized" when I was sitting in a smoky Tokyo bar with a Frenchman, Australian and a Brazilian while a *shihan* warbled that Irish ballad "acrossu de gren ... andu downu de mountainsaiiiiiidu ..." The point is participation with the group and to let people be themselves—at least a little bit. A *Hombu shihan* said to me one evening, when we were out as group and I sat there stiffly alert, pouring beer and politely lighting his cigarettes and changing his ashtray, "*Wi-ri-ya-mu; ree-raku-su!*"[88] Translating, "It's easy to sit there with a serious face saying nothing; it's harder to enjoy yourself while still remaining aware and alert." He had a point. Still, I reckoned it's best not to relax too much too soon. There are limits to how honest and frank and lively one should be, even when drunk, in Japan. Also, particularly in business, Japanese can use an apparently innocuous night out entertaining to try to observe and catch the true nature or character of a person—*en vino veritas*. Is he "wet" (ウエット, *whet-to*) or "dry" (ドライ, *du-rai*)? Emotional or logical? Japanese can be distrustful of highly logical types, as they may be prone to behavior based less on the warmth and trust of the mutual relationship and more on cold logical principles regardless of the relationship. In my case, I didn't want judgments about my background or personality (or lack of it) to interfere with my opportunities to learn, so I did try to keep some things hidden. *Neko wo kaburu* (猫を被る, ねこをかぶる) —literally, "hide the cat," meaning keep calm; hide your intent.

Still, these were festive and heartfelt gatherings ... sometimes even argumentative ... but rarely dull and could often include horseplay. One cold winter's evening it snowed over a foot (approx 0.305 m cm) while we were inside enjoying some fish and beer. As we all left the *izakaiya* for home, a *yuki gassen* (雪合戦, ゆきがっせん, snow battle) broke out— sensei, *deshi*, students all furiously firing away with snowballs. Is it proper etiquette to miss or hit your teacher? Your *sempai*? Years later, I was actually

---

[88] William; relax.

invited by a Japanese client to join their team for a *yukigassen* competition held annually in *Sobetsu, Hokkaido.* Yes, the Japanese have turned the spontaneous snowball fight of childhood into an organized event that has grown into a global competition under rules governed by the *Yukigassen* Federation. Really.[89] Norway's a powerhouse apparently, closely followed by the Finns.

Early days in my time in Tokyo, we frequented this old wooden *izakaiya* (居酒屋、いざかや) a snowball's long toss from the *Nuke Benten* shrine where fifteen to twenty of us sat on the tatami, crowding 'round a large rectangular lacquered table, deferentially pouring beer for one another after a hard evening's training. The place had been frequented for years by aikido teachers and students. Of course the evening's menu included *sashimi,* but on some more adventurous evenings it might include deep fried sparrow, tuna stew (complete with floating eyeballs) and so on. The eyeballs—a "delicacy"—went "pop" when you crunched 'em. In East Asia, it often seems that the things people eat periodically to avoid starving have later been labeled as "good for your health" or "delicacies." The master was a gentle and generous spirit who was getting on in years and, according to some, had a real gift for food poisoning at least one of us monthly. In a sort of culinary Russian roulette, I dodged the bullet— maybe he liked me—but another local place on *Fuji Terebi Dori* (Fuji Television Street) got me good ... twice.

Good ol' "J.D. Heaven," which was short for "Jack Daniel's Heaven" or, in my view, better dubbed "Just Done Heavin'." Twice, within minutes of returning home from eating my steak dinner, I was beset by rapid and violent reverse-peristalsis. Yum-yum. JDH was a massive wooden barn-like themed restaurant developed around Jack Daniel's whiskey and the U.S. Wild West. Managed by a kindhearted smiling Nigerian and staffed by Japanese in cowboy garb, it was one of a kind, and not only for the apparently carefree approach to kitchen hygiene. Arguably the highlight of the place—for men—was the Gents, which had a urinal befitting its Western theme. Patrons could mosey up to one wall and relieve themselves onto a floor to ceiling glass-encased diorama of a West Texas prairie, complete with soil, a steer's skull, cactus and the painted pink and azure

---

[89] Skeptics can look at www.yukigassen.jp.

skies of a Western sunset. I am guessing that management hadn't reckoned that J.D. (Jack Daniel's) comes from the rather Eastern Southern state of Tennessee. Good thing, or maybe we would've been whizzing into porcelain versions of Davy Crockett's coonskin cap or onto a diorama of the Alamo—"take that Santa Ana!"[90]

Don't get me wrong, Japanese more often than not absolutely nail (with alarming authenticity) recreations of foreign cultures. And Tokyo is chockablock full of them: bars, restaurants, clubs, events, etc. The annual Tokyo Highland Games leap to mind—yes, you can toss the caber and dance the Highland Fling in Japan—where one Japanese *oji-san* was annually dressed to perfection in his Highland garb: kilt, sporran, kilt-hose, sgian-dubh, ghillie brogues, capped with a Tam o' Shanter and holding a brass-handled walking cane.[91] He looked every bit the very Laird o' the Manor. Another festive spot we frequented for *nijikai* or other nights was *Acaraje!* – a Brazilian-themed bar near Roppogi that projected films of Brazilian football and Carnival on the walls, while patrons sipped caipirinha's and danced the samba, lundu, forro or other Latin dances into the wee hours of the morning.

Tokyo is my favorite city on the planet. Not the prettiest; you'll never confuse it's skyline with Hong Kong, Edinburgh, Rio, Paris or San Francisco, though it has its quiet beautiful spots. If they'd just put the electrical wires underground, as much of earthquake-prone California has done, it would improve the look by half at least.[92] A co-worker visiting from Beijing was shocked how green Tokyo was. Tokyo is certainly one of the liveliest cities in the world, yet not in the distinctively aromatic and chaotic way of say Saigon or Bangkok. It has more focused energy; a sharper edge. It's a massive, sprawling, incomparable mix of modern high-rise offices, crept up upon by post-war single-story and low-rise commercial buildings, residential apartment blocks and single family houses, with the occasional wooden structure that has survived the WWII fire bombings

---

90   Read about General Santa Ana at www.pbs.org/weta/thewest/people/s_z/santaanna.htm part of *THE WEST*, an eight-part documentary series for U.S. public television.

91   For the basics on Highland kit see www.tartansauthority.com/highland-dress.

92   Of course, they won't put the wires underground because that might put their old friend the maker of the concrete electrical/telephone poles out of business; couldn't do that. I jest, but that's definitely Japanese-style thinking as opposed to American or Chinese, which is, "Can someone else do it cheaper? Okay. Ba-bye, old friend."

and natural disasters, and sprinkled with the odd park, temple, graveyard or shrine. Wikipedia claims this about Shinjuku ward, where the dojo is located: "The prefecture is part of the world's most populous metropolitan area with 35 to 39 million people (depending on definition) and the world's largest metropolitan economy with a GDP of US$1.479 trillion at purchasing power parity in 2008, surpassing even New York City, which ranks second on the list ..."[93] It is notoriously expensive and can live up to its reputation, but if you know where to go to eat, shop, and live, you can get by comfortably.

Two words to remember to help your wallet and have some fun:

- *Nomihodai* (飲み放題, のみほうだい) all-you-can-drink; bottomless cup.
- *Tabehodai* (食べ放題, たべほうだい) all-you-can-eat; smorgasbord.

Some restaurants have a kind of "happy hour" in the evenings, during which you can eat, say, all the *shabu-shabu* you can get down your gullet for 2-3,000 yen plus *nama biru* (生ビール, draft beer). We would go and gorge ourselves to save a few yen.

Though Tokyo had been a bit overwhelming on my first visit in 1992, I became quite comfortable with it in 1994 when I was there training for a month. It is surprisingly walkable, unlike Los Angeles or Beijing. In Tokyo, most of you will walk more than you have ever walked in your life. To the subway, from the subway. To the market, from the market. To the dojo, from the dojo. And so on. Daily. I (the diehard Californian) sold my car before I moved and never looked back. Haven't owned one since. No gas. No insurance. No parking. No traffic jams. One friend describes Tokyo as a series of connected villages, and that matches my sense and experience of it. Our neighborhood had a *sushi-ya, tonkatsu-ya, sento* (public bath), *kusuri-ya* (drugstore), coin laundry, cleaners, tofu shop, fruit and veg seller, market, etc. ... and, because people walked rather than drove to get

---

93   See http://en.wikipedia.org/wiki/Tokyo.

their daily business done, the shops were replicated by other small business owners in the adjacent area and the next and the next.[94] The pedestrian-based shopping and errand life also meant that people were a lot less fat and otherwise unfit than in the U.S. or other automobile-based societies with their colorless "warehouse shopping."

The lively amazing city itself, "The Big *Mikan*," was an integral part of my aikido adventure.[95] To be engaging in cultural study of Japanese *budo*, albeit a modern or *gendai budo*, with links to the ancient past in this most modern of cities only added to the sense of wonder. The quality of everything in Tokyo is particularly striking. Those of you who are "foodies" will know that Tokyo has at times had more Michelin-starred restaurants than the combined scores of Paris, Hong Kong, New York, L.A. and London.[96] But it's not just these high-end places. Even average restaurants have amazing food. You can get a two-dollar cup of coffee that's good or a ten-dollar cup of coffee at a specialty coffee bar that actually tastes so good you nearly think it was worth ten dollars. In a bar that has the feel of a Zen monastery, you can get a cocktail mixed and served by someone with years of *sado* (tea ceremony) and *ikebana* (flower arranging) in the perfect cut crystal for that particular beverage—the perfect drink. It still never ceases to amaze me. No fakes. No corners cut. No fake dumplings made of cardboard. No building of elaborate copies of Apple stores to sell bogus iPhones. No cheap wine relabeled as connoisseur in flawless copies of genuine bottles with famous labels. Real.

Most major cities have one or maybe two areas known for food, drink and nightlife. Tokyo has seemingly endless sources of nightlife entertainment, all supercharged by neon lights floor to ceiling and humming with liveliness (though it's not as if I had time and means year one to be out enjoying it). In Shinjuku, there's colorful Kabukicho where a Häagen-Dazs ice cream shop might be next to a soapland ("happy massage" shop), which is next to a *sushi-ya,* which is next to a sex show, which is next to a discount shop, which is next to a noodle shop, a cinema and a *sento* and on and on. Nestled in amongst the ordered chaos is a wee Scottish pub—

---

[94] A *tonkatsu-ya* is a diner specializing in deep-fried pork cutlet, *tonkatsu.* http://japanesefood.about.com/od/pork/r/tonkatsu.htm

[95] *Mikan* is a mandarin or satsuma orange.

[96] See the list at www.fine-dining-guide.com/michelin-guide-tokyo-2012-full-pr and www.cnngo.com/tokyo/eat/tokyo-regains-heavyweight-crown-world-food-capital-327460.

Hazelburn—with every conceivable single malt and lager, bitter, porter or ale you can think of from "God's own country."[97] Thursday nights at The Dubliner near the east exit they had a live Irish band with Japanese players on the Uilleann pipes, bodhrán, fiddle and mandolin. With a pint of Guinness in hand, standing there you could have thought you were in Dublin ... during a Toyota convention.[98]

South of Kabukicho on the Yamanote line, there's Shibuya, home to the famous "Shibuya Scramble" (a six-way crosswalk across the boulevards), *Senta-gai* and *ko-gyaru* mecca "109."[99] A few stops north on the Yamanote line lies the poor man's Shibuya, Ikebukero. There are foreigner haunts like Roppongi with places, at that time, like "shot bar" Geronimo's, pick-up dance joint Gaspanic, tastelessly decorated African-theme bar Magumbo, '80s disco joint Castillio's, sleazy bar Motown and authentic Irish pub Paddy Foley's (shipped over piece by piece from the Emerald Isle, if you believe them) to name but a few grains of sand on the beach. There's Korean hostess heaven Akasaka Mitsuke. Arrive at about 6:30 for *yakiniku* (Korean barbeque) and you will see all the babes heading off to work. The *Shitamachi* area is on the other (eastern) side or underbelly of town, and so on. Quite frankly, every area around any station has its little pockets of food and fun. About a month or so after I moved to Tokyo, I thought ... had I come here in my twenties, I'd be dead by now.

And while you are wandering the streets and alleyways, better not forget to look up! One of the more distinct things about Tokyo is how vertical it is. There are a lot of high-rise buildings, and unlike in the West, it's not just office space upstairs. There may be shops in the basement, a tea and cake shop on the ground floor, an array of restaurants on floor two, bars above that, karaoke above that, hostess bars above that, another variety of bars, etc. etc. You might walk down the same street for fifteen years in Tokyo and then one day by chance glance up, catch sight of a sign, say on the eighth floor, and think "Eskimo Salsa Bar? Huh; wonder what

---

[97] Find for yourself www.wood-river.co.jp/hazelburn or http://metropolis.co.jp/dining/bar-reviews/hazelburn.

[98] See/hear the fiddle, guitar and bodhrán at The Dub at www.youtube.com/watch?v=eEooJA6rweY and find your way there. www.dubliners.jp/shinjuku/index.html.

[99] Get a sense of The Scramble www.youtube.com/watch?v=A8MaRKSV1gk.

that's all about?" and then drop in. Ten years later, we might come back to visit one evening finding you there doing the Lambada in your muk-luks—Rico Suave meets Nanook of the North.

I remember taking my Scottish business partner to Tokyo for the first time in 2005 (he'd likewise introduced Beijing to me). He confessed that he'd never seen anything like it. Took him to infamous Roppongi and a bar where the patrons were, as usual, shoulder-to-shoulder down the length of the long wooden bar—dancing—whether they wanted to or not, they were packed in so tightly. A favorite graffiti was still there on the wall: "Simon 1997, Please don't hit me." Simon had been a lifeguard at the American Club pool who had made the mistake of shagging the wife of an English executive and former rugby player. Yep, "POW." Deserved it. This night, a lone Japanese salaryman, in standard summer-issue short sleeve, white, collared, shirt with a handy plastic pocket protector and pens in his shirt pocket, was gyrating enthusiastically to the music. We bought him a beer. Have I ever seen anyone happier? "A foreigner just bought me a beer! A foreigner just bought me a beer!!!" Frosty Corona in hand, both arms thrust skyward, he spun into happy-feet overdrive. Well; maybe I've seen one happier guy in East Asia—the Chinese guy at the Beijing Olympics, with his big ol' shorts hiked up to the armpits of his t-shirt, who caught "boogie fever" while the bikini-clad cheerleaders wiggled and jiggled during a timeout of the Woman's Volleyball final. The cameraman zoomed in for a closeup of his ecstatic face, which basically read, "Now, THAT'S a proper cultural revolution." Anyway, my business partner really admired the good-natured celebratory spirit of Tokyo nightlife. No one sitting around a bar or pub, posing, having ridiculous diva or comical gang-sta attitudes, just people who had worked hard all day cutting loose and having a laugh at night without bothering anyone else.

When you are out on the town, you do need to keep your wits about you for the occasional bad egg, particularly in foreigner bars. As the then second and now third-largest economy (on a purely GDP basis), people come from all over the world to Japan to make their fortune. Many people come from parts of the world where life is cheap. I remember that a South American soccer player was stabbed in the eye by another foreigner in a bar in Roppongi while I lived there. Generally, it is extremely safe, but fights do occur, even with locals, and are most likely (and stupidly) alcohol related. I confess to being drawn into the stupidity on occasion. Sorry; no details. Most of these entertainment areas have their local *ya-kuza* (mafia) presence, so you do need to be careful if you have a "misunderstanding" with any of them. People like that are one mobile call away from quickly having you surrounded and taken off for a "blanket party" (blanket over your head, you getting thumped with bats) or worse.[100] The old phone call "rat-pack" attack happened to a very tough and handy aikido friend of mine after a run-in with a few street punks on motorbikes. What started as an exchange of words quickly escalated into a twenty-against-two fight for their lives. For the most part, though, you are safe and sound in Tokyo and could probably strip naked, cover yourself in 10,000 yen notes and walk down the street at midnight and not a soul would bother you.

In all seriousness, if you go to Tokyo to live and train, not only are you studying martial arts at the source, you have the opportunity to experience and enjoy one of the world's greatest cities. Have fun but be a good guest and, if you go out at night, be aware—as you should do anywhere. Do that and you can have an amazing time; there really is no place like it on Earth! Drink it in!

---

[100] Sushi knives are best left to cutting fish, not being slipped between ribs. Watch Kyung-Tack Kwak's film *Chingu* (친구, Friend) if you are a visual learner. See www.youtube.com/watch?v=8O-f9jiYfho, www.facebook.com/pages/Chingu/110231942337889 and www.imdb.com/title/tt0281718/.

Spring

To Iwama, and Beyond!

"Testing 1, 2, 3"

審査
(*Shinsa*)

"No one is a failure; you can always serve as a horrible example."
— *Dr. T. W. Gillespie*

Hombu Dojo is a <u>very</u> big place, with thousands of students. If you are from abroad, training there, you're nobody special ... just another visiting foreigner. Some people who move to Japan to live in Tokyo and train at Hombu Dojo never quite make the adjustment to their new lower station in the dojo. Perhaps they were *uchideshi, kenshusei,* or even an assistant instructor in their home dojo. Maybe they were otherwise a notable student, close to the local teacher or even teaching back home. In Japan, they find themselves toiling in relative obscurity and isolation—both inside and outside the dojo. Not everyone can handle that kind of loss well (or the perception of loss).

Lost in Translation

I remember one relative "newbie" to Japan telling me exactly that after Miyamoto sensei's 07:00 beginners' class. It was about a year after I had left Japan (after years living there). I had returned to Tokyo on business and to train. He was finding his relative anonymity as a student in Japan a difficult adjustment, particularly after his prominent position at his home dojo. I chuckled (to myself) when he added, thinking aloud, that of course if he spent many years at Hombu he could become like "Joe Doe" (a friend and *kōhai* of mine who was still living there). My friend was no more or less known than any number of the foreigners who had spent say more than four to five years at Hombu Dojo and spoke a bit of Japanese. I guess it was a matter of perspective. The truth is that while Joe Doe, myself and many, many others may be known there by face and name, we are just visitors passing through. When we leave, other foreigners will come to take our place. It was also rather ironic that this newbie, but relatively experienced *aikidoka,* who had spent countless hours at home seeking *mushin* (無心, むしん, no-mind, free from obstructive thoughts) through the study of aikido and *zazen* (座禅, ざぜん, seated Zen meditation), was so concerned about where he fit in at his new dojo. I just listened and smiled, wondering if all this fretting wasn't the real obstacle to a positive experience training in Japan. Why not just practice and let go of the rest? In the end, people will respect you more and you'll benefit better from your training.

Gaming the System

Anyway, I digress. The topic is testing at Hombu Dojo for rank – *shinsa* (審査, しんさ). In fact, another way some people seek affirmation, recognition or prestige is through the pursuit of rank. If you become a regular member at Hombu Dojo you will be able to test for rank just like any other Hombu student, provided your teacher at home finds this acceptable (presuming you maintain that relationship). If so, it is polite if not otherwise advisable to seek, well in advance of any exam, the permission of your teacher in your home country. Do you really want to return home having done as you pleased? "Oh, by the way sensei, I'm *nidan* now." Maybe I'm old-fashioned. Years after my move to Tokyo, I started training in another martial art, but due to my work, I was training in two different cities.[101] I didn't care about rank. I was interested in learning and acquiring very specific skills. However, it became slightly awkward as, eventually, both teachers promoted me but not at the same time since I was always coming and going. One day, the teacher in one city watched me during *randori* and at the end of class he calls me up in front of the class and hands me a new belt (to my surprise and slight embarrassment). I joked with my fellow students that they were just tossing "the old man" out of the beginners' class. What was I going to do, say "no thank you"? It's the dojo of a world champion. So, when I returned to the other city and class, I still wore my white belt until I took the examination nearly a year later in that dojo. It just seemed the courteous thing to do (plus each teacher's technique and focus was sufficiently different, in my view). Before living in Japan, or maybe before being exposed to Japanese culture, I'm not sure I thought the same way about considering how my actions may affect other people. Probably still don't do it

---

[101] I could tell you which one, but then I'd have to kill you. The ninja blood oath requires it. Oh, whoops.

enough.

Given the size of Hombu Dojo and the lesser or more appropriate emphasis on rank in Japan, the decision on whether or not you are allowed to take a test is very mechanical. It's based simply on the number of hours of practice (one hour per day), timely filling out of the proper form, paying the appropriate fee and, in the case of some *dan* ranks, writing an essay in Japanese. Don't panic. Write it in your native tongue and then have it translated. Well.

At my initial dojo, testing for rank was done solely at the discretion of the chief instructor. By using this method (and other means) he sought to minimize a student's focus on obtaining rank. In fairness, that dojo did so many community demonstrations annually (ten to twelve per summer at various temples for *nisei* week festivals around L.A. plus one at the Japanese American Theater before an audience of over a thousand people) that a student had ample opportunity to do aikido under some form of pressure, so examinations were not really integral to a student's development.[102] The teacher watched your daily practice, considered your attendance, attitude, etc. and if he felt you deserved the rank, you were tested or simply promoted, though always with appropriate traditional gaps between each promotion.[103] There was no leaping from one *dan* to another in a year or some such thing. Doubtless, it was harder than some places and easier than others. It was what it was.

At Hombu Dojo, however, if according to the dojo records you have put in the time on the mat (in accordance with the posted testing standards) then you can usually take the test for your next rank. Often so many people are testing that this can and does lead to some questionable personal decisions to test (and unusual outcomes), I believe. Some foreign students seem particularly determined to test the very minute they complete the bare minimum number of hours for the next level, and they often pass, too. Isn't this a global issue?

---

[102] The Nisei Week demonstration at the Japanese American Theater in L.A. was particularly interesting (and pressurized) because my first teacher organized the participation of many of his friends, e.g., well-known martial artists like *Kareteka* Fumio Demura, Jeet Kun Do and Escrima legend Danny Inasanto and *Judoka* Hayward Nishioka. See www.jaccc.org/theatre.php.

[103] Traditionally, this meant a year for each level of rank (at least). So between *shodan* (初段, first degree) and *nidan* (弐段, second) was two years or longer. *Nidan* to *sandan* (参段, third) was three years or more. *Sandan* to *yondan* (四段, fourth), four, and so on. He wasn't building a group of dojos or an organization so that wasn't part of the equation.

In all martial arts? Rank inflation? What's the cause? Trying to make a living off of martial arts? Empire building? Some well-meaning modern desire to be "inclusive," so everybody passes the exam?

I suppose rank doesn't mean so much in the end anyway. It means at least that wherever you took the exam you could demonstrate the *waza* at a level to the satisfaction of that particular teacher on that particular exam (or during your daily practice) and ticked whatever other box that needed to be ticked to satisfy that teacher. Some people seem to be really deluded about rank. A friend who lived in Hombu Dojo over a year liked to sardonically (but all too accurately) say that when most people get *shodan* they think they're tough, when they get *nidan* they are unbeatable, at *sandan* bulletproof and at *yondan* invisible. However, as another guy I know (several traditional martial arts black belts plus a "BJJ" black belt) mirthfully quipped: "most of them couldn't break a grape in a food fight." More on this later. Aikido practice is principally *kata keiko* (forms practice), not fighting, and some people cannot and will not ever make the leap between good practice and practical application of the art, though they can still benefit deeply from practice.[104] Anyway, people receive rank, for all kinds of reasons so I tend to judge the level of a person, if I judge them at all, by how their movement looks and feels in practice and not by what rank some other teacher bestowed on them in their dojo or particular organization.

In the end, the inescapable fact is that not everyone can achieve the same level of proficiency in martial arts, and that is a good life lesson. You shouldn't measure your own success by comparing yourself to others. Not everyone has the same talents. Not everyone has the same good fortune. Everyone does have the opportunity to give their utmost effort with the talents and fortune they do have. I've always admired the legendary University of California, Los Angeles (UCLA) basketball coach and American national treasure John

---

[104] I'm not saying someone needs to make this leap. Aikido is what it is and that is more than just *bugi* (武技, ぶぎ, martial skill). It's that, plus. "At the core of the practice of aikido, more than anything else, is a continuous hard training and disciplining of one's body and mind in order to develop wisdom. In the event of a confrontation, beast-like behavior aimed solely at protecting oneself and injuring the opponent must be avoided at all costs. To develop the determination to resolve a confrontational situation with omniscience and omnipotence (that is, using not merely technique but applying the entirety of one's abilities and wisdom) is *bugokoro* (武心, ぶ ごころ, budo's spirit/mind). One must realize that aikido is neither more or less than the expression and embodiment of this *bugokoro*." Mitsunari Kanai *shihan*, from the Preface of his book *Technical Aikido*. www.aikidosphere.com/articles/shihankai_articles/kanai/technical_aikido_preface.php

Wooden who, though he was from the Midwestern U.S. (basketball-mad Indiana), had an almost "East Asian" approach to the practice and play of basketball. He never stressed winning but focused instead on mastery of the fundamentals and teamwork. Winning (or losing) would be a natural extension of one's ability, preparation and effort and that of your opponent, plus serendipity. This approach resulted in his UCLA teams winning seven consecutive national championships and ten national championships in twelve years.[105] Coach Wooden defined success as "peace of mind attained only through self satisfaction in knowing you made the effort to do the best of which you are capable."[106] Not everyone is "dealt the same hand" in life; do your utmost with what you have received and don't worry about the rest. Among other things, the study of aikido should liberate us to penetrate and destroy our self-delusions, not sustain old ones or create new ones. To me, it is incumbent upon the student to have a bit of restraint not to take advantage of the testing system. Even if you slip through, your fellow students will all think you're a joke. As a friend in Tokyo said, whose grandfather was a famous swordsman in Japan and student of O-Sensei, "better to be a good *nidan* than a lousy *yondan.*"

When I first arrived at Hombu Dojo, there were some built-in quality control mechanisms. Ichihashi sensei was notorious among the foreign students as the "smiling assassin"—watching student tests with a pleasant, smiling, almost admiring look on his face and then (usually deservedly) failing people, *whoooosh*, with a big flushing sound. He failed one foreigner on his *sandan* test three times and the guy had the hutzpah to complain that it was "racism." No; I knew the guy and he had about reached the limits of his ability—plateaued—or at least reached the limit of his development from that amount of practice. It wasn't racism. He just wasn't good enough yet (and maybe never would be). Ichihashi sensei passed away a number of years ago, and my feeling was the gradings became a bit easier, but that might be my imagination. It's difficult to strike the right balance, but speaking personally, all dojos should be a bit stricter about passing people, which would discourage people from rushing to take their tests and help maintain high standards within aikido.

---

[105] See http://en.wikipedia.org/wiki/UCLA_Bruins_men%27s_basketball#The_John_Wooden_era and http://sports.yahoo.com/blogs/ncaab-the-dagger-college-basketball-blog/no-1-untouchables-ucla-seven-straight-national-championships-130051388--ncaab.html.

[106] See www.coachwooden.com for more, including his Pyramid of Success.

Basically, there are three ways to get promoted at Hombu Dojo—perhaps four if you count monetary donation as a legitimate basis for promotion, which I don't fully understand.   First is by general examination.   Second is by successfully completing the Aikido Academy course. Third is by recommendation, which is announced at *Kagami biraki* following the new year.   One and two typically only apply up to *yondan*.   There is no testing after *yondan*.   Thereafter, rank is honorary with the formula being something like: a good relationship with a teacher, years of practice and some special service to aikido, e.g., opening a dojo.[107]

Testing Dates

Hombu Dojo has many students, and students come there from other dojos to take examinations as well.   If I recall, gradings occurred bi-monthly for *dan* grades and monthly for *kyu* ranks.   The tests are ordinarily held on the third-floor dojo.   Test days are Sundays at 13:00 and Monday mornings at 07:30 sharp.   Morning class ends early, at 07:00.   Those who are testing or who want to stay and take *ukemi* remain in uniform (presuming you took the morning class). Check with the dojo for details, as things may have changed in one way or another.   Be on time.   If you cannot be on time, be early and changed into your proper clean uniform, warmed up and ready to go.

Techniques

The dojo publishes a syllabus of techniques required for each rank. It's on the Aikikai Hombu Dojo website as well, and there is a chart listing the requirements that is posted on the wall of the main dojo on the third floor and in the dojo on the fourth floor.   If you are testing for *dan* grades, you may have some minimal weapons work.   If you have never studied weapons, it is incumbent upon you to do so before testing.   A number of students and teachers who are Hombu Dojo members are quite skilled. There are many dojos in Tokyo and elsewhere in Japan where you can study *jo, bokken, iaido*, etc.   Find one and train.[108]   Ask one of your *senpai*

---

[107]   Writing a frank book like this one is probably a death blow to promotion. LOL.

[108]   Some people foolishly criticize Hombu Dojo for not having weapons instruction. There are historical reasons behind the absence.   And anyway, how is the dojo going to have weapons instruction with such a huge membership? Have a weapons class a few times a week and a

at Hombu Dojo.

Procedure

One challenge on test day, especially one of the four *dan* rank days, is the fact that you usually have to sit *seiza* for a very long time. The tests start with fifth *kyu* tests and proceed up the ranks to *dan* grades. Your *seiza* skills will be sorely tested.

It may be helpful to have your *uke* prearranged. Before I left for Japan, I had always understood that your *uke* for the exam should not be a higher rank than you, but I am not aware of any official policy on this point at Hombu Dojo or some cultural norm. I had one high-ranking friend who loved to perform and took *ukemi* for anyone and everyone who asked, so I called him an "*ukemi*-whore," as any good male friend would do. Think about it, though; doesn't it seem silly that if you are testing for *nidan*, a *yondan* is taking your *ukemi*? Have a bit more self-belief; take a bit of risk. To me, a better attitude would be, "I don't care who takes my *ukemi*. I will do my best aikido."

When they call you up and tell you to "*hajime*," you know the drill.[109] Bow to O-Sensei, bow to the teachers, bow to your partner, wait for the technique to be called out and then start. Stop when they say stop. It's a fairly standard approach overseas as well, in my experience, and should be familiar to you.

Oh; no photographing or videoing during the exams.

Essay

As mentioned, *dan* rank testing may require an essay on aikido. When I was there, it had to be in Japanese. Find someone skilled to help translate yours if you cannot write proficiently in Japanese. I have no idea what I wrote it on, and the computer I used is long gone, as is the document. Certainly my knowledge and understanding has changed, as well. I know

---

hundred-plus people would show up, at least. It's completely unworkable. (One teacher actually was teaching a small invitation-only weekly *iaido* class at Hombu Dojo.) Enjoy Hombu Dojo for what it is and what it offers. Don't whine about what you think it's not. Tokyo has many dojos where traditional weapons can be learned. I used to arrive early for practice and do *suburi* on the third or fourth floors and practice *iaido* at home. There are many solutions if this concerns you.

[109] *Hajime* (始, めはじめ) means to begin, start.

now how much more I don't know.

Testing Tales

If you test at Hombu Dojo, relax and savor the experience. You're studying martial arts in Japan! Wow. While your performance on the examination may or may not be exemplary, it may prove memorable, whether you like it or not.

- The Hidden Blade -

Though I was not there, I don't doubt the veracity of this story as several of my friends witnessed it. Another friend of mine from the U.S. was testing for *san dan*. Apparently, he was demonstrating *tanto tori kote-gaeshi* when the *uke* suddenly let go of the *tanto* as he took *ukemi*. The blade flew up in the air over *nage*'s head and landing snugly, but softly, between his *keikogi* and the back of this *hakama* (proving yet again that "shit happens"). *Uke* jumped up. As *uke* and *nage* frantically scanned the *tatami* for the missing *tanto*, the teachers and students burst into raucous laughter. Order was restored and my pal passed, plus he had a great story to tell. Well done.

- Le Miserable -

Another test that had to be seen to be believed was the young fellow from France who was apparently a weekend student at the dojo. At least that's what I heard, that he trained at some other dojo and came to Hombu on the weekends. I had certainly never seen him before. Well, I did see his test for *ikkyu*. Incredibly, throughout the test he kept instructing and even scolding his *uke*. Loudly. Unashamedly. "No, no; not like that!" Now, generally speaking, this kind of behavior is so bizarre to a Japanese person that I think at first they weren't exactly sure what to do. Maybe they hoped that if they ignored it and gave him a chance he would realize his folly—no, idiocy—and stop. When he didn't have the hoped-for epiphany—one teacher finally said, quite forcefully, "Stop talking and do the technique." He F-A-I-L-E-D. Gloriously. With panache!

Again, the point is, don't be nervous about your test. Be enthused! Be excited! You are taking a martial arts examination in Japan! How many people can say they have ever done that? Enjoy the moment and remember that whatever mistake you do make or think you have made, someone else has probably already made it there and maybe even bigger, badder and bolder. If not, well then, as my father said, "Remember! No one is a failure. You can always serve as a horrible example." Hopefully he didn't have his son in mind when he said it. LOL.

Budo U

武道大学
(Budō Daigaku)

Imagine it. You can go to university in Japan and study *budo*.[110] I'll write it again, in case you missed it. In Japan, you can go to university and study *budo* … as your major. Well, I didn't write it exactly the same way, but you get the point. You're asking where? *Kokusai Budō Daigaku* (国際武道大学, International Budo University) in Shinga, Katsuura City, waaaaay out towards the end of the peninsula of Chiba prefecture, is a private university with a curriculum focusing on budo and sports-related education. Its department of martial arts includes: aikido, judo, karate, kendo, kyudo, naginata, shorinji kempo and sumo.[111]

Short of going "old school" *a la* Will Ferrell and becoming a university undergraduate again, you can briefly experience life at "Budo U" by participating in the annual International Seminar of Budo Culture (回国際武道文化セミナー, *Kai Kokusai Budo Bunka Se-mi-na*.[112] Yes; it's a Budo-fest, a Budo-fiesta, a Budo-extravaganza, a Budo-palooza! Call it what you will, but for twenty-four years, the Budokan (yes, of Cheap Trick, Bob Dylan, Iron Maiden, etc. "live at" fame), sponsors a weekend seminar of practices and lectures, most recently the venue being the *Nippon Budokan* Training Center adjacent to International Budo University, for foreign black belt-level practitioners of Japanese martial arts. I attended on several occasions and it was a unique and thoroughly enjoyable experience, though the food made airline grub seem like *haute cuisine*. *Mazukatta!*[113]

The seminar is usually limited to about a hundred participants, and there are other conditions for attendance, according to the website:

---

[110] If by chance a non-martial arts enthusiast reads this, budo (武道) means martial way.
[111] See www.budo-u.ac.jp.
[112] See www.nipponbudokan.or.jp/shinkoujigyou/semi_english.html.
[113] Past tense of the adjective *mazui* (不味い、まずい) meaning was unappetizing; unpleasant (taste, appearance, situation).

(1) Applicants must be foreign practitioners of modern *budo*, over eighteen, and be resident in Japan. They must, in principle, have obtained *shodan*, at least.

(2) Applicants must understand either English or Japanese. (Both languages will be used during the seminar.)

(3) Applicants must, in principle, be recommended by an organization belonging to the Japanese Budo Association. Alternatively, they must belong.

Each day had morning and afternoon training sessions that involved practicing your own budo and then trying another *budo* form: aikido, iaido, jukendo, karate, kendo, kyudo, naginata, shorinji kempo or sumo. Each teacher was a true master, and I don't use that term loosely. I have had the curious experience recently of hearing someone describe himself as a "master" of a particular martial art after just twelve years or so of practice. Hmmmmm. I've done aikido more than twice as long, always with a highly trained and skilled teacher and wouldn't dream of using that term to describe myself or anyone else other than the few true life-long dedicated "masters" I have met over the years in martial arts. It's better to show some restraint, I believe, in how often we bestow rank and honorific titles on people. The more they are used, the less meaningful they become.

It was an extraordinary event, with extraordinary opportunities and some extraordinary people. I was able to meet and practice with *aikidoka* who practice in *Yoshinkan*, *Iwama* and other schools. One year, a friend who spent fourteen years in Japan, and I roomed with two long-time students of Saito sensei from *Iwama Dojo* and had an excellent time training, eating and drinking together. The biggest decision of the weekend was which *budo* to try?

I was always interested in Karate, especially the hand conditioning whereby your mitts literally become weapons. Boxing is great; it has excellent footwork, defense and conditioning, but you are punching people with pillows on your hands. Muay Thai is the same, though your shins become like granite. I've seen an Okinawan karate drill where you thrust your "knife hand" into and through a thicket of bamboo poles, packed tightly into a heavy ceramic jar.[114] Each strike tears up but eventually toughens up the hand blade. Pointless musings here, however, because at the seminar, I didn't have enough time to give it a go (Karate, not the hand conditioning). Shorinji kempo? Very cool getup (chest armor for *kumite*); very curious about it; never got to it. Just not enough time. Jukendo? Bayonet is irrelevant, you say? Right. Apparently not if you're Scottish (why is that not surprising):

> OUTNUMBERED British soldiers killed 35 Iraqi attackers in the Army's first bayonet charge since the Falklands War 22 years ago.
>
> The fearless Argyll and Sutherland Highlanders stormed rebel positions after being ambushed and pinned down. Despite being outnumbered five to one, they suffered only three minor wounds in the hand-to-hand fighting near the city of Amara.
>
> The battle erupted after Land Rovers carrying 20 Argylls came under attack on a highway. After radioing for back-up, they fixed bayonets and charged at 100 rebels using tactics learned in drills.
>
> When the fighting ended, bodies lay all over the highway and more were floating in a nearby river. Nine rebels were captured. An Army spokesman said: "This was an intense engagement."
>
> The last bayonet charge was by the Scots Guards and the Paras against Argentinian positions.[115]

The term "wild-eyed Highlander" was coined for a reason. The only surprising thing to me about the skirmish is that the Scots didn't ditch the bayonets and go with head-butts, aka the "Glasgow Kiss," the martial art refined by their Lowland cousins. "Does yerrr Motherrr sewww? Have

---

[114] Chinese Wushu and other martial arts have similar hand conditioning exercises as well.

[115] Read *Bayonet Brits Kill 35 Rebels*, 17 May 2004 www.thesun.co.uk/sol/homepage/news/article88661.ece See too the official site of the Argyll and Sutherland Highlanders, whose motto is *Sans Peur!* (Without Fear.) www.argylls.co.uk

herrrr stitch this!" BAM!!!! As Glaswegian comic Kevin Bridges quips, "I mean, aye, we're the murder capital of Europe, but one year we got voted the UK's friendliest city. So we'll batter ye and take yer money, but we'll give ye directions to the hospital."

I brought my *iai-to* (居合刀, いあいと, practice sword) for classes taught by an all-Japan champion. Sensei's movement was "like butter." Having me in his class must've felt like violin virtuoso Itzhak Perlman teaching a kindergärtner. "Okay; 'Twinkle, Twinkle' once more; taking it from the top!"

Kendo was a laugh and utterly exhausting. If you've done some *bokken* work or *iaido*, then your body has an aptitude for the basic movements though the technique and intention are very different. We put on the armor. Very cool. We drill and learn a bit. Excellent. Time for *shiai*. Great. I face off with my best buddy from Tokyo and we go "bat-bleep-mental" on each other. We collide; *shinai* clashing at the *tsuba*. I knee him in the stomach, push back, screaming "*men!*" calling out my smash on his helmet. (You call your shots in kendo.) Next, it's step on his foot, bump him (a variation of an old "give me your lunch money" playground trick), spring back and cut—WHACK! My pal gave as good as he got—clean and dirty. The sensei was bent over laughing, saying that was old-school kendo and you can't do that nowadays. It was great fun; until, dripping with sweat, exhausted, I looked to my right as we changed partners and saw my next opponent – a 6'-7" (2 meters) German *karateka* looking grim.[116] I have done a handful of martial arts over the years, and the next few minutes were probably the hardest I've ever had to fight back in anything. I was exhausted going into my match with über-mann. We screamed out our strikes: "KO-TE," "MEN," "DOU!!"[117] Somehow I managed to survive, without getting my skull bashed in or puking into the wire facemask of my helmet.

In the early morning session, some friends and I gave *Naginata* a foggy-headed try, but absolutely not just because we were battling severe hangovers and the woman sensei was assisted by female university students. No way! That's our story and we're stickin' to it.

---

[116] Is there another kind? I am half-German and enjoyed the Brit comedian of Iranian decent whose heavily accented shtick includes, "I am the only Iranian comedian! Which is three more than Germany." To my German volk, it's not that we are laughing at you; we are laughing with you while you're not laughing.

[117] Wrist! Head! Stomach!

Of course, how could I possibly miss the opportunity to don a *mawashii* (回し, まわし, sumo wrestler's loincloth) and step into the *dohyō* (土俵, どひょう, sumo ring). The one lady *judoka* in the class laughed convulsively when we all paraded out in our loaner white-belts and nothing but. She had maintained her modesty by wearing hers over her judo trousers and keeping on a thick t-shirt. A sumo belt's a snug fit. You hope the launderer's done his job since the last user. Sumo is tough, tough, tough training. The hard gritty clay and sand floor, the massive sweaty bodies, the pushing forward with your arms, the pushing down into the earth with your legs. You gain new respect for just how big, strong, flexible and, yes, fast these guys are, and our assistants were just aspirants for the big leagues. My friend and I took on fighting names, of course: *Shiroyama* and *Kanada-no-hana* (White Mountain and Flower of Canada).

First, we learned how to do *shikko* (四股, しこ, sumo wrestler ceremonial leg raising and stomping). Planting your feet squarely on the floor, slightly outside each shoulder, you tilt to your left and raise your right hand and right leg skyward (or as skyward as flexibility permits) and STOMP, thudding your foot into the clay and dropping your backside towards earth. The instructor explained that they do something like two hundred-fifty of these to start practice and another five hundred (at least) to finish it. Next we learned how to slide our feet and push our opponent—a drill they do thousands of times. One guy stands in the center of the ring, placing his weight forward on one foot, knee bent, hips square, the other foot behind as a brace against the impending collision. You rush forward, smashing into his chest and push, push, push, shoving and sliding him across the clay to the other side of the ring. Turn around and do it again. Maybe he slaps the pusher on the back of the head, exposing a lack of balance and sending the rusher forward in a tumble onto the sandy clay. It's exhausting but great fun, and that unusual surface is great training for your balance.

Then it was time for matches. My opponent only outweighed me by ninety-five kilos, tipping the scales at one hundred seventy-five kilos. I reckoned I could *irmi* (enter) right by him and then turn and push him out. Oh "the best laid plans o' mice and men." I got about halfway behind and "thunk." His tree branch of an arm shot out, "clotheslining" me cold to a dead stop. Grab of the *mawashi* and a twist. I was toast. The woman *judoka* nearly pulled off the upset of the day when her opponent came forward, with a push she went for a hip throw (*o-goshi*) with all she could muster, dropping low, and had the wrestler up on his tiptoes, eyes saucer-sized in shock, only for him to shift his weight and save himself, just, and then usher her out of the ring. I left with newfound respect for how well-trained and powerful these athletes are and for the severe hardship and sacrifice they endure to try to reach the *makuuchi* (幕内, まくうち) division, the top-level professional sumo, which is limited to just forty-two wrestlers (*rikishi*, 力士, りきし). It's extraordinary.

It would be a shock if the judo sensei was not considered one of the art's superb late 20th century competitors and teachers. I guess my belief actually needs to straddle the 20th and 21st centuries. Katsuhiko Kashiwazaki won a silver medal at the world championships in 1975 and a gold medal in 1981 (at sixty-five kilos) and a number of other championships, including a world Sambo championship in Russia. Nobuyuki Sato, co-author with Kashiwazaki sensei of the superb book *Fighting Judo*, wrote in its preface:

> It has been said of Kashiwazaki and his judo that "he is a man who created art from effort." If I can make a comparison between Kashiwazaki and Yasuhiro Yamashita: the latter is an exemplary product of a system designed to create judo champions. He was nurtured by that system as a prize flower cultivated in a garden. Kashiwazaki, on the other hand, is like a flower which sprang up among weeds, training as he did in Northern Japan, whilst teaching in a high school.

He retired from competition in 1982, coaching internationally in England, Canada, Germany and locally at International Budo University and is considered a "*newaza*" specialist.[118] In his book *Shimewaza Master Class*, he remarks how old writings on *jujutsu* admired the ingenuity and beauty of *sankaku-jime* but also noted that it was very dangerous as it exposed your femoral artery/vein to attack (and potential death) by a bite from

---

[118] Newaza (寝技, ねわざ) is the term for "ground fighting" in jujutsu, then in judo and then in judo's modern progeny: Olympic Judo, BJJ, Kawaishi-ryū jujutsu, *Kosen Judo*, Sambo, etc.

your opponent.[119] [120] The remark illustrates how times have changed and highlights the difference between the safety of a sport/match-fight and life and death survival. As you can see on YouTube, Kashiwazaki sensei is smooth, clean and clear on the ground. When I met him, he was incredibly humble and pleasant and a very helpful instructor. I would have loved to study judo from him in an earlier time of my life. His one senior student scared the hell out of us all. "Rumpelstiltskin" someone (definitely not me) dubbed him for his stocky but diminutive stature, large-chiseled *samurai* head and deadly technique.[121]

I've lived in Beijing now for going on eight years, following eight in Tokyo. Two and a half hours by plane but worlds apart, but China's a new adventure. The People's Republic of China is basketball mad. It's on the TV daily.[122] The official NBA ads on Chinese TV proclaim "NBA; where amazing happens" but you don't always have to buy a wildly overpriced ticket to "roundball" or turn on the telly to see such things. At Budo-fest, Kashiwazaki sensei obliged for free. A regular attendee when I was there was a massive *Shorinji kenpo* practitioner – African-American guy, nice fellow, built "like a brick shithouse," as the crass but aptly descriptive saying goes, who was about six-foot-one and nearly 300 pounds. What I saw happened so fast that I can't fully recall all that I saw. In fact, I reckon I didn't "see" it all even when it was happening right in front of me. During class, there was some look or comment of incredulity from the American block of granite and like a coiled leopard Kashiwazaki sensei leapt, planting a foot on the Yanks thigh/hip, one hand whipping out one side of his *keikogi*, and the next thing you know, the poor foreigner is fast asleep, having been so stunned (or stubborn) as to fail to tap in response to the deftly applied choke.

---

[119] *Shimewaza* (絞め技, しめわざ) are strangling techniques, "chokes."

[120] Sorry to disappoint fans but no; the Gracies didn't invent the "triangle choke," and no, "Japanese" jujutsu was never just a battlefield art. Duh. The apocryphal internet story is the G's added *sankaku-jime* after seeing it in a judo book. Who knows? See the artery/vein www.innerbody.com/image_cardov/card41-new.html

[121] Courtesy of The Brothers Grimm www.grimmstories.com/en/grimm_fairy-tales/rumpelstiltskin.

[122] NBA is on along with endless daily, no, hourly, dramas about Imperial Japan's 1930's invasion of Republican China (played by obviously Chinese actors with badly dubbed Japanese, like an old Godzilla film's English without "da Monsta.")

One morning session, we shot off for *Kyudo* (弓道, きゅうどう, Japanese archery). Class was held outdoors or, well, nearly outdoors since the building we were in had a wooden floor, three wood-paneled walls and a high ceiling, but where a structure would usually have a fourth wall, there was no wall at all, nothing but an open, straight and true path to a wooden building about fifty meters away that housed a line of straw bale targets. The serene silver-haired *shihan* was of indeterminable age, maybe seventy something, maybe 170 something. He was so zen'ed-out he practically hovered, gliding across the hardwood floor like Yoda. Impressive presence. After a brief, but sufficiently complete, explanation and flawless demonstration, we each had to select a bow from a rack containing thirty or forty of them and were instructed how to bend it to "string it."[123] Each bow was numbered. The higher the number, the stiffer the bow and stronger the flex. Naturally, in yet another of a lifetime of acts of over and under estimation, I went for the highest I could find, a twenty, which was like five digits higher than anyone else more sensible was using. It was like stringing Ulysses' bow.

Kyudo is incredibly difficult, even with the right equipment, and nothing like Western archery, or even Korean or Chinese archery—apart from a bow that's supposed to launch arrows at and into a target you are aiming to hit. The bow is gripped tight in your sturdy leather-gloved left hand. Arrow in your right. Fumbling done; arrow now strung; you raise the bow straight up your body's centerline and at the apex of your lift, draw it down while stretching your arms wide—you "open your chest—pulling the bow forward and drawing the bow string back in equal parts, arrow eager for release. Eyeing the target keenly, you loose the string to let your arrow fly true. Phhhttt!!! A loosened grip on the bow lets it rotate freely in your left hand, and it revolves in your grasp as the bow string follows its forward energy, swinging round like a gate to strike the back of your extended arm. Oh, whoops! No; the arrow's on the ground at my feet. Clakkk!!!

Drawing the string to shoot my twenty gauge? Ha. The beads of sweat dripping down my forehead from stringing it never left. *Kyudo* put the T in technical and D in difficult, especially with my mind chattering away while aiming to fire. One thing is for certain. I <u>can</u> hit the "broad

---

[123] You must unstring it after each use so that the bow doesn't become misshapen and ineffective.

side of a barn." Did it. Literally. Fired one right off the roof of the target shed. A couple of "worm burners" skimmed along the dirt in front of the targets. I think I managed to bounce one off the target—sideways. I confirmed that while there are dummies for Kyudo, there is no "Kyudo for Dummies." Practice, practice, practice. Kyudo makes neurosurgery or even golf look like child's play.

It was particularly interesting that the most crowded class was aikido, usually by a significant amount. People were ever curious to try it and always surprised by it when they did. You can't watch videos or live aikido practice or demonstrations and really understand it. You have to feel it for yourself. Like some senior martial artists who have joined my class in Beijing, there's a sudden look of surprise on the face, and the body flinches at the unexpected loss of balance; gravity finishes the job as down they go. Aikido is fundamentally experiential, not conceptual. It has to be tried with a qualified instructor before you can even begin to conclude anything about it and even then, as you train for years, you may find your conclusions were incorrect or incomplete.

There were also discussion groups after lunch and in the evening plus an annual guest speaker of some kind. Three of them really stood out, for various reasons.

Samurai Sprinter

The first one was the rather unique Kono Yoshinori, a Japanese *bujutsu* master (武術, Japan's classical martial arts) and "expert" on body technique (身体技法, *Shintaigihou*) who interestingly enough began his martial arts training in 1971 at the Aikikai Hombu Dojo, training primarily under Yamaguchi sensei. According to his published bios, his martial arts C.V. apparently includes *Kashima Shin-ryu kenjutsu* and studies of the technique of remarkable *bujutsu* practitioner Kuroda Tetsuzan. Kono sensei describes himself as a researcher of the proper and most efficient use of the body based on traditional *bujutsu* and in 1978 established the *Shoseikan, Bujutsu Keiko Kenkyukai* (Martial Arts Training Research Association).

The theory of his lecture at the seminar could be summarized as "Japanese used to be really really fast (and otherwise move very well) until they learned Western running methods (and other Western sports methods) and that ruined them." It seemed at the time like stereotypical *Nihonjin ron* (日本人論、にほんじんろん) rubbish and his audience let him know it.[124] He was derided and dismissed by a large number of the participants. Perhaps fairly; perhaps unfairly. I don't know. I didn't see enough of what he was presenting to decide.

In his article "*Perceptual warfare in the classical Japanese martial arts: What a person anticipates and perceives when he contacts someone else's body*," Akira Iwabuchi of Daito Bunka University, Tokyo, Japan penned the following concerning Kono sensei:

> According to *Kono*, the classical Japanese martial arts are a form of "perceptual warfare" whose techniques are intended to outwit an opponent's anticipation in body perception. When the opponent's anticipation is outwitted, his perception is momentarily disrupted. During this disruption, he cannot fight with his full strength and can therefore be defeated even by quite a weak force. Kono believes that the body skills to outwit an opponent's anticipation made it possible to develop seemingly miraculous techniques such as are recorded in the episodes (Pranin & Kono, 1992).

> This unique character of the classical Japanese martial arts, as well as other aspects of traditional Japanese culture, disappeared after the opening of Japan to the world in 1854. Civilization and enlightenment rapidly occurred, and in place of the training methods of the classical Japanese martial arts, those of Western sports were adopted under the guidance of the Japanese government. Consequently, not only modern martial arts such as judo or aikido, but also so-called "classical" ones such as jujutsu, were changed in nature and converted into modern sports (e.g., "Tairon," 1999).[125]

---

[124] *Nihon jin ron* are written works theorizing about Japanese cultural or racial uniqueness; a type of thinking that I have found is not limited just to Japan in East Asia (or elsewhere).

[125] *Perceptual Warfare in the Classical Japanese Martial Arts*, July 1999, www.jcss.gr.jp/iccs99OLP/p2-41/p2-41.htm. Presented in 1999 at The 2nd International Conference on Cognitive Science

In fact, Kono sensei has received some recognition for his application of his interpretation of *bujutsu* principles to modern sport.

TIME MAGAZINE
Monday, Aug. 09, 2004

When sprinter Shingo Suetsugu races around the track wearing his high-tech spikes and aerodynamic suit, he has another less visible secret weapon: he practices ancient techniques used by samurai and ninja to move more swiftly through the streets of Edo-era Japan. Suetsugu, 24, credits a centuries-old practice called nanba for the bronze medal he won in the 200-m race at last year's track-and-field World Championships, which made him the first East Asian since 1900 to land a medal in an international sprint competition. [126]

I remember Suetsugu well. Lean; even slight; built like a Whippet. In fact, I was watching the athletics meet in Japan when he set the Asian record of 20.03 for 200 meters while slowing down in the last twenty meters to ease across the finish line ten or fifteen meters ahead of his closest competitor.[127] How could you not like this kid? At some point, though, Kono sensei became Suetsugu's coach. In fact at the *budo* seminar, Kono sensei had demonstrated his "*namba*" running style of ancient Japan, where the arms and legs move in unison on the left side and then the right side, to the incredulity of the audience.[128] The left hand surges forward with each left leg stride and the right hand forward with each right leg stride, rather than the usual opposite leg opposite hand. All I know for sure is that Suetsugu's career seemed to lose its surge after taking bronze at the Worlds in 2003, and I always wondered if someone had tinkered with him a bit

---

and the 16th Annual Meeting of the Japanese Cognitive Science Society Joint Conference.
[126]   Time article republished at www.martialartsplanet.com/forums/showthread.php?t=19453.
[127]   A time that was very impressive until Usain Bolt came along and exploded conceptions of sprinting.
[128]   *Namba Aruki* – a Style of Walking Practiced in Old Times in Japan. See www.tofugu.com/guides/namba-aruki/ or www.youtube.com/watch?v=DC66NZj8pJ4.

too much.[129] I don't know if that bronze medal was pre- or post-Coach Kono. Maybe Suetsugu's success in Paris that hot summer's evening in 2003 had nothing to do with Coach Kono's methods at all.[130] Or, maybe it had everything to do with it, and indeed some knowledge really was lost when Japan opened to the west and "modernized." It's certainly worth further research, regardless of awkward first impressions.

Samurai Swimmer

Living in Japan it sure seemed like there was "a Way" (道, *dou*) or "*waza*" (技, わざ, technique or art) for just about any undertaking. Whether it's making and pouring tea or sharpening a pencil, it just seemed like these folks have examined "how-to" to the point of perfection, or inching ever closer to it. Ever hear of *sui-jutsu* (水術, water techniques) or *nihon-eihou* (日本泳法, にほんえいほう, traditional Japanese swimming)? Yep; there is samurai swimming.[131]

> "The development of swimming in Japan dates from ancient times. When Izanagi no Mikoto came down to the province of Hyuga 700 years before the accession of the Emperor Jimmu to the throne, it is said that he bathed in water. From the time of the Gods through the Ancient Times there have been many myths concerning swimming. Later swimming became a kind of military art and was used in time of battle, in river and sea. Swimming was as natural to the Japanese as walking, because Japan is surrounded by sea, and in all quarters,

---

[129] Suetsugu later fancied himself a 100-meter man rather than a 200 phenom and skipped the 200 at the Sydney games. The 100 is not his race, though he has clocked a respectably quick 10.03 during his career, just short of the Japanese and former Asian (and current for Mongolic peoples) record of 10.00 by *Koji Ito* in 1998.

[130] Suetsugu's 200-meter bronze medal at World's, Paris 2003.
www.youtube.com/watch?v=7qGsxi9zBhY

[131] Forget for the moment *suibajutsu*, the art of swimming a horse across a river (水馬術, すいばじゅつ). The All Japan Swimming Association presently recognizes 12 classical swimming traditions. See www.koikeryu.com/master.html. They are known collectively as *Nihon Eiho* (日本泳法, にほんえいほう, Japanese swimming styles). Each *ryu-ha* has its own emphasis or expertise, based in part on local geographic and aquatic conditions. For more, find a copy of The *Nihon Eiho 12 Ryu-ha Soran* (日本泳法12流派総覧, traditional Japanese swimming school guide) which is a comprehensive book on Japanese swimming traditions.

there are many rivers, streams, lakes and swamps. In the Tokugawa period the ways of swimming in the river and in the sea became varied. The differences of depths and currents of rivers gave rise to distinct styles of of swimming."[132]

Kobudo (古武道, こぶどう, pre-Meiji martial ways) includes schools teaching the art of swimming and fighting in water. You can learn how to swim in armor, how to swim with a weapon, how to fight in water, how to swim with your hands tied, how to swim silently, how to swim long distances, how to cross rapid streams, how to shoot a flintlock musket or bow while treading water (in high demand nowadays), open-water swimming and so on.[133] Makes some sense. While Japan was not, until after *Meiji* restoration and the building of a modern navy with the help of Scottish expatriate Thomas Glover and the shipyards of Aberdeen, a maritime power in the global sense of, say, Spain, The Netherlands or the Britain, it is surrounded and linked by seas both oceanic and inland.[134] Learning to swim sure beats drowning.[135]

---

[132] From "Swimming in Japan," Published by the International Young Women and Children's Society Tokyo, Japan 1935. www.ishof.org/exhibits/pdf/japan1.pdf

[133] The "and so on" includes, amongst other things, swimming while standing upright (*Tachi Oyogi*), techniques for negotiating waves (Teishin nuki Oyogi), methods for resting in water (Yasumi Oyogi), *Suisho* or *Ukimi Sho* (the practice of calligraphy whilst floating), (calligraphy while swimming), *Haizen Oyogi* (serving food and drink while swimming), *Sakenomi Oyogi* (serving of sake while swimming) and even swimming while juggling bowling balls and singing the Catalina-Madelina song (ボーリングボール ジャグリング カテリ と ナ-マドリ ナの歌 うながらの泳ぎ). Okay, I made up the last one, but it could happen.

[134] From Dunkeld, or in Scots Gaelic *Dùn Chailleann* meaning Fort of the Caledonians, home to a favorite folk singer of mine Dougie Maclean), Glover was a titan in the industrialisation of Japan. His shipbuilding company later became the Mitsubishi Corporation. See www.visitdunkeld.com/thomas-glover.htm.

[135] Setting aside for the moment the myriad of straits, channels, rivers and lakes of the island nation, Japan is surrounded by the Pacific Ocean to the east, the Sea of Japan (if you are Japanese) or East Sea (if you are Korean) to the west, the East China Sea to the southwest, and the Sea of Okhotsk to the north.

One year, the seminar offered a lecture and practicum by Koga Tadao *shihan* of *Kobori-ryu Tosui-jutsu.*[136] We were all told to bring our swimsuits.[137] In the supplement provided as part of the study materials for the 14th International Seminar of Budo Culture, Koga Tadao Shihan wrote:

> "There is an order of education for the development of the warrior that reads '*Ichi soku, Ni: sui, San: tan, Yon: gei*' (One: legs, Two: water, Three: guts, Four: art). The first of these criteria suggests that the development of good health is paramount, the second that mastery of swimming should be achieved, the third that courage should be cultivated, and the final criteria concerns the martial arts."

Soon we were all in the pool, splashing about. Beat the lecture hall. A number of my fraternity brothers at UCLA had won NCAA and Olympic gold medals in swimming or were water polo players, and I had become a competitive triathlete, with swimming being a strong suit (particularly for someone who did not swim competitively since youth), so I was eager to see how Toga sensei moved in water. Impressively. Effortlessly. Especially for a guy in his sixties, I suppose. We were taught the *tosui* leg movement and various other strokes, each of which actually take years to master. It was challenging learning new movement, physically tiring and otherwise fascinating. The human ingenuity alone was impressive.

It wouldn't have been us (my group of friends on the weekend) without a bit of mischief. Circumstances obliged with opportunity. Naturally, we took the kickboards and stood on two or three of them at a time,

---

[136] Founded around 1700 in *Kumamoto* by Muraoka Idayu Masafumi, *Kobori ryu Tosuijutsu* was practiced as part of the martial training of the local warriors right up until the Meiji Restoration, according to Toga sensei. *Tosui* is a circular leg kick that allows the practitioner to tread water, reportedly while keeping the upper body above water (even while wearing armor and carrying arms). The art became not solely concerned with physical technique, but the development of the mind and spirit through swimming embodied in a set of ten teachings called the *Suigaku Gyodo.* See "*Kobori-ryu Tosui-jutsu,*" by Koga Tadao. Published in the program for The 14th International Seminar of Budo Culture (March 2002), sponsored by the Nippon Budokan Foundation and International Budo University.

[137] Koga Tadao is the Eleventh Generation *Shihan* (Teaching Master) of *Kobori Ryu* Tosuijutsu. Born in 1945, Koga Shihan entered the tradition in 1958 and in 1993 received the '*Bosui no Maki,*' the highest level of recognition in the tradition. In 1994, president of the *Kobori ryu Tosuikai* (an organization for the preservation and promulgation of the tradition). He also received the level of *Hanshi* from the *Nihon Suiei Renmei* in 1990. Koga Shihan is presently employed as a professor at Yatsushiro National College of Technology.

magically raising ourselves out of the water like we were experts at the standing stroke. And, naturally, one of Toga sensei's assistants was a gorgeous Japanese woman who we each proceeded to wave to for assistance, over and over again.

While I lived in Japan, Eastern Europeans began moving to Tokyo— The Wall having fallen not long before. Three Bulgarian lads, one of whom had trained very seriously in Greco-Roman wrestling in the "Russian system," all joined Hombu Dojo following various adventures in the world. As we were all treading water around Miss Gorgeous-*deshi*, grinning stupidly like school-boys and jockeying for position to be next for "help," one of the Bulgars, tall, dark and handsome Kiril, looked over at me and said in thickly accented English, "You g't yurrrrr blue eyes out of herrrre!" I nearly drowned; I was laughing so hard. Recovering with a final splutter and one more gasp, I glanced up at the spectator balcony, and there was the Hombu Dojo *shihan* laughing heartily and shaking his head at us. No drownings. Some learning.

Samurai Master

The highlight of all the speakers I heard over the years was the year Tada sensei of Hombu Dojo was the featured speaker. The students were spellbound. You could've heard a hair hit the floor during his lecture. Here is a man who joined *Aikikai*, *Ichikukai* and *Tenpukai*, all on the same day apparently, and went on to train seriously and steadfastly within each discipline. His presence and piercing raptor-like gaze alone was enough to silence what could be on occasion a rather skeptical and boisterous, even confrontational, crowd.

He is a living testament to the value of training the mind, body and spirit systematically and continuously. Back then he moved like a man in his thirties or forties and he was in his seventies. I heard from some in attendance at the All Japan *Aikikai Embukai* in May 2011 that this has not changed. He'll probably just disappear into The Force one day. We meet someone so well-trained and refined like Tada *shihan* and think "wow"; impossible; but if asked how he did it, it would not surprise me if his reply paralleled Michelangelo Buonarroti: "If people knew how hard I had to work to gain my mastery, it would not seem so wonderful at all." That's what was staggering. To think what this man had chosen to endure and how it had transformed him. His exhibiting genuine humility when blessed with exceptional talent and extraordinary training is perhaps what's most amazing.

There were always surprises, and one of the foreign translators got his when confidently explaining in English for a young Hombu Dojo teacher, whose stature could be described as "vertically challenged." The teacher had given a detailed explanation in Japanese about how each person has to adapt whatever art they study to his own body. "I am not tall and have to work around this difference," he said in Japanese, as one example. Well, the translator's choice of word for difference was "handicap," which the moment it was uttered was met with a roar of "IT'S NOT A HANDICAP!!" from the teacher in perfect English. The group howled in laughter, particularly because Kanazawa sensei hadn't uttered a word of English all weekend until that moment.

There were opportunities to be out with the teachers as well, away from Tokyo, in a far more relaxed setting. One night a friend and I were out with two Hombu Dojo *shihan* at a local *izakaya* down by the waterfront and really enjoying the discussion, food and drink. One teacher, remarkable not only for his fluid technique but his big heart and sense of mirth, blurted, while snapping his posture upright to attention, "Oh! *Dai senpai!*" when the local grandfather, who by the look of it enjoyed his drink, shuffled in towards his usual stool. Smiles, waves and laughs were exchanged and naturally, grandfather was invited (and accepted) to join us on the tatami for the rest of the evening. [138] I witnessed this kind of goodhearted playfulness on numerous occasions on nights out in Japan and noted the general lack of attitude and posturing (aggression) too prevalent in the West.

Like so much of my experience in Japan, there really was (is) nothing like it. And all these extraordinary experiences unfolded from the simple "Yes" I had finally spoken in reply to a lingering sense since 1992 that my destiny lay in Japan. "Yes, man yes!" chants the passionate self-help seminar crowd in the Jim Carey film comedy, *Yes Man*. "Yes always leads to something good." "Never avoid opportunities. They may come in any form," claims the seminar pamphlet in the film. After taking on a seminar

---

[138] He was the good friend of a student in our group in fact; who'd been invited).

covenant to embrace the power of "Yes," Carey's character, formerly un-shakable "No Man" Carl Allen, finds himself saying "Yes" to everything that comes his way. Scanning the local coffeehouse's bulletin board, he hears himself saying aloud: "I <u>do</u> want to take guitar lessons! I <u>do</u> want to learn how to fly! Yes, I <u>would</u> like to learn Korean!" acquiring various skills that come into play in unforeseen ways in his life. As Carl's girlfriend-to-be later remarks, "The world's a playground. You know that when you're a kid, but somewhere along the way everyone forgets it."[139] While I certainly don't recommend indiscriminately saying "yes" to anything and everything that comes your way in life, maintaining a sense of wonder, openness and joy in living will make your journey a lot more enjoyable and make you a heck of a lot more fun to be around. It's easy to be a cynic or a critic, but nobody likes you much.

---

[139] See the trailer at www.youtube.com/watch?v=4WUr6P4mUso.

The Grunion are Running!

大学生
(*Daigakusei*)

I was born in Garden Grove, California (now home to "Little Saigon") and at about three years old moved to adjacent Anaheim (then) another new, clean, cookie-cutter community behind "The Orange Curtain" (Orange County or "the O.C." if you prefer) in "So-Cal" (Southern California), as some say.[140][141] As a young child in Anaheim, I used to climb up into the windowsill of my parents bedroom with my big sister to watch the Disneyland fireworks blast off every summer's evening. When I was seven, we moved to "No-Cal" (Northern California) to Burlingame, a quiet, almost quaint, commuter town fifteen miles (twenty-four kilometers) south of San Francisco on the bay side of the peninsula, aptly dubbed "Boringame."

I can remember not wanting to leave So-Cal. After all, it was home to Mickey Mouse and the beach. Even at that young age, it had made its impression on me and I dearly loved Los Dodgers y Los Lakers y Los Rams (the local baseball, basketball and gridiron teams). But when I heard from my folks that the new house had a wooden shed, a well and a creek next door? "Wow!" I was down with the move. "A creek?" There were adventures to be had! Of course, I couldn't have known it at the time but I would return to So-Cal at eighteen for four years of university, three years of law school, a professional career and the beginning of my aikido training.[142]

As a result of my dual upbringing, unlike many Californians I am not afflicted with the divisive So-Cal versus No-Cal mentality from which the state has suffered historically. It's a long and deep rivalry or even dislike

---

[140] Orange County is notoriously conservative politically.

[141] Back then O.C. WAS full of orange groves, before the Irvine Ranch was sold off and development ran wild to the very limits (or beyond) of public tolerance.

[142] I actually had my first class in 1977 in San Francisco but didn't stick with it as it was too far from my home.

(somewhat like Northern and Southern England or Northern and Southern China). I prefer to enjoy the best both have to offer and there's plenty on offer—a large population of East Asian immigrants and culture is certainly one of them. Typically, in So-Cal it's Japanese and Koreans (though let's not forget the big Viet and Taiwanese communities) and in No-Cal it's Chinese (southerners historically, but that's changing).

It's probably better to spend one's formative years in No-Cal where you can grow up a bit slower (if that's still possible anywhere in a now-wired world) but for university days and while you're young and single, then L.A. and the sun and surf are heaps of fun. Even after we moved north, we continued to spend every summer at the beach in So-Cal in (then) sleepy and (still) picturesque Laguna Beach at a old wooden bungalow my folks rented from friends. Two of my dad's seminary classmates and their families stayed in two other cottages on the same property, which certainly made it a tough crowd for the inevitable Jehovah's Witness or Mormon missionary who dropped by. So though I moved north where the beaches (and the surf) are far less hospitable, the So-Cal beach life remained in my blood.[143]

One So-Cal surf event that I was always curious about but never actually saw was the running of the grunion, not to be confused with the Running of the Bulls of Pamplona or The Snipe Hunt of North-America. [144][145] "The Grunion are running!" Hearing this at about eight or nine

---

[143]   Head north from Malibu and the water grows colder. Well before you reach the San Francisco peninsula, the sea becomes much more hostile. Think wild coastlines, head-numbing cold waters, wetsuits, booties and even hoods for surfing, plus massive surf and monstrous sharks. Fun!

Surf
- http://en.wikipedia.org/wiki/Mavericks_(location)
- www.youtube.com/watch?v=4Fqg43ozz7A
- www.surf-forecast.com/breaks/Mavericks

Sharks
- www.fearbeneath.com/category/habitat/california/
- www.time.com/time/magazine/article/0,9171,950217,00.html
- http://animal.discovery.com/videos/weird-true-freaky-great-whites-and-the-red-triangle.html
- www.greatwhitesharks.tv/shark-attack-fatalities.html

[144]   Hemingway wrote about it; friends of mine have done it but it is not without risk.
www.spanish-fiestas.com/spanish-festivals/pamplona-bull-running-san-fermin.htm
www.youtube.com/watch?v=DHO116nzdWw

[145]   Hold the flashlight behind the paper bag and imitate their cry "Heeersnipe! Heeersnipe!"

years old on holiday in Laguna Beach, I couldn't help but wonder, "Who are the Grunion, where are they going and why are they running to get there?" Turns out a grunion is a fish and they were "gettin' busy" (spawning). Every spring into early summer. Like clockwork.

> "The California grunion (*Leuresthes tenuis*) is a member of the New World silversides family, *Atheriniopsidae*, along with jacksmelt and topsmelt. Their usual range extends from Point Conception, California, to Point Abreojos, Baja California. Occasionally, they are found farther north, to Monterey Bay, California, and south to San Juanico Bay, Baja California. They inhabit the nearshore waters from the surf to a depth of 60 ft. ....
>
> Grunion are the object of a unique recreational fishery. These fish are famous for their remarkable spawning behavior, which evokes an 'I don't believe it!' response from people seeing or hearing about it for the first time.
> Grunion leave the water at night to spawn on beaches during the spring and summer months. For four consecutive nights, beginning on the nights of the full and new moons, spawning occurs after high tides and continues for several hours. As waves break on the beach, grunion swim as far up the slope as possible. The female arches her body and excavates the semi-fluid sand with her tail to create a nest. She twists her body and digs into the sand until she is half buried, with her head sticking up. She then deposits her eggs in the nest. Males curve around the female and release milt. The milt flows down the female's body until it reaches and fertilizes the eggs. As many as eight males may fertilize the eggs in a single nest. After spawning, the males immediately retreat toward the water while the female twists free and returns with the next wave.

The light blinds the Common Snipe and they run right into the bag. Really. http://en.wikipedia.org/wiki/Snipe_hunt

> While spawning may only take 30 seconds, some fish re-
> main stranded on the beach for several minutes.

> Spawning occurs from March through August, and occa-
> sionally in February and September. Peak spawning is late
> March to early June.[146]

Sad thing for the fish is that they make a good fry-up and people go down and catch them mid-orgy. There are rules for the catch, however: a fishing license, 16 years and older, "hands only" capture (no holes in the sand to entrap), no bag limit, but take only what you can use—it is unlaw-ful to waste fish.

This kind of seasonal cycle is miraculous. A Rolex, Hublot or Girard-Perregaux may all be beautiful chronometers sinfully coveted by consum-ers, but nature needs no Swiss-tinkered timepiece to follow its mysterious, innate, temporal rhythms. It happens harmoniously.

Daily life in Japan, even in the modern urban centers, is closely linked to the local natural phenomena: oceanic (tsunami), atmospheric (*tsuyu*, *typhoon*, snow, heat), geologic (mountainous terrain, volcanoes, earth-quakes) and seasonal (*kouyou* and *sakura*).

With spring in Japan come *sakura* (桜, さくら, cherry blossoms) – emblem of the Emperor. Cherry trees are indigenous to the Japanese archipelago and for centuries it has been the national tree. Cherry blos-soms are glorious and pure.

> Sleeping under the trees on Yoshino mountain
> The spring breeze wearing cherry blossom petals
> —*Saigyo*

From at least the *Man'yoshu*, the earliest Japanese poetry anthology, the cherry tree has captivated the Japanese psyche. It's an almost mystical fascination, and rightly so, because a cherry tree in full blossom is a mag-ical thing. Cherry trees can be ancient and vast, with thick dark branches stretching out high and wide. The tiny blossom petals fall from those lofty

---

[146]   Department of Fish and Game, California Grunion Facts www.dfg.ca.gov/marine/grunion-schedule.asp

heights, like pale pink powder-light snowflakes on a winter's day.

Shining spring day
Falling cherry blossoms with my calm mind
—*Ki no Tomonari*

With the flowering of the *sakura* come *hanami* (花見, はなみ, literally flower viewing) – festive picnics under the blossoms. Across Japan, people head to their favorite park, cemetery or other spot abundant with cherry trees to enjoy the fleeting beauty of the delicate blossoms that remind us of the brevity of youth and life but signal Spring's promise of renewal. Flowering and falling within a few days, the blossoms are symbolic of human life. With each falling flower, we see time is passing and sense our own mortality.

The radiance of cherry blossoms, their scent,
ever fresh with every passing year –
so man grows old, eternally.
—*Ki no Tomonori – Kokinshu 84*

Fortunately, *hanami* are much more festive than mournful, though there's a touch of melancholy or nostalgia. Better to celebrate life rather than fret over death. In Tokyo, favored locales include: Ueno Park, Aoyama Cemetery and Shinjuku Park. Picture hundreds, even thousands of people sitting under the pale pink blossomed trees on big bright blue plastic tarps (who knows why) or large pieces of cardboard jigsawed together for ground seating - all guzzling beer, swilling sake and gorging on *senbei* (rice crackers), *onigiri* (rice balls) or other local delicacies. There's lots of chatter and laughter, and singing often breaks out. It is a far more spirited occasion than the zen calm contemplation one might stereotypically (and erroneously) expect of a nature viewing by Japanese. For Japanese, witnessing the blossoming of the cherry tree, the falling petals, is a reaffirmation of their connection with their past and with each other – an expression of interpersonal, communal and national solidarity. Less poetically, but simply, the flowers are beautiful and it's a lot of fun.[147]

At Hombu Dojo, spring (and fall) heralds the arrival of the *daigakusei* (大学生, だいがくせい, college students) in droves. Many universities have aikido clubs and ten, twenty, thirty, forty students at a time arrive weekly at the dojo from schools on near every island in the Japanese archipelago. By planes, trains and automobiles, they trek to Tokyo rendezvousing at Shinjuku train station to make the fifteen-minute walk to the dojo *en masse*. You see them on the street herding towards Hombu.

> In this shimmering spring day,
> ah, with ever anxious heart
> the blossoms are falling
> —*Ki no Tomonori – Kokinshu* 57

How to spot them? As is the case in Japan, there is often a standard uniform integral to the identity of a group and its members. Male *daigakusei* are usually attired in a dark blazer, gray trousers, white shirt and tie, and each young woman sports her best plain dark suit and white shirt. Each totes a gym bag holding their *keikogi* 稽古着 (practice uniform*).*

Arriving at Hombu, they assemble in the dojo *genkan* (玄関, entry way) and in unison with great gusto *aisatsu* (挨拶, greet) the dojo staff at the front desk: "We are from [XYZ] University. Thank you very much." Thus begins their five to seven days of daily training: 6:30, 8:00, 3:00 and 5:30 classes, quickly grabbing meals outside the dojo, getting "pissed" (drunk for you non-Brits) at dinner, washing up at the local *sento* and then sleeping on the fourth floor of the dojo until wake-up call at 05:30 to do it all over again. Builds character.

For those of you who know little or nothing about student life at a Japanese university, up to high school is typically where the serious studying gets done. For most, university is four years of play before subjugation to company "life" as a salary man or "OL" (office lady). Typically, a university student will join one club on campus, e.g., tennis, judo, chess, etc. and loyally participate in all its activities. The club is <u>the</u> focus of their

---

[147] Autumn means the *kouyou* (紅葉, autumn leaves) when the vibrant myriad greens of a Japanese summer flame to brilliant reds, oranges and golds that will fade towards bleak winter with each falling leaf.

social activity at university, other than consuming mass quantities of alcohol and disgorging their stomachs to claim top marks in "Making Station Pizza 101." Years later, I worked part-time in Tokyo helping aspiring Japanese graduate students with their applications and essays to law school and business school in the U.S. It was amazing how little they had for their resumes during university years other than whatever club they had joined.

So what, you may be asking? Why the hack anthropological observations? What does this mean to you as a student at Hombu Dojo or as a visitor from abroad who happens to arrive during *daigakusei* migration? Crowds. Morning class is ordinarily crowded—anywhere from fifty to eight *aikidoka*. Add twenty to forty *daigakusei* and you have near-gridlock. So if you are coming from abroad and only have a few days or a week to practice, you may want to visit when the students are not. On the upside, the classes at 08:00 and 03:00 are fuller than usual and often invigorated for it. In any class, these kids are really *genki* (元気, げんき, full of energy) and particularly eager to practice with foreigners be they male or female and be ye large or be ye small, no matter. In fact, some leap at the chance to practice with a "foreigner." The migration of *daigakusei* to Hombu Dojo are a welcome infusion of enthusiasm and energy in my experience.

Wishing to die under cherry blossoms in spring
Cherry blossom season in full moon time
—*Saigyo*

To Iwama,
and Beyond!

合気神社大祭
(*Aiki Jinjya Taisai*)

O-Sensei died on 26 April 1969 at the age of eighty-six. If you consider that he was born in 1883 and if you appreciate the many hardships he had endured in his training and life, then his longevity is all the more impressive.[148] It's impossible for us to accurately imagine and fully understand the depth of feeling and sense of loss of those around this extraordinary person at his passing: his wife of sixty-seven years, his sisters, his children, his friends, his students, all *aikidoka* and so on. It's amazing how one life, lived well, can touch so many lives so powerfully and so positively. And the ripples continue to flow outward.

What begets genius? The hand of the Almighty God? Blind chance? Some precise mathematical formula of talent + opportunity + vision + inspiration + commitment + perseverance + experience x other factors? Or is it some more mystical quantum alchemy that's beyond our earthly understandings? "Genius, by its very intensity, decrees a special path of fire for its vivid power."[149] This much is for certain: once touched by it, how can you not feel a crushing sense of irreparable loss when it's gone? It's easy, maybe even typical, to decline into destructive thinking: "If only I had listened more! Watched better! Worked harder! Met sooner!" It's constructive to be thankful for the privilege and good fortune of the experience you've had, great or small, and carry that forward positively into

---

[148] A pioneer's life in Hokkaido? The Russo-Japanese War? Surviving "The Wild Wild East," Manchuria? Disease alone was likely to claim most well before their eighties. Antibiotics weren't even discovered until 1928 by Scottish biologist Alexander Flemming.

[149] Phillips Brooks (1835-1893), Harvard graduate, Massachusetts Episcopalian clergyman, abolitionist, author and professor. See www.preaching.com/resources/past-masters/11548006/, www.gutenberg.org/browse/authors/b#a5551 and www.finestquotes.com/author_quotes-author-Phillips%20Brooks-page-0.htm.

your own life and into the lives of others. Even so, that's not much consolation. Nothing wrong with grieving deeply.

My original teacher's move to Japan to live in and train at Hombu Dojo had to be delayed a year due to a family illness. Consequently, he just missed meeting O-Sensei. He spoke occasionally, outside of class, of his experiences in Japan from 1969, including his time in Iwama training with Saito sensei and how nothing had been touched in O-Sensei's study room in the Iwama dojo, out of grief and respect for the loss of their dear teacher. Cleaning out the personal belongings of a loved one after the person's passed away has a sharp finality to it, as if disturbing his belongings will end the chance that he will miraculously reappear, back among his things. Glancing at O-Sensei's workspace, my teacher had noticed a collection of books/scrolls and he couldn't resist slipping into the room one day and quickly writing down each and every title he could. Over the years, he found, bought and read every one, which I believe because I have never seen anyone read faster in my life, and, in law, I have met some very intellectually gifted people.[150]

In remembrance and respect of O-Sensei's extraordinary life and the gift of aikido, Hombu Dojo holds two events each April. The first is at the dojo. On the twenty-sixth of April, people gather there for *Shinobukai* (偲ぶ会, remembrance gathering) where we watch two films about O-Sensei's life and, since his passing, one concerning Second *Doshu*, *Kishomaru Ueshiba*. Some speeches are made. Some toasts of sake follow. Then the three films. It's an unadorned, thoughtful remembrance of a great man and the extraordinary son who followed him.

The twenty-ninth of April is *Shōwa* Day (昭和の日, *Shōwa no hi*) in Japan, an annual national holiday that observes the birth of the Shōwa Emperor (Hirohito, from 1926 to 1989) and encourages public reflection on the regrettable events of his reign over Imperial Japan (大日本帝国, *Dai Nippon Teikoku*). On that day, *aikidoka* trek to Iwama in Ibaragi prefecture to commemorate the Art of Peace and its founder by visiting the Aiki shrine and O-Sensei's old dojo, and perhaps climbing the nearby mountain *Atago san* (愛宕山, あたごさん) where O-Sensei and his deshi would practice from time to time. The gathering is known officially as the

---

[150] Although, some lawyers questioned whether they had put their intellect to the highest best use.

Aiki Jinjya Taisai (合気神社大祭, あいき じんじゃ たいさい) or the Aiki-shrine grand festival.

Making the pilgrimage to Iwama for the first time should be a thrill for even the most jaded *aikidoka*. Getting there is an easy two-hour train ride on the Joban line from Ueno or Nippori stations in Tokyo, and the trains are usually filled with others recognizable as making the trek. On arrival at quaint Iwama-*eki* (岩間駅, いわまえき, Iwama station), a pleasant ten-minute walk to the dojo follows. Located in the Yoshioka district of the town of Iwama, the Ibaraki dojo (茨城支部道場, Ibaraki Shibu Dojo), sits on a quiet (now) residential street, abundant with trees and greenery. It looks like something from a bygone era because it is—an old, single-story, wooden Japanese dojo. It's an architectural treasure that celebrates the natural beauty of wood and the considerable skills of Japanese carpentry in rendering it.[151]

Run by the Aikikai Foundation, the dojo was established under the supervision of O-Sensei and completed in 1945 and originally called *Aiki Shuren Dojo* (合気修練道場, harmonising drill dojo). It was later moved to the present-day location and expanded from twenty-four to sixty mats. After the Founder died, the dojo was in the care of Saito Shihan, who served as chief instructor until his passing. The Aikikai renamed it *Ibaraki Shibu Dojo* and Isoyama Shihan, who began training at *Aiki Shuren Dojo* in 1949 (at age twelve), serves as its chief instructor.[152] The Aiki shrine sits in an adjacent clearing amidst a hoary grove of tall, deep evergreens, with a few blossoming trees. There's an undeniable majesty, beauty, serenity and sanctity to the setting. Everything was as I expected (having seen it in films), but on a scale somewhat smaller or more intimate than my imagination had invented in its enthusiasm over the years leading up to the visit.[153]

A brief religious ceremony is conducted inside the shrine by white-

---

[151] Regrettably, it was damaged in the 2011 Tōhoku earthquake but thankfully has been repaired.

[152] Summarized from Wikipedia (which can suffer from errors, bias or both). See www.en.wikipedia.org/wiki/Iwama_dojo. See too the *Hombu* website at www.aikikai.or.jp/eng/ibaragi/ibaragi.htm and the *Ibaraki Shibu Dojo* homepage at www13.big.or.jp/~aikikai/index.html.

[153] You can get a glimpse of the shrine at www.mustlovejapan.com/subject/aiki_shrine/spot335.html and have a bird's eye view via Google Earth: Aiki shrine, Iwama, Kasama, Ibaraki.

robed, black-hatted *Omoto-kyo* priests, which includes some chanting and haunting ancient music. To my untrained eye, it looks a lot like Shinto ceremonies I have seen. The tunes certainly add to the mystery, but you won't find yourself humming them afterwards.[154] The current Doshu gives a very brief offertory demonstration of aikido techniques (*hōnō embu*, 奉納演武). Reading the amusing book *Angry White Pajamas*, about a Brit journalist's year in Tokyo in the Yoshinkan intensive training program, I laughed (at him) when he described the demo at the Aiki shrine as being somewhat overly compliant on the part of the *uke*. The area in the shrine is about the size of postage stamp, *Doshu* was rather elderly at the time, it's a demonstration of *kata*, what's the *deshi* supposed to do? Try to block *Doshu*? It showed at least one big gap in the guy's learning during his "intensive" year.[155] *Iwama, Yoshinkan, Aikikai,* whatever; there is always some guy telling you "It's not like back in the day" or "We have the real stuff." How about we all just do aikido? Hell, visit three different dojos in one "style" and you'll see three different expressions of the art. For certain, if I entered other dojos of various aikido "styles," I would learn plenty at each place. Find your own way! Anyway, on the twenty-ninth of April at the shrine (in the shrine, actually) there is a brief, simple demo. Short. Simple. Not a *shiai* (試合, しあい, match). The ceremony is a beautiful ritual of remembrance, thanksgiving and prayer for the Founder and Second *Doshu* Kishomaru sensei, and for the continuing development of aikido and its aspirations and contributions towards peace in the world.

Following the ceremony, there's a massive picnic. A time to eat and drink together, see old friends and perhaps make new ones. Back in the day, *Saito* sensei was still running the dojo and it was interesting meeting Iwama students. Naturally, some exuded "we have the real aikido" smugness, but others were cool. Cuts both ways regarding Tokyo people, too. Not my concern. Better to look for something to like in every person I meet. After the festivities, people pack up and head up Mount Atago (by foot or by car and then foot) to visit the mountaintop shrine. Others just head back home, passing on the hill hike. Either way, the festival is a

---

[154] Regardless of my own views, I found an article by Homma Shihan regarding the event very thought-provoking. www.nippon-kan.org/?p=1168.

[155] Other than that, it was a fun read, but principally for his capturing aspects of how wacky life in Tokyo can be for foreigners.

thoroughly enjoyable day trip from Tokyo and a rite of passage for any *aikidoka*—the past is prologue.

My first year in Japan, I attended *Shinobukai* and planned to go to Iwama for the *Aiki Jinjya Taisai*, but as the Bard of Ayrshire wrote: "The best laid schemes o' Mice an' Men, Gang aft agley, An' lea'e us nought but grief an' pain, For promis'd joy!156 I was <u>supposed</u> to go with friends from *Saitama ken* (Omiya) who had visited my dojo in Los Angeles years ago. Really lovely people. I've heard that people from this area actually have a reputation for being particularly good-natured even beyond the typical *tatemae* pleasantness of most Japanese. The "plan" was that I would catch the train up from Tokyo. At their station, I would step out on the platform, where they would be waiting. They would play "Spot the Big Tall White Guy." Once spotted, we'd all get on the train and off we'd go for the event. Simple. Yet, "there's many a slip twixt the cup and the lip."

So the night before, I am out in the Ebisu district of Tokyo looking for a particular pub to meet some friends. Going on three months in Japan now. I'm standing on the corner across from the station, trying to filter out the neon and noise enough to figure out where's the bar. I spot a white guy, walk up and ask for directions: "Excuse me. Do you know how to get to What the Dickens?"157 I look at him and start thinking, "Hey; I know this guy. I know I know this guy."

"Brendon Monis?" Yep; hadn't seen the guy in fifteen years, and in the middle of Tokyo, he's the one guy I choose to ask for directions. He'd been living in Tokyo the past five years. "It's a small world after all; it's a ..." Sorry; it's stuck in your head for at least three days now, but it had to be sung.

Stranger still, Brendon was going to What the Dickens, too. Once we got there, we sat at a booth in the back, leaning forward on the wooden table shouting over the band's blaring horn section. We proceed to get completely "o-bli-ter-ated," while recounting not only all our *My Old School*

---

156 From Scottish national poet Robert Burns's poem *To a Mouse* written in 1785 in the Lowland Scots dialect. In English? "You make plans but shit happens and you're left with zilch or worse."

157 It's a British pub with live blues, jazz and other music, exhaustive beer menu and no cover. See www.whatthedickens.jp.

tales but catching up on our lives since, discovering that we were both in the midst of sorting out difficulties with particularly fetching members of the fairer sex. A number of his friends and a few of mine joined us, smiling politely at our inside jokes and old tales that we found so hysterical. At closing, the *njikai* (second party) was at his apartment not far from Nishi-Azabu. At that point, stumbling up to that "fork in the road," that's when good sense should've kicked in and I should've headed home, but instead I foolishly reckoned, "Oh, I'll still make it home and to the station in the morning. No problem!" Problem.

Though by nature and habit an early riser, I awoke at about noon sprawled in my shorts on the couch at Brendon's flat, with little recollection of how I got there, having: slept through the alarm I'd set, missed the train to Saitama to meet my friends (who never Spotted the White Guy), missed the train with my friends to Iwama and missed my first chance to attend the memorial. Whoops. Yeah; big whoops. Of course, I phoned and eventually reached a foreign student that I knew from the Omiya dojo, told him flatly what happened (it didn't deserve an "explanation") and apologized profusely. He instructed me in what to say to the teacher from this dojo. I got real-time experience in how to apologize in Japanese. Like so much else in that country, it's an art form.

Moushiwake arimasen (申し訳ありません)! This literally means "there is no excuse." It's a serious and formal expression that should definitely be used to superiors. It shows a stronger feeling than *Sumimasen* (すみません). You are just accepting your part in the event and not making any kind of explanation or excuse or attempting to shift blame elsewhere. If you are apologizing that something has been done, *Moushiwake arimasen deshita* (申し訳ありませんでした) can be used. Like *Sumimasen* (すみません), *Moushiwake arimasen* is also used to express gratitude. *Shitsurei shimashita* (失礼しました) is a formal expression, but it doesn't show as strong a feeling as *Moushiwake arimasen*. You might use *shitsurei shimashita*, for example, if you bump into someone you do not know. It all depends on how polite you want to be. That's an art form in Japanese.

This situation definitely required an "M.A." A big one. In ALL CAPS.

I telephoned the sensei and I said it, sincerely—"*MOUSHIWAKE ARI-MASEN*"—and I shut up and listened, repeating "sorry" (*sumimasen*) when it was clear some acknowledgement was required. Sincerity counts a great deal in Japanese culture, and they can be very forgiving for even egregious errors if your apology is appropriate and sincere and you are truly repentant. Of course, eventually he asked me (knowing full well, having already spoken with his foreign student) what the hell happened? In broken Japanese and English I told him. "Old classmate. *Guuzen*. So drunk."[158] Silence. He chuckled. "Don't let it happen again." Fortunately for me, too, in Japan being shit-faced and acting the fool (on occasion) covers a myriad of offences. He was forgiving, and they invited me to participate in the All Japan Aikido demonstration (*Embukai*) with them and to attend their special practice with (Third) *Doshu* a month later. The fences I'd broken were mended, thankfully, and I certainly appreciated the sensei's kind-hearted wife taking me aside at the dinner and reminding me that moderation and balance were key in life. I smiled in genuine gratitude, swearing to myself to resist the "Call of the Wild" next time. English novelist W. Somerset Maugham claimed "excess on occasion is exhilarating. It prevents moderation from acquiring the deadening effect of a habit." True enough Maugham-san, but pick the right occasion.

It was an important early lesson in Japan. Relationships matter. Punctuality matters. Reliability matters. Consideration for others matters. Apologizing matters.[159] My stupidity and selfishness had caused a lot of trouble for other people. I recognized it, put my hand up, "my bad," accepted my part and tried to move forward positively. To me, aikido training is not just about learning martial techniques. Through our training, we strive to become stronger in many ways, but we should also strive to become more generous, unselfish, compassionate and forgiving people who accept responsibility for and learn from our errors (in action and inaction), rather than making excuses. *Moushiwake arimasen*!

---

[158] *Guuzen* (偶然, ぐうぜん, (by) chance; unexpectedly; suddenly; accident; fortuity.

[159] They all matter if you want Japanese people to take you seriously, though one friend at Hombu Dojo, American, is "Mr. Teflon." Nothing sticks. It's near legendary how he can be unreliable, but in his case it's forever "charming." He's just a very likeable guy in any language.

After my missed-adventure to Iwama,   I had to scoot out of Japan. In my "aikido sabbatical" first year, I only had a tourist visa, which meant that I couldn't stay in-country more than three months at a time. The U.S. wouldn't let Japanese citizens (or anyone else) remain longer than three months so *quid pro quo* from the Japanese government to U.S. visitors. People from many other countries can stay much longer in Japan, e.g., six-month working holidays from the U.K, Canada, South Africa or Australia. Me? I had to leave and plan how to make sure they let me back in when I returned. Of course, I'd thoroughly investigated and considered getting a student or cultural visa, but felt it was more hassle, money and obligation than it was worth.   Going out-and-back quickly to Korea or China or other spots in East Asia for a weekend would only enhance my adventure and lend perspective.160

The first out-and-back "visa run" was easy. Being American, in particular fitting the Japanese stereotype of an American (tall, white, blond, blue eyes), and having a professional job (attorney), the first exit and re-entry wasn't a problem. "Why on Earth would a California lawyer be staying in Japan to work illegally?" I didn't make the rules but was willing to exploit their discriminatory views. Visa trip number one, I flew to Hong Kong for a weekend with the thought of perhaps going to the Philippines, Vietnam or Cambodia if the spirit moved me.

Hong Kong! I'd been before in '94 and was excited to return because it was just before "Handover." What a fascinating place. Conceded by the Chinese Qing Dynasty to Britain, under the Treaty of Nanking (Nanjing), after some old-fashioned imperialist bullying (a timeless and most unfortunate human misbehaviour best left behind us), it officially became a Crown colony in 1843. When Britain took possession, the island was described as "a rock with hardly a house upon it". The neighbouring islands supported scattered fishing villages, while the Kowloon peninsula and the New Territories to the north had settlements of rice farmers of several large clans. Despite long odds, this lush, rugged, mountainous "rock" in the Pearl River estuary, with a natural deep water harbour, proceeded to develop from a forgotten backwater of the Chinese and then British Empires into one of the most dynamic modern cities and a global

---

160 I had heaps of frequent flyer miles from my work.

trading and financial powerhouse.

Hong Kong! East meets West. The South China Sea, the mountains and skyscraper skyline all help place Hong Kong firmly in the pantheon of the world's best cityscapes, alongside New York, Paris, Sydney, San Francisco, Rio de Janeiro, Edinburgh and Cape Town to name a few.[161] The people, the places and the attractions are imbued with a sense of the Age of Empire (Chinese or British), of adventure or fun: the Yue, the Han, the Hakka, Arab and Outer Barbarian traders, Victoria (or Fragrant) Harbour, Hong Kong Island, Lantau Island and the Big Buddha, New Territories, The Peak and Peak Tram, Kowloon and the Peninsula Hotel (legendary "Grande Dame of the Far East"), Causeway Bay, Wan-Chai, Central and the double-decker trolley (the Ding-Ding) that links them, Happy Valley Race Track and the Hong Kong Jockey Club, Admiralty, Repulse Bay, Big Wave Bay, tai-pan (大班), hongs and the trading houses of Jardine, Matheson and Swire, the Star Ferry, junks and floating restaurants, cobblestoned stylish watering hole Lang Kawi Fong, opium dens and Suzie Wong, Flagstaff House and Government House and the still active Triads, the now renamed Royal Hong Kong Police Force and the now gone Brigade of Gurkhas. Set the zoom just right and a Google Earth view of modern Hong Kong might reveal it as a place of extraordinary geographic beauty, visible and palpable history, extravagant wealth amidst humble poverty, glorious architecture—past and present—wearing against tropical decay and typhoon, all slightly blurred by the hum and

---

[161] Surrounded by the South China Sea, Hong Kong Island is a lushly green, mountainous, volcanic rock sitting just south of the Tropic of Cancer on latitudes similar to Calcutta, Havana and Hawaii and shares longitude with Bali and Perth. It's just 1,095 sq. km (423 sq. miles), though they are continually expanding it by reclaiming land from the sea (too often from the harbour). The island of Hong Kong is 80 sq. km (31 sq. miles), Kowloon peninsular is 47 sq. km (18 sq. miles), the New Territories is 794 sq. km (306 sq. miles), and the remote islands total 175 sq. km (67 sq. miles).

whir of relentless trade.[162] [163] [164]

In the expanse of human history, however, Hong Kong (as we know it since British "development") is just a blade of spring grass. No doubt lots occurred on or principally around the island before Royal Marines rowed ashore at Possession Point (水坑口, Shuǐ Kēng kǒu, water hole or puddle mouth) in the winter of 1841, planting the Union Jack, "claiming" it for Her Majesty Queen Victoria and setting Hong Kong on its dynamic, but unlikely, course to global prominence.[165] Clinging to the outer fringe of "Bumfung" Canton (now the PRC province of Guangdong), Hong Kong was largely a neglected, if not forgotten, corner of that period's Chinese empire, a backwoods of scattered communities of farmers, fishermen and pirates (the maze of isles and inlets affording ideal cover and swift access to the Pearl River and prey). The northern rulers in Beijing looked down on the southerners (as is sometimes the case today) and southerners (as is the case today) took solace in Chinese wisdom: 天高皇帝远 or tiān gāo huángdì yuǎn or heaven high, emperor far or better: "the heavens (or mountains) are high and the emperor is far away." Even after the Brits took and kept it for a bit, the place was a vice and plague ridden boondocks, deep in the shadow of Shanghai, which was East Asia's premier trade, financial and style centre until after World War II. The revolution, Great Leap Forward and Cultural Revolution set Shanghai back a smidgen, though it's making up for lost time. China's big enough to have

---

[162] Hong Kong offers excellent outdoor activities and some good beaches with surf, so long as they have the occasional water quality (sewage) issue controlled. There were six fatalities from shark attacks (typically Tigers) in the 1990s so most public swimming beaches have shark nets, though Darwin Award winners occasionally swim over them.

[163] A favourite of celebrities, leaders, writers and singers, The Peninsula (built in 1922) is a throwback to a romantic age of travel by ocean steamliner, Pan Am's "China Clipper" or the Trans-Mongolian railway and the elite who could afford such luxurious travel and lavish accommodation. The British signed their articles of surrender to Imperial Japan at the Peninsula in 1941. See e.g., www.willysthomas.net/Peninsula.htm, www.flyingclippers.com/M130pichistory.html

[164] Hong Kong took advantage of its political and economic freedom under Britain and developed a famous film industry, particularly for martial arts or police/gangster genres. Despite recent decline, it has produced stars such as Bruce Lee, Jackie Chan, Jet Li and Donnie Yeun and directors John Woo and Stephen Chow. www.lovehkfilm.com

[165] "We landed on Monday, the 26th, at fifteen minutes past eight, and being the bona fide first possessors, her Majesty's health was drank with three cheers on Possession Mount." So wrote Captain Edward Belcher in his 1843 book *Narrative of a Voyage Round the World*. Volume 2. p. 147–148. First possessors? Hmmmm.

more than one special city.

The new Hong Kong International Airport, Chek Lap Kok (赤鱲角機) is a feat of engineering, if not a work of art, winning a number of prestigious awards. However, landings at the old Hong Kong International Airport, "Kai Tak" (啟德機場) were a white-knuckle thrill-ride. Located on the west side of Kowloon Bay in New Kowloon, opposite Hong Kong Island and its stunning skyline, Kai Tak was flanked to the north and northeast by rugged hills (10 km away) some as high as 2,000 ft (610m). East of the runway, the hills were less than 5 km away. Just south of the airport was Victoria Harbour, and not much further south was Hong Kong Island, with hills up to 2,100 ft (640m). It had one runway, built by reclaiming land from the sea, that jutted out into Victoria Harbour. Three sides of the runway were surrounded by water, while at the north end, multi-story buildings stood just across the road. Picture a shoebox with one of the short end sides missing (the two long sides and one short side being the hills and tall buildings of Kowloon and Hong Kong) and picture a big hole down the middle of the box (the harbour) with one strand of cardboard extending out into the hole (the runway). Now imagine a tiny plane flying into the box on the left side, making a tight right turn and landing on the left side of the box onto the little strip of cardboard that sticks out into the hole—stopping just in time not to drop through the hole (the harbour).

Real-time planes flew in—mountains to the left, the harbour and Hong Kong Island to the right—and made a big right-banking u-turn, belly towards the mountains, to line up the runway for touchdown. It was spectacular, and so close to the high-rise buildings on final approach that through the plane window I saw a guy on his couch watching telly. The U.S. television's History Channel program *Most Extreme Airports* ranked Kai Tak the world's sixth most dangerous airport.[166] Once safely touched down, disembarking from the plane down a portable stairway for the walk across the shimmering hot tarmac to customs and immigration seemed of another age.

Thankfully, my United flight south from Tokyo had a happy landing at Kai Tak. It sounds cliché that on the flight I met a stewardess, a beautiful curvy lady from Bhutan, with a thoroughly charming British accent.

---

[166] See www.youtube.com/watch?v=T36xY3sQFEY.

This was pre-911 days and security was more relaxed, but not so relaxed that I was allowed to get off the plane during boarding to buy batteries for my Sony Walkman. (It's '97 kiddos, and the options were: cassette tapes, mini-discs or CDs).   I'd found my row and seat and then realized "Whoops; no juice for tunes!" The stewardess reminded me leaving the plane was a no-no. Later in the flight, she'd deliver me a bottle of red wine as consolation. I reckoned it would be rather ungentlemanly of me not to return some favor, so a few days later we shared an evening meal in Mid-levels, and while the food proved a disappointment, the company didn't. After-dinner drinks on the sheltered patio of a hidden Lang Kwai Fong bar included a steamy South China torrential downpour. One day I'm fighting over other people's money in a law firm in downtown L.A., the next I'm in Hong Kong having dinner with a Bhutanese stewardess before returning to Tokyo for martial arts study. Alas, the romance was not to be, as I remained captivated by my wife-to-be (who was studying for her M.A. in Seoul) and the shapely stewie was struggling with a hometown Himalayan relationship with sectarian strains (a close friend of the king who was a Buddhist but she a Catholic, him nicknamed "Massive" for his oversized head) and overcoming a bad dating experience with a *furyo gaijin* in Hong Kong. *Zannen* (残念, ざんねん, too bad).   Still, charming female company is always a pleasure in my view, and the evening added texture to the adventure.

I was staying with a school friend (and his wife and two children) who was working in finance in Central and living the expat-life in an old house on a quiet street in the hills of Repulse Bay. He'd studied Mandarin (due to his family's leather business) back when everyone else was studying Japanese. While studying in China in the mid-eighties (people still in grey or green Mao suits and clutching their little red books), students would rush up to Chris at school and ask things like "Chris! Chris! What is the difference between a brook, a creek and a stream?" Uhhhhh. Good question. Being an international ambassador for your country and the standard bearer of the (American) English language is never easy. Chris and I had known each other since third grade, schooled together all the way through UCLA and have one of those uncommon friendships that despite separations of years or miles, the next meeting is like you saw each other yesterday. You just pick up as if the gap never occurred.

I could come and go as I pleased. Chill by the community pool. Enjoy their Filipina amah's cooking. Whatever. I rested, healing up from three months of relentless training. I thought of Japan and considered my path a bit, though, frankly, "when eating, eat; when drinking, drink." My mind stayed where I was, doing what I was doing. Along with my dinner date, I made a few other visits into Central, revisiting The Peak and some other familiar historical sites. After all, Hong Kong was being "handed over" in just a few months and I wanted to breathe in the last of its colonial freedoms. At the time, there was a lot of angst over exactly what would happen when the keys to the city were handed to the communist regime of the PRC. Mostly, I just relaxed and enjoyed the posh accommodations and being part of a family.

Chris would be relocating to the U.S. soon and his Mrs. wanted to furniture shop, so I joined the retail raid. Doesn't sound so enticing, but this foray involved taking a sleek hydrofoil, skimming west 60 kilometres, to explore the antique markets and other offerings of Macau, Hong Kong's (then) poorer "Portuguese cousin." The first and last European colony in East Asia, the Portuguese arrived in the Pearl River delta in 1513, well before the English (circa 1635 and not yet "British"), and Macau soon became a trading centre which they administered until "handover" in 1999. With the permission of the Emperor of China, Macau monopolized trade between China and Japan and between those two East Asian nations and Europe. Since I visited in 1997, it has been transformed into a major gambling centre (from the seedier one that it was) to rival Las Vegas, but in many ways it remains a harmonious blend of things Portuguese and Chinese, including the gentle old architecture like former cathedral Ruínas de São Paulo (大三巴牌坊) and the streets and plaza of Largo do Senado (議事亭前地).[167]

Flagging down a black taxi, we sped towards Coloane (路環, Lou Wan) the southern, mountainous and less developed island of Macau. Through Portuguese trade and Catholic evangelism, there'd been historical ties between Macau and Japan. Ahead was the baroque-style Chapel of St. Francis Xavier, the sacred relics of which include the remains of twenty-six

---

[167] See photos at www.big-world-out-there.com/c/china/macau/ruins-of-st-pauls.htm and www.big-world-out-there.com/c/china/macau/senate-square.htm.

foreign and Japanese Catholic priests who were crucified in Nagasaki in 1597, as well some of the Japanese Christians killed during the Shimabara Rebellion of 1637, a populist revolt of samurai and peasants led by a sort of Jeanne d'Arc of Japan, sixteen-year-old Christian samurai Amakusa Shiro, a charismatic figure with purported mystical powers. But I was a guest; my friend's wife's agenda was historical furniture— antiques—not historical sites, and it was lunch time. Ponte da Amizade, Estrada do Istmo, driving over the silt brown waters of the Pearl River Estuary then onto the island on our way to Hac Sa (black sand) beach, I rolled the window down.

The strong salty breeze blew hot and, for who knows why, brought a moment's reflection on (or visceral reaction to) the past three months in Japan. My time in Tokyo felt like trying on a new suit of clothes that, being novel, weren't entirely comfortable yet, but fit so well that it didn't need a stitch of tailoring. In a word, perfect.

Perfect, at least until we got to Hac Sa for lunch at famous Fernando's. This restaurant serves Portuguese fare, which includes what can only be described as the crack-cocaine of brick-oven roasted chickens. Two bites in, and you're eating it by the fistful. Snarfing like the Donner Party post-rescue.[168] "Bring more bird!" If you weren't hooked yet, the pusher masquerading as a waiter brings equally addictive, fresh, warm-baked sweet-bread. Could I ever leave? Not without adjusting my belt a notch. As the mad Scottish father, Stuart MacKenzie, in Mike Meyers' nutty comedy film *So I Married an Axe Murderer* exclaims about Colonel Sanders and his chicken: "... he puts an addictive chemical in it that makes you crrrrave it forrrtnightly ...!" Finger lickin' good, and then some.

The visa run to Hong Kong proved a most excellent adventure, but I couldn't wait to get back to Tokyo and the dojo. So, with a final salute of the Noon Day Gun, I left Hong Kong and dreams of a greater South East Asia excursion for another day. I arrived back at Narita refreshed and ready to hit the mats. Getting back into Japan for another three-month stay on a tourist visa proved as easy as a South China Sea breeze. This time.

---

[168] See http://nevadacountygold.com/about/history-east-nevco/donner-party and www.pbs.org/wgbh/americanexperience/films/donner/.

Making a Spectacle
of Yourself

武大会
(Embukai)

My experience in 1992 at Hombu Dojo and traveling in the Japanese countryside had nurtured the seed of a dream that I might live in Japan one day. In May 1994, I visited Tokyo for the second time, specifically to train at Hombu Dojo and otherwise test the waters again. At the multinational law firm in Los Angeles where I was working, partners received four weeks vacation (holiday), associate lawyers three weeks, and staff two weeks. Americans are a funny bunch when it comes to time off. Most workers get their two weeks a year, while many Europeans seem to enjoy six or even eight weeks a year. Two weeks to jump into the Winnebago and drive off to "Wally World," like the Griswolds of film fame, or wherever.[169]

In Japan, like America, there's a frugality towards work vacation days. No doubt in part it's due to a suspicion that idleness is wastefulness, which would make any Protestant proud of the Japanese work ethic. But a slightly different social contract seemed at play. Japanese typically receive two weeks of personal holidays, but they often didn't take their allotted days (though it's changing). American thinking seemed something like, "Look, pal; you take two weeks off and I'll pull at the oar while you're gone, and then I'll go and you do the same for me; What d'ya say?" Japanese were like "Oh, I couldn't think of inconveniencing you by taking a break; shall we keep working together?" When they did take leave, they returned with gifts for the office—*omiyage* (お土産, おみやげ, present;

---

[169] "Winnebago" is a brand of "Recreational Vehicle," a sort of gasoline-guzzling house on wheels—"mobile home"— that a few holidaymakers rent to travel the highways and byways of the U.S.A.

souvenir)—typically cookies, candy or snacks of some kind to be shared by co-workers.

Anyway, spring '94, I still had all three weeks of my vacation coming and, not being Japanese, I was intent on taking it and stretching my stay in East Asia to the fair limit. First, I flew 14.5 hours from L.A. to Hong Kong, where my firm had an office. While in Hong Kong for a week (staying with the same friend I'd visit in May 1997), I would visit my firm's office, do some work and visit some clients and prospects, all with the intention of submitting timesheets and not burning vacation days. That was the plan, at least. With lawyers there's ever the possibility (always) of a discussion (an argument) to be had in the end, and one had to be prepared for it and that the outcome could go against you. It was almost part of the training of young lawyers—crossing swords with the partner managing your work, with caution, mind you. Too aggressive and you could find yourself in trouble (if not sacked). Too soft and you could find yourself disregarded (if not sacked). Anyway, that skirmish would come later.

It's an odd thing traveling that far, going from east to west to get to "the Far East." Think about it; from a Hong Kong perspective, I'm coming from the east.[170] From a California perspective, I'm going west. All I knew for sure was that the jet I was on was chasing the sun the entire trip. Pull up the window shade mid-flight and there was the glaring light of day, even though my body clock read well past midnight. Nine hours, three movies (on the screen hanging from the ceiling, kiddos), a Bloody Mary, two meals and a beer later, I washed down a sleeping pill with the last of the red wine, finally capitulating on my determined quest for natural sleep. Five and half hours later, I woke on approach. "Put away your tray table and make sure your seat is in the upright position." The plane touched down gently at Kai Tak International Airport. I managed not to tumble down the stairway while deplaning and wandered bleary-eyed and zombie-like across the tarmac and through immigration, shaking off the last of the narcotic.

This was pre-handover Hong Kong, and it still had its British sensibilities. But it was also pre-SARS Hong Kong, and "Honkers" were at their very rudest.[171] What a contrast that was for me from my first

---

[170] Typical LAX-HKG flight path. www.gcmap.com/mapui?P=LAX-HKG
[171] Some long-time residents I knew remarked that the city changed after SARS (and handover)

experience in East Asia in 1992 when I'd visited Japan. In Hong Kong, there was no hiding the disdain locals held for *gwailo*.[172] In Japan, even if deep down they harboured the same dislike, harmony was preserved for the good of all by the same good manners used amongst themselves. Despite some inhospitable locals, it was fantastic experiencing dynamic, exotic, magnificent Hong Kong for the first time. The lush green, hilly terrain. The stifling heat. The smothering blanket of humidity. The sparkling harbour. The glittering skyline. Clear skies, pre-PRC industrial air pollution. Full English breakfasts, with H.P. brown sauce. Outdoor escalators sweeping you up the steep hillsides of Central-Mid-levels.[173] The shameless haggling of traders at the Jade Market pushing fakes. (Mis)Calculating Hong Kong dollar prices into Greenbacks mid-barter. Walking wide-eyed through a Kowloon open air food market: civet cats, monkeys, turtles, insects and other critters that you could buy to wok. All still very much alive and kickin'. Never seen anything like it, or smelled. Further amazement at the races at the Hong Kong Jockey Club in Happy Valley; we left a few races early (penniless) and found traffic outside at a complete standstill. Gridlocked. Engines off. Doors open. Chinese drivers stood beside their cars, ears bending towards the crackling car radio, listening to the final races and cheering on their bets with a cackle of Cantonese.

Back then, my friends lived way around the other side of the island in peaceful, picturesque Stanley. Their high-rise flat offered spectacular views of the South China Sea, surrounding islands and Shek-O peninsula on the southern coast of the Hong Kong Island. In my enthusiasm, I imagined that I could see all the way to mainland China. The PRC wasn't yet in its pell-mell industrial-boom phase. It was still difficult for them to acquire luxury goods, even if one of the greater-among-equals was somehow flush with cash. However, the resourcefulness of Chinese people is a continuous wonder. One afternoon, standing on their balcony, a Mercedes sedan came screaming down the twisting road, speeding for the Stanley harbour. Hong Kong police were in rapid pursuit. Sirens wailing. The sea at the waterfront would end the chase. Nope. The car sped onto a waiting cigarette boat (engine at the ready, rumbling like thunder) where

---

and people became a bit more neighbourly.
[172] "Ghost man" (鬼佬) in Cantonese; a pejorative term for Westerners.
[173] See them at www.12hk.com/area/Central/MidLevelEscalators.shtml.

it was swiftly strapped down tight. The dagger-sleek jet boat launched forward, rocketing across the water past lazy Chinese junks waiting for wind in their sails. But wait! Police boats appeared from around the point—lights and sirens blinking and blaring—and the chase continued. At least I suppose it did, as far as PRC waters. Hopefully, the Merc was fully insured.

Over my jet lag, rested and restored by my Hong Kong adventure, I flew on to Narita airport, zipping down to Tokyo Station on the Narita Express. My first visit to Japan in '92, I had stayed in hotels and various *ryokan* (inns) around the country. Frankly, Tokyo (apart from aikido) had been the least desirable part of the journey. It's hyper-drive urban life was rather overwhelming and my Japanese was at its nadir. This time I knew a bit more of the local tongue, had some friends there (locals and expats) and was determined to get to know Tokyo better and see whether or not I would really enjoy living there, as I believed I wanted to do. This time too, fortuitously, I had a free place to stay—a massive 10,000 USD per month flat—courtesy of the guy who ran the derivatives desk at Morgan Stanley Tokyo. It was the kind of place only foreigners (whose companies pay their rent) or extremely wealthy Japanese could afford. An American I met there pitched for the Yakult Swallows baseball team who played home games at nearby Meiji Jingu Stadium.[174] My host, Tim, was a very generous, very hospitable East Coast American who opened his huge, extremely comfortable and convenient home to me for the three weeks I was there. It was an artificial test of Tokyo life, though, because I would probably enjoy living in luxury like that anywhere on Earth.

For those of you good with numbers, that's sounding like four weeks of vacation (a week in Hong Kong and three weeks in Tokyo) at a job that gives you three weeks vacation. However, as the law teaches us, "What is the rule?" "What are the facts?" "Does a particular set of facts fit within the rule or outside the rule?" There; now you don't have to go to law school. Anyway, I had brought gifts with me and planned to pay respects to some firm clients, meet some local lawyers and work half-days at the firm's Tokyo office for at least a few days. Perhaps for the first week, I would attend aikido classes for half the day and go to my firm's Tokyo

---

174 See http://tokyoswallows.com/about-2/going-game/.

office for the other half or vice-versa. Between my visits to the office in Hong Kong and the time in Tokyo, my "vacation" time would be well within the "three week" rule. That's the position I was taking and would defend at all cost.

Tim was an old pal of my Hong Kong buddy, from their days at Salomon Brothers investment bank, proving that the oft-held conviction that "all investment bankers are wankers (and that's an insult to wankers)" is, at least in two instances, most unfair.[175] Tim was very busy, very dedicated to his work, but graciously gave me the run of his place. He even threw a house party, and we went out on the town a couple of nights. It was the kind of hospitality that's not easily repayable. While in Tokyo, I had planned to see a friend who had inspired me to follow my dream of living in Japan, but he had died suddenly in Japan in March in a mountaineering accident. He had been a classmate at UCLA. My stay would include meeting many of his personal friends and professional colleagues and piecing together in my own mind what his life had been like in Japan. I had seen him in San Francisco in January, and he was exuberant about how great it was to be in Japan and how living boldly was the answer to life's questions. His death would help change my life.

But this book is about my life in Japan in 1997, not 1994, and I mention this prior trip because it influenced my decision to move, and it also offered my first chance to attend "Embukai" or rather, the *Zen Nihon Aikido Embutaikai* (全日本合気道演武大会), the All Japan Aikido Demonstration. Most of you will know that every year for the past fifty years there has been a demonstration of aikido at the *Budokan* displaying the skills of the various teachers from Hombu Dojo, from around the country and even from overseas. I say first "chance" because chances are opportunities and can be lost. Don't we all drop the ball on occasion? No? I can't help but chuckle whenever I meet people who are rather full of themselves, for whatever reasons. Self-deception comes too easily to too many of us. I mean, we all come into life helpless, gurgling, peeing, crying,

---

[175] At some point, Samurai attitudes towards money-making changed, as this purported quote by Mitsui Takatoshi (1622-1694), founder of the Mitsui empire reveals: "A great peace is at hand. The shôgun rules firmly and with justice at *Edo*. No more shall we have to live by the sword. I have seen that great profit can be made honorably. I shall brew sake and soy sauce and we shall prosper."

crapping little blobs, entirely dependent on the love and care of others, and often go out the same way in old age— in diapers. In between, most human lives are filled with so many stumbles, fumbles and bumbles that one needs to be in major denial to truly be self-impressed, assuming one is at all self-aware.

I remember a scene from the film *Defending Your Life,* starring comedian Albert Brooks and Meryl Streep, as two very different recently departed souls who find themselves in "Judgement City," a sort of purgatory between their last life and their next life. Their most recent past life is put on trial to decide whether or not they have learned and grown enough to move on to a higher level of existence. In the adversarial court proceedings, the prosecution and the defense show video clips of the defendant's life to prove their points. Streep's life is sublime but for the senseless bathroom fall at home that ended it. Brooks' classically neurotic character, Daniel Miller, on the other hand, dies after picking up his brand new convertible BMW and driving it head-on into a bus when he leans over to pick up CDs he's dropped in front of the passenger's seat. His life? At one point, his merciless prosecutor submits into evidence "a compilation of misjudgements; half of them fear based, half of them just stupid. ... 164 misjudgements over a twelve-year period." Next we see: Brooks leaping in futility onto the windscreen of his car (keys locked inside) as it rolls slowly out the driveway; Brooks happily brushing his teeth, vigorously gargling—with face wash, not mouth wash—and then spewing it across the mirror; Brooks "getting had" at a used car lot, salesman guffawing as he drives the clunker off the lot; Brooks table-sawing wood and cutting the saw stand in half, as it (and the wood) falls neatly in two pieces on either side of him; Brooks starting a hedge trimmer, losing control and cutting a patio-table umbrella in half, Brooks sitting inside his car, trying to unlock the driver's door from the inside by threading a coat-hanger through a gap in the window to hook the door handle, Brooks falling off his roof while installing a TV antennae ... [176] You get the picture. Take any life; there's cringeworthy footage aplenty. Hopefully for us all, this is only Hollywood, and the damning footage remains in the dusty vault of distant memories.

---

[176] See an overview at Imdb.com. www.imdb.com/title/tt0101698/

Anyway, I had arrived in Tokyo having forgotten that it was the week of the *Embukai*. Yes; how could I? The evening before, I had gone out to dinner solo in Omotesando and met two Japanese girls who were keen to chat with a foreigner. Problem was, my Japanese wasn't so hot yet (certainly not *nampa-waza* level), one spoke no English but pretty good Spanish, and her bubbly chubby friend some English.[177] I am a Californian, which means I studied Spanish from second through ninth grade (until I foolishly quit, having enough foreign language study to get into UCLA). Certainly "Donde está el aeropuerto?" would finally come in handy chatting with these J-girls. Either way, I never pass on a game of "International Charades": a few words and hand gestures, and you've got a conversation. "First word (1 finger held up) sounds like (tugging your ear lobe)?" It was an entertaining evening that kicked off in an Italian restaurant better known for showing old Hollywood films on the wall than for its food. The conversation literally was Japanese, English and Spanish. As a Southern friend would say, "fucked-up like a pile of coat-hangers." Charades changed locales and went late into the morning, so I decided to skip "morning class" and attend later in the day. When I arrived at the dojo, I found a sign on the door. Unfortunately, I could not read it, but obviously the place was a ghost-town for some reason. The whistling wind, tumbling tumbleweeds and coyote howling in the distance were dead giveaways. If I could have read the sign or if I had my thinking-cap on properly, I would have gathered that it was the day of the *Embukai* and if I had dashed over to Kudanshita and the Budokan I would have had a gander.

The octagon-shaped Budokan is usually packed for the event. Dojos come from all over Japan to participate. *Aikidoka* come from overseas, as perhaps some of you have done.[178] Before and after they demonstrate,

---

[177] *Nampa* is Japanese for picking up women. (ナンパ, 軟派, なんぱ flirt; scam; scope; skirt chaser). *Waza* (技, わざ) is *technique or art*. *Nampa-waza*, well, you get the idea: your techniques for chatting up women.

[178] A friend of mine was the minder for Steven Segal when he came and demonstrated one year. "Big as a house. Polished off a huge platter of sushi; solo." Who knows for sure, but the current girth of "The Great Pissed Off One" (as another friend fondly refers to Steven Segal the actor) makes one wonder. I only saw him once, in slimmer days in L.A. in front of my old health club—The Sports Club LA on Sepulveda, just south of UCLA. Big dude.

participants usually sit up in the stands and watch the other demonstrations. On the floor of the Budokan, light green tatami mats are set up to form five large squares—like Wellington at Waterloo. (Have a look on YouTube). Each square block of tatami is for a different demonstration. One square sits in the center and then diagonally off each corner of the four corners of the center square sits one of other squares. Each of the four corner squares is bounded by mats of another color: red, yellow, blue, green and white (in the center). This makes it easy for the participants and the viewers to know where a group is demonstrating. It's described in the program by color.

Annually, among other things, you got to see Isoyama sensei spectacularly hoist someone up over his head and toss him, Watanabe sensei receive oohs and aahs (plus a few cackles) while extraordinarily pliable (and compliant) *uke* writhe as if receiving The Cruciatus Curse and Tada sensei wows the crowd at the end just before Doshu provides a smooth and sharp demonstration of aikido. Each of the older teachers are living testimony that aikido training is the longed-for fountain of youth. I mean, if you saw Tada sensei walking down the street, based on his movement you might think he was a thirty-year-old man, not a (then) seventy-plus-year-old man. I also remember thinking one day after Arikawa sensei's class, "Boy; some dumb Tokyo street punk could make a massive mistake one evening trying to prey on sensei." "*Hora*! *Ji-ji* give me your subway money!" CRUNCH. SNAP. In fact, I thought he was going to punch my ticket one day in his class. I was practicing with two of his long-time students and *uke* "Nial and Nari." The class was crowded with *daigakusei*. We were on a tiny patch of tatami in the back corner. Nari threw me, I took *ukemi* onto the wood and with the "lightest of touches" (that's my story and I'm sticking to it) I tapped the bottom back window pane with my left foot. KER-SMASH! CRASH! There was that distinctive tinkle-tinkle-tinkle sound of the last shards and splinters of the glass settling on the roof below. Arikawa sensei was up front near the *shomen*. At the first sound of breaking glass, he looked up and across the room, then rolled like a boulder to the back where we were standing … or was there a flash of light and suddenly he appeared next to me? I forget. Actually, he walked up to me, and without uttering a word reached down, grabbed my foot and lifted it up to inspect it. Now, even on the warmest of days, I am not the most limber guy in the room, but terror can motivate us to exceed our perceived limits. Sensei's eyes scanned my foot, now held head high. He dropped it, kerplunk, as he turns muttering "*daijobu*" (okay) while walking away. "Shorts change; can I get a shorts change here!" Mercifully, I was spared; probably only because of my training partners. Now there are bars in front of the window and thicker glass.

In 1997, I decided not to participate in the event because I wanted to watch it all and film it. I finally participated in *Embukai* in 1998 with the people from Omiya who I mentioned previously. Did so again twice more with the Hombu Dojo group. Normally I just went and watched. Some of my friends took *ukemi* for teachers from Hombu Dojo. You are wondering how does it happen that a Hombu Dojo teacher asks you to take *ukemi* for him/her at *Embukai*? Who knows for sure? It seems to require some shifting thaumaturgical formula of abilities, circumstances and timing, few or none of which I have ever possessed to any sufficiency, including: having a close relationship with a specific teacher who is demonstrating, speaking good Japanese, your teacher back home having a close relationship (particularly senior) with a teacher who is demonstrating, using you as *uke* being good for the development of aikido in your home country and being particularly adept (or adequately so) at taking *ukemi* for the particular teacher who asks you. As far as relationships with teachers went, after my experience with my teacher in Los Angeles, I was an avowed *ronin* in Japan. I pretty much kept everyone at a safe distance, though I certainly enjoyed meeting them all and was ever grateful for what I learned from each one. I stole what I could from whomever I could. I climbed up the ranks in one class to the point of being called for first *ukemi,* but that was more because all my foreign seniors had returned home than because of any skill or relationship with the teacher. I was like athlete's foot; I wouldn't go away, so I had to be dealt with.

Now one job I coveted at *Embukai* was thumping the *taiko* (太鼓, たいこ, drum). There is a huge taiko just inside one entrance to the floor of the Budokan, which is used to signal the start and end of your demonstration. It's timed (obviously). A young friend of mine got to watch the clock and bang the drum for a bit one year, and that looked like good fun. BOOM and, if you don't get off the stage, BOOM again. I don't think I ever heard more than two thumps, but some demonstrators do need a polite reminder (BOOM) to "get off the stage!"

Embukai are not exclusive to Aikikai. Many martial arts hold such events. A friend in the Tokyo legal community practiced a bit of Yoshikan Aikido. He was a very pleasant American but always seemed a little too concerned that I appreciate this other branch of the aikido tree. I already did. I was fine with it. Great. You do another type of aikido. Cool. He invited me to attend the Yoshinkan Aikido *Embukai* and, naturally, I went, and it was both interesting and enjoyable. Smaller. It included some reg-imented 1-2-3-4 type demonstrations *en masse,* which seemed consistent with the suggestion I'd read somewhere that the "changes" Gozo Shioda had made to his expression of aikido were chiefly pedagogical. It was all interesting, but I was there to see the high-level teachers, and they were impressive. Perhaps not surprisingly, their aikido looked a lot like some Aikikai instructors' aikido. To me, the most important thing in studying anything is a good teacher (there are many) and committed, energetic, dedicated practice, rather than a particular "style."

I'm a martial arts *otaku* and I would love to have seen every *embukai* of every martial art in Japan, at least once. One event that always seemed to some-how escape me every year was the annual *Kobudo* demonstration at the *Budokan,* the *Nihon Kobudo Kyokai,* as it's known officially. As I recall, the Japan *Kobudo* Demonstration is held at the *Budokan* every February (it has been at locations in the country other than the *Budokan*), presented by the *Nippon Budokan* and the Japan *Kobudo* Association, and has been held annually for the past 34 years or so.[179] In 2009, participating schools included:

1. *Ryushin Katchu-ryu Jujutsu* (柳心介冑流柔術)
2. *Shosho-ryu Yawara* (諸賞流和)
3. *Iga-ryu Ha Katsushin-ryu Jujutsu* (為我流派勝新流柔術)
4. *Kiraku-ryu Jujutsu* (気楽流柔術)
5. *Tenjin Shinyo-ryu Jujutsu* 1 (天神真楊流柔術)
6. *Tenjin Shinyo-ryu Jujutsu* 2 (天神真楊流柔術)
7. *Hasegawa-ryu Yawarajutsu* (長谷川流和術)
8. *Daito-ryu Aikijujutsu* (大東流合気術)

---

[179] Nowadays you can see it on the Internet. www.youtube.com/watch?v=zn-p19C8MAQ&dist=PLA0AE606C652B2AFD

9. *Kito-ryu Jujutsu* (起倒流柔術) ……

down the list through to numbers 76, 77 and 78: *Ogasawara-ryu Kyubajutsu* (小笠原流弓馬術), *Nito Shinkage-ryu Kusarikamajutsu* (二刀神影流鎖鎌術), *Takeda-ryu Aiki no jutsu* (武田流合気之術).

I've learned that there are two principal classical martial arts organizations in Japan: the *Nihon Kobudo Kyokai* (日本古武道協会, Japanese Classical Martial Arts Association) and the *Nihon Kobudo Shinkokai* (日本古武道振興会, Society for the Promotion of Japanese Classical Martial Arts). Well-recognized schools are usually a member of one or both (sometimes both) of these associations.[180]

To this day, Japan offers an unparalleled amplitude of indigenous martial arts, each one organized, categorized and systematized as the locals (and few, if any, others) have the cultural gift for doing. And martial arts are (or at least were) connected generally to the ethos and daily culture of Japan in a way I have not seen in any other country, in my experience, in East Asia or otherwise.[181] I have yet to see someone on The Tube in London carrying an English longbow, but in Tokyo it was not surprising to see *kyudoka* with their gear slung over one shoulder walking through the subway station.

All year round in Tokyo, not only at such *embukai*, you can find just about anything you could possibly want to find for martial arts: *kobudo, gendai budo* or *kakutougi*.[182] You'll find *jiujutsu* (pick your *ryu-ha*) and its offspring judo (you want *Kodokan* or its ground-fighting arm *Kosen?*) There's karate aplenty (pick your *ryu-ha*). Stealthy *ninjutsu*? Yep. There are weapons dojos: *ken, yari, naginata, kyu* (on foot or on horseback?). Whatever you fancy! How to kill people with a toothbrush and dental floss (or in the case of one lawyer in my Tokyo firm, the lack of use of both, "*hakuiki-*

---

[180] See www.nihonkobudokyoukai.org/, www.koryu.com/library/gbuyens4.html and www.nipponbudo-kan.or.jp/shinkoujigyou/kankeidantai_03.html.

[181] I have noticed it a bit in Korea as well.

[182] *Kakutougi* (格闘技, かくとうぎ) are one-on-one fighting matches or combat sports, without weapons. Boxing would be a Western version, as would Mixed Martial Arts. *Vale Tudo* or "UFC" are *kakutougi-kai* (格闘技会, かくとうぎかい), martial arts or rather combat sports competitions. As the good book says, "what has been will be again, what has been done will be done again; there is nothing new under the sun". (Ecclesiastes 1:9)

jutsu").[183] Okay. I made that last one up ... but only about the toothbrush and floss, not the lawyer with the eye-watering pungent breath. And then there were the local hybrids and foreign imports: Pancrase, *Shooto*, BJJ, Submission wrestling, Boxing, MMA, Muay Thai, Wushu (Yokohama has a huge Chinatown), Western fencing and so on. All you have to do is look around a bit. iPhones at the ready; there's probably an app by now.

Many of my friends in Tokyo were (and still are) studying other martial arts as well as aikido. *kyudo, newaza, kenjutsu, sōjutsu* (槍術, spear), etc. One friend studies at the dojo of famed judo *newaza* specialist Hirata sensei under his successor.[184] Another does aikijiujutsu. Others *ken* or *jo-jutsu* or karate and some BJJ. I fancied studying boxing at one point (Japan has produced a number of world champions) and found a very old-school gym in the slightly dodgy *Uguisudani* area of *Shitamachi*, met the manager, learned how to wrap my hands and so on, but in the end there just weren't enough hours to add serious study of the sweet science to aikido, a new wife and professional work, and give each one the right amount of time, energy and commitment. Hell, another friend even started his own *ryu-ha*. Serious as a heart attack. Koichi Tohei was his children's class teacher at Hombu Dojo. My friend is about fifty now and was a close dedicated student of Arikawa sensei.[185]

Perhaps it's easy, over years of practice, to grow weary or even cynical towards events like the *Embukai*, but gatherings of this kind are important for the collective spirit of the art and the preservation, exhibition and promotion of it. It's easy to criticize, to tear down, to dismiss; but how can one contribute positively? That's the more challenging question, which is why so many people ignore or choose not to answer it—opting to be a sneering, snarky, little username sitting behind the safety of a computer screen. The answer lies in supporting the event, in ways great or small, to the best of your ability, whether you are living in Japan or afar. For example, in Japan, it has been on television, if I recall, and with the Internet and social media (for better or worse) a live international webcast might be a possibility. Going to

---

183 Exhaled air techniques: *hakuiki* (吐く息, はくいき, exhaled air; one's breath) plus *jutsu* (術 じ ゆつ, art; means; technique). This guy's breath could stop a rutting rhino's charge. ぷんぷん!

184 Search *Kosen* Judo Hirata. See www.youtube.com/watch?v=xjidQQz1yjM.

185 Nariyasu Enku Toyosaki, Founder of Self-Defense Aikido Genshinkai & Iaienkukai http://homepage2.nifty.com/self-defense-bushido/index.html

the event during your lifetime, if you live outside of Japan. Attending if you do live there. And so on. The *Embukai* is the singular annual mass celebration of our mutual pursuit. As an annual mass gathering, a celebration of the art, it should serve as a focal point and inspiration for every aikido practitioner, something that should be enjoyed locally and internationally to the fullest.

Don't miss it, like I did back in 1994! Oh; and what of my boss? My four weeks off? Well, I'd landed on Sunday and was back in the office early on a Monday. There's a seventeen-hour time difference between Tokyo and L.A., so jet lag hits hard. WHUMP! Despite a valiant effort and several stiff coffees, about an hour after lunch, I was slumped over in my chair, forehead smack on my desk, snoozing on a pile of papers, Post-its and office supplies. In my slumber, I must've heard someone coming because I suddenly jerked upright, wiping the slobber off my cheek and making best efforts to look alert. My boss, a superb trial lawyer who was notoriously confrontational (though surprisingly benevolent and a good teacher to me), knocked and called me into his office. "Got a second?" I nodded and shuffled down the hallway. In his office, he sat; I stood. He called me out on the extended absence. "Hey, you took four weeks vacation!??" I looked at him. "Really? I don't think so. I visited clients and did some work in both the Hong Kong and Tokyo offices, so it was a business trip and a holiday. I believe the days off comes to a bit less than three weeks, actually." He stared . . . thought . . . blinked a few times . . . studied me . . . paused and said, "Clever. I'll give you that one. Now get to work! Oh, and get rid of that paperclip stuck to your forehead."

Summer

雨降って地固まる
ame futte chi katamaru

after the rain, earth hardens

Wet Behind the Ears
(and everywhere else)

梅雨
(Tsuyu)

Many film aficionados claim the two "best" films (or at least most influential on directors) ever made are Orson Welles' *Citizen Kane* and Akira Kurozawa's 1950 film *Rashômon*.[186] Set in twelfth century Japan and using a series of flashbacks to tell the story of the murder of a samurai and rape of his wife on a forest road by an infamous bandit, Tajômaru (played brilliantly by Toshiro Mifune), Kurozawa cleverly examines the philosophy of justice and, in particular, the nature of truth when our understanding of truth relies so heavily on the frailties of human perception and character.

The film opens with a peasant sloshing through the puddles and muck as he sprints towards shelter from a downpour. He dashes into the burnt-out ruin of an old gatehouse named *Rashômon* (羅生門) where he finds a priest and another peasant (a woodcutter) already taking refuge from the storm. The two seem in a state of shock as they reflect on a trial they have just witnessed. The "horrible" story then unfolds as the woodcutter, who discovered the corpse, recalls the testimony of the only reported direct witnesses to the crime: the bandit, the wife and the samurai, whose spirit is channeled through a shamanistic medium (a *miko*, 巫女, みこ): "I am in darkness now. I am suffering in the dark. Cursed be those who cast me into this dark hell!"

Concerning the singular event, each eyewitness recounts a structurally similar story but with drastically different details. There was a murder and a rape, or was there? Which version, if any, is the truth? What is truth? Watching this cinema classic for the first time, I felt it was brilliantly told and deeply substantive, but I also made a more mundane observation: "Damn; does it rain hard in Japan!" Little did I know; boy, does it ever.

---

[186] Watch *Rashomon* at www.spike.com/video-clips/asqxfw/rashomon.

Years later one night, caught out in *Shinjuku* during a deluge, searching for some bar my friends were in safe and dry, I half expected to see a bearded guy in a robe leading pairs of animals onto a boat. Welcome to "rainy season" in Japan!

Technically speaking, Japan has two rainy seasons. The first is *tsuyu* (梅雨, つゆ) meaning "plum rain" since it coincides with the fruit ripening, which runs sometime May to July depending upon where you are in Japan. It's less poetically but perhaps more accurately referred to as *baiyu* (黴雨, ばいう, "mold rain") and occasionally by the rather sterile *samidare* (五月雨) literally "Fifth Month Rains" (in a Japanese traditional calendar). The second, perhaps lesser known or less oppressive, "rainy season" is known as *Sazanka Tsuyu* (さざんか梅雨, "Camellia rainy season" which apparently bloom then) arrives mid November and lasts into early December. Whatever you choose to call them, it's the spring-to-summer version that'll be the indelible climatic and atmospheric experience for most of you, unless you hail from parts on this blue planet between the Tropic of Cancer and Tropic of Capricorn. As a CNN story I read on *tsuyu* aptly put it, those "June showers bring ... uh, more showers."

Now, just because it's rainy season don't think that Tokyo necessarily gets the most rainfall in June or July. According to the Japan Meteorological Agency (JMA), September is the wettest month, but that's based on the total precipitation in the month, not a measure of how many days it rained during the month, and is skewed by typhoon activity.[187] Typhoon season actually overlaps with *tsuyu* and runs May through to October, with the heaviest storms arriving in August and September. Even when they miss Tokyo, there's plenty of rain.   In fact, typhoons don't hit Tokyo often; only two or three did while I lived there, but when one of these tropical-born tempests does strike the capital, it's an extraordinary experience, inside the safety of solid shelter. The wind howls; rain shrieks down in sheets (when it's not falling sideways); the windows shake; the buildings creak (and sway, if tall enough). But afterward, when the storm has passed, has the air ever smelled so clean or the sky been so crystal

---

[187] Japan Meteorological Agency www.data.jma.go.jp/obd/stats/data/en/normal/normal.html

blue?[188]

The length and strength of *tsuyu* varies. The ever-helpful JMA, a useful source for residents or visitors, provides regional averages of starting and ending dates.[189]

Region	Start	End
Okinawa	May 8	June 23
Southern Kyushu	May 29	July 13
Shikoku	June 4	July 17
Kinki (incl. Osaka, Kyoto)	June 6	July 19
Kanto (incl. Tokyo)	June 8	July 20
Northern Tohoku	June 12	July 27

For you Weather Channel junkies, rainy season is caused by an "itch." A very big "itch," the ITCZ (pronounced "itch") or Inter-Tropical Convergence Zone, to be precise. Observable from space, the ITCZ is a low-pressure band of clouds that encircles the Earth between approximately 5° north and 5° south of the equator, which is created by the convergence of the trade winds of the northern hemisphere with those of the southern hemisphere. The ring of clouds can extend for thousands of miles or be broken into a series of segments.

Within the ITCZ, the intense equatorial sun evaporates water, forcing moist air to rise until it cools and comes back down as precipitation.[190]   It's a daily convection cycle: liquid turns to gas, clouds form, building into thunderstorms, and by late afternoon the water comes back down in sharp showers. The ITCZ follows the sun and Earth's celestial orbit so as the northern hemisphere spring shifts into summer, with the tilt of the Earth's axis towards the sun, the ITCZ shifts north, pushing warm wet air before it. *Tsuyu* occurs when moist tropical hot air moving northward from the ITCZ collides with northern cold Siberian air, trapping an east-west rain front that stretches from the China coast east to Taiwan and northeast over the Korean peninsula and

---

[188] What is a Tropical Storm? http://worldlywise.pbworks.com/w/page/25349490/Unit%202%20Section%20C%20-%20Causes%20and%20effects%20of%20tropical%20storms%20and%20responses%20to%20them

[189] Japan Meteorological Agency www.jma.go.jp/jma/indexe.html

[190] See www.youtube.com/watch?v=q0wRv0C1wxo.

Japan.[191]

Tsuyu in Japan typically lasts about fifty days or so. Skies are dreary gray; it's not so hot, but the humidity is sky high. (I returned there May 30 through June 10, 2011 and it was bizarrely cool, in fact.) As the chart below from Japan-guide.com (via the JMA) shows, it doesn't rain continuously. It varies, not only how often but how it rains: a series of short showers, intense downpours, days of drizzle. It comes down, however, in the many different ways that nature delivers, short of "cold hard rain": snow, sleet and hail.

June

City	Max. Temp	Min. Temp.	Rainy Days	Rainfall	Sunshine
Sapporo	21 C (70F)	12 C (54F)	7 d	51 mm	187 h
Tokyo	25 C (77F)	19 C (66F)	12 d	165 mm	120 h
Osaka	27 C (81F)	20 C (68F)	12 d	201 mm	150 h
Fukuoka	27 C (80F)	19 C (67F)	12 d	272 mm	148 h
Naha	29 C (85F)	25 C (76F)	11 d	212 mm	182 h

July

City	Max. Temp	Min. Temp.	Rainy Days	Rainfall	Sunshine
Sapporo	25 C (77F)	17 C (63F)	8 d	67 mm	176 h
Tokyo	29 C (84F)	23 C (73F)	10 d	162 mm	148 h
Osaka	31 C (89F)	24 C (75F)	10 d	155 mm	186 h
Fukuoka	31 C (87F)	24 C (75F)	11 d	266 mm	183 h
Naha	31 C (88F)	26 C (80F)	9 d	176 mm	243 h

There will be some sunny days or bits of days. When they come, seize the day, including opening up and airing out your flat, hanging laundry, etc. Humidity remains the fundamental challenge. Everything seems to get moldy, and fast: clothes, shoes, keikogi, apartment, etc. Food goes bad faster. Skin wounds heal slower. Typical warm wet weather stuff.

Getting through a rainy season comfortably involves coming up with

---

[191] The location of the ITCZ varies throughout the year. It remains near the equator over water but over land (where temperatures vary) the location of the ITCZ can vary as much as 40° to 45° north or south of the equator.

your own strategy, depending on your working, living and training situation. To cope, I don't think you'll need to resort to Whacky-Gadget-Happy-Japan solutions like Dehumidifying Coat Hangers, Eco Shoe Driers, Neem Trees (repel mosquitoes, flies, and cockroaches who thrive in *tsuyu*) or other Akiharbara delights, but you may wish to explore it for fun. God knows what's been invented since I left. To me, the only essentials are hydrating properly, an umbrella at the ready, a timely cold shower, at least two *keikogi*, a good attitude and a bit of 我慢 (がまん, *gaman*, perseverance), which any aikidoka should have in abundance. Depending on your personal need for comfort, options might include:

- a lightweight waterproof jacket,
- an air conditioner (a bit expensive) or at least an electric fan,
- mosquito net for your bed (if you plan on keeping windows open),
- a "sweat" towel (手拭い、てぬぐい、*tenugui*), maybe the one you received for completing winter or summer intensive practice, or handkerchief (手巾, しゅきん, *shukin*),
- a folding or other hand fan (扇子, *sensu* or 団扇, *uchiwa*) or just grab one of the plastic ones they hand out at train stations,
- eating cooling foods like *zarusoba*,
- cold showers or the cold-plunge bath at your local *sento* (if they have one),
- the occasional laundromat dryer for your *gi's* (clothes are typically line-dried outside in Japan, which means longer drying times and dashing out to take in laundry before it gets wetter).

Be prepared for rain at any time. Every 7-11, Lawson, Family Mart, Sunkus or any number of other convenience stores is stocked with the basic gear you'll need. You can pick up a cheap plastic umbrella for about 300 yen or a disposable raincoat for as little as 100 yen. Hell, rain became so predictable that every time I brought my "brolly" it didn't rain, so I started leaving home without it and bought one if it did.

While *tsuyu* is a little uncomfortable and gloomy, it has its positives (always look on the bright side of life). It's part of the cycle of nature.

The rain is vital for rice farming and causes many flowers to bloom, so public parks and hikes have a very different look this time of year. There are fewer tourists and other travelers, so visiting popular places can be more enjoyable. The air is cleaner; I don't have allergies, but pollen and pollutants can be very bad in Tokyo. With cleaner air, the city and sites become more attractive: temples, gardens and hot springs, the clouds and wetness altering usual perspectives. Sitting in a *rotenburo* (outdoor hot-spring), rain drops falling all around you, bouncing and rippling the steaming waters, while you savor the dripping landscape, is incredibly soothing.

At times, there are some seriously heavy rains. That opening scene in *Rashômon* where the peasant is running through the mud towards shelter, rain pissing down? I've been that guy on the streets of Tokyo, if only slightly better dressed. Biblical downpour. No umbrella. Sloshing through the streets. Scrambling for cover. Soaked to the skin. Lightning flashing. Thunder booming. Counting the seconds between flash and boom, it was way too close for anyone right-minded to be outside.

I used to help a friend teach aikido at St. Mary's International School on Saturdays. Four hours of packed children classes, divided by ages, with the instructors taking most of the *ukemi* for the kids until they hit high-school age. (My friend reckoned one injury to a child, and it's very bad for the program). It was a good day's work for him and the two or three other instructors helping out, especially if we went back to Hombu Dojo for practice afterward. I'll never forget taking the train back from *Futako-tamagawa* (God, I love saying that fast) and stopping at Shibuya to grab some Chinese food with my pal. We were sitting upstairs in the restaurant on *Sentagai*, the pedestrian shopping street that heads up and away from the Shibuya-Scramble crosswalk, having a draft beer, when skies opened and every faucet in heaven got turned on full. Like a flash flood in an Arizona canyon, a fast running river formed, coursing down Sentagai, that was nearly a foot deep. Just as fast as it came, the rain stopped and it drained off. With all the neon lights and boombox blasted music coming from the shops, the thunder and lightning, it was surreal.

Rainy season can really go out with a bang, with some of the biggest thunder and lightning storms imaginable. In the eight years I lived in Japan, whatever train I was waiting for was late on only two occasions. Think about that for a second. Twice. Once was the Tohei-Shinjuku line at Akebonobashi station and who knows why. They get one time gratis, a "mulligan" as golfers say. The second time was at the end of *tsuyu*, but it hardly counts, either. The Yamanote line (if you're from London, that's a Circle Line that works all the time) was stopped dead in its tracks when it got zzzzzapped by a bolt of lightning. There was a blitzkrieg-like lightning storm that night. The sky turned pitch black and the sparks flew. It was as if nature was saying, "Shock and awe my ass; get a load of this!"

Another night, I was off to meet my mate for his birthday bash in Shinjuku. Crappy clear plastic 7-11 umbrella gripped tightly, while the devious wind pressed it down 'round my head. Phone pressed to my ear, shouting into it, wet up to my knees, water sloshed in and out of my loafers like a car-wash sponge, as I pound down the pavement in what I think is the right direction.

"*Moshi-moshi?*"

"Yeah; Gene; it's Bill."

"Hey Bill! Great; we're in *£$%% b^r."

CRRRRRACK …... BOOOM! Lightning strike … nearby.

"Where?!!"

"We're in $£"%^£"$$£$." CRRRRRACK … BOOM!!

Peering out from under my umbrella through the hiss of rain and flash and smash of *Raijin-sama* (雷神様, らいじんさま, god of lightning), like some soaked samurai in a *chambara* film wearing a wide-brimmed straw hat, I don't feel the slightest bit like singin' in the rain. I feel like not getting electri-fried, so I backstroke into some adjacent bar and wait out the storm while sipping a frosty cold *dai-joki* of Asahi Super Dry.[192] *Sa-ppari!*[193]

A few months in Tokyo and I was already feeling I'd stay long-term. I waited, though, to complete my sabbatical year to make certain the feeling

---

[192] 大ジョッキ, だいジョッキ, large beer mug.

[193] さっぱり, feeling refreshed.

stuck. I loved living there and would eventually go back to work at a law firm in a superb situation that still easily allowed me to train daily. But work changed the game for coping with *tsuyu*. My flat was only about 500 meters from Akebonobashi station (heading up the street towards Nuke Benten corner and Hombu Dojo) but during *tsuyu* (or summer), if I walked down the hill in my suit to the subway station for my work commute, by the time I got to the bottom, I would be sweating so profusely that I looked like I had jumped into a swimming pool. So, I used to zip down the hill on my *mama-chari* bicycle, jump off, quickly lock it up in front of the station (with the many other bikes) and dash down into the cool(er) underground station before I got too sloppy.[194] There's a good strategy and *waza* to everything in life.

The flaw with this approach was that you weren't supposed to park your bike in front of the stations—despite ample area to do so in many places. In the U.S. or China, they would probably charge you to park there in order to make money but in Japan, no-no. Still, people did it. Generally (and stereotypically), in my experience, Japanese are incredibly well behaved and rule followers. On occasion, however, rules are broken with aplomb. For example, umbrellas and bicycles do seem to get "appropriated" periodically. Umbrella takers are probably drunk and grab the wrong brolly coming out of the pub. Understandably. A few (mildly) rebellious junior high or high school students might fit the profile of incidental bike thieves. Mine actually got pinched once by a junior high school girl, according to the police when I went down to pick it up.

So, the day I came up out of the station to discover my bike was missing, along with all the other bikes, I was like, WTF? A mass theft! My friends clued me in that Shinjuku ward workers periodically visit each station with a truck and clean out all the bikes, loading them onto the flatbed and hauling them off to a large open air storage yard next door to Shinjuku *koen* (park) in the shade of a grove of massive cedar trees. I trekked down to the yard, paid my 2,000 yen fine and picked up my bike, which involved searching for it out of hundreds of others, buying a ticket in a machine to pay the fine once I found it, taking the ticket up to the

---

[194] *Mama-chari* is short for mother's chariot, a common nondescript black, gray or dark blue bicycle of tank-like steel construction.

window at the trailer that serves as an office, signing "*ze papers*" and ped-aling off. And then the next time, and then the next time, and then the next time. About once every one or two months, but it was often enough that the staff recognized me, and we would both smile and laugh every time I showed up. I thought they might erect a statue to me like the famed pooch Hachiko in Shibuya—the unrepentant, inveterate, wayward *gaijin*—since my fines probably put some of their kids through school.[195] Actually, it wasn't so much, and when I explained my strategy to them, they thought better of me. First, it was seasonal. Second, I had to get to work in good shape and not too stinky for my co-workers and clients. Third, spread across the course of a year, the benefit outweighed the cost. Fourth, the disobedience of me and people like me meant they had jobs. They re-flected for a moment, then nodded, saying "*Mm, naruhodo*" (成程, なる ほど, indeed).

Tsuyu was just one more aspect of the forging experience of adjust-ing to life in Japan. In Southern California, everything had been easy: the weather, travel by car, sitting in chairs, familiar places, the routines, old friends. Being pushed out of one's comfort zone can be an im-portant part of learning, learning to thrive in any circumstance, and that indeed "wherever you go, there you are." Heck, but for my move to To-kyo, how else would I ever have experienced "brolly condoms," the plas-tic baggies that are dispensed at the entrances to department stores and some other buildings during *tsuyu* for you to slide onto your umbrella be-fore entering (keeping floors dry) and then drop into a receptacle when you leave. There's an umbrella rack out front of Hombu Dojo. Don't take yours inside. Do take yours (and not someone else's) when you leave. "Now which one of these eighty virtually identical black umbrel-las is mine, hmmm?" "Eenie, meenie ..." In the end, the best time to go to Japan is whenever you feel like going.[196] Don't let a little wet weather douse your dream. [197]

---

[195] See Northland Akita at www.northlandakitas.com/hachiko.htm or the Project for Public Spaces at www.pps.org/great_public_spaces/one?public_place_id=989.

[196] See www.japan-guide.com/e/e2273.html re: weather and travel to Japan.

[197] Visit the climate prediction center of NOAA's (the National Oceanic and Atmospheric Administration) National Weather Service www.cpc.ncep.noaa.gov.

"I'm Boiling!"

暑中稽古
(*Shochugeiko*)

Heat waves shimmering
one or two inches
above the dead grass.
—*Matsuo Basho (1644 - 1694)*

When I was five and a half years old, "the stork" brought my family a baby girl, my little sister Dayle. I thought it was pretty cool to be a big brother, not knowing that little sisters are basically human video cameras that record and playback to mommy and daddy everything that big brother does. "Billy drove the car! He really did!" she shouted, when at ten years old I pulled my "park to neutral" stunt, rolling my parents' sedan (me at the wheel and baby sis in the back) out the driveway and across the street, bouncing off our elderly neighbor's ivy-covered fence before coming to a halt. Thankfully, I lived to tell about it, though my father considered a summary execution. As mentioned, my family summer holidays were spent at the beach in Southern California—a month every summer. My dad's idea of good vacation was to relax: board-shorts, sandals, butt in the sand, stack of good books, bit of Frisbee, ocean swims, body surfing, squeeze in three good meals and that's your day. If it's not heaven, it's just next door. Even after we moved to Northern California when I was seven, we would trek down to So-Cal for a month in Laguna Beach, usually in August. Baby sis got the middle seat in the back of the sedan for the 400 mile drive down from the Bay Area. This was pre-iPod days; hell, it was pre-Walkman days. It was a long drive for children, for anyone. I can't remember if the car air conditioner wasn't working or if it didn't have one and we were limited to "4-65 air conditioning"—roll down all four windows and go sixty-five miles an hour. I do remember baby sister moaning (at about four to five years old) most of the way down: "I'm boiling. I'm boiling," because it was a hot ride south in summer.

Summers in Tokyo are hot, too. Damn hot. At least ninety (35C) degrees and ninety percent humidity. Sweltering. Of course, it's not fry-an-egg-on-the-pavement Vegas hot or melt your shades to your forehead Saudi Arabia hot or even California hot. California hot? Yeah, why do you think they call it Death Valley?[198] While temps may be in the high forties in those places, they are all dry. Tokyo is sticky hot, smothering hot, steamy East Asia hot. If you are not already a Japanese speaker, you will quickly become acquainted with words like *atsui* (暑い, あつい, hot) or *mushiatsui* (蒸し暑い, むしあつい, humid, literally "steamy hot"). If you are from a humid climate, you should feel right at home June to the first bit of September in Tokyo. If not, *ganbatte*.

On some indeterminable collectively scripted day, as spring shifts to summer, Tokyo salary men suddenly start wearing identical white short-sleeve shirts. Carrying their jackets neatly folded over one arm, a Japanese folding fan may be held in the opposite hand, fanning away, trying to keep themselves cool. Women carry *higasa* (日傘 , ひがさ, sun umbrellas) shielding themselves from the UV rays. And the mercury climbs. All the trees and plants are a lush green in a way I had never seen green before. *Semi* (蝉, せみ, cicada) hum in the trees so loudly that an amiable bookish friend from Canada remarked on his arrival, "Wow, those electrical power generators are really noisy." Uh, yeah, and they are about as big as your thumb, and thousands of them will fly around if you shake any adjacent tree.

One foreign *dai-senpai* (over thirty years in Japan) told me how much hotter Tokyo had become over the years (and that was nearly ten years ago) due to relentless commercial and residential development. High-rise buildings by Tokyo Bay blocked the cooling sea breezes, and all that concrete and asphalt that was poured and poured and poured for the city to grow and grow and grow is a giant heat trap. He spoke of the old days traveling by train to Mount Takao and seeing nothing but farms after about fifteen minutes heading out of Tokyo for Hachijoji.[199] Now it's solid development nearly all the way there. With global temperatures on the rise, the situation's not improving. The summer of 2010 was reported as the hottest in the 113 years that Japan has been recording temperatures.

---

[198] Hottest, driest, lowest place in North America. www.nps.gov/deva/index.htm
[199] Go see it! www.takaotozan.co.jp/takaotozan_eng1

According to Japan's Fire and Disaster Management Agency, 132 people died nationally, with another 30,000-plus hospitalizations, as temperatures soared and held between 35-38C for months.

I leave it to your personal faith in science to decide whether or not the northern hemisphere has found itself at the mercy of the polar jet stream in summer due to natural, human-made or human-assisted global warming … but there is no doubt that Tokyo is hotter in summer. During my July 2010 visit, when I quietly voiced surprise to my training partner as a teacher stopped class and allowed students to take a brief water break, my friend informed me that earlier in the summer a student had passed out from the heat after class in the street in front of the dojo. I was fortunate. That week, a typhoon was approaching. The breeze brought brief relief.

In my first year, temperatures in summer were often in the thirties too, with ninety-plus percent humidity. Despite the fact that all my foreign friends in the Hombu-hood thought I was completely mental, I made it year one without an "air-con" (エアコン, wall hung air cooling/heating unit for the tatami room in my flat). My mantra (thanks to Thoreau) was "Simplify, simplify, simplify," so I didn't buy one. The flat was on the top (third) floor and received morning sun, which meant that it was cooler later in the day. Summer nights I would leave the windows and sliding glass door open and switch on my high-speed fan, setting it to blow back and forth across the room and onto me as I slept on the futon. The biggest challenge was finding how the *ka* (蚊, か, mosquitoes) were getting into the flat at night, plugging the breach and then hunting down and murdering each and every one of the the little Draculian bastards. Still a bit of blood splatter up high on one wall, I suspect; "Gotchya!" I coped and slept pretty well that summer. Being exhausted from aikido helped. For year two though, when I had a girlfriend, I bought an air-con. Thoreau had his point, but as Einstein supposedly remarked, "Make things as simple as possible but no simpler."

Summer practice proved a bigger challenge than winter. Six months into my move, Japan remained very new to me, so of course I joined in the midsummer practice at Hombu Dojo—*Shochugeiko* (暑中稽古, しょちゅうけいこ, midsummer training). It's another ten days worth of morning classes (like the midwinter practice but in a sauna).[200] The sun rises early in Tokyo (no daylight savings time) and it gets hot fast, if it ever cools down much over night. It was more challenging still because I was determined to maintain the same training schedule — two to five times a day (except Sunday) — despite the weather, using the sweltering summer to really test, push and expand the limits of my physical, mental and spiritual endurance. And during *shochugeiko,* I increased to three to five times a day and added a Sunday because it's a requirement of the event. It was very, very difficult; not the least of which was having enough dry uniforms. Two current teachers at Hombu Dojo had yet to enter the dojo as *deshi* at that time, and we often trained together during that intensive week. It's interesting how such shared hardship, though brief, forges lasting friendships.

One friend from the U.S. did back-to-back practices on a stifling August day and lost six kilos (of water weight). Along with heatstroke, "prickly heat" can become a challenge, particularly if you wear a heavier *keiko-gi* year round. Prickly heat? Yes, prickly heat. Before my wedding in October 1999, I taught some private students advanced English to make some extra cash. One student worked for the drug giant Merck, and as a gift he gave me a copy of the famous Merck Manual, which describes virtually every known medical condition. Don't read it unless you are prepared to fear having contracted a frightening number of them—simultaneously. According to the Merck Manual, "Prickly heat (miliaria) is an itchy skin rash caused by trapped sweat. Prickly heat develops when the narrow ducts carrying sweat to the skin surface get clogged. The trapped sweat causes inflammation, which produces irritation (prickling), itching, and a rash of very tiny blisters."[201] It feels like your skin is on fire, but you can cope with some medicated talc powder, a lighter *gi* and some other sensible measures. Year one I just pushed on and through, completing the course and receiving my certificate despite my double-stitch *gi*.

There are various ways to cope with the elements both on and off the mat. On the mat, make sure you are very well hydrated. "K-So". Use supplements or specialty drinks to keep your electrolytes and other minerals topped up. If you train in consecutive classes, find some means to

---

[200] You don't have to do *asageiko* but it makes it a bit tougher.
[201] See www.merckmanuals.com/home/sec18/ch206/ch206b.html.

cool down between sessions, e.g., a shower. Find some way to dry out your uniform a bit between classes— cleverer still, bring two *gi*, hang one upstairs, change between classes. Dry off as well as you can after showering and try a good medicated talc powder. Some of you won't need to take any or all of these steps. I didn't bother, but if you are susceptible to extreme temperatures, you may wish to be a bit smarter about it. Off the mat, again, keep well hydrated, which is easy enough in Tokyo. When you arrive in Tokyo, you can't help but notice that there are drink vending machines everywhere. They are typically stocked with warm drinks in winter and cold drinks in summer. Even beer. Imagine that in the U.S. or U.K. Beer vending machines. Unsupervised! They contain all kinds of health or "vitamin water" drinks that will be new to you. After purchasing his "bevi" of choice from a vending machine, a friend visiting from America looked at the plastic bottle and commented, "Who is Pocari and why am I drinking his sweat?"[202]

Even Hombu Dojo has a vending machine; it's on the first floor. One of the drinks in stock may be of particular interest to you if its enhanced performance claims are true: VAAM. VAAM stands for Vespa Amino Acid Mixture, which is a chemical compound secreted by the larvae of the Japanese giant hornet, or *Vespa mandarinia japonica,* a *Japanese subspecies* of the Asian giant hornet (*Vespa mandarinia*) dubbed the "yak-killer."

I don't know about you, but I tend to keep well clear of anything or anyone that has the words "Yak Killer" attached to its name, or frankly any "[Hardy large beast with a thick hide] Killer." "Allow me to introduce my friend, Boris the Yak Killer." With a body length of about 50mm (two inches) and a wingspan of about 76mm (three inches)—the bee, not Boris—this insect is known in Japan as *O-suzume bachi* (大雀蜂, オオス ズメバチ), literally the Giant Sparrow Bee.[203] I remember seeing a dead one, preserved in liquid in a jar, at *Kakashi*, our neighborhood *tonkatsu-ya* that served as the principal eating and watering hole for the *deshi* and many foreign students back in '97.[204] *Kakashi* was about the size of a walk-in

---

[202] Pocari Sweat is a famous sports drink in Japan. http://pocarisweat.jp/
[203] Chased by a sparrow bee www.youtube.com/watch?v=JbTdfCxyv1U; Hang a hornet nest to ward off other hornets. www.youtube.com/watch?v=hwvRrb9F9TI.
[204] *Tonkatsu* sounds a lot better than deep-fried pork cutlet, but it's great and, apart from the addiction that is breakfast bacon, I'm not a pork fan.

closet, consisting of seven or eight tall metal stools at a rustic wooden counter, behind which the kindhearted master worked his magic with the help of his moody—mostly grumpy—but sometimes charming wife. He made an addictively good *tonkatsu* set for 540 yen (*tonkatsu*, cabbage, pickles, rice, miso soup) not to mention a mean *mabu-dofu*.[205] One night, a *deshi*, who has a big thirst, and I drank all the beer in the place ... literally all the beer. "One more please," holding up the bottle.

"It's all gone."

"Huh, what do you mean it's all gone?"

"You drank it all."

"All?"

"All."

Anyway, the bug was huge; unbelievably so. "What ... is that?" I asked. The whole shop laughed, though perhaps a bit nervously. "*Suzumebatchi!*"

Years later in Beijing, I saw a National Geographic special all about the bug entitled *Hornets From Hell Offer Real-Life Fright*.[206] You've heard it said: "Mad as a hornet"; yep this is one irked insect. It hibernates all winter and wakes up hungry and cranky—definitely not a "morning person." Nat- Geo filmed part of the program up in the mountains of northern Japan searching for a hornet's nest. Combat pay anyone? Now, like all hornets, *suzumebachi* have a barbless stinger, allowing it to sting repeatedly. Oh, perfect! So basically the film crew—despite their head-to-toe special plastic protective boots, gloves, suits and helmets—had to run like hell after filming for a bit because the wee bastards were so relentless that eventually they were stinging right through the hi-tech gear. Tamagawa University entomologist Masato Ono is quoted online as saying the sting feels "like a hot nail being driven into [your] leg."

But wait! There's more! The stinger contains venom. Of course it does! Wikipedia claims:

---

[205] The Japanese take on the Chinese dish of spicy tofu. See, e.g., www3.nhk.or.jp/nhk-world/english/tv/kitchen/archives2011080801.html

[206] Nat Geo www.youtube.com/watch?v=2P7Q1ncgcoY&feature=related or see a guy's "pet" bee at http://softypapa.wordpress.com/2011/10/08/my-pet-suzumebachi-asian-giant-hornet-2/

- The venom contains at least eight distinct chemicals, some of which damage tissue, some of which cause pain, and at least one which has an odor that attracts more hornets to the victim.
- The venom contains 5 percent acetylcholine in higher concentration than bee or other wasp venom. Acetylcholine stimulates nerve fibers, intensifying the pain of the sting.
- The venom is not as deadly by weight as some other bees or wasps (less toxic than honeybee venom) but the large quantity of venom means one of the greatest toxicities per sting.
- The venom has an enzyme that dissolves human tissue.

If you head to the mountains in spring (when they are hungriest), summer or fall (before they hibernate), you may run into them or they into you as the *Mainichi Shinbun* reported in 2009:

> "At about 12:25 p.m. on Sept. 20 on Mt. Oe near Kyoto, a swarm of the giant killer hornet *suzumebachi* attacked runners taking part in the Yosano Mt. Oe Mountain Race. Thirty runners out of the field of 370 were stung as they ran on the mountain's hiking trails, some receiving multiple stings.
>
> Race officials helped incapacitated participants to return to the start via cars at road access points along the course. While most of the stings were mild, five people were injured badly enough to be taken to the hospital after police received word of the attacks from a nearby campground and from race officials. One athlete remained in the hospital to receive further medical treatment."

Fortunately for us, their principal target is the European honeybee, not us. Imported to Japan for its honey producing prowess, a Euro-bee hive is virtually defenseless against the big Japanese beasts. Five times the size of the honeybee a few attacking *suzumebachi* can clean out a hive in minutes—biting the heads off the valiantly defending bees. The Japanese honeybee, you ask? *Ahh so. Senryaku!* (戦略, せんりゃく, strategy; tactics). When the hornets make the mistake of attacking a Japanese honeybee hive, the worker bees quickly unleash their "shake and bake" defense. In a testament to the power of coordinated collective action, the bees envelop each hornet, creating a bee-ball with a hornet core, and then shake-shake-shake, shake-shake-shake, shake their booties. The vibration by the bees literally cooks the hornet, since the J-bees can withstand a body temperature higher than their massive attackers.[207] On its way to hornet heaven, the *suzumebachi* probably feels like you will in a double-stitch *gi* during midsummer intensive training.

Fortunately for us, it's not all bad news from the bird-bee. The larvae of the Sparrow Bee produce "VAAM," which is ingested by the adult hornets giving them legendary strength and endurance. If reports are to be believed, a *suzumebachi's* wings flutter up to 1,000 times a minute and it can fly at speeds of up to 25 miles an hour, cover 60 miles a day and lift objects in excess of six pounds. All this from a bug that weighs-in (on average) at 0.09 ounce (2.5 grams). It's a mightymite, due to its special home brew.

Takashi Abe, a biochemist at the Institute of Physical and Chemical Research in Japan, discovered the purported benefits of VAAM, which has been synthetically recreated for a sports drink.[208] Dr. Abe claims that the amino acids generated by the larvae expedites the metabolism of fat for use as energy and also promotes better hydration of the body.[209] Naoko Takahashi, record-setting gold medalist in the women's marathon at the 2000 Olympics in Sydney is a zealous convert to VAAM and attributed her ability to train so hard to the sports drink in part. So if you find yourself fading in summer practice, maybe a jolt of hornet juice will help get your buzz back.[210] If not, just visualize being chased down the mountainside, their barbless stingers locked on that bulls-eye on your behind. That should keep you moving.

---

[207] "Massacre in the hive," Mail Online, 13 January 2012 www.dailymail.co.uk/sciencetech/article-2086250/30-Japanese-hornets-kill-30-000-European-honeybees-video.html

[208] See VAMM Japan. www.vaam.jp

[209] See paper by Prof. Abe on VAAM. www.vespapower.com/assets/images/articles/VespaPdf3EffVAAMixtureEin.pdf

[210] If they don't sell it in the vending machine on the first floor, try the convenience store at Nuke Benten corner. Careful if you have allergies!

Climb Every Mountain

富士は日本一の山
Fuji wa Nippon ichi no yama

Lo! There towers the lofty peak of *Fuji*
From between *Kai* and wave-washed *Suruga*,
The clouds of heaven do not cross it,
Nor the birds of the air soar above it.
The snows quench the burning fires,
The fires consume the falling snow.
It baffles the tongue, it cannot be named,
It is a god mysterious.[211]

Indeed, the mountains of Japan are beautiful, inspiring and even mysterious. While you're there, the peaks can become part of your training experience, if you like, by embracing the physicality of climbs, revelations of nature and remote solitude as a kind of *misogi* (禊, みそぎ, purification). A friend of mine is the grandson of a famous Japanese swordsman and he'd tell stories of his grandfather disappearing into the mountainous wilderness for months at a time as part of his training regime. For me, Fuji-san itself actually played a pivotal role in my moving to Japan.

An estimated seventy-plus percent of the country is mountainous terrain. Each of the main islands has at least one significant mountain range crossing it that offers remote wilderness. Honshu alone has the Hida Mountains (飛騨山脈, *Hida Sanmyaku*) or "Northern Alps" (北アルプス, *Kita Arupusu*), the *Kiso* Mountains (木曽山脈, *Kiso Sanmyaku*) or "Central Alps" (中央アルプス, *Chūō Arupusu*) and the Akaishi Mountains (赤

---

[211] From the *Man'yōshū* 万葉集 ("Collection of Ten Thousand Leaves") which is an eighth century compilation of Japanese poetry from the *Nara* or early *Heian* periods. The *Nara* period (奈良時代 *Nara jidai*) being from AD 710 to 794 with the establishment of the Japanese capital of *Heijō-kyō* (now Nara) and the *Heian* period (平安時代 *Heian jidai*) being named for the capital city of *Heian-kyō* (now Kyōto) and the years AD 794 to 1185.

石山脈, *Akaishi Sanmyaku*) or "Southern Alps" (南アルプス, *Minami Arupusu*). Readily accessible nowadays, they are superb for hiking, skiing/boarding and other outdoor adventures.[212] They may not be the tallest in the world, but they must rank among the most picturesque and serene. Strengthen your body, soothe your psyche, revive your spirit; get out of the dojo and climb them.

Japanese Buddhists believe a mountain is a gateway to another world, and when you live in Tokyo you need to visit "other worlds" from time to time to escape the pace and lack of space. In particular, they revere the "Three Holy Mountains" (*Sanreizan*, 三霊山) of Japan: Mount *Ta-te*, Mount *Haku* and of course Japan's tallest and most iconic peak, Mount *Fuji*. The characters for Fuji-san are 富士山: 富 (wealth; enrich; abundant), 士 (gentlemen, warrior) and 山 (san for mountain, not the honorific for a person) but these pronunciations are the *on-yomi* or Japanese pronunciation of the Chinese pronunciation of the *kanji* (Japanese is difficult this way, *on-yomi* and *kun-yomi* for each Chinese character borrowed ages ago) and I have read that *Fu* and *Ji* were selected merely for the sound, not the meaning. Some say its name comes from the ancient Ainu (アイヌ) language, the aboriginal people of northern Japan, and means "everlasting life." Others claim the name is from the *Yamato* language and refers to a Buddhist fire goddess.[213]

Whatever the origin, the mountain has been venerated for centuries, being the subject of countless creative works by poets and painters and even the object of religious worship. There are some 1300 Asama shrines (浅間神社, *Asama Jinja* or *Sengen Jinja*) in Japan dedicated to the Shinto worship of the spirits (神, *kami*) of volcanoes. A shrine to *Sengen-Sama* (浅間), a Shinto goddess of nature, is on the summit (along with noodle restaurants, trinket shops and drink vending machines).

Rising to 12,388 feet (3776m) above sea level, it is the thirty-fifth tallest mountain in the world. An active volcano and not part of a range of mountains, Fuji-san overwhelmingly dominates the surrounding landscape. It looks massive even when viewed from Tokyo some sixty miles

---

[212] See the Seven Cities Japan Alps site. www.japan-alps.com/en/

[213] *Yamato-minzoku* (大和民族) is the dominant ethnic group of Japan.

away. On some trips back to Tokyo from Seoul, I would see it clearly from the air, standing colossal even from 35,000 feet. Fuji-san has to be one of the world's most beautiful mountains. As the locals claim, "三国一の山" (*Sangoku ichi no yama*)—the best mountain of the three lands: India, China and Japan. Nationlistic leanings aside, it does possess an inexplicable yet undeniable allure. A good friend in Tokyo was a Swiss accountant (how exciting) and he had seen a mountain or two in his day. Yet he was absolutely enthralled by Fuji-san; admittedly so. Perhaps it's the lack of competing heights that gives Fuji-san a unique nobility and visible power. In a glimpse, we catch the enormity of the geologic up-heaval that formed it. Certainly, its symmetry (though deceiving) adds to its distinctive beauty, as do the seasonal changes and their effect on view-ing the mountain. Perhaps it is the imperfection of its beauty that Japa-nese (and we) find so appealing. Fuji-san is a geologic expression of that distinctly Japanese aesthetic, *wabi-sabi* (侘寂, わびさび), which admires, among other things, the beauty of the imperfect, impermanent and in-complete in nature and art.

The mountain is certainly more beautiful from a distance and more imperfect up close. In climbing Fuji-san, one trudges up a big pile of red/black rock and dust. It's a volcano, folks! It last erupted from De-cember 16, 1707 to January 1, 1708, covering Tokyo (then Edo) in ash. Geologists predict that Fuji-san will blow its top again. Ten years, fifty years, 100 years, 1000 years? Who knows? Geology is far more patient than people. Maybe you will be "lucky" during your visit. One of the most unique instructions I have ever received as a hotel guest was the "In Case of Volcanic Eruption" evacuation card posted on the wall of our room in a remote country-inn in *Hokkaido*. If I recall, it advised quickly dropping your shorts and kissing your rear-end *sayonara*.

Just as it is for locals, climbing Fuji-san is a rite of passage for many visitors. The first ascent was reportedly made by a monk in the seventh century. "Okay; done with *zazen*; had some tea; swept the steps; raked the sand garden; hmmm. Wonder what 'nothing' is like up there?" It was then climbed regularly by men (women were finally allowed on the summit in the Meiji Era) and the first reported non-Japanese, Sir Rutherford Al-cock, to ascend was in September 1860 and was also the first British dip-lomatic representative to live in Japan. The first non-Japanese woman to summit is reported to have been Lady Fanny Parkes, the wife of the British ambassador, in 1867, in defiance of the ban on women. Those plucky Victorian Brits!

A Japanese proverb advises something like, "a wise man climbs Fuji-san once but a fool twice." I may be a fool, but I only climbed once. I had to, as catharsis, or *misogi* if you prefer. A friend from university had died while climbing Fuji-san in March 1994 while it was still capped with snow. A sturdy guy at about 187 cm and 90+ kilos, he took a fatal tumble—literally blown off his feet—when he let go of the rope line while reaching down to fix his crampon (spikes attached to your boots for climbing snow/ice) and a powerful gust of wind sent him 3000 meters down the mountainside. As a website regarding the peak warns:

> Climbing outside the official season is **extremely dangerous** without alpine climbing experience and equipment. Nearly all facilities are closed in the off season. The weather, unpredictable any time of year, is downright vicious in the winter (temperatures below -40°C have been reported up top) and there are cases of people being literally blown off the mountain by high winds. All roads to the 5th station are shut out of season so you will have a long walk up. But if you insist, you're strongly encouraged to at least file a climbing plan with the Yoshida police.[214]

I still remember the phone call that March from my college pal "Swanny" in San Diego, Doug's best mate in university. I was at my desk grinding the last bit of work before dashing to evening practice in Little Tokyo. "Bill ... Doug's dead!"

I sat; stunned. When you hear shocking news like that, it's just that. Shocking. Hit by the cliché "bucket of cold water." You hear it, but it just doesn't make sense, as if the messenger was speaking gibberish. "Hello. Broccoli asphalt!" So you're silent, repeating the words in your head, or maybe managing a "What?" in reply.

---

[214] See http://wikitravel.org/en/Mount_Fuji.

As the first words were sinking in, I heard, "He's dead. He fell and died climbing Mount Fuji."

"He what?!!" Swanny gave the fatal details.

By sheer chance, I had seen Doug two months prior in a bar in San Francisco on "Super Bowl Sunday."[215] We hadn't spoken in years. I learned how he had boldly moved to Tokyo a few years earlier to work as a lawyer and was thriving in his new globalized life that preceded the globalization craze of the late nineties, early noughties and since. He learned that I was a student of aikido and that I'd visited Japan previously. He spoke with conviction and power, encouraging me to end a dying relationship, leave my slavish job and move to Japan—if that's what I wanted from life. His testimony was influential towards my decision to ditch Los Angeles for Tokyo, but his death proved instrumental.

Two, maybe three hundred people showed up for Doug's memorial service and burial in Los Angeles. It was astounding. While always a likeable guy, Doug had not been particularly extroverted in university, but when I met him in January 1994, I could sense the growth that law school and adventure abroad had imparted. He'd gained self-belief and grown in stature. His enthusiasm was boundless and infectious. When he said he was living life to the fullest, you believed him. However, at the service, I learned that it was not all work and play in Japan; he had taken up philanthropy, e.g., packing in medical supplies to remote villages in Southeast Asia. Since I'd last seen him, he'd been transformed by his experiences, and his transformation had positively affected the lives of those around him. Moved by his life and untimely death, his law school classmates would help establish a scholarship in his name:

Douglas M. Raskin
Memorial Scholarship

A scholarship established by classmates and friends of Douglas Michael Raskin, Class of 1987, who died in 1994 at the age of 33 while climbing Mount Fuji in Japan. The scholarship is awarded to a third or fourth year student who exemplifies the spirit of adventure, sense of humor,

---

[215] See www.nfl.com/superbowl/46.

love of life, and caring for others exhibited by Douglas Raskin.[216]

So, following the tragic news of my friend's death, I traveled to Tokyo for the second time, in May of 1994, stayed for three weeks, trained daily at Hombu Dojo and tested the waters for a life in Japan. I sought out many of Doug's friends, piecing together a fuller picture of his life abroad. While my trip was tinged with sadness over my missing friend, it was still a fantastic experience. I returned home with renewed appreciation for life's impermanence, for its value, for the possibilities and practicalities of a life in Japan (and with improved aikido). I can't recall exactly when I decided irrevocably to move. Was it during that spring trip in '94? Was it after my chance meeting with Doug in S.F.? Or was it before that, following my first visit to Hombu Dojo in 1992? Whenever that switch flipped, once I was got back home after the '94 visit, the decision became a plan and the plan became action. I trained harder, worked harder (socking away two years worth of bonuses from the law firm) and otherwise completed arrangements for my move. Finally, off I flew to start my own adventure. Climbing Fuji-san, out of respect for my friend's life, would be part of that journey.

However, I didn't undertake that mountain pilgrimage until much later. In July 2001, midweek in hopes of reduced crowd, the Mrs. and I (we had married in October 1999 in Princeton with a subsequent party in Seoul) caught the bus at the west exit of Shinjuku station for *Kawaguchiko*, a picturesque lake beneath the west slope of Fuji-san, figuring we would hang out through the afternoon, slowly climb that evening and watch the sunrise the next morning.[217]

July and August are the official season to climb Mount Fuji. The weather is milder and most of the snow has melted. Mid-July until the end of August, schools are on vacation so it's crowded. Weekends are even busier. Mount Fuji is the most climbed mountain in the world, with

---

[216] See www.usfca.edu/law/jd/financialaid/scholarships/usf/.
[217] See Kawaguchiko at www.japan-guide.com/e/e6906.html or the Kawaguchiko Chamber of Commerce site www.kawaguchiko.or.jp.

hundreds of thousands climbing annually. On a busy day, your uphill view will be the bum of the person in front of you while you all snake up the mountainside like slaves in a golden-era Hollywood biblical epic directed by Cecil B. Demille.[218] In the words of National Geographic:

> "Climbing Fuji isn't the snap many people think. Yet every year, during the July-August climbing season, some 400,000 mostly enthusiastic tenderfoots (20,000 on a good day) scramble for the summit of Japan's mighty beacon. For the Japanese, Fuji (early Chinese characters for which mean "without equal") is unrivaled in its capacity to stir a sense of national identity even in a society that is more individualistic than in the past."[219]

Four main trails ascend Mount Fuji. Ten stations are found on each trail. First stations are at the base; tenth stations at the summit. Each station offers basic amenities and spartan lodging, all of which are rather expensive. Most people travel to a fifth station by bus and then begin their climb, though one slightly eccentric and extreme friend did start at a first station. From the fifth station (on the path we took), it's a steep, deliberate climb that requires no technical mountaineering skill. Simple persistence will do.[220]

Growing up in California, I had previously spent a fair amount of time in the Sierra Nevada range and had climbed the highest peak in the continental U.S., Mount Whitney in Eastern California, via a mountaineering route rather than the gentle walk around the back on the Whitney Trail.[221] At 14,500 feet, Whitney was a challenge for the body and the mind. At over 8,000 feet, the air is thin, and once over 10,000 feet, the body stops processing protein well—"straight pipe" as a Southerner on our climb referred wryly to his intestinal tract at high altitude. To climb

---

[218] See www.cecilbdemille.com/.
[219] See Nat Geo at http://ngm.nationalgeographic.com/ngm/0208/feature3/.
[220] I have read that there are technical mountaineering routes for the true outdoors-person.
[221] Learn about Mount Whitney climbs from the National Parks Service www.nps.gov/seki/planyourvisit/whitney.htm or www.summitpost.org/mount-whitney/150227 and the Mountaineer's route first climbed by John Muir www.summitpost.org/mountaineer-s/155528. It's worth a look on Google Earth.

Whitney, one first goes to Whitney Portal (if one has any sense), spends the night at 8,500 feet, climbs to 10,000 or so, camps and then summits the next day—up and down since Whitney can have very unstable weather and is notorious for lightning strikes. We reached the summit (three of us out of twelve) but not without genuine risk. Our guides ran short of enough rope to safely traverse a glacier about 1000 feet beneath the summit. One misstep or a bit of unstable snow/ice and you had yourself a final thrilling 3,000 foot slide to certain death. One guy was developing altitude sickness. What to do? Knowing when to turn back is vital when mountaineering (and in other things). In this instance though, one of us asked "why not go straight up?" The guides offered us a choice. One guide would take some down, the other up. So one guide, me and another lawyer (a former U.S. Army Ranger with mountaineering experience in the Alps while serving) roped together and climbed the north-east face rather than go all that way and turn back. Aikido training helped actually. A calm and focused mind. Good balance. One strong hand hold. One sure step. Another. Step by step. Typically, though, in mountain climbing the sensible thing is to descend when you have the slightest uncertainty over weather, terrain, equipment or health.

Fuji-san did not offer that level of risk that July day with my wife, but it always poses challenges, and you do need to be ready for gusts of wind, falling rock, rapidly changing weather, hypothermia and altitude sickness. One website reports "on average, around four people die and over a dozen are injured every year on Fuji by hypothermia or falling rocks." Don't win a "Darwin Award" and become a statistic! Be prepared; use common sense. Walk a bit. Take a break. Have a drink and a snack. Enjoy the view. Walk some more. It's not a running race to the top, though they do have them. Seriously. There are individual races, including one to the summit from Fujiyoshida City Hall that is 21K, and an *ekiden kyousou* (駅伝競走, えきでんきょうそう) or long-distance relay race up and back down.[222]

The traditional approach is to climb from a fifth station over two days,

---

[222] For details on the Fujiyoshida race, see the official website www.fujimountainrace.jp/forms/top/top.aspx or the city's website www.city.fujiyoshida.yamanashi.jp/div/english/html/race.html. For the relay from Gotemba, see www.fujisannet.jp/data/article/1532.html. The downhill leg is always good for a few wipeouts, e.g., www.youtube.com/watch?v=40Piye38uTo.

staying halfway up the mountain in one of the huts at the seventh or eighth station, then rising early to complete the climb for the "Buddha's Halo Sunrise" or *goraiko* (御来光, ごらいこ) on the volcano's rim. You witness the sunrise on the highest point in the Land of the Rising Sun. If you do not spend the night halfway up the mountain, then you face climbing from sea level to nearly 13,000 feet in about ten hours, including your bus trip and depending on how fast you climb. Go too quickly and you will suffer from altitude sickness, which is very uncomfortable at least and life threatening at worst. If you are set upon severely, head back downhill immediately. I have heard enough urban legends about people found wandering senselessly on the mountainside (or found dead) that there is probably more than a kernel of truth to the high altitude (and hypothermia) tales. The walk up usually takes four to eight hours, depending on your pace, the weather and your susceptibility to the elements. Plan for three to five hours to descend. One more thing: as the Ministry of Education song about Fuji-san goes *"Kaminari-sama wo shita ni kiku,"* something like "Below we hear the Lord of Lightning." Watch the weather closely; don't get zapped.[223]

When we arrived that summer's day, the weather was postcard perfect. Blue skies, not a cloud. Remember it may be a sizzling 40°C in Tokyo, but Fuji-san makes her own weather, and it will be single digits on the summit during the day and below freezing at night. I remember it being quite cold at the top, even though we were well prepared for the climb. It was not so crowded that day, thankfully. The climb was strenuous, but not overly. We stopped at some huts along the way to have a look inside, a bit of rest and use "the facilities." We were thankful that we had brought plenty to drink and some good snacks. You need to renew your energy during the climb. As we passed the ninth stage, we looked towards the goal above and saw the wooden gate (*torii*, 鳥居, とりい) that you must pass through to reach the tenth stage and summit. Like horses to water, we quickened our pace, despite the mild headache from the altitude and

---

[223] A young partner at my L.A. law firm came to the office one day proudly displaying photos of how he had walked up the Whitney Trail, an easy Class 1 approach from the west. (www.summitpost.org/whitney-trail/156374) He'd reached the top during a serious gale. Rain, hail and severe wind. Sensibly, his brother had turned back. I looked at the photos and thought, "What an idiot." Mountaintops and lightning go hand-in-hand. The guy was lucky not to have been fried.

fatigue from the thin air.

The view from the summit was extraordinary. Like nothing I had ever seen before or since. I reckon that part of the feeling that day on Fuji-san was that we had journeyed from sea level (or thereabouts) to nearly 13,000 feet (3700 meters) in a matter of hours. This is very unusual for mountain climbing.[224] Our reward was the panoramic vista and a belief that we could see across the breadth of Japan. The summit or crater rim actually has eight peaks. Called *ohachi-meguri* (お鉢めぐり) in Japanese (which I believe means "eight times crazier"), some climbers do make the one-to-two hour walk around the rim for a photo at *Kengamine* (剣ヶ峰) peak, which is Fuji's (and Japan's) highest point. As it would happen, it is on the opposite side of the crater rim from *Yoshidaguchi* Trail side, so we skipped it. We just sat quietly and gazed at the still expanse below. I quietly contemplated my friend's passing, tried to imagine that winter's day and said a private prayer. We had a warming bowl of noodles at mountain-top hut, a good rest and made sure to send friends and family postcards from the post office on the summit. Really; there may not be a "train to the top," but there's a post office.

Soon we were becoming a bit concerned about getting back down before dark. So, after some more photos of the view and me inching curiously towards the interior rim for a better look into the volcanic crater (and my wife ordering me to move back from the edge), we began our trip down the mountain. At points, we were literally leaping and sliding in the scree like skiers on snow.[225] We are from California, after all, so an "X-games" style descent was in order. We bounded back to Gogomae just as the sky finished darkening, only to discover the place was completely shut down. It was looking like we would have to spend the night at the fifth station parking lot, but then *Sengen-sama* or someone else on high smiled on us again. A car pulled into the lot (I forget what he was there for) and this Japanese driver didn't tear off in a panic when he saw a tall *gaijin* (me) waving him down to stop. I asked for a ride. He said, "No problem." I reckoned, two of us, one of him,

---

[224] As I in my Whitney climb, typically you will start climbs of 2,000+ meter peaks from a much higher altitude than sea level and, depending on the height, will take steps for your body to acclimate to the altitude before summiting. Climbing Fuji-san and going from sea level to 3776 meters in a day is ambitious.

[225] Hikers follow a different path down than up so descending and ascending traffic do not conflict.

it's Japan (which means the likelihood of a kook exists, but lower, and the likelihood of a gun is zero). So we hitchhiked back down to a train station near the base and made it home safely. All's well that ends well, though my Vasque climbing boots never did lose the red volcanic dust.

For me, it had been special trip in memory of a friend who had been instrumental in my moving to Japan. I would certainly recommend the climb—at least once—to anyone. Get out of the dojo, go climb a mountain, if not the mountain—mighty Fuji-san.

> "Each and every master, regardless of the era or place, heard the call and attained harmony with heaven and earth. There are many paths leading to the peak of Mount Fuji, but the goal is the same. There are many methods of reaching the top, and they all bring us to the heights. There is no need to battle with each other—we are all brothers and sisters who should walk the path together, hand in hand. Keep to your Path, and nothing else will matter. When you lose your desire for things that do not matter, you will be free."
>
> —*Ueshiba Morihei*

Notes on Climbing Fuji-san

Suggested Gear

Rucksack, sturdy broken-in hiking boots, good wool socks, layers of clothing (if you climb in shorts like I did, bring some nylon or Gortex sweats), thermals, wool hat, rain gear, gaiters (for the descent, keeps the rocks out of the boots), flashlights (extra batteries), water or other drinks, snacks, multi-tool or Swiss army knife, small first aid kit, sunblock, cash, bus schedule, mobile phone (fully charged), number to call for an emergency or taxi or car from fifth station (if you miss the last bus, as we did) and of course a camera (extra batteries). If you are really paranoid, bring a whistle, topographical map and a compass.

Websites of Worth

Fuji -san info
www.japanguide.com/e/e6901.html
http://gojapan.about.com/cs/mtfuji/a/climbmtfuji.htm
http://englishtreejapan.tripod.com/mt-fuji.htm
http://live-fuji.jp

Fuji-san huts
www17.plala.or.jp/climb_fujiyama/mountain_huts.html

Health
www.altitude.org/altitude_sickness.php
www.nlm.nih.gov/medlineplus/hypothermia.html

Map
www.webcamgalore.com/EN/webcam-map/Japan/Mount-Fuji/city-3982.html

Photos
www.asahi-net.or.jp/~ud6m-kizm/N_P_I_J/Fuji/Fuji_san.html

Tales
www.fuckedgaijin.com/forums/viewtopic.php?t=19186

http://climbjapan.blogspot.jp/2013/01/winter-mt-fuji-some-climbing-strategies.html

Temple lodging
www.shukubo.jp
http://eng.shukubo.net/temple-lodging.html

Volcanic eruptions in Japan
http://homepage3.nifty.com/hyamasat/eruption.html
http://ngm.nationalgeographic.com/ngm/0208/feature3/map.html

Yamanashi prefecture site
www.pref.yamanashi.jp/english/tourism/mtfuji/index.html

Weather
www.wunderground.com/global/stations/47639.html

Webcams
www.myworldwebcams.com/asia/japan/mount_fuji.html
https://twitter.com/Fujisan_Photo

Watering Holes
and Haunts

水を遣る，それで憑く
(*Mizu wo yaru, sorede tsuku*)

Sensory Overload

A condition in which an individual receives an excessive or intolerable amount of sensory stimuli, as in a busy hospital or clinic or an intensive care unit. The effects of sensory overload are similar to those of sensory deprivation, including confusion and hallucination.

- Mosby's Medical Dictionary, 8th edition. © 2009

Sprawling, frenetic, thrilling, kinetic: Tokyo can wind your life up like a top, if you let it. The population, the pace, plus bits of what you see seems somewhat familiar, but in truth, anything you recognize is the thinnest veneer of the modern Western world spread over a highly unique ancient East Asian culture. This can be disorienting and alienating for newcomers, as the popular 2003 film *Lost in Translation* tried to depict, a film which I have invariably heard was enjoyed by people who have no or little experience with Japan and is equally routinely despised or disregarded by those who do. You will also have difficulties communicating, unless you studied seriously at home, and that will become tiring and frustrating, particularly if you lose perspective and patience. Yes; for newbies, Tokyo can be oppressive and become overwhelming especially in summer: the heat, the high-rises, the concrete, the crowds.

O-Sensei reportedly wrote, "Your mind should be in harmony with the functioning of the universe; your body should be in tune with the movement of the universe; body and mind should be bound as one, unified with the activity of the universe." Inspiring words which are all the more challenging to follow in the hyperdrive universe of Tokyo. The locals and the "lifers" seem to handle "The Big *Mikan*" with surprising calm, some of which no doubt is merely on the exterior, but until you are similarly experienced and thick-skinned, how do you cope?

To maintain your *wa* (和, harmony), seek ways to balance the stimulus equation. Find escapes within and from Tokyo—your oasis or sanctuary, as it were, because Tokyo can be maddening, maybe even drive you mad. Don't get me wrong. I'm not being alarmist. "Oooh Tokyo. So overwhelming. Scary." Far from it. I found it exciting—a welcome daily adventure. But some won't feel that way, and an ounce of prevention is worth a pound of cure. Even Superman had his retreat, his "Fortress of Solitude."

Fortunately, escape is not far away. It can be as simple as an evening stroll down a quiet residential street. The back streets of most any Tokyo neighborhood are remarkably quiet at night, and the scale is rather intimate since the streets are often narrow and meandering. Or maybe you'll find it visiting the grounds of a particular temple or a quiet wooded area in town, like in Shinjuku or Ueno parks. Maybe you can find it in a rooftop bar or hidden coffeehouse or restaurant where, once you walk through the *genkan,* you feel miles removed from the hustle outside. It's vital for your sanity to find some kind of refuge from the grind of any city, particularly this unfamiliar one that travels at light speed. I had several methods: *asageiko*, *zazen*, late afternoon snoozes on my *tatami* in spring and summer (windows open, breeze blowing through, sumo on the tele), using a favorite set of stone stairs next to the peaceful Shinto shrine *Tenjinsama* when I would walk to Shinjuku, walking along the stone-lined foot path of Shikino-michi on the way past Kabukicho from the dojo—wooded, cooler, calmer until you walk out past *Mister Donatsu* onto *Yasukuni-dori* and get blasted by the neon, noise, sidewalk and street traffic. These small quiet spaces exist all over town and possess sustaining if not restorative powers. Have fun searching out and finding yours. Savor them once you do.

Swimming is always a great way to cool off in summer and, if you feel the need, Tokyo has many public pools and water parks, like Summer-land.[226] The problem with most of these places is that everyone else in Tokyo (and their aunts, uncles, cousins and more distant relations) has the same idea as you. "Let's go for a swim!" The water can be extremely crowded, as the YouTube video "INSANE Wave Pool in Tokyo" shows.[227] I see the people; where's the water? Year one, I didn't have the time or interest, frankly, but years later, I did go to a waterpark with my Mrs. and her friend, and it was a real laugh and a great way to beat the heat for a day.

If you want a proper swim, then the Tokyo Metropolitan Gymnasium is a great place for serious training that is not too far from Hombu Dojo.[228] Coached by fraternity brothers from UCLA who were Olympic gold med-alists in swimming and water polo players, I used to be a fairly competitive triathlete and I didn't give up swim training when I started aikido. Swim-ming has helped rehabilitate most of my aikido aches, pains and injuries over the years and is highly complementary to martial arts training, in my view. Swimming utilizes natural movements and timing, involves extended ranges of motion and creates highly functional and flexible musculature. A properly structured workout (including interval training, hand-paddles, a pull-buoy, paddle board) can provide exhausting cardiovascular training while improving your strength. Plus the buoyancy of water spares the body the pounding of land based exercise.[229]

If you do seek to cool off poolside or add it to your training regime, be prepared for the fact that you may be prohibited from entering water-world if you have tattoos. Seriously; tattoos (*irezumi*, 入れ墨, いれずみ) are usually considered (in modern Japan at least) a mark of the Japanese underworld (gangsters), and you will routinely see signs posted banning tattoos (and hence the wearer) from public swimming pools, spas and hotsprings.[230]

---

[226] For Summerland see www.summerland.co.jp or for a list of pools see www.sunny-pages.jp/search/tokyo_leisure/water_parks_pools.

[227] See www.youtube.com/watch?v=inA-36YRV0Y.

[228] Find the Metropolitan gym pool here. www.tef.or.jp/tmg/en_pool_top.jsp

[229] Search the web for your own swim workout or join a masters swim program for a bit to get some coaching.

[230] On Japanese and tattoos see: *The view of tattoos in Japanese society*, June 29, 2012, http://japan-dailypress.com/the-view-of-tattoos-in-japanese-society-295623/, or *In Japan, Tattoos Are Not Just For Yakuza Anymore*, Janurayr 2, 2013, www.japansubculture.com/in-japan-tattoos-are-not-

Given its extraordinary transport system, getting out of Tokyo is a breeze, and usually involves completing the simple standard equation of big station + fast train + slower train + (walk V bus V taxi). Currently in the U.K. and in California (and elsewhere in the U.S.) there is lots of moaning over plans to build high-speed rail networks ... the kind that Japan, Korea and France have had for some time and that the PRC is in the process of building using French, German and Japanese technology. People in the U.K. and U.S. don't know what they are missing, so they resist change. If they truly understood, they would want high-speed rail NOW, pausing ever so briefly to wonder why the hell it wasn't built years ago. The Germans and Americans might contend otherwise, but an Englishman invented the linear induction motor for the magnetic levitation train, for goodness sakes![231] The U.K. would be radically changed for the better, if there were high-speed rail lines linking London and key points north up the left and right sides of the country straight up to Glasgow and Edinburgh. Two hour-plus travel times (into city centers) with no airport hassles.

In fact, transport is so easy in Tokyo that in winter, my wife and I would wake up some weekends and say, "Hey, let's go snowboarding." Up. Quick shower. Grab our gear. Into a cab—fifteen minutes to Tokyo station. An hour and twenty minutes on the *Shinkansen* towards Nigata into *Yukikuni* (snow country), a ten-minute bus ride and we were boarding. If you plan a little, you can even *takubin* (宅急便, たっきゅうびん, express door-to-door delivery service) your luggage to the destination in advance of your departure. It's easier still for you nowadays, with the Internet and so many more Japanese speaking or being willing to try to speak English. However you do it, get out and do it. There is a substantial connection between nature and aikido, so go explore and enjoy the amazing beauty of the Japanese countryside, make it part of your training or simply a revitalizing retreat from Tokyo.

For me, the former coastal capital of Kamakura (鎌倉市, かまくら) became a favorite easy trip over the years. The power center of Japan's first shogun *Minamoto no Yoritomo* and acting capital during the *Kamakura*

---

just-for-yakuza-anymore/.
[231] Each country claims the invention.

jidai (鎌倉時代, Kamakura period) from 1185 until 1333, which saw the ascendency of the samurai class and establishment of feudalism, it's a bit over an hour by train from Shinjuku station on the JR Shonan Shinjuku Line, depending on whether you catch a direct train or are required to change at Ofuna Station. Disembarking at Kita-Kamakura station, I would stroll from temple to temple, drinking in the history and breathing in the fresh air along the way. Descending the weathered stone steps of Shinto shrine Tsurugaoka Hachiman-gū (鶴岡八幡宮) into the center of the city of Kamakura, I would catch the quaint three-car electric train (Enoden, www.enoden.co.jp) and head down the coast to Hase station for a walk inland to the *Daibutsu* (大仏, Great Buddha) at Kotoku-in temple (高徳院, www.kotoku-in.jp). The visually compelling, ninety-three ton, 13.35 meter-high cast bronze statue of Amida Buddha sits serenely on the temple grounds, exposed to the open air. When I first visited, I read a plaque (with some incredulity given the distance from the sea) that claimed that the last building housing the statue had been washed away in the tsunami of 20 September 1498 and had even moved the statue. After the March 2011 Tōhoku earthquake and tsunami, I'm a believer and wonder how anything historical has ever managed to survive.

Of course the mountains are nearby Tokyo and, depending on how high you climb, usually much cooler. Nearby and remarkably remote Chichibu Tama Kai Kokuritsu Kōen (秩父多摩甲斐国立公園, *Chichibu-Tama-Kai* National Park) borders Tokyo, Saitama, Nagano and Yamanashi prefectures. Covering more than 1250 km², it has eight peaks over 2000 meters. There are rivers, waterfalls, gorges, mountain hikes on ancient paths and roads and Shinto shrines to be explored, including:

- Mount Mitake (929 m) has been worshiped as a sacred mountain since antiquity. The Musashi Mitake Shrine, a Shinto shrine established during the reign of Emperor *Sujin* in 90 B.C., sits on the peak. The shrine holds many events throughout the year, including ascetic training.[232] *Shukubo* (宿坊. しゅくぼう. pilgrims' lodgings) are available on the mountain and a stay may include

---

[232] www.mitaketozan.co.jp

taki no misogi.[233]

- Mount Mitsumine has the 2,000 year old Mitsumine Shrine.[234] Mitsumine san was also the wilderness retreat of famed Korean karate master Mas Oyama (Chae Yeong-eui, 최영의, 1923 – 1994) where for a reported fourteen months he underwent his solitary mountain training in developing *Kyokushin* ("search for the ultimate truth") karate. For those of you who have not seen it, the Korean film of Oyama sensei's early life in Japan developing his art, *Fighter in the Wind* (바람의 파이터). *Baramee Pai-teuh* in Korean, Wind's Fighter), is well worth watching (despite its embellishments for the sake of storytelling) for its portrayal of Koreans living in post-WWII Japan as much as for the fight scenes.

> "The greatest fruit of my stay in the mountains was that I trained my physical and mental strength during the day and confronted my inner self at night. Of course my skill in karate was greatly developed, but more fulfilling was the strengthening of a great mental state, a state developed far in excess of that before entering the mountains."
> —Oyama Masutatsu

- Daibosatsu Tōge (大菩薩峠, "Boddhisattva Pass") was made famous in the novel by Nakazato Kaizan which was the basis for the 1966 *chanbara* (チャンバラ) film of the same name, directed by Okamoto Kihachi but dubbed *Sword of Doom* in English. "The sword is the soul. Study the soul to know the sword. Evil mind, evil sword." Climbing to 1,897 meters, the pass runs between Kōshū and Kosuge past 2,057 meter-high Mount Daibosatu (大菩薩嶺, Daigosatsu-rei). It was an important transport route historically, and you can trod the path of samurai, merchants and

---

[233] www.hkr.ne.jp/~komadori/komadori.html
[234] www.mitsuminejinja.or.jp

peasants long since passed while taking in the views.[235]

- The Arakawa River (荒川 Arakawa) can be explored from its source via the "Chikuma River Upstream Course" (千曲川源流コース), a mountainous trail in Nagano-ken stretching from Mōkiba (毛木) to 2,475 meter Mount Kobushi (甲武信岳) that also borders Saitama-ken and Yamanashi-ken or via river excursions on traditional wooden boats (with whitewater sections if you like) from Nagatoro (長瀞).[236]

Confucianism advocates self-cultivation, including the study of history. I found that visiting historic places, particularly those of notable natural beauty and power, where extraordinary events occurred, was inspirational to my training and my daily life in Japan. You get a glimpse of ages past and, if your mind is open, acquire a deeper appreciation of time, its value and the transience of your life. As a sign in the changing room of my first dojo read, "Not Even a Million Dollars Can Buy Back a Minute of Your Life." Too true. Although, it has to be said that a million bucks could be helpful given enough minutes left on the clock.[237]

If the mountains aren't your thing, there is always the beach (between rainy season and jellyfish season). I'm from California, so perhaps I am spoiled (though not as spoiled as a Hawaiian or Australian) when it comes to sun and surf, but about an hour and a half's train ride from Shinjuku or Shibuya there are several passable beaches around the *Miura* peninsula: Chigasaki, Zushi, Enoshima. I have never been but hear that Boso Hanto is a cleaner, less crowded option. I did some swimming and surfing in some of these places years later, and they weren't the cleanest of beaches. Massive shipping traffic sails in/out of Tokyo harbor, and sailors toss every manner of thing overboard: empty ships' bilge, etc. I half wondered

---

235 www.daibosatsukankokyoukai.net
236 See www.naganoken.jp/mount/chichibu/okuchichibu/kobushigatake.htm and for the river trip https://plus.google.com/116023904214250044448/about?hl=ja and www.outdoorjapan.com/travel/operator_details/28.
237 For a useful interactive map of the park and its relation to Tokyo see http://iguide.travel/Chichibu-Tama-Kai_National_Park/Activities#/Map. For a list of all the national parks in Japan, see the Ministry of Environment website www.env.go.jp/en/nature/nps/park/index.html and related Bio-diversity Center of Japan www.biodic.go.jp/english/jpark/jpark1R_e.html.

if I would wipe out and come up with a colostomy bag on my head or some other illegally dumped waste. However, there are nice beaches in Japan. In fact, O-Sensei was born in Tanabe in Wakayama-ken, and not far from some of the best reef-break surfing in the country, according to www.japansurf.com, like Gobo or Isonoura. You can make a pilgrimage to Wakayama-ken for aikido (or surfing), but that's for another chapter.

If you want cleaner waters closer to Tokyo and a bit of wilderness to boot, then head to the *Izu* peninsula (伊豆半島, Izu-hantō). A little over sixty miles southeast of Tokyo by train, the picturesque, hilly, forest-covered peninsula stretches out into the Pacific Ocean between Sagami Bay (相模湾, Sagami-wan) to the northeast and and Suruga Bay (駿河湾, Suruga-wan) to the southwest. The Tōkaidō *Shinkansen,* with stations in Atami to the northeast and Mishima in the northwest, will get you there the quickest. From Tokyo, you'll probably want to go to *Atami* and then change to a local Izu line there. The east side of Izu is peppered with small seaside villages, each with *ryokan, minshuku* and *onsen* all the way to the southern tip. The Izu peninsula JR Itō Line and the Izu Kyūkō Line provides service along the east coast of the peninsula down to Shimoda. Central Izu is served by the *Sunzu* Line as far as Shuzenji. The west coast of the peninsula is less developed and has no train service. Japan has surprisingly wild places still and Izu has deer, wild boar. If you drive down you should notice many tidy small plot farms growing *wasabi,* as *Izu* is a famous producer of the green horseradish.

My favorite spot in Izu is Shimoda, way down at the tip of the peninsula, where in 1854 the U.S. squadron of "black ships" under Commodore Matthew Perry anchored and forcibly opened feudal Japan to world (Western) trade after 250 years of self-imposed isolation. I believe we used the diplomatic phrase, "Open up or else!"[238] Shimoda is an extraordinarily beautiful place, with palm trees and white sand beaches: Tatado, Ohama and Shirahama. Sitting on a longboard in twelve to fifteen feet of water at Kisami-Ohama, gorgeous bodyboarding girls left and right, a decent slow rolling left break, I look down into the water and can see the sandy bottom. I'm in Japan surfing; what's not to like?[239]

---

[238] See http://shimoda-city.info/index_e.html.
[239] See a satellite map of Shimoda at http://mapsof.net/shimoda.

Shimoda holds a key place in Japanese and world history, and there is a museum about the opening of Japan and a three-day Black Ship festival each May to commemorate events. A number of the city's temples are historically relevant as well:

- Gyokusenji Temple, where Harris opened the first U.S. consulate in Japan in 1856. (www.asahi-net.or.jp/~qm9t-kndu/gyokusenji.htm)
- Ryosenji temple, where on 29 July 1858 the Treaty of Amity and Commerce (日米修好通商条約, *Nichibei Shūko Tsūshō Joyaku*) was signed between Japan and the United States. (www.izu.co.jp/~ryosenji/index.htm) (This more comprehensive treaty followed the 31 March 1854, Convention of Kanagawa (日米和親条約 *Nichibei Washin Joyaku*, "Japan-U.S. Treaty of Amity and Friendship") concluded between Commodore Perry of the U.S. Navy and the Tokugawa shogunate.)
- Chōraku Temple where on 7 February 1855 Russia and Japan signed their Treaty of Commerce and Navigation between Japan and Russia (日魯通好条約, later called 日露和親条約), establishing official relations between Russia and Japan. (www.izu.co.jp/~p-boo/chorakuji.html)
- Hofukuji Temple, erected for Tojin Okichi, a geisha who was ordered to serve (three days to three years, depending on which story you believe) as "female attendant" to the first U.S. diplomat in Japan, Townsend Harris. When Harris left, Okichi was supposedly shunned by the Japanese as *"Toujin"* (唐人, とうじん, a barbarian, being the mistress of a foreigner) and years later, she committed suicide by drowning. Much of the Okichi story seems more legend than fact. Some historians say she and another young woman merely served as housekeepers for a short time. Gossip then spun the legend.

Visiting the temple grounds, you can begin to imagine how remarkably foreign these initial cross-cultural encounters must have been (as strange as an alien space invasion) and how resourceful the Japanese proved in quickly "modern-izing" their country rather than ignoring the technology and "handwriting on the wall," as some of its East Asian neighbors did.

Surrounded by lushly green hills, the dense foliage, the bamboo, and the palm trees give Shimoda a tropical feel in summer. Hot. Humid. Fecund. Teeming. At night, the surrounding hills and fields come alive with croaking, chirping, creaking, sneaking, preying, darting, feeding as nocturnal creatures engage in nature's circle of life. Japanese poet Shiki Masaoka may have wistfully penned:

> After killing
> a spider, how lonely I feel
> in the cold of night!

but Shiki san's eight-legged victim was no kin to the daughter of "Shelob" that I battled and killed in my and my wife's room at our pension at Kis-ami-Ohama, Shimoda. We came back from dinner, on night two of our stay, that's night two, bored reader, night two (meaning the beast was prob-ably in there the first night, too), and there she is clinging high on the wall. (The spider, not my wife.) Bugger was the size of a salad plate and of the Huntsman variety, if I know my Discovery Channel. While I am not arachnophobic, I confess I had visions of the film *Arachnophobia* where the gigantic and deadly poisonous arachnid-antagonist hitches a ride from the Amazon jungle to the U.S. on the fresh corpse of the scientist it had bitten being shipped home for burial. By the time it gets back to the U.S., the body looks mummified, having been sucked dry of fluid by its stowa-way spidey coffin-mate. Having vanquished my foe, I turned out the lights for sleep; "Honey, stop playing footsie, OW!"

There's not as much human nightlife in Shimoda. There's an outdoor bar at a place called Ernest House (after Hemingway, www.ernest-house.com) if you don't mind a clientele of foreign "banker-wankers" from Tokyo. In Shimoda city, not far from Hofukuji temple, there was a "reggae bar" the size of a phone booth (that's a "phone booth" mobile-phone babies, a "phone booth"; Google it) with its walls painted black, a few reggae posters on the wall, a fully stocked bar and a DJ manning the turntable. Had two extraordinarily good times there. The first time I was

with a fraternity brother from UCLA days, the very one I had run into
guuzen in Ebisu in April on my way to the pub What the Dickens for a pint.
Months later, we were in Shimoda and he introduced me to this Japanese
walk-in closet of a bar that's an homage to Bob Marley. The next morning,
after an indefensibly long evening playing the juvenile (but still amusing)
drinking game "quarters" over cups of tequila with some locals, I was up,
stumbling across the sand, Bob and his Wailers' tunes still wailing in my
head, and falling face first into the cold Pacific surf: "Get up; stand up!"
Not the best hangover remedy, but a surprisingly effective first step in the
day-long recovery process.

The second time, years later, I was with a best mate from Tokyo, Canadian, and we were away for a final "guys weekend" since we were both
getting married in two months … on the same day—he in Tokyo and me
in Princeton, New Jersey. Miraculously, I found "the Bob Bar" again. We
walked in and it was packed with young women holding their fifth-year
high school reunion. I remember asking one, "Are all the girls in Shizu-
oka-ken this pretty?" "Yes," was her emphatic unabashed reply. My pal
and I both got married anyway; willingly; happily. That's our story, and
we're sticking to it.

From Shimoda (or Tokyo), you can travel by conventional ship or hydrofoil to the Izu Islands, Ojima, Niijima, etc. Stay in a *minshuku* (small
inn) there and you'll feel a million miles away from chaotic Tokyo and
return rejuvenated.[240] Hakone is another close getaway. Buy an Odakyu
free pass and you can travel by rail, cable and pavement all about the area
famous for *onsen* and views of *Fuji san*.[241] Fashionable relaxed Karuizawa,
frequented by John and Yoko back in the day, is in Nagano-ken about an
hour by *shinkansen* from Tokyo station. At one time, it served as a post
town on the 530 kilometer Nakasendo Trail, a key route through the
mountains linking Kyoto to Edo. You can walk the trail, or maybe the
fifty-three stations of the Old Tokaido road.[242] Check with Oxalis Adventures (www.okujapan.com) or Walk Japan (www.walkjapan.com). You
can probably arrange some really outstanding and rather unique adventures. And I've only mentioned bits of the island of Honshu (because

---

[240] See www.tokyo-islands.com/v3/e_contents/niijima/top.html.
[241] Visit www.odakyu.jp/english/freepass/hakone_01.html.
[242] See www.japan-guide.com/e/e5205.html and www.artelino.com/articles/old_tokaido.asp.

the trips can be done quickly and less expensively.) Hokkaido and Kyushu, for example, offer extraordinary history, scenery and cuisine. On Shikoku, you can walk the eighty-eight temple pilgrimage.

Japan was ever full of surprises. Being from California, outdoor playground extraordinaire, it was wonderful discovering that equally there is so much to do outdoors in Japan. With the benefit of hindsight, this makes sense. Japan is blessed with miles of coastline, mountains, lakes and rivers and even wilderness. There is a certain rustic, hearty, earthy nature to the Japanese. It's revealed in their old architecture and by their building material of choice (or necessity given the seismology), wood. The only limit to your adventures will be your imagination and your wallet. It's even possible to make your travel part of your formal training experience because other cities and towns have their own dojos, though I advise finding a way to get an introduction rather than just showing up unless you speak a fair bit of Japanese.[243] Some temples offer lodging and opportunity for *zazen* and ascetic training. Personally, I try to live the phrase "the whole world is my dojo," watching, studying, learning, training … hourly, daily, weekly, monthly, annually. The point being to strive to live a fuller, deeper, engaged and enriched life not only for my benefit but for the benefit of those who I encounter each day—to affect positively my points of contact with the world, however small and insignificant they may be. Each of us has the freedom to make this choice daily.

Oh, if you do go to Izu and by chance stay in a remote mountain inn and if in your room you happen to find a videotape in the VCR (or a DVD player nowadays I guess) and when, out of curiosity, you turn it on to watch it, you see a bunch of static, then a creepy lady in a kimono combing her hair in the mirror (and looking in the mirror back at you), and then you see a well in a field and a pale, thin, eighteen-year-old girl in a nightgown climbs out of it, stringy wet hair hanging down in front of her face, and begins staggering towards the screen … run! Watching

---

[243] In 1992, I had shown up unannounced at a *dojo* in Kyoto. My Japanese was very limited at the time and the telephone (that's landlines, kids) was the only way to communicate short of face-to-face. It's easier to say "no" on the telephone. I showed up. A foreigner, German student, was there early. I helped set up the mats. When the teacher arrived, he wasn't thrilled, but since I had set up the mats I was allowed to practice. The first hour was just with the German. The second hour, having passed the vetting process, I was permitted to practice with the general membership.

ultra-creepy Japanese horror flick *Ringu*, adapted from the first novel in the 1990's "Ring Trilogy" written by Koji Suzuki: *Ringu* ("Ring"), *Rasen* ("Spiral") and *Rupu* ("Loop"), was another of those only-in-Japan moments for me. FYI, the original is much better than the glitzy U.S. remake that draws from the 1956 film *The Bad Seed* (making the ghoulie-girl a ten-year-old child instead of an eighteen-year-old teen) and playwright Peter Shaffer's '73 *Equus*, i.e., a bunch of horses die. Following my first year, *Ringu* was on Japanese TV one evening, in Japanese, no subtitles. Me, my wife, a Canadian aikido pal and his Japanese wife, were all watching together in the dark, naturally. I was catching about 15-20 percent of it, my wife 40-50 percent, my pal 50-60 percent (he'd studied the longest) and since his wife was catching all of it, she was voted to translate vital bits for the rest of us. Every once in awhile it's okay to take advantage of Japanese politeness. The amusing thing was that she was getting creeped-out twice—once watching and listening and then again while translating. Didn't sleep right for weeks. We watched in late winter when the static electricity can really build up in Tokyo … even turn on appliances that are on "standby" … like our TV. Truth. I am standing in the kitchen and suddenly our TV turns on ... to static … just like for the victims in the film. My high-level brain sighs, "Damn static electricity," but my primitive brain screams "Here comes *Sadako*!!!!" Shorts change please! Can I get a shorts change here?

In Japanese culture, summer rather than winter is the traditional time for scary stories because they have a "chilling" effect (or distracting effect) from the heat. Amusement parks in Japan will feature haunted house attractions or *"obake yashiki"* in summer to help customers cool off by "sending shivers down their spines." Summer (August specifically) is also viewed in Japanese Buddhism as the time when ancestral spirits return for a visit, and during *O-bon* Japanese visit family graves. In his work, *"Nihon no Yūrei"* ("Japanese Ghosts") Haruo Suwa, professor emeritus of Gakushuin University, states the first documented ghost tales are from the Heian Period (平安時代, *Heian jidai,* 794 to 1185) but belief in supernatural beings were common well before that time. According to Suwa sensei, prior to the import of Buddhism to Japan, notions of heaven and hell did not exist. Recognizing the divine all around us, Shinto believed that humans were transformed into spirits after death, and spirits were considered to be harmless or even favorable. Only after Buddhism spread from India to Tibet to China to Korea and ultimately to Japan did ghosts become terrifying and harmful to the Japanese.

You gain some appreciation of the significance of the supernatural in Japanese culture merely by considering the number of words for ghost (spirit, specter or apparition and some double for monster). An abbreviated list could include: *bakemono* (化け物, ばけもの), *boukon* (亡魂, ぼうこん), *henge* (変化, へんげ), *hourei* (亡霊, ぼうれい), *konbaku* (魂魄, こんぱく), *mononoke* (物の怪, もののけ), *obake* (お化け, おばけ), *onryo* (怨霊, おんりょう), *seirei* (精霊, せいれい), *shiryo, shirei* (死霊, しりょう, しれい), *youkai* (妖怪, ようかい), *youma* (妖魔, ようま), *yūki* (幽鬼, ゆうき), *yūrei* (幽霊, ゆうれい), *yūkai* (幽怪, ゆうかい) and so on ...

Yūrei is the generic term and folkloric equivalent of a Western ghost. Comprised of two *kanji*, 幽 (*yū*), meaning "faint" or "dim," and 霊 (*rei*), meaning "soul" or "spirit," *yūrei* are generally believed to be souls kept from a peaceful afterlife due to some event in life. Like Western ghosts, a *yūrei* may be tied to a specific place where a life tragedy occurred or it can be linked to certain people, remaining until some past emotional conflict (love, jealousy, hatred, grief, vengeance) is resolved. In the Japanese supernatural, different circumstances produce a variety of spirits of varying intentions:

- *Ayakashi* (あやかし): a ghost appearing at sea during a shipwreck;
- *Chouchin Obake* (提灯お化け, ちょうちんおばけ): a ghost appearing as a demonic lantern leading people astray;
- *Funayūrei* (船幽霊): *a ghost of one who died at sea;*
- *Goryō* (御霊): *powerful spirits of nobles, capable of pestilence and natural disaster;*
- *Hitodama* (人魂, ひとだま): a *disembodied soul appearing as a supernatural fiery ball;*
- *Konaki Jijii* (子泣き爺, こなきじじい): a ghost appearing as a small old man that has a baby's cry to attract humans;

- *Jibakurei* (地縛霊, じばくれい): a ghost tied to a specific physical location;
- *Mononoke* (物の怪, もののけ): a (vengeful) ghost or specter;
- *Noppera-bō* (のっぺら坊): a faceless ghost;
- *Oni* (鬼 (おに, き): a demon;
- *Onryō* (怨霊): a strong, typically female ghost who returns for revenge;
- *Shuramono* (修羅物): Ghosts of samurai who fell in battle;
- Seductress *yūrei*: a spirit seeking a relationship with a living person after passing into death;
- *Ubume* (産女): spirits of women seeking to care for their still living children;
- *Zashiki-warashi* (座敷童/座敷童子): house ghosts of children, causing mischief but bringing good fortune.

Yūrei were popular subjects in Japanese art forms like *Ukiyo-e* or *Kabuki*. In Tokyo, only in August, you can see Edo period prints of *yūrei* at Zenshoan temple, which maintains a priceless collection of some fifty roughly 200-year-old silk paintings.244 A common theme to Japanese horror tales is the *onryō*, which is a spirit bound to earth by a burning desire for *vengeance*. Powerful, angry and relentless, th*ey are generally female; go figure*. Often portrayed wearing white, like a traditional Buddhist burial kimono, pale-looking, with long stringy unkempt black hair, arms stretched forward, wrists dangling and sometimes legless, or if bipedal then crawling or walking with awkward, twitching movements. They may be emitting guttural, croaking noises. They have been supernaturally transformed from human to *kami*.

One night I took a shortcut with a friend, on our way from Aoyama to Roppongi, by walking through the massive Tokyo cemetery Aoyama Bochi (青山霊園). No spooks spotted, but maybe that's because I wasn't passing through during the "time of the three oxes" (two to three A.M.), which is the most haunted hour, according to Japanese legend. I did catch a ride one night from a long-time Tokyo taxi driver who swore that he saw

---

244 See 全生庵 at www.theway.jp/zen.

strange things in the cemetery as he would drive by it at night, perhaps confirming a sleazy co-worker's claims about "getting busy" with some girl in the graveyard one night. There is, however, a well-known Tokyo taxi driver tale of a young woman who waves down a taxi for a ride (the passenger's door of Tokyo taxis opens and closes automatically, so don't touch the doors), gets in, gives an address and upon arriving the cabbie turns to find nothing in the backseat but a pool of water. Turns out he has driven to the home of a family whose daughter died years ago in a car crash one rainy night in Tokyo.

My wife attended high school in Okinawa. It's a beautiful, fascinating place, if somewhat tragic due to the battle of Okinawa in WWII. It retains elements of its own very distinct cultural past—now an interesting blend of things Okinawan, Japanese and Chinese—having for centuries been the ancient and independent Kingdom of Ryukyu (with its own language, a subfamily of the Japonic language family). Some claim that at some point it became a tributary state of the Ming Dynasty (1368 to 1644) of China, but the island kingdom was definitely invaded in 1609 by *Shimazu Tadatsune*, Lord of *Satsuma* (a feudal *Daimyo* domain located in present-day *Kagoshima* prefecture, Southwestern *Kyushu*) establishing definitive Japanese control over the islands ever since. Okinawan friends told my wife that it is not unusual for one person in each generation of an extended Okinawan family to possess the "gift" of seeing ghosts (霊感, れいかん, *reikan*), like the young boy in the popular M. Night Shyamalan film *The Sixth Sense* or Stephen King's book *The Shining*. "You're dead." "Redrum!"

Since living in London (at least part-time), I have gone on two "ghost walks" and both were quite entertaining—one through the ancient City of London and the other in The West End. London has a rather grisly history, including plague burial pits (some holding victims tossed in while still alive), hangings, decapitations, serial killers (Jack the Ripper), haunted houses (50 Berkeley Square), a haunted Underground.[245] There seems no end to "Haunted London." With its own unique history and culture, dating back thousands of years, Japan has a rich supernatural tradition and Tokyo its share of reported haunts.

---

[245] See the spooky Tube at www.youtube.com/watch?v=8ZzHtxf9TNI.

The Yotsuya district, not far from the dojo, is the setting for perhaps the most famous Japanese ghost story, *"Yotsuya Kaidan"* ("Yotsuya Ghost Story"). Based on the supposedly true story of Lady Iwa (O-Iwa, who died some time in the first half of the seventeenth century), it has been retold so many times by so many people that there is no definitive version. Adapted for *kabuki* and numerous films, it is a tale of vengeance by a young woman O-Iwa Inari, a real person, who lived in the Yotsuya area of Edo. O-Iwa san was betrayed by her philandering and social-climbing *ronin* husband, Iyemon, who with the help of family servants slowly poisoned her, causing gruesome bloody facial disfigurement. Seeing her horrid reflection in the mirror, she sadly tries to make herself presentable by combing her long hair, only for it to tear away in bloody clumps. O-Iwa dies horribly, cursing her betrayers, but her wrathful spirit returns to exact revenge by slowly tormenting them all—her hideously scarred face appearing in windows and mirrors—and finally killing her husband. Basically, it's a heartwarming story that features baby dismemberment, insanity, torture and a person who has his face eaten off by rats. If claims are believed, her ghost still roams the streets of Yotsuya and remains extremely dangerous. Some do take this seriously, as stage, TV or film productions concerning her story are known to pay homage at her shrine beforehand or to set an extra place at cast gatherings, etc. to appease her vengeful spirit.

You can visit two shrines with different takes on Lady Iwa (a five-minute walk from Yotsuya San-chome station on the same street) and visit her grave:

- O-Iwa-Inari Tamiya Shrine (於岩稲荷田宮神社) in Shimanom-achi, Yotsuya.
- Yoh'un-ji temple.
- Myogyoji temple, Somei Cemetery, Sugamo—*Four* minutes on foot from Nishi Sugamo Station (transferred to its present location from Iga in Yotsuya Ward in 1909).

If you hunger for more of haunted Tokyo, see:

- "Bloody Tourism" www.cnngo.com/tokyo/play/tokyo-sites-re-call-grisly-tale-oiwa-535888#ixzz1JUr0Gual
- James Seguin De Benneville (1917) *The Yotsuya Kwaidan or O'Iwa Inari, Tales of the Tokugawa, Volume 1 (of 2)* www.guten-berg.org/files/19944/19944-h/19944-h.htm or www.wattpad.com/22019-the-yotsuya-kwaidan-or-o'iwa-inari-ta-les-of-the?p=2
- Lafcadio Hearn, Author of 1904 book *Kwaidan: Stories and Studies of Strange Things.* http://lafcadiohearn.jp/tokyo/index.html. The 1965 film adaptation won the Special Jury Prize at the Cannes Film Festival and an Academy Award nomination.
- "Tokyo: Town of Terror" http://travel.cnn.com/to-kyo/play/tokyo-map-terror-143802
- Haunted tours: www.meetup.com/Haunted-Tokyo-Tours or www.hauntedtokyotours.com

However, you don't even have to leave your comfy couch (or *futon*) in order to frighten the bejesus out of yourself in an effort to forget the heat. The Japanese do an incomparable job telling their ghostly stories in film. While they have produced graphic, violent, slasher, splatter, gorefest, de-praved type cinema over the years, it's the more restrained, atmospheric, often spiritual and eerie style of films that have made an impression on Western audiences. Relying on a deliberate pace and mood that builds towards terror, they are often moralistic and rooted in Japanese mythology, Shintoism or Buddhism—a primal energy that simmers beneath the sur-face of modern industrial technological Japan. Having written that, there are also campy, wild and wacky films like *Versus* (2000) which somehow manages to combine s*amurai, yakuza*, flesh-eating zombies and reincarna-tion, all into a single highly entertaining, if not entirely cohesive, film.

In addition to the *Ringu* series, these are worth a watch with the lights off if you enjoy the genre:

Audition (1999) Director Takashi Miike explodes the sappy Japanese romantic comedy when a bachelor's buddy convinces him to hold a fake audition for a film part so that he can meet babes. He does, but who or what is she? Things go wildly wrong. Did I mention brutally and horrif-ically?

Dark Water (仄暗い水の底から, *Honogurai mizu no soko kara*) (2002) Hideo Nakata, director of Ring and Ring 2, returns to familiar territory of the vengeful spirit and water. Creepiest of all may be the sterile apartment building.

Ju-on (呪怨, じゅおん, Curse-grudge) (2002) directed by Takashi Shimizu (who studied under Kiyoshi Kurosawa) is a classic place haunting. A murdered housewife dies with a burning grudge and a curse is born linked to the place of death. Encountering the place leaves you cursed and your death spreads the curse beyond the place.

Shikoku (死国) (1999), directed by Shunichi Nagasaki, is a Buddhist ghost story of sorts. Fiddle with the first *kanji* a bit and Shikoku (四国, the Four Countries), smallest and least populated of Japan's four main islands, becomes Shikoku (死国 the Dead Country). After many years, *Hinako san* returns from Tokyo to her childhood village in rural Shikoku to discover that her dear friend *Sayori* died fifteen years before in a drowning accident at sixteen years old. *Sayori's* loving mommy (a spiritual medium or *miko*) misses her daughter (and planned successor) very much. So very much that for the past fifteen years she has been walking the famous *Shikoku* eighty-eight shrine Buddhist pilgrimage (四国遍路, *Shikoku Henro*, www.tourismshikoku.com/features/o-henro) ... backwards! Will her sixteenth trip open the door to Shikoku? Indeed, *"some things are better left dead."*

Shutter (2008) An American remake of the 2004 Thai horror film, directed by Masayuki Ochiai and set in Tokyo. What are those odd cloudy shapes appearing in the photos? It's a cautionary tale of sorts for Western men visiting Japan.

I know; I know. "I ain't afraid of no ghosts." But if all this supernatural stuff leaves you feeling even a bit *kimiwarui* (気味悪い, きみわるい, creepy), looking over your shoulder and wondering, how would I stop a spook? If you do find yourself face-to-face (or face-to-faceless), "Who you gonna call?" ゴーストバスターズ？ Well, holy water and crosses may not help keep Shinto-Buddhist Japanese ghosts at bay. The tradition is *ofuda* (御札, おふだ, amulets) inscribed on wood or paper with Buddhist sutras, or Shinto shrines provide an *oharai* (御祓い, おはらい, purification ritual) to remove bad mojo with wooden wands and chants—

Expecto Patronum, *kudasai*! If the ancient approach doesn't suit you, techno-Japan may have just the answer. Float over to Akihabara or online and pick up a "ばけたん2ストラップ" (*Baketan* 2 Strap) for your mobile phone. Replacement to the *Baketan* 1 (you missed it?), the manufacturer Solid Alliance claims their gadget offers twenty-four-hour specter detection and protection, as the *Baketan* 2 can read rhythms of "ultra-waves" and use "spatial algorithms" to turn spirit sounds into electronic sounds, warning the user of any supernatural presence. Quick press of a button and you're protected. Uh-huh. Hopefully it doesn't ward off Ultra-man too, in case a giant rubber monster attacks Tokyo while you're there.[246]

Years ago, I asked my father the theologian about ghosts, and he replied, "Well, they might exist; they might not, but I don't believe in them." Aforementioned, Suwa sensei confesses that even after all his studies he can't decide whether ghosts exist, but it's an indisputable fact that many Japanese believe in supernatural spirits. Let's not forget that the Omoto-kyo (大本教, おもときょう, Great Origin Faith, www.oomoto.or.jp) religious sect, a sincreistic amalgamation including elements of Koshinto (古神道), Japanese folk-spiritual and divination traditions and another *Shinto* sect Konkokyo (金光教), which had a profound influence on the founder of aikido and his development of the purpose of his art, had links to the supernatural.[247] Synthesizing sources, the sect was founded in 1892 by Deguchi Nao (1836–1918), a peasant housewife, who at fifty-six years of age claimed to have been possessed (神憑り, かみがかり, *kamigakari*) by the *kami Ushitora no Konjin* (a guardian spirit of metal) and compelled to pen the Omoto-kyo scriptures, *inter alia* professing the universal family of humankind and open criticism of Japanese society. I don't know if it's accurate or not, but an appealing description I read by a reviewer of a book on Omoto-kyo wrote something like, "it incorporates the *Shinto* appreciation of nature and beauty, a Buddhist eschatology of

---

[246] Get yours at www.apparestore.com/gadgets-apps/baketan/.

[247] In the late 1870's Shinto became the official state government and over the years certain Shinto sects were officially recognized: Tenrikyo, Konkokyo, Kurozumikyo, Fuso-kyo (which included Omoto-kyo), Izumo-oyashiro-kyo, Jikko-kyo, Misogi-kyo, Shinshu-kyo, Shinto-shu-seiha, Shinri-kyo, Shinto Taisei-kyo, Ontake-kyo and Shinto Taikyo.

enlightenment for all sentient beings, a Christian call to universal fellow-ship and realization of the Reign of God, the political sensibilities of an oppressed peasantry, and places a premium on esthetic expression."

In 1919, O-Sensei met the second leader of Omoto-kyo, Deguchi Onisabur (born named Ueda Kisaburo in Kameoka, 1871–1948), in Ayabe while returning home to his dying father in Tanabe. Do we accu-rately call Deguchi the spiritual teacher of O-Sensei? However one de-fines that relationship, this talented artist (writer, poet, calligrapher, sculp-tor, and ceramist) and notably eccentric fellow claimed, according to some, to be an incarnation of *Miroku Butsu* (Maitreya Buddha) and authored the *Reikai Monogatari* (Tales of the Spirit World), an eighty-one-volume work describing his travels through spiritual dimensions. I have read that O-Sensei believed he had a guardian *kami* known as *Ame-no-Murakumo-Kuki-Samuhara-Ryu-O* ("Heavenly, Awesome, Enlightened Dragon King").

Don't misunderstand me. I am not judging Omoto-kyo one way or the other, or any believer. Today, with our 21st century sensibilities, such beliefs may sound bizarre to many (forgetting that quantum physics can seem no less fantastic), but in context, it's not so extraordinary given cen-turies of folk and Shinto belief in countless *kami* (and other spirits) influ-encing nearly every aspect of human life. I am even less quick to judge because the human heart yearns for meaning and "There are more things in heaven and earth, Horatio, Than are dreamt of in your philosophy".[248] I never met any of these people and have no personal understanding of them or their religious experiences. It's a mistake to comprehensively pro-ject one's own level of consciousness onto people of one's own era, let alone those of another time and another land. Mentioning Omoto-kyo and its recognition of the supernatural merely highlights the deep Japa-nese belief in an unseen spirit world. Whether you are a zealous Dawkin-sian rationalist skeptic or an "I do believe in spooks, I do, I do, I do" Cowardly Lion in need of some courage, joining in the "spirit" of things in summer in Japan can be good fun, plus studying the origin and nature of Japanese spiritual beliefs will deepen your understanding of the people and their culture. Who knows, maybe it will even help you beat the heat.

---

[248] William Shakespeare, Hamlet Act 1, scene 5, 159–167.

Honorable Ancestors

御盆
(O-bon)

So August arrives in Tokyo and it gets hotter still—damn hot. If I hear one more well-meaning person volunteer the bloody obvious—"*Atsui desu ne*"—I'm gonna lose it. Well, actually, such crusty cynicism only bubbles up after simmering in Japan for several years. Year one, it's all very fresh and I find myself, aloud or in my head, stupidly parroting back, "*Ehh, so desu ne.*" (It's hot isn't it. Yes, so it is.) Anyway, August: "It's hot enough to boil a monkey's bum," as an Australian philosopher once said, but there I was (Tokyo not Australia) still practicing every day but Sundays.[249]

Unquestionably, there are more difficult things in life than practicing aikido several times a day in 30-plus degree heat and ninety percent humidity, but it isn't exactly easy either and, unlike many of life's challenges, you can choose not to do it. I had that choice. There was no teacher back home to disappoint. There was no peer pressure. It was up to me. Like Woody Allen reportedly said, "Eighty percent of success is showing up." Through the years in Japan, I met plenty of people who arrived at Hombu Dojo claiming they were going to train a lot and then rarely saw them. However, summer of '97, I was still very excited to be in Japan and just kept telling myself that summer practice was all part of the "forging process," the heat-up-the-iron-near-molten-before-hammering-out-the-impurities phase. Just about the time I was beginning to convince myself, despite the methodical debunking I'd seen on the Discovery Channel, that humans can actually spontaneously combust, the dojo closed for *O-bon* (お盆, 御盆, おぼん, Lantern Festival or Festival of the Dead).

O-bon is the Japanese version of an annual Buddhist celebration held to commemorate one's ancestors. The word is a shortening of *Urabon-e* (

---

249 Philosophy Department of the University of Woolamaloo.
    www.youtube.com/watch?v=qJkO-EKRVd0

于蘭盆會 or 盂蘭盆會), which is derived from the Japanese transliteration, *Urabanna*, of the Sanskrit word Ullambana, which apparently means something like "hanging upside down" and is an oblique reference to the dead being in a state of suffering and in response to which we should be merciful.[250]   The origin of O-bon's observance in Japan is lost in ancient history, but scholars guess it may have started in some form in some places as far back as 600 to 700 AD following the arrival of Buddhism in Japan.[251]   Buddhism traveled to Japan from India, adopting and adapting preexisting local practices, e.g., Taoist, Confucian, Shamanistic, etc., and disregarding or discarding some doctrine, along the stages of its eastward journey.[252]   Like other East Asian Buddhists, the Japanese came to consider mid-August a spiritual season.[253]   The belief is that during *O-bon* the spirits of relatives return for three days to visit their relations.   The living

---

[250]   Originating in India, Ullambana commemorates one of the Buddha's first disciples, Maudgalyayana (*Mokuren* in Japanese), who demonstrated admirable filial piety (however at odds this Confucian ideal may be with Buddhist tenets against worldly attachment) in seeking out The Buddha for a way to secure salvation for his suffering mother who had been reborn to a lower hellish realm. The Ullambana Sutra (actually penned hundreds of years after Buddha attained Nirvana) is a discourse on filial piety and achieving religious merits towards salvation by offerings to ancestors made on the fifteenth day of the seventh month.

[251]   The *Nihon Shoki* (日本書紀) records the introduction of Buddhism to Japan as 552 AD, though some monastic records claim an earlier time. At some point in the sixth century, the twenty-sixth king of Baekje (one of the then three independent Korean Kingdoms) sent a delegation to the Japanese capital of *Nara* including monks, nuns, an icon and sutras.

[252]   It is a common, often ethnocentric, misconception that a particular cultural practice in one East Asian country is a simple transplant from an adjacent neighbor. However, ancestor-themed observances are not unique to any particular people or continent, occurring in a variety of forms in Africa, Asia, Europe and South America at the least. It makes sense that it is part of the collective human conscience. You are thankful for your life. You realize it's a gift from those who went before you. You miss those who you knew while they were alive. You wonder about those you never knew and annually take time to remember them.

[253]   Ullambana spread to China sometime in the sixth century, where it blended with Taoist and folk religion traditions. Now, many ethnic Chinese in the People's Republic of China, Taiwan and amongst the global diaspora observe Ullambana as "The Ghost Festival." The Chinese are a "spirited" bunch, having painted the whole country red to ward off ghosts, and the seventh month of the lunar calendar is Ghost Month (鬼月) and the fifteenth day of that month is Ghost Day when spirits return to visit the living. Notions of filial piety are at odds with original Buddhist tenets, but apparently Confucianism influenced the faith when it reached China. Actually, the Chinese hold three fundamentally ancestral observances: Qīngmíngjié, (清明節, Pure Brightness Festival in spring) and Chóngyángjié (重陽節, Yang (Double 9) Festival in Autumn) and Ghost Day. With the first two non-Buddhist events, the living seek their dead ancestors by tending to their graves. In the third, the ghosts of relations (older or younger) come see the living. "Okay, let's do two at your place and one at ours; hǎo ma?" From what I saw in China, Ghost Festival is a more somber occasion than the highly festive *O-bon*.

gather at their ancestral homes to welcome them back and honor the departed through various customs, including visiting grave sites and making various offerings. It's sort of a less macabre Japanese version of Mexico's Día de los Muertos.[254]

So when is *O-bon*? Well, as I wrote, it's in August, er, well; is it? As part of the Meiji restoration, Japan switched in 1873 from the Chinese lunar calendar to the Western Gregorian solar calendar and different regions reacted differently to the change, causing *O-bon* to be celebrated on different dates in different regions.[255] So there are three different *O-bons*: "*Shichigatsu Bon*" in July (fifteenth day of the seventh month of the solar calendar), "*Hachigatsu Bon*" in August (fifteenth day of the eighth month of the solar calendar) and "*Kyu Bon*" (旧盆, Old Bon) celebrated on the fifteenth day of the seventh month of the lunar calendar, and so it differs each year. I've mentioned that Tokyo seems like a series of connected villages, and this was apparent during *O-bon*. Tokyo sets the official date of *O-bon* as July 15, but in my extended neighborhood, there were a series of *O-bon* celebrations around that time, every few blocks it seemed, and not all on the same days.

Over time in Japan, *O-Bon* has broadened (or diminished) into a modern day family reunion, with people leaving the metropolitan cities for their hometowns and (more recently) holidays abroad. I've told you about Japanese and taking holidays. "Oh honorable co-worker, I couldn't dream of inconveniencing you by taking a holiday and leaving you to work alone, so why don't we both take a very short holiday at the same time? Perhaps we can invite the whole nation to join us?" In fact, *O-bon* (in August) is "summer vacation" for Japan. Things slow down in Tokyo; it gets pretty quiet, and trains and other public spaces seem comparatively empty. The dojo closes for about a week (in 2011, August 8 to 13). Most shops close

---

[254] "DDLM" is a convergence of the Catholic holidays of All Saints' Day and All Souls' Day and a preexisting Aztec death cult (a common syncretic practice employed by the church in spreading Catholic Christianity). It's a national holiday in Mexico, October 31 through November 3, whereby family and friends gather to pray for and otherwise remember the dead.

[255] Japan first adopted the Chinese lunar calendar, which meant *O-bon* was celebrated around the fifteenth day of the seventh (lunar) month, which roughly coincides with August. However, with the change of calendars, *O-bon* came to be officially set in the solar seventh solar month of the year (July) in the Tokyo area but observed in mid-August in much of the rest of Japan. Consequently, companies in Tokyo will allow time off in August for workers to return to their provincial homes.

for a few days before and after *O-bon*.[256] Like "Salary Man Bad Haircut Day," *O-bon's* not an official Japanese national holiday, but *O-bon* seriously competes with Golden Week and *O-Shogatsu* for top observance in the Japanese calendar year.[257] Culturally, it is very important and another peak travel time. Urbanites with roots in the provinces travel en masse to their hometowns to visit family—living and departed. Recently, people have sensibly started staggering time off so holiday travel is more typically between August 6 and August 21, with the busiest domestic travel days being the two days before *O-bon* and two days after it. If you are planning a visit or just moved to Tokyo, bear in mind that for about three weeks in August, airports, train stations, and roads are choking with travelers.[258] Fares and accommodation rates rise accordingly. The word "extortionist" comes to mind.

Once they do get home, people renew family ties and local roots by thoroughly cleaning their houses before the arrival of their spiritual guests, cooking special foods and feasting together (being sure to set a place for the unseen). They make very typically Japanese, delicate, meticulously beautiful food offerings, placing them in the home's Buddhist altar (*butsudan*, 仏壇, ぶつだん) and may further decorate with flowers and with a paper lantern (*chouchin*, 提灯, ちょうちん), which is lit to guide the spirits of the deceased home as part of *mukae-bon* (迎え盆, むかえぼん, welcoming bon). Some places may allow outdoor fires (*mukae-bi*, 迎え火, むかえび, welcoming (bon) fire) in addition to *chouchin* placed inside or hung outside of the home. The point is, "Yo; ancestors; it's this way (in case you forgot)!" It is customary to attend to the graves of their ancestors and, depending on a family's religiosity, pray and chant sutras in the home and perhaps also visit a temple.

There are city, town or village festivities as well, such as firework displays and of course *Bon-odori* (盆踊り, おどり, Bon dance) held in parks,

---

[256] Public schools typically go on holiday from mid-July through to the end of August.

[257] For a list of official holidays in Japan see http://en.wikipedia.org/wiki/Public_holidays_in_Japan.

[258] A 2010 Ministry of Labor survey found 85 percent of larger companies (1,330 with over 30 employees) set their summer vacation in mid-August over *O-bon*. The average holiday was nine days. The longest sixteen days. For 2011, a major travel agency projected domestic *O-bon* travelers (July and August) at 80.45 million (about two out of every three Japanese) and overseas travelers at 3.33 million. That's a lot of folk on simultaneous walkabout.

gardens, shrines, or temples. *Bon-odori* is a dance of joy for one's ancestors and for life, done because the Indian monk *Mokuren* (in Japanese) supposedly danced with joy when his mother was released from her suffering after he had completed the rituals advised by The Buddha. The dance differs significantly from one locale to another.[259]   Basically, dressed in *yukata* (cotton summer kimono) or *jinbei* (甚平, じんべい, a pajama-like cotton jacket and shorts worn by men in summer), the dance is done in a circle around a wooden *yagura* (櫓, 矢倉, やぐら, turret or tower) or a stage strewn with lanterns or electric lights. *Taiko* drums beat the rhythm. Movements may relate to an area's history, geography or another local distinction. Some dances may employ a particular type of fan, sticks or other device to add syncopated rhythms to the drumming. There may be chanting, shouting or singing in accompaniment. In my neighborhood in Tokyo, it was accomplished with a recording blared over a loudspeaker on a wooden tower constructed in the local playground between Akebonobashi and Nuke Benten crossing. My wife is an extraordinarily charming woman. Basically, I married her so people wouldn't think I was all bad. Seeing her enthusiastically jumping into the dance circle with our neighbors at our local *O-bon* festival was a treat. The locals loved it. Oh, how the world has changed and shrunk in a very short number of years—a Korean (American) welcomed to dance *Bon-odori* in Tokyo. She hadn't a clue, but did what you are supposed to do if you are new; fake it with gusto. Like aikido, watch and copy. Watch and copy. With practice, you catch on. Me? Real men don't dance. And anyway, my *jinbei* was at the cleaners.

O-bon* ends as it started, with fire. At *Okuri-bon* (送り盆, おくりぼーん, seeing off or sending off *bon*), the last day of the festival, people use *chouchin* to guide spirits back to the grave. *Okuri-bi* (送り火, sending off *bon* fire) may be lit in some locales telling the spirits to go back. In Kyoto, a giant kanji, 大, and other figures burn bright on a mountainside (*Daimonji*, 大文字).[260] In areas adjacent to the sea, lakes or rivers, people may gather at the water's edge substituting the *okuri-bi* with setting wooden or

---

[259]   See www.bonodori.net.
[260]   See it come and go in 2010 at www.youtube.com/watch?v=VlV6MMNiCLs&feature=related.

straw, candlelit lanterns (*Tōrōnagashi*, 灯籠流し, とうろうながし) adrift on the water as a farewell gesture. As with the date of *O-bon*, customs vary regionally, but in each instance, it's most certainly a celebration, not only of the deceased but of the living.

I don't know whether or not it was from being around East Asian culture for many years, a momentary flash of maturity and wisdom, aikido and the study of martial arts (with the emphasis on honoring our teachers and seniors, from whom we receive so much) or something else, and I can't identify any particular epiphany, but at some point while in Japan, the clouds parted and the sun shone and I realized just how much I owed my parents and their parents and so on. I sat down and wrote a long letter to my maternal grandmother (at that point in her early nineties; she passed her driver's test in her little pale yellow Volkswagen Beetle at ninety years old and lived independently until ninety-eight-and-a-half years old), Oma (grandmother in German). Oma, Alice Heilshorn, was born in the town of Arnstadt, in Thuringia, in Central Germany, where Johann Sebastian Bach is thought to have penned his *Toccata and Fuge in D Minor*. The second daughter of a German industrialist and my Grossi (great grand-mother, who I knew and lived to ninety-three and a half) who was from Hamburg. Yes; that makes her a "Hamburger." Oma was a tomboy and rather athletic: hiking, mountain climbing, skiing, dance, gymnastics. She led an idyllic life of privilege in a twenty-plus room home. However, World War I changed all of that. They lost everything. Her father had died earlier, and back then there wasn't much help for single mothers. At seventeen, Oma decided to leave Germany. The family had an aunt in Southern California, so she set off for the U.S. via ship from Hamburg, across the Atlantic, through the Panama Canal and up the Pacific Coast to San Pedro (L.A.'s harbor). Her aunt put her to work on their chicken ranch in the San Fernando Valley. Later, Oma met and married a Swiss immigrant from St. Galen (my grandfather) and they had a child, my mother, Barbara Alice. However, their happy new American life changed when my grandfather died in an automobile accident. My mother was just over one year old. Faced with being a single mother, Oma returned to family and friends in Germany. However, in 1936, friends there advised her to leave for America, as an infamous mustached Austrian was gaining power. Good advice; so Oma and little Barbara (now four years old)

moved back to Southern California with Grossi and escaped the devasta-
tion of the Second World War. Oma found work in a book-binding factory in Los Angeles and worked her way up the ranks. Grossi raised my
mother.

So, one day I wrote Oma and thanked her. How could I express a
proper thank you? It's impossible. Now that I am a father of a baby girl,
I appreciate how much love, sacrifice and care goes into raising a child
well, and how each life is built upon the effort of countless preceding
lives. Despite the gross inadequacies of words, I thanked my grandmother. Thanked her for all her sacrifices. Thanked her for persevering
when faced with so many challenges and disappointments. Despite the
hard hand life had dealt her at times, my mother and her three children all
had a life because Oma had refused to give up.[261] We can't control everything in our lives, but we can choose daily to strive to control our attitude
and our effort. Whether you believe in an afterlife or not, I do believe
that remembering the fore-lives (of your ancestors) and that your life is a
gift built on their struggle and survival is humbling and inspiring.

I don't have any particular memories of O-bon from year one in Japan.
Not surprising; I was focused on training and knew that when the dojo
closed in August for the holiday I had to leave to renew my visa. That
would be a very serious challenge. There was good reason for concern.
Where to go? Go for how long? When I returned, would I clear immigration? Would they actually grant me a nine-month stay in Japan (with
just two past brief exits)? Without a long-term visa? Or, would they think
I was working illegally or doing something else, or just not like the look
of me and deny me entry? It happens. There was absolutely no guarantee
that I'd be readmitted. Prayers to ancestors and higher places!

Why not just get a long-term visa? Who knew how long I'd actually
stay? Of course, I thought I'd stay for a year, but would I really? The
dream of something and the reality of it can prove very different. Even
so, it wasn't self-doubt that stopped me from going through the visa application process. It was common sense. I knew I'd get at least six months
in Japan (one exit in the middle), and because of where I came from (Cal-

---

[261] At ninety-eight and a half years, Oma lived long enough to see her beloved "Los Angeles
Angels" finally win The World Series.

ifornia), what I did professionally (lawyer) and how I looked (stereotypically respectable). I figured I would get another three months and maybe
even six if I had a very clear explanation with supporting documents. If
I failed, I would spend the time and effort on a cultural or study visa.
Remember, the Internet was in its infancy. Good information was tougher
to come by, and I figured that with my boots on the ground in Japan, I
could tap the real-world experience of other foreigners.

So, after six months in Japan, my inevitable confrontation with immigration would require considerably more planning and strategy than the
lost weekend I spent in Hong Kong in spring, plus a good measure of
luck. I prepared my supporting documentation: a wallet full of credit
cards and a file folder of bank statements (showing I had plenty of cash
to support myself without working), my *Aikikai yudansha* book (to evidence that I was there studying aikido), my California Bar Card (law license), proof of a place to live and so on. To maximize my chances, I
needed to stay away a bit longer this time, so the stereotypical visa-sprint
to Seoul was out of the question. I flew down to Bangkok.

Thailand was wildly fantastic; the postcard-perfect backdrop for yet
another East Asian adventure (that would go global in the end). Threading through the day's rising thunderheads, my JAL jet touched down at
Suvarnabhumi Airport. The trip southwest from Japan had been une-
ventful, just how I like my flights. I cleared customs and sped off for the
hotel, rolling down the taxi window to take in all the unfamiliar sites,
smells and sounds of Bangkok. The place I'd booked was shockingly in-
expensive given its quality and centrality. I'd been cooking simple meals
at home or eating out cheaply for six months in Tokyo, while training like
mad, so I treated myself to a decent place with a daily buffet. If anything,
I have difficulty maintaining weight, and I was working out so much in
Japan that I had to be careful that I ate and drank enough. Not only was
I doing heaps of aikido, but *suburi* also, and a Navy Seal exercise program
I had discovered, which involved various types of pushups, pullups, hand-
stands and, go figure, swimming. My first teacher used to remind us, "The
whole world is your dojo," and I had really taken that to heart in Japan,
trying to do everything with enthusiasm, concentration, dedication and
energy, particularly physical activities. Whether climbing stairs up and out
of a subway station or walking to the dojo for practice, it didn't matter.

It was all to make me stronger or better in some small way. One of my friends had the same mentality, so if we were teaching aikido at The British School, for example, where we had to carry the tatami up two flights of stairs to set up the mats, we grabbed two at a time, balancing them on our head or back, and ran them up the stairs. Back down when we were done. This was particularly foolhardy on my part, because my friend was ninety-eight or ninety-nine kilos of sinew, and I was about seventy-nine or eighty then (eating to get back to eighty-three). The hard work paid off, though; when I left Japan during *O-bon* for my second visa run in August '97, I was perhaps the fittest I'd ever been. Even my pinky fingers had muscles.

For the next few days, in the searing heat and stifling humidity of Southeast Asia, I walked and rode (in a tuk-tuk or dragon boat) all over Bangkok, visiting temples and palaces, watching Muay Thai from ringside seats and enjoying amazing Thai street food—sweet, salt, sour, lime—chasing it down with refreshing Singha beer. It certainly fulfilled any desires for the exotic. I wanted to head north to Chang Mai, Chang Rai and the Burma and Laos borders, but it was pissing rain up there. Having had my fill of big cities, I flew down to the island of Koh Samui for a few days of board-shorts and beach. I needed the rest, frankly, and the sea has healing powers for mind, body and soul.[262] I wasn't some smug back-packing traveler looking for a hidden corner of the kingdom still untouched by tourist development to "live" the local experience. Certainly by 1997, Koh Samui was already a flourishing tourist destination. Give them a break; after centuries of subsistence agriculture and fishing, it's probably not a bad way of life for many, if not most. As Thailand's third largest island (about 230 to 240 square kilometers) and having a population under 50,000 (at that time) it still had its mountain jungles, coconut trees, white sand beaches, turquoise waters and coral reefs. Located in the Gulf of Thailand, about 35 km off the peninsula and just 700 km south of Bangkok, it was simple to get there and a good hub for hopping off somewhere else, since it is surrounded by something like fifty or sixty other islands, and its airport offered numerous regional flights. All I needed was a towel, patch of sand, a book and the ocean. It would all be

---

[262] "Koh" is Thai for island but no one seems entirely sure of the etymology of "Samui," though some say it means "safe haven."

there and more.

Landed. Stowed my gear. Hit the beach. If the dreary weather wasn't going to cooperate so that I could go free diving or scuba, then I would make the best of it somehow. Through the light drizzle, I spotted an equipment rental shack on Chaweng beach. Back home I used to Jet-Ski in the So-Cal surf, thanks to a friend who owned two. Real stand-up Jet-Skis, not sit-down user-friendly Wave Runners. Speed straight-in towards shore, tight u-turn in the white water, then speed straight back out, using the incoming wave like a ramp to launch yourself (and the ski) skyward: "You will believe a man can fly." On the island, I immediately hired a Wave Runner since Jet-Skis weren't available.

Aikido is an interesting discipline in so many ways. For example, it's improved my skills in just about every other physical activity. My skiing improved, my basketball improved, my snowboarding got better, my surfing improved, and so on. Other aikidoka have told me the same. A friend in Japan says his boxing improved, for example. I don't know if it's the footwork, the perpetual right-side/left-side practice (doing things with your weak hand is good brain training), highly developed balance, the fearlessness required for high-level *ukemi* or something else, but it has this effect and, having studied some, I don't think every other martial art does this. Speaking of snowboarding, out one evening in Tokyo in a group that included three *shihan*, two from Hombu Dojo, we were all feeling rather happy, and one teacher known for his skiing/boarding prowess in addition to his shockingly skillful aikido —"X-Games sensei"— said, "William! Do you snowboard?!"

"Yes, sensei; a little."

"Do you jump?!"

"Yes, sensei; only small ones."

"I did a seven-meter jump!!" he says with gusto, then leaning back and folding his arms across his chest in satisfaction. "Then, I told my student; you must do! (Long pause.) He broke his collar bone ... bahahahahahaha!"

I remember laughing with him and thinking, "No wonder I am frightened taking your *ukemi*."

Fortunately, water in its liquid state is more forgiving than as a solid (ice or snow), so back on Koh Samui on the Wave Runner I reckoned, correctly, that if I held the handlebars just right, I could stand up on the rails of the hull and ride it like a Jet-Ski. *Yari yasui.* Could I get my shoulder wet when turning acutely? (It could happen.) There was as a small swell rolling towards shore so, vrrrrrrroom into shore, sharp about-face, speeding back out, I was getting five to seven feet of air under the hull. Kasploooooosh!!!! Tight u-turn. Gun it towards shore. Do it again. Then I figured out that by moving waaaaay to the back end before a landing, I could sink the craft halfway up the hull and then try to do a 360 on its stern, bow pointing skyward. Quickly sliding my feet forward, it would level out and tear off across the water again—hopefully with me still attached. It was good balance training. Like aikido and so much of life, it had a rhythm or spacing and timing to it. After twenty tries or so I nearly had it, when I saw the rental dude sprinting into the water up to his waist, waving his arms frantically, having realized that he'd rented to a nutter. Fortunately, no cracks in the hull, so my full deposit was returned, though I was banned from further watercraft rentals.

Back on land, I rented a motorbike, a Yamaha 250 Enduro, the kind of bike that has so much torque you have to lean out over the gas tank to keep it from doing a wheelie if you goose the throttle. Rode all over the island. Helmetless, shirtless, wearing only board-shorts and flip-flops may not be the smartest riding gear, but have I ever felt more alive than while whipping down a quiet island back road, past rows of palm trees and the occasional beautiful wooden Thai house? One day, at the very moment I was about to foolishly agree (in an inebriated state) to get a Celtic knot tattoo round my bicep at a very dodgy establishment, I bumped into friends from Tokyo, who wisely talked me out of the ink, no doubt saving me from Hepatitis B or C or both (or worse) from the well-worn tattoo needles.

Days later, with the skies still gray, dismal and dripping and me tired of being waved to by "women" with all too narrow hips, big hands and Adam's apples, I hopped a flight to Singapore on a Thai Airways German-built Fokker turbo-prop to check out a former trading post of the East India Company, turned ultra modern city state and financial center, off the southern tip of the Malay Peninsula. Made it safely to Singapore in a little over two hours, despite our pilot's comforting opening remarks of "well, there's a typhoon advancing and we may have a very bumpy ride, folks". Who cared? I was living life as it should be lived – moment-to-moment, fully, whatever the circumstance. One sure intention of my sabbatical was to live a simple life, fully engaged in each minute of each day. I had intentionally cut many of my life's conventional moorings to drift from the sort of safe havens we all construct to deceive ourselves into a false sense of security and (complete) control over our lives. Of course, I didn't want to recklessly tempt The Fates either, so the right balance was required. My thought wasn't about big trips and bold moves but about mindfulness, fearlessness and appreciation of all things and moments great and small—to reclaim that sense of wonder about life that we lose as we "grow up."

After a few days and extraordinary local food (a blend of Chinese, Malay and Indian) in equatorial hot-and-steamy but sterile Singapore, the Switzerland of East Asia, I abruptly decided to fly back to L.A. to tidy up some loose ends, including preparing my motorbike for long-term storage (a black, Kawasaki Eliminator, 600cc, shaft driven, water cooled, cross between a street and drag bike. Still in storage today; it only has 550 miles on it!) The original plan had been to ship it when I moved, but months in Tokyo had taught me riding a bike there was a death wish. I also wanted to test my desire to be in Japan. From Singapore, I flew in one go six and a half hours to Tokyo, then eight and a half hours to L.A. Landing in L.A., I quickly took care of business, saw some friends from university days, and went to a house party in Santa Monica Canyon (where a good friend who I used to train with for triathalons had settled down). Nothing had changed. Not a thing. Within minutes of landing, I wanted to return to Japan as fast as possible. I flew back out through Seoul in a gambit to rekindle things with my wife-to-be (that would prove successful) and then, I faced "high noon" with immigration and customs at Narita.

Now, when you consider where I had been over the past seventeen days: Tokyo, Thailand, Singapore, L.A., Seoul and now Tokyo, alarm bells were probably set off with customs officials as I was landing. "Drug mule!" On the flight back to L.A., I had been musing that this is how jet-setters live. "Hmmmm, where will I go today?" Of course, they travel in an entirely different cabin class. Sensibly, in Seoul, I'd shaved off the goatee I'd grown while in Thailand and presented myself to immigration officials at Narita airport in my best well-dressed clean-cut white-boy look (albeit a suntanned one). Blew past the passport entry official. No problem.

Collected my bags and rolled my baggage cart up to meet the blue-suited customs official–the final hurdle to re-entry—and handed him my passport. Slowly flipping through it, without looking up, he very deliberately asks in English, "Where are you from?" "California," I reply. "You were in Japan before?" "Yes." "Where did you go before Tokyo?" "Thailand, Singapore, L.A., Seoul and now Tokyo." "Why did you go?" "Sightseeing and to see friends." "What were you doing in Japan?" "Studying aikido." "Why are you back?" "To do the same." "Where do you stay?" "Akebonobashi." He looks at me, sizing me up, his eyes narrowing, revealing a certain incredulity. His gaze returns to my passport. He starts flipping pages again and repeats each previous question. Methodically. Calmly. Now, I was a trial lawyer in state and federal court in California for about nine years before moving to Tokyo and later switched from "the dark side of The Force" to transactional legal work. While I'd begun to view commercial litigation as essentially fighting over other people's money and tired of it, I remained very grateful for the training and experience. It is mentally challenging work and unforgiving of errors. In court in particular, mistakes are not suffered lightly. You can get fined or even tossed into jail. "What's the difference between God and a U.S. Federal District Court judge (they too are appointed for life)? God doesn't think He's a Federal District Court judge." I know a thing or two about questioning people and about being questioned under pressure. Good thing.

"Where are you from?" "You were in Japan before?" "Where did you go before Tokyo?" "Why did you go?" "What were you doing in Japan?" "Why are you back?" "Where do you stay?" He soothingly, soporifically repeated each question. "Shields up, phasers on stun," I thought as I carefully repeated each prior answer. Then, at the very end, when you think it's all over, he pitches the "fastball": "WHERE DO YOU WORK?!!" and looks up from my passport glaring. "Ah, the old slow-ball, slow-ball, slow-ball, slow-ball, FASTBALL trick," I thought. "Where do you live? What do you do? Where do you work? When did you beat your wife?" Make the witness feel comfy, establish a rhythm and then hit them fast with the real question. Of course, I had been in the country previously on a tourist visa and was not permitted legally to work. If I hesitated or otherwise blundered, like saying I was teaching aikido (though I did that for free) or said I might look for work, I was finished. Deported. Admission was up to him. In situations like that, the less said, the better. And, the more politely that you say less, better still. Mustering my best expression of innocence and mild surprise with a pinch of puzzlement, I looked back at the officer saying, "Do you mean in California? I am not allowed to work in Japan." He stared at me incredulously, sighed and waved me through, reluctantly handing me my passport. My mind shouted *"Kachimashita!"* (victorious) but I dared not breathe a sigh of relief until I walked through those automated sliding doors and into the Arrivals lobby. I was back!

Thankfully, that was my only close shave with deportation. However, you meet all types of people at Hombu Dojo and my mild challenge at immigration was hardly as harrowing as the lovable, but reckless, *aikidoka* from Queensland who rather insanely years back had gone "on walka- bout" that included passing through Iran shortly after its war with Iraq in the 1990s. Having used the last of his money to buy a bus ticket to the Turkish border, his bus was stopped in transit, searched, and police shot a passenger on the roadside for allegedly carrying multiple pass- ports for sale. My friend was worried, of course. Especially so, be- cause smack on top of his clothes in his rucksack was his black address book (it's pre smartphone days kiddos) which had a sheet of paper with a list of names and phone numbers of friends in Israel who he hoped to visit during his travels (forget that the Israelis might not let him in, given his passport stamps from Turkey and Iran). Just the kind of circumstantial information that could be "misunderstood" in less rational parts of the world, with the holder winding up dead as a spy. The bus (and my friend) made it to Iran's border with Turkey. Between the double barbed-wire fences, a metal Quonset hut straddled the bor- der. Step out one door and you are in Iran. Step out the other door and you are in Turkey. My friend and his fellow bus travelers filed into the hut and lined up facing a desk where their luggage would be searched by Iranian officials and they would pay their visitor's exit tax before being welcomed into Turkey. Note. "Pay their exit tax." Ex- actly. He had no money. Nothing.

When his turn came, he boldly strode up to the table with a big smile on his face. He put his rucksack on the table for inspection and handed over his passport. Still smiling. The Iranian official opened the bag, rum- maging hastily through it with one hand while taking the passport with the other. Glancing, my friend could see the address book in the backpack bobbing like a cork on a sea of clothes and other kit. The official looked at his passport, looked up and barked, "You pay money!"

My friend smiled broadly, holding both arms open, palms up, then closed his hands, leaving only the index finger of his right hand extended and replied, "Yes, no money," while wagging his index finger for emphasis.

"NO! YOU pay money now!" blurted the irked Iranian official. My friend smiled bigger, gestured with both hands, palms open and up, waving outwardly, hip high, on either side of his trouser pockets, saying "No money; yes, no money!" and nodding his head in almost gleeful affirmation.

"NO, NO! YOU! PAY MONEY!!" screamed the official.

My pal raised his voice too, but not as loud and with a positive enthusiastic tone, smiling bigger still and vigorously nodding, "Yes, no money; no money!! No money!!" With the growing line of people behind my friend getting restless, the frustrated (and slightly baffled) guard threw his hands up and waved the crazy foreigner through, tossing his passport and the rucksack at him. Had Twitter existed back then, my pal's daily tweet might have read: "Dodged a lethal bullet today from gun I foolishly pointed at my own head." Fortunately for me, after my mild brush with immigration in the summer of '97, getting out of (and back into) Tokyo proved light-years simpler (particularly after I got my long-term visa in 98). Yes; no money!

I've had a bit of a laugh about the weather in Japan, but I truly loved summers there. The heat and the rain. Rain-brollys, sun-brollys, fans and sweat towels. Even in such a technologically sophisticated city, life was affected by the rhythms and forces of nature. In Los Angeles, though I was regularly outdoors swimming in the ocean, running in the soft sand or in the Santa Monica mountains, daily life seemed too often a tedious cycle of artificial environments: "house-pod to car-pod, to work-pod to car-pod to house-pod," with a gulp of fresh air at the dojo sandwiched into each day.

Tokyo summers meant sweat-drenched practices and the summer scent of Hombu Dojo tatami, the windows and wall fans of the third-floor dojo rattling like sabres when a storm would pass through. If I close my eyes and dream, I can feel the breeze of the beach, hear the buzz of the bugs and recall a frosty cold pint of lager in a beer garden. Summer was filled with new sights and sounds. Fireworks festivals are a summer mainstay—*Hanabi*—throngs of people walking about the streets, many women in *yukata* and a few bold men dressed in *jinbei* negotiating the asphalt streets in *geta*.[263] Probably my favorite firework ever was in Ibaragi, not far from Iwama dojo where one explosion displayed the glowing face of *Anpaman* (アンパンマン) the popular children's *anime* character. I remember too one Sumida River Fireworks Festival (隅田川花火大会, *Sumidagawa Hanabi Taikai*, near Asakusa the last Saturday of July) so windswept and rain-soaked that the show amounted to: "Boom; ooooh; purple cloud!" "Boom-ba-boom; ahhhh; red cloud," "Boom; boom; boom; ohhhhhh, yellow cloud" with each burst of gunpowder high above nature's cumulonimbus ceiling.

My ancestors may have been looking down (or up) and wondering what the hell whitey was doing in the Land of the Rising Sun, but I was loving every minute of it and found myself thankful for every day of the experience and for my whole life leading up to it. My father had tried to teach me early days to live with a sense of gratitude and joy. My aikido training and exposure to Japanese culture in Los Angeles had reinforced this somewhere along the way, at the very least to be mindful of the moment. My time in Japan completed the process. Living each day with a sincere sense of gratitude for what you have received, rather than a sense of entitlement to or longing for what you may lack, will help you live a far happier life, one that you and your honorable ancestors can be proud of at the end of your race.

---

[263] Like a kilt, it takes a real man to wear jinbei (甚平, じんべい) well, in public. http://ja.wikipedia.org/wiki/甚平

Autumn

This thing called parting
Has no color
Yet it seeps into our hearts
And stains them with loneliness.

—Ki-no-Tsurayuki (ca.868 - ca.964)

Views of Japan and
the Street Fightin' Man

紅葉
(Kouyou)

How clear the chimes resound
of the temple bells.
The hills of Kamakura,
filled with autumn winds!
—*Kunen Kaneko (1876–1951)*

My adventure was heading into fall. Autumn, the season with the sweep and swell of a Beethoven symphony—beauty, poignancy and power. With fall in Japan comes *kouyou* (紅葉, こうよう, autumn colors; leaves changing color) a natural phenomenon only slightly less revered by the Japanese than the *sakura*. By October in the north and November or even December further south, the leaves of verdantly green Japan are flaming reds, oranges, yellows and golds. Kamakura, which is near Tokyo, is one good viewing spot. WTF? Another chapter poetically extolling the natural wonders of yet another season in Japan? Can I get a "second," so I can commit *seppuku*?[264]

Nah. Who wants to read that?! Hence the chapter title *atemi* to jolt the senses.[265] Patience; I'll get there, 'cause in [never] sleepy Tokyo town there is room for a street fightin' man. First, back to nature's wonders: don't mess with Mother Nature.

Fall is the best time of year in Tokyo. It's the best season in Northeast Asia, in fact. By far. Of Japan's six seasons (the standard four plus the two rainy ones), autumn has the best weather. It's fantastic. Crisp, clear blue skies. Easier temps. Dry air. In September, there's a bit of push-

---

[264] Most of you know that *seppuku* is the ritual suicide of cutting open one's belly, which is known more commonly to Westerners as *hara-kiri*.

[265] As many of you know, *atemi* (当て身, あてみ) is a strike to the body, often to a weak or vital point.

pull between summer and fall, but generally the season is a weather-friendly and Hombu Dojo-friendly time to visit Tokyo. If you are living there, it's a good time to intensify your training.

Returning from my visa-run summer of '97, that's exactly what I did. I didn't spend time gazing at the foliage other than the glimpses you catch as you travel around town. I hit the mats with renewed vigor—three, four and five times daily while keeping up that strength/fitness regimen devised by a Navy Seal.[266] I was in Japan for training and I could feel my year gathering speed, so it was time to squeeze it for every drop. Temps were cooling. Days were getting shorter (remember there's no daylight savings time in Japan).[267] Even the pace of Tokyo seemed to slow; or maybe, since I'd been living in Japan for about nine months, I was beginning to catch the city's rhythm. By autumn, my routines were well established. I knew my way around town pretty well. For awhile there, I figured I knew how a prairie dog feels daily. Using the subway, I bundled along underground, popping up here and there to scurry around a bit before dashing underground and home. Taking longer walks and occasional late-night cabs, I'd gathered a better sense of Tokyo above ground. It was starting to feel like home.

While fall is viewed as the season of decline, for me in '97 it was a time of renewal both in my practice and otherwise. My wife to be—who was studying for her master's degree in Seoul—and I patched things up.[268] The Japanese call it ロング ディスタンス ラブ (rongu disutansu rabu, long-distance love) and it does add challenges (this was pre-Skype, kiddos, the infancy of the commercial Internet) but it worked for us. Seoul is just a two-hour flight away from Tokyo, and it's an amazing city, especially these days, with all the architectural and other beautification works, like the

---

[266] *Navy Seal Exercises – The Cutting Edge Total Body Workout* by Mark De Lisle, U.S. Navy Seal, 1996, ISBN 9654093-0-9.

[267] Following the War in the Pacific, the U.S.-led occupying forces imposed daylight savings time from 1948-51, May to September annually. Daylight savings time proved predictably unpopular with the locals. Days were longer, so people just worked longer (dawn to dusk). Shorter nights, so they slept less. The initiative was abandoned in 1952, after Japanese sovereignty was restored. Over the past thirty years, there have been periodic movements to reinstate it for saving energy, increasing recreational time, combating global warming, etc.

[268] On 23 October 1999, we would wed in Princeton, New Jersey, with kilts, bagpipes and hanbok (한복).

Cheonggyecheon (stream) that flows through downtown.[269]   Given my tenuous visa status, I reckoned that if I stayed in Japan another three months
straight they'd never let me back in when I returned, so I'd hop a flight to
Seoul for a weekend if I felt like it. Angela could be in Tokyo or I could be
in Seoul in six hours door-to-door. I spent the better part of an early October
day walking all over Seoul's historic Jongno-gu (district). Streets lined with
golden-leafed ginkgo trees, the lively Insa-dong art district, I drank in the sites:
Gyeongbok Palace, Changdeok Palace, Changgyeong Palace and Unhyeon
Palace—smaller but each more beautiful than the Forbidden City (unless
you're wild about the color red) and each placed carefully and thoughtfully
amongst the surrounding mountains to "capture energy and promote prosperity".[270] Seoul is an excellent weekend getaway from Tokyo, especially if
you have to do a "visa run." There is lots to see and do: great food and drink,
historic and cultural sites, martial arts, the DMZ (wave to their kooky northern brothers and Dear Leader 3.0), mountain temple stays and so on.

- City of Seoul www.visitseoul.net and http://english.seoul.go.kr
- Happkido www.hapkido.or.kr
- Ssireum www.cnngo.com/seoul/play/ssireum-legacy-old-days-
  727634
- Taekwondo www.wtf.org/wtf_eng/main/main_eng.html
- Tae Kyon www.taekyun.org/yui
- Temples http://visitkorea.or.kr/ena/SI/SI_EN_3_4_5.jsp and
  www.templestay.com

What the hell? Another chapter on cultural sites, Asian cities and
weather? Now relationships? Ahhhhhhh! Run! Alright, alright. Give us
the riff, Keith!

---

[269] See http://discoveringkorea.com/2008/12/09/cheonggyecheon/ or www.worlddesigncapi-
tal.com/world-design-capitals/past-capital-seoul/.
[270] According to David Mason, Professor of Cultural Tourism Studies at Seoul's Kyong Hee University, Korean geomancy (somewhat akin to Chinese fēngshuǐ) is known as Pungsu-jiri-seol
and is a derivative of Chinese Daoism and Seon (Zen). In brief, it concerns principles of har-
monizing manmade objects and structures with Wind, Water, Earth and life energy or Gi
(Chinese Qi and Japanese Ki) in a particular landscape. http://san-shin.net/Pungsu-jiri.html

Ev'rywhere I hear the sound of marching, charging feet, boy
'Cause summer's here and the time is right
for fighting in the street, boy
Well now what can a poor boy do
'cept to sing for a rock 'n' roll band
'Cause in sleepy London town
There's just no place for a street fighting man.[271]

—Sir Mick Jagger and Keith Richards
Rolling Stones, Street Fighting Man

Well, it was no longer summer, but there had been fightin' in the streets from time to time, though I can't say that I am proud of the fact. Everyone who studies aikido—no, everyone who studies a martial art—wonders at some point if it "works." It's human nature, though it's worth noting that all humans have a better and a baser nature, and we should all strive for the former. Aikido *keiko* seeks to point us in that more positive direction with its broad and noble objectives of self-cultivation. The weathered wooden sign above the door to a traditional dojo may for very good reasons read 学術道 (*gaku-jutsu-do(u)*, study or learning, technique or means, and way). Learning is lifelong, and reflecting The Way in ourselves in our daily lives is important, but what of *jutsu*? If you didn't at least wonder, after years of training, if you have any legit skills, some folks might wonder about you. Believe me; for a number of sound reasons, nobody with any good sense should be particularly eager to test his or her martial abilities. You want to pit yourself against other people in a physical, mental and spiritual battle? Take up a sport, even a fighting sport if you like. Nothing good comes from real fighting, with very few exceptions.

And be mindful that your ability to use your martial arts is limited by the cold Darwinian cruelties of life. Oh. Sorry! This is the point in the book where if you think aikido (or any martial art) is magic, you had best stop reading. Your chances in any scrap can be summed up with a simple Cartesian coordinate system. You have your X-axis and your Y-axis. The model could be more complex (with additional axis and dimensions:

---

fighting spirit, strategy, tactics, etc.) but let's start with something simple and central. The X-axis charts your *waza* (技, わざ, technique; art). How much *waza* do you have? How developed are your skills? The Y-axis charts your ability, your God-given talent (*zairyou*, 材料, ざいりょう, ingredients; materials).[272] Are you a big, fast, strong, young dude? If so, then you don't need much *waza* to defeat most people. On the other hand, if you are not particularly gifted, then you had better hope you have developed enough skills to overcome your lack of ability. Even then, the higher up the ability axis your opponent charts above you, the more *waza* required to compensate for the disparity, if you are going to have a chance of prevailing. In many cases, you could study an art forever but never overcome someone who is just too physically gifted for you. This is the brutal truth. This is "real." You had better take it to heart if you want to avoid errors in judgment that could result in you suffering serious bodily harm. Just because you study a traditional martial art or MMA or whatever system of self defense does not mean you have a Z-scar on your forehead and can defeat all foes like the boy wizard Harry. "*Expel-o Delusion-o!!!!*" Unless you are sufficiently trained (and able) to overcome the superior ability of your opponent, the same guy who took your lunch money in high school will have it again. As the group Bowling for Soup sings in resignation, "High School Never Ends."[273] There's another double espresso being served up on this in a later chapter, so amble up to the barista counter when your number's called.

Even if you are properly prepared and adequately able bodied, does might make right? My first teacher confided in me once that using martial arts on an untrained person can be one of the highest forms of abuse. Despite his penchant for hyperbole, he had a point. It all depends on the context and your restraint—the recognition and appropriate execution of which are reflections of your training. And, if you do respond physically by necessity or a lack of sufficient restraint, are you able to respond proportionally? Given the actual measure of the threat? I mean, if you study

---

[272] I've heard it said that the Chinese soul is expressed in jade, the Korean in ceramics and the Japanese in wood, so perhaps it's no surprise that a *kanji* in words concerning "talent" is 材, ザイ, きさい, lumber; log; timber; wood; talent. What's the wood like at the core of the structure? It makes all the difference.

[273] Bowling for Soup, "High School Never Ends," www.youtube.com/watch?v=jrxI_cuTX4A&feature=relmfu

Thai boxing and someone bumps you, intentionally or not, and you kick him in the leg, breaking it, or elbow strike him in the head, opening up a big gash, or worse? Is that appropriate? Who cares, some say? Well, in the U.S. and other places, you could find yourself on the wrong side of the law rather quickly. I heard from an American in Tokyo that a former student at the American Club who wasn't very good at aikido but was phenomenally strong physically had "lost his rag" in public and gotten himself into serious legal trouble as a result. Aggravated assault is no joke. Neither is civil liability for injuries inflicted.[274]

Once, in a laughably harmless context, while playing American "gridiron" in a league with other lawyers—the "two-hand touch" version, not the tackle version—a much bigger fellow, about six-foot-three, 225 pounds, tried to throw me (six-foot-one, 180 pounds) on the ground by grabbing my shirt at each shoulder and then trying to swing me and toss me down.[275] He was angry and he meant it. I planted my feet (wearing cleats or "studded boots" if you prefer), cutting down inside one of his arms at the elbow, pushing up on the other one and strongly turning my hips in the direction he had been trying to spin and toss me. Worked like a charm - *kokyu-nage*. Up he went and then—THUD—down he went. I quickly knelt and pinned him down using *suwari-kokyu-ho* (a riskier prospect on someone who knows their way 'round on the ground). The big man's face went from angry red to frightened white as he struggled to get up but somehow could not, as if held by some unseen force. I wasn't holding him—just extending my muscles and touching his arms in the right spot as he tried to come up (and putting him back down). The referee finally noticed something was up and came racing over. I quickly stood up, throwing my hands up in the air and then out wide to the side with a "What? Don't ask me" expression on my face. My African-American pal who is about six-foot-five and 250 pounds (and studies martial arts) was the only person on the field (pitch) who knew what had just

---

[274] Check out the law review article *Super Human in the Octagon; Imperfect in the Courtroom: Assessing the Culpability of Martial Artists who Kill in Streetfights.* www.law.emory.edu/fileadmin/journals/elj/60/60.6/Kunen.pdf

[275] Only lawyers' basketball league has more poor sports than lawyers' football league, though there were also exceptional athletes in both in L.A. I actually saw one lawyer playing in a b-ball league game "take his ball and go home" (having loaned it for use in the game) after becoming distraught over the officiating. "Wah, wah." Big baby.

happened, and he was bent over belly-laughing. It was all instinctive; I didn't stop and ponder first. He was trying to toss me, so I stopped it. *Kaeshiwaza* (返し技, かえしわざ, counterattack; reversal). An objectively unnecessary, but relatively restrained response. Harmless enough. No broken bones. Play ball! Frankly, walking away is usually if not always the better option.

I remember hearing a story in Japan about someone likewise choosing to fight rather than walk away from a big bully during a night out. From the description, the bully sounded like a jerk and deserving of a lesson, but the situation, as I heard it, presented an alternative path—walking away (not running away). Outside, the smaller (but highly trained man) quickly used his judo to knock the bully down (*tachiwaza*, 立ち技, たちわざ, standing technique) and then positioned himself (*newaza*, 寝技, ねわざ ground technique) to choke the bully unconscious (*shimewaza*, 絞め技, しめわざ, choke or stranglehold).[276] Done; right? No; apparently, once the bully was asleep, the trained man began abrading the bully's face on the pavement—as a "lesson" for him. This is what martial arts teaches us? Sure, the guy may have been a bully, but if we retaliate without (or with insufficient) restraint, the attacked becomes the attacker, and the burden of responsibility (and blame) shifts. We can prove to be little or no better than the jerk who picks the fight. Worse, some might say, because we should know better.

What is the spirit of *budo*? *Bushidō* valued seven core and three associated virtues. The seven being: Rectitude (義, *gi*), Courage (勇, *yū*), Benevolence (仁, *jin*), Respect (礼, *rei*), Honesty (誠, *makoto*), Honor (名誉, *meiyo*), Loyalty (忠義, *chūgi*) and the three: Filial piety (孝, *kō*), Wisdom (智, *chi*) and Care for the aged (悌, *tei*). To me, aikido is imbued with these ten principles plus the considerable wisdom of the Founder. Study aikido and I believe it is your duty to emulate these character traits to your utmost and to pick yourself up and try again when you inevitably fail to do so.

Take even my novice's word for it, street fighting is a very risky affair and should be avoided except for moments of absolute survival. People

---

[276] Setting aside the issue of weapons for the moment, old *Jiu Jutsu* always had three levels or stages of fighting: *tachiwaza* (standing), *suwariwaza* (seated/kneeling) and *newaza* (lying down).

do *kata keiko*, the forms practice which is the core of aikido training, and believe they are invincible, while having little if any clue how to actually apply, on a noncompliant opponent, the technique that they have committed to muscle memory. People watch MMA matches or study it thinking that it is "real" fighting, but it's not. Not even close. It has aspects of real fighting, but it also has referees, rules, physicians, uniforms, gloves, mouth-pieces, protective cups, focused preparation, a predictable contained environment, one-on-one opponents, a scouted opponent, timed rounds, no weapons and no (or limited) foul play.

Anything can happen in a street or, as I prefer, a "spontaneous" fight (or survival confrontation). Life would prove this point for me years later in Tokyo when I was out with some old friends one September evening. One guy, a Canadian, hadn't had a night out in years. He managed the family business (diligently) and had the Japanese mother-in-law from hell. The poor guy really needed to blow off some steam. He and another West Coast Canadian pal and I were joined by three other friends, one a Dan Aykroyd lookalike, another a tall, rangy Kiwi (who I knew from Japanese TV acting jobs), and a recent addition to Tokyo, a Russian sailor who was a pal of the Kiwi. The evening proved bizarre, even for Tokyo. Just the setup sounds like the beginning of a bad joke. "Two Jews, an Arab, the Pope and a penguin walk into a bar ..."

We rendezvoused at one of the notorious establishments of Tokyo—Gas Panic—a bar where a friend from Hombu Dojo was a bouncer (the elevator GP, not the original). The entire inside of the bar was stainless steel—floor to ceiling—a big metallic cube. Stainless standing tables; there are no chairs. When the night's done, they can (and do) probably clean the place out with a fire hose, sending a good bit of the night's festivities down a drain where it belongs. Everyone has to have a drink in their hand or they must leave. The music is thumping: rap, rock, pop, dance; it's a relentlessly catchy playlist. Young mini-skirted women climb up and dance on the bar, grasping onto a metal bar suspended from the ceiling for stability. In theory. In practice, they occasionally take drunken nose dives into the gyrating crowd. It's exactly the kind of place you take your mother to ... well, not exactly. Well, not at all. In fact, for you chroniclers, you tear out and burn that diary page. In other words, it's a helluva lot of fun. Japanese are typically (or perhaps stereotypically) a serious and reserved bunch but a friendly and festive tribe when they party. The place had a happy, positive, celebratory and harmless vibe that was generally devoid of the posing, posturing and glowering you can get in night spots in the West.

The evening started off with a twist as, shortly after his arrival, the Russian sailor disappeared into the unisex toilet with the Kiwi's English language student, after her overtures towards the rest of us fell on deaf ears (or near deaf from the music). Apparently, they needed a quiet place for language exchange. No doubt. He returned to the table with his hand bleeding, which he says he cut on the stainless steel interior while bracing himself. Must've been an enthusiastic washing-up. Hand wrapped up with a napkin tourniquet, "Alexi" stayed. Hours later, we were all increasingly well oiled and bouncing to the pumping music while dodging lit cigarettes in the hands of the swaying, bopping, inebriated celebrants surrounding us. Soon after, they're going mad to a hyper-version of RedNex' *Cotton Eye Joe*. Eventually, we recovered our better sense (or it got too late for the marrieds) and decided to call it a night. We exited into the street and started walking up towards the subway station or to hail a taxi or take whatever route that led swiftly home. Me and my pal with the monster-in-law stopped in an alley to water the local shrubbery and then walked up to the *kosaten* (交差点, こうさてん, crossing; intersection) and saw a commotion between a cab driver and a thick-set, middle-aged man who had a certain air of authority and toughness about him. Both were out of their vehicles, having collided or nearly so, and the *oji-san* is berating and bullying the taxi driver (who are usually pretty tough in Tokyo). Our other mate (an aikidoka since he was fourteen years old) was standing about five meters away in the street in front of the stopped cab, listening and watching. I was walking towards him and ask, "Hey; what's going on?"

He replied, "The taxi stopped, got bumped by the other car, the other car then tried to force its way through scraping the side of the taxi, then this asshole (he points at the middle-aged guy) jumps out ..."

Well, it turned out *oji-san* knew some English. Upon hearing "asshole," up strode "C-battery-shaped-man" to my friend, barking in rough and menacing Japanese. "*Horrrrrrrrrra*!!!" [277] Now my pal was the object of

---

[277] You have to really roll your rrrrrrrr's to sound like a yak when using the expletive (ほ ら, hey!

this guy's "affection." I calmly set down my briefcase (I had come straight from the law firm), neatly folded my coat, placed it on top and started walking towards my friend and his assailant (he had already committed assault—causing fear of battery. Assault plus unlawful touching is battery). "BAM!" *Oji-san* popped my friend in the eye. Lead right.

ZOOM!!! Me and my very stout friend with the monster-in-law are on *oji-san* in a flash. My friend who got popped is stunned he didn't watch his *ma-ai*.[278] My large friend grabs *oji-san* in front; me in back—by the shoulder and clothes at the sleeve. I try to toss the guy *irimi-nage* but realize my beefy friend is pulling the other way. *Henkawaza!*[279] I turn my hip quickly, generating power in the same direction as my friend … executing the throw. Yeah; executing the throw of <u>all three</u> of us. There was so much force in our combined synchronized movement that all three people went airborne—nearly street parallel (it was also slick, as it had been raining before). SMASH. They both hit the pavement; three quarters of me did, too. The other quarter—my head—hit the base of the concrete and steel construction barrier that divided the sidewalk from the street (a thumb's width forward from the right temple, just above the hairline). Hit the coarse, sharp steel edge of it (it's a steel box with poured concrete inside it and a white-metal railing embedded in the concrete). Blood spurted everywhere, but I didn't even realize it. "Tis but a scratch!" I bounced up; *oji-san* was coming to his senses. My friend quickly sat on him. At some point, the bottom of someone's shoe left a pristine print (Church's, size 12 US) on *oji-san*'s face.[280] Must've happened in the scuffle. Japanese ran up to say, "Leave the poor guy alone." My friends told them to back off (in Japanese); the "poor guy" just assaulted us and the cab driver.

The "poor guy" started coming to and was cursing us furiously. He had little hope of getting my 120 kilo pal off him but was struggling to reach into his pocket for his mobile phone. My foot on his arm stopped that. "Bambi" (picture a deer staring transfixed into the headlights of an

---

look! look at me!).

[278] *Ma-ai* (間合い、まあい) is a concept that is central to aikido and other Japanese arts, which incorporates the issues of both spacing and timing (interval or distance) between opponents.

[279] 変化技、へんか わざ change or variation technique.

[280] English made Church's footwear was founded in 1873 by Thomas Church and his three sons. See www.church-footwear.com/en/UK/new-flex-sole.

oncoming car before impact), as we were now calling my friend who got popped in the eye, was nursing his wound.[281]   A pretty young Japanese woman walked up to me and handed me her cutesy little pink Hello Kitty handkerchief to sop up the blood, which I finally realized was flowing down my right temple and cheek.   Another foreigner used his mobile phone to take pictures and emailed them to me, which I later forwarded to a few select friends.   One martial arts pal in California replied, "Did the city of Tokyo send you a bill for your big melon (my head) damaging their construction equipment?"   Ho-ho-ho.   I've heard them all.   "It's got its own weather system."   "It looks like an orange on a toothpick."[282]   How droll. Now, this scrap went down about a month before my wedding. Yes; I went a bit mental before I got hitched, even though it was high time I grew up. (The Peter Pan suit was pinching at the knees, and I never did look good in green.)

The police showed up. *Oji-san* was mouthing off at them now. "Gee, who is this guy," we all start thinking aloud. A crowd of about thirty or forty people have gathered now. The cops stood him up, slapped him around a bit, cuffed him and put him in a patrol car.

Other cops in another patrol car whisked me off to a nearby hospital for an x-ray of my noggin and five stitches in it and then it's back to the police station for statements. Blood had been spilled, a big thing in Japanese culture, according to my pals who have lived there for double-digit years and have Japanese wives.   My friends were both fluent, very polite and married to locals, which the cops loved. Turned out that the cops had seen me on television before, too. True. I was in some T.V. commercials and T.V. shows for laughs from time to time and made some decent money.[283] They had seen a recent commercial I'd done for a home alarm system where I played an astronaut co-piloting a space shuttle mission with Japanese. When my character (the ever-

---

[281]   In fairness, my friend skillfully played the hero another evening at *Ebisu* station when he saw a local slapping around his girl friend. My friend ran up and grabbed the jerk and said "Stop! Hurt her again and I beat you." The bully ran away. Remember, Bambi did grow up to become King of the Forest.

[282]   *So I Married an Axe Murder.* "Head! Move!" www.youtube.com/watch?v=qRmLGYSc0XQ

[283]   Appeared on the pop group Smap-Smap's variety show playing a cop and the matrix baddie, was cast as a swordsman for an auto commercial, a fake German (my grandma is at least) in a racist show documenting how strange foreigners are during a trip to a hot spring and sightseeing in Japan (Germans, Italians, Africans and Frenchmen …. all faux foreigners but one or two).

lurking lecherous foreigner) grabs the pilot's photo of his eighteen-year-old daughter exclaiming "That's your daughter!!!???" The homesick Japanese pilot turns the shuttle around to "Go Home!" and check on his baby girl. Buy a home security system and lock her away from the barbarians was the message, I guess. Anyway, the vibe with the officers had lightened significantly.

It also turned out that *oji-san* was a local *kumicho* (組長、くみちょ, boss – typically *yakuza*) and we would've been dead meat if he had reached his mobile phone. We could hear the cops choking him out in the other room after he started shouting and fighting back. "Aaaccchhhkkkk!" What is the sound of one yak choking? Silence. Once satisfied with our stories, the cops binned the reports (so nobody undesirable could get our addresses later and pay us a visit), sent us home, told us to stay clear of the area for a good while and that was that. Somehow, a week or so later, the lawyer for the yak boss reached Bambi by telephone and offered to meet to give him some money. I calmly told my friend, "ARE YOU MEN-TAL?!!" "DO NOT MEET HIM!!" And, at last, that was that.

But there were good lessons in it. Stay away from trouble. Even if you are prepared and clearheaded, anything can happen. Anything. My head turns a bit to the right and the steel edge hits my eye socket. Towards the left and back, it hits my brain stem, and I'm a veg or dead. Anything can happen. I've never since worn slippery leather-bottom dress shoes for work.

Indeed, Tokyo can be less safe than it seems. For certain, the annual dearth of gun-related deaths in Japan means that either gun control works or the Japanese can't hit the side of a barn door.[284] Still, there are the occasional crazies, knife-wielding angry youths and alcohol-fueled citizenry who are in close physical contact with you due to the prevalence of public transport and because Tokyo's a walking city.[285] Remember, too,

---

[284] The only gun violence I heard of while in Tokyo was one *yakuza* shooting another dead at a hotel near the dojo.

[285] Occasional (rare) knife crime is a more realistic threat, particularly at the hands of some hormonally crazed junior high school kid (if news reports are to be believed). Though Japan imposes the death penalty, it's hardly a deterrent (if it ever is) for minors. In Japan, you are an adult at twenty: for criminal justice, drinking, smoking, betting at horse tracks, voting, signing contracts, marriage without parental consent, etc. You can drive at eighteen. Periodic efforts to lower the age of adulthood to eighteen are strongly opposed due in part to access to vice and finance. Inexplicably (and inexcusably) the national age of sexual consent in Japan is

that until 2010, Japan (which is the size of California, in case you have forgotten, and has a population of roughly 126,000,000, which is less than a tenth of the PRC) had the second largest economy in the world on a gross GDP basis. [286] In other words, lots of people come to Japan from all over the world to make money. Tokyo is filled with foreigners "on the make" by means both legitimate and less so. The visiting crowd includes some badly behaving first-worlders and some feral third-worlders. In some of those third-world places, life is pretty cheap. If you are out in a place that foreigners frequent, you need to be aware of your surroundings and alert to the possibility of trouble.[287] Alert, not paranoid or solicitous of it. Traditional aikido training should cultivate a kind of awareness or mindfulness that is useful for just such situations. It's one of the fundamental benefits of the teaching method. Your wits will keep you out of far more trouble than your brawn will overcome once it starts. Believe it.

There are grittier neighborhoods in Tokyo as well. Ikebukero, Uguisudani … I mean it's not South Boston or the Bronx or Glasgow's East End, but there can be spots of trouble. Hombu Dojo is just a short walk from the *yakuza* run nighttime playground Kabukicho that sits just east of Shinjuku station's east exit. As a lawyer walking through Kabukicho for the first time, I couldn't help but think about … zoning. There seemed no rhyme or reason to the businesses: *kaiten-sushi*, sex-toy shop, movie theater, noodle stand, karaoke bar, hostess club, hand-job shop, book store, blues bar, tempura restaurant, donut shop, art supplies, blowup-doll museum. It's a mysterious steaming bowl of neon noodles. And, more than once, Kabukicho has proved a testing ground for students (and future teachers) from the dojo. There's a well-worn, apparently true, story of a particular Hombu Dojo *shihan* who in his younger days used to walk through a particular Shinjuku neighborhood on his way to the dojo for training. Word is that local thugs, demonstrating consistently bad

---

thirteen, according to the Japanese Penal Code Articles 176 and 177. However, prefecture ordinances prohibit sexual activities with minors under eighteen.

[286] Gross domestic product figures can be misleading. End of 2010, the U.S. economy was ranked first on a GDP basis but eleventh on a per capita basis. The People's Republic of China was ranked second but about one-hundred-twenty-fifth on a per capita basis. Japan third but thirty-eighth on a per capita basis. There are other statistical ways to make economic comparisons. Reminds me of the statistician judging the shooting contest. A shooter misses twelve inches to the right of the bullseye. Then twelve inches to the left. And the statistician shouts, "Bullseye!!!" "Lies, damn lies and statistics," as the saying goes.

[287] It's a big mistake to presume that other people share your same consciousness, your way of thinking.

judgment, accosted him on a series of occasions. Eventually, the local *kumicho* sent a polite letter to the dojo requesting in effect "Please have Mr. X walk some other way to the dojo rather than through this neighborhood. I have too many men in the hospital." True; the *chimpira* (ンピラ, ちんぴ, young hoodlum, small-time yakuza punk) were hassling him as he walked through their turf and they received the worst of it.

For the most part, the local gangsters leave foreigners alone, though some of their hired help (often Nigerians or Chinese) will try to hustle you into some scam hostess bar or sex show joint. Ignore them; just keep walking. There are legitimate establishments in the area though, which are worth patronizing, but if you visit, watch yourself. If you get into a scuffle, you may think you are having an altercation with one person, but you have no idea how many allies are watching, and you are just one *keitai* call from being surrounded in great numbers.[288] It won't end well.

So discovered three friends of mine one afternoon after practice: Yank, Canadian and an Aussie. They weren't in Kabukicho but in a bar in a suburb of Tokyo. For whatever reason, two of them had gone outside. Words were exchanged with a local tough. A mobile call, the next thing my friends were surrounded by a horde of *bousouzoku* (暴走族, ぼうそうぞく, the kanji literally means "violence run tribe" referring to clubs of motorbike/scooter-riding delinquents run wild).[289] They had clubs, pipes and Lord knows what else at the ready. It was on in a flash. Moving, slashing, flying, bashing. My Canadian friend and the large Huntington Beach, nutty rude-boy pal (MMA character Tank Abbot hails from H.B.) fought for their lives. Literally. They just kept moving and punching and moving to keep their feet. Fall to the ground and they would be beaten senseless, maybe even to death. They got dinged up pretty good. Scrapes, bruises and cuts, including a pipe blow to the back of the head requiring serious stitches later. But as suddenly as it had ignited, it extinguished; perhaps because they had inflicted a few casualties and blood had been drawn. Who knows?! Spontaneous fighting has an unpredictable rhythm. One friend confided later that he "could've done better." But I reckon he and the

---

[288] *Keitai* (携帯, けいたい; ケイタイ; ケータイ) is something carried (in the hand); "handheld" and is a colloquial abbreviation of *keitai denwa* (携帯電話) mobile telephone or cell phone.

[289] *Bousou* (暴走, ぼうそう) means running wildly; reckless driving; runaway; rampage. *Bou* – 暴 outburst; rave; force; violence; cruelty; outrage. *Sou* – 走 run. *Zoku* – 族 tribe; family. Remember, how a *kanji* is read depends on its position in the word so these aren't always read this way.

other guy did pretty well by surviving. It could've turned out much worse.

Aikido doesn't generally attract the toughest crowd (more on that later), but there are a few exceptions, and I met some of them in Japan. One had boxed, with an aim for a professional career, before taking up aikido. Another was a New Yorker who also trained both judo with the police and at an old *newaza* school. Another was a tough guy from a former Soviet satellite. His father had tried to keep him out of trouble by putting him into a Greco-Roman wrestling club (Soviet training system; think bone-shatteringly exhausting workouts timed to the second). He claimed to have been in countless fights on the mean streets of his hometown, and I found no reason to doubt him. He reckoned it was time to stop brawling when in one melee of about forty people outside a nightclub, he found himself sitting on the cobblestones with his head against the front bumper of a car, a pistol pressed against his forehead by a standing assailant. Fortunately, police arrived and pistola-boy ran off. Before Japan, this guy had adventured in West Africa pursuing business opportunities with friends, but somehow got lured into local unsanctioned no-holds-barred bare-knuckle prizefighting. African *vale tudo*, so to speak. I had heard (I had friends who trained there) that he had checked out a westside Tokyo BJJ academy and given everyone a very hard time given his wrestling background. He wasn't the biggest guy, but damn if he wasn't one of the toughest I'd meet in Japan. Fortunately for me, he was just starting aikido but great fun to practice with. Fortunately for him, he found inner peace in Tokyo through aikido, *zazen* and *misogi* and has gone on to become a fine teacher in his home country. He's one of many friends, seniors and juniors, who I miss.

"I know you can fight. But it's our wits that make us men," counsels Malcolm Wallace in the film *Braveheart* to his young son William who is keen to join the impending battle against the invading English. Wise words, as it's generally better to use your brains rather than your brawn to avoid or extricate yourself from situations. There used to be a tastelessly decorated but oddly compelling African-themed *gaijin* bar nestled back on a side street behind Roppongi *kosaten* called Magumbos. It was a popular spot for foreign hostesses both before/after work and on their nights off. For a couple of friends keen on *gaijin* women, it was a frequent haunt.

The size of a large walk-in closet, it had an oval-shaped bar (like an African warrior's zebra-skin-covered shield). There was just enough room for someone to walk between the wall and your barstool. Spears, shields, masks and headdresses adorned the walls, and on one wall hung a large oil painting of a Zulu warrior of unsurpassed kitsch. One Saturday night, while waiting to meet friends in Roppongi, I wandered into Magumbos, took a stool at the bar and ordered a cold bottle of beer. A weedy, slightly nerdy Pakistani fellow had the stool on my right. We chatted a bit. The stool to my left was open. The place was half-filled but still busy because the patrons were thirsty. Three relatively young large guys walked in. One sat in the stool next to me and two stood behind. They're French or at least spoke French and, since I didn't hear the *quack-quack-quack* of Quebec French, I reckoned they're French. I don't remember how or why, but they start hassling the guy on my right. Verbally. It's important to stand up to bullies and for the bullied. So, since they're talking across me to their victim, I figured I had the right to speak. It was irksome that they're mocking this guy. I hadn't said a word yet, so I took a swig, put my beer down on the bar with my hand closed around it, and said "Oi! Leav'em alooone," in my best (worst) Scottish accent.

Frog in the seat said, "Oh, and where are you from?"

I turned, grinned and said, "I'm frrrom Glasgo(w), Jim."

My words were met with an abrupt shocked silence, from all three, like I'd tossed a bucket of icy loch water over their heads. If you know your Euro-cities, then you know that for years Glasgow has been considered one of its roughest and toughest.[290] Suddenly the guy next to me tensed, sat up straight and thrust out his right hand to shake, saying, "Really nice to meet you."

The other two chimed in, "Oui; nice to meet you."

"Aye," I replied, as I sipped my beer and kept an eye on them. It could've gone badly, but it didn't. We left on good terms and they stopped picking on Mehmood.

I was out with an aikido teacher from Saitama one night in 1994 in Tokyo and was at that point where you get tired of "Harroooo! Whereyoufrom?" A(nother) drunken salaryman had cornered me on the

---

way out of the restaurant as the sensei and I were putting on our shoes. "Fuck off, ye cunt" would've been a typical Glaswegian response, but instead I turned, smiled and said, "Ich kanst Englisch gesprechen. Ich bin aus Deutschland." (How does he know my German is crap?) The poor guy looked so stunned and sad I nearly said, "Nah; dude; I'm from California!" I didn't, though, and the sensei, who witnessed the whole exchange, was laughing himself silly.

Sometimes things happen, though, that make you lose restraint or trouble just won't take "no thanks" for an answer. When I moved to Tokyo, I was already thinking of staying beyond my planned one year for training. I was helping my friend teach aikido at the American Club just down the road from Roppongi, and occasionally some of the students wanted to go out. Roppongi is probably the most famed eating, drinking and entertainment area where foreigners and locals mix. It used to be just a happy fun spot, but years after I moved there, it began to turn a bit "pink" with Chinese *japayuki* trying to hustle me to agree to a *"massaji, massaji"* to which these days I usually reply in Mandarin, "Why are you in Japan? I thought Chinese hate Japanese people."[291] If only I had an iPhone to capture their stunned expressions. "OMG; that horse speaks two languages!"[292]

Anyway, one notorious Roppongi spot was the bar Motown House, the original. As mentioned, I had reconnected with my old university classmate, and he and his pals used to hang out there (among other spots). The bar was always packed. Always had people dancing. Always had the same handful of sad local girls on the make and their sadder middle-aged

---

[291] *Japayuki* (じゃぱゆき, ジャパユキ) is a derogatory term for Asian women working in Japan as "entertainers." It is derived from wordplay concerning *karayuki* (唐行き, からゆき), which refers to the historical occurrence of impoverished Japanese families sending girls or women to go (行き) overseas (唐国) to earn money as prostitutes. Before your mind leaps to prostitution here, it's more common that the work is as dancers, singers, hostesses, and strippers, though don't rule out the world's oldest profession. Add the honorific *san* and it becomes *japayuki-san* (ジャパ行きさん) meaning literally "Miss Gone-to-Japan." For the curious, read Wiki, and for the overly curious pick up a copy of the *Pink Box: Inside Japan's Sex Clubs* by Joan Sinclair. No; I have not read it.

[292] A Scottish mate of mine's strategy when hassled by guys or girls in the streets to go to a "girlie bar" was to say "Hey, yeah; well I love tits, but my friend here is gay as a Maypole; sorry." His other gem was when some telemarketer called him asking annoyingly if he'd like to speak about switching broadband providers, to which he replied, "I'd love to talk about it but first ... what are you wearing?"

targets, plus, on occasion up at the front, there was the added color of a (patently obvious) transvestite or transsexual or two. Who knows why? But the music was good, the drinks skillfully poured, the beer cold, the vibe happy and the natural wood classic-pub-look made it rather homey. Filled with a few friends, you could have a fun time.

Since I was already thinking of staying beyond my year sabbatical, it was worth networking a bit. I met a group from McKinsey Consulting, a group with an unlimited expense account, for example. They introduced me to a new drink … the "John Stockton" (now maybe the Steve Nash, Chris Paul or Ricky Rubio, after more contemporary NBA stars with skilled hands). Brandy snifter, chartreuse, light it, cover it quickly with your hand and it creates a vacuum so the glass sticks firmly to your palm,which allows you to turn it upside down and pretend to be dribbling or passing it left and right like a basketball. When ready, lift the lid and down it. Tokyo is a work hard, play hard kind of place, and those in martial arts are little different. In fact, when you are out on the town, best be mindful that a lot of other foreigners in Japan are there studying martial arts. I once saw a foreign guy in Motown step back abruptly and accidentally bump another foreign guy. As the bump-er turned to have words with the bump-ee, the bump-ee's friend "took the back" of the bump-er, choking out the bump-er out (*ushiro hadaka jime*, rear naked choke) and letting him slump to the floor 'till he awoke to a view of the patrons' footwear.

My classmate's pals were an interesting collection of American misfits. Thanks to my friend's big mouth, they all soon knew that I was in Japan studying martial arts full time. Usual dumb questions. Usual misconceptions. Usual skepticism. One of his friends, a twenty-four-year-old American guy, just wouldn't leave it alone. The drunker he got, the more obnoxious he got. That night I had invited out a *kōhai* from Canada for some fun. He was on a tight budget, so I bankrolled him. We had met a couple of ladies there and were sitting on stools at one of the high tables near the front door. The twenty-four-year-old Yank was a pest. He took my *kōhai*'s seat when *kōhai* headed off to the lavie, and when I reminded him when *kōhai* returned, the guy said, "I'll arm wrestle you for it!"

I said, "Okay; but win or lose, you get out of his seat and leave, deal?"
"Deal."

I gripped his hand tightly, tensed up like I was going to rip his arm off, and when our friend said "go", I went absolutely limp. Nothing. The back of my hand slapped the table in defeat. "You win!" I waved bye.

Everybody laughed. I give him credit for getting up and walking off. He'd "won," after all, and the deal was win or lose, he'd go.

But soon he was back for more. Up to this point, he had only been pestering me. What did I care? Then he suddenly started in on aikido. Baiting me. "Aikido is bullshit. The Ueshiba's are full of crap."

I looked up and snatched the bait in my teeth. "Alright; have it your way; let's settle this outside," I said, gesturing to the door with a smile on my face. *A verbis ad verbera:* from words to blows. Out we went. I was careful to go quickly enough that he didn't try to shove me down the steep metal stairway you must climb to get into the bar from the street. (The one where straight men habitually look up women's skirts as they walk into the bar.) Turn left at the bottom, another left, fifteen meters down the small street, left again and you were in a dark alley behind Motown. This kid was blathering all the way there—about his fighting prowess. We squared up and he started taking off his coat, telling me he had done this so many times. I don't know if it was my hanging out with the Canadian mafia the past months or his annoying chatter, but I stepped forward, grabbed his right arm with my left hand and reached over his left shoulder with my right, pulling his jacket up and over his head. NHL hockey shirt style. Whump. Upper cut. Slide my right hand from his back and jacket to his right shoulder and stepped back, pushing his right arm up with my left at his elbow to toss him *kokyu-nage*. He went stiff and pulled back, and as he did I stepped in, right arm reaching over his left shoulder past his ear in an arc—*irmi-nage*—plus I added a leg sweep, *o-soto-gari*, though at that point in my training I had never played judo before. Only seen it. There went his balance. Down went his head. Up came his feet, where his head used to be. And ... BAM. "Down goes Frazier!" Flat on his back. Hard. Now say hello to Dr. Marten.

The annoying foolish kid was shocked and stunned. I didn't press the fight. He frantically scrambled to his feet and dashed away, thirty meters down the alley to the main street—faster than a coursed hare. He stopped at the boulevard to look back, and I gestured like I was going to chase him.

Off he sprinted. The guy never bothered me again. He apologized later, in fact; as did I. I probably could've avoided it, but what was I gonna do? He had "offended the Shaolin Temple." And, what on Earth was he thinking? He knew I had been in Japan for six months and done nothing but practice all day long. As a "headhunter," he spent his days sitting at a desk cold-calling people to place them in new jobs. Unless he was some kind of physical phenom, trained in martial arts for years previously, or both, the outcome was predetermined. Honestly? It was satisfying to shut him up, but I was happy nothing but his pride got hurt, surprised how clearheaded I had been during the brief scrap, amazed by the principles of aikido and happy to get back inside with my friends and complete the evening without further incident. It was an interesting lesson to see what "worked" and what didn't. Notably, it didn't last round after round. No one (but him) ended up on the ground.[293] And the ground hits a lot harder than people do.[294] Never forget that the bodies of normal people are not conditioned for the kind of shock you take daily in practice. Your body is being forged day after day to endure impact. It's akin to how a Muay Thai boxer conditions his shins, but aikido forges the entire body.

I'm not going to bore you with every actual or near altercation I ever had in Tokyo or anywhere else (and I certainly don't condone violence or fighting). Most, if not all, were avoidable if I were a bit smarter or more restrained.[295] Many were the result of someone or both consuming too much alcohol. However, while the oft said "your aikido doesn't work" may be true sometimes, "but my aikido works just fine" can complete that statement. Both the mindset that aikido cultivates—avoiding direct collision/conflict—"works" and the various skills it cultivates are all beneficial to self-preservation: a heightened acuity, clear and calm mind, excellent balance, a hardened body, a strong spirit, the ability to move quickly and freely in any direction, to read and destroy your assailant's balance and so on. If you are concerned about actually using aikido technique, the problem isn't aikido, but it may be how you practice it.

If you truly wish to learn to apply your aikido, *oyouwaza* (応用技, お

---

[293] Tellingly, none of the fights have ended up with the participants "on the ground."
[294] Don't take my word for it. Review the Kodokan's scientific research. www.kodokan.org/e_info/research.html
[295] In one I'll describe later, my life literally was at stake.

うようわざ, applied technique), then your practice/training must include the kind of drilling and other training that develops your ability to do so. *Kata-keiko* is just the foundation. If you think life's foes are going to take *ukemi*, like aikido people do, then you are fooling yourself. I used to practice on the second floor at Hombu Dojo in the beginner classes for several reasons, including to study and feel how normal people move (while handling them gently). Non-aikido people typically get stiff, fall down and it hurts them. *Ukemi* is why people watch aikido videos, get confused and think, "Oh, that's so fake." No; you cannot watch aikido and understand it. You have to feel it to appreciate it. What you are usually seeing in videos are two skilled people—one who knows how to do the technique and one who knows how to receive the technique safely (protecting herself without resisting).[296] It is the basic method of training by which technical skills (and a new body) are slowly built and from which all the other many benefits of aikido training flow. Generally, people misunderstand the nature and purpose of *ukemi* so they misunderstand aikido.

I remember practicing with a *kōhai* of mine who is my height but usually weighs anywhere between 115 to 130 kilos. His thighs are the size of a fit man's waist. He's just a big lad. He had been a butcher in Canada before moving to Japan. He had also done blue-collar construction his whole life, so he had that kind of elemental strength that most physical laborers possess. Given other opportunities earlier in life, it would not surprise me if (like some of my university classmates) he would've been in the National Football League being paid to level people with "de-cleater" body blocks.[297] In training, he had a habit of "blocking" people whenever they would attempt *kata-tori nikkyo* or *katate-tori nikkyo* on him. He could block all but a few. However, one day in Masuda sensei's class, sensei walks over and tells him, "Grizzly (sensei's nickname for my friend).[298] Don't resist. Let your wrist stretch. Let them learn. You develop flexible strength. Not rigid strength. Some partners you can stop. What if you cannot?" He held out his wrist for my friend to grab and invited him to "block"

---

[296] If *uke* is always just capitulating, that is "fake". "OK, now I go here and you fall down."

[297] A "de-cleater" is when you hit the other guy so hard that you knock him out of his cleats (studded football boots).

[298] Sensei called me "Los Angeles" or "San Francisco" whenever he called me up for *ukemi*, because he couldn't remember my name or which city he liked better. He just knew I was from California.

his technique, with predictable results. In aikido, we give our training partners a "real" grab ... just "real" enough that they can still train and develop themselves.[299] We increase the energy as they develop. As *uke*, we train ourselves for the people we cannot resist. We develop our *ukemi;* we forge a new body: strong but flexible, hardened but not stiff, stable but responsive.

Ol' Heraclitus also claimed "a man's character is his fate," so I'm not particularly proud of the run-ins I've had in life. But, for better or worse, I've had a measure of "hands-on" experience using my aikido and the practical application of aikido technique continues to be of interest to me. However, in Japan, in life, be wiser than I've been at times. Stay out of trouble and harm's way. Use the autumn (and every other season) to savor nature's incredible offerings in Japan.[300] Nature will remind you that time is passing. Ground yourself in the reality that you cannot escape your mortality. That you should use your time wisely. That you should live life in harmony with its natural timing. That your life is a wondrous (though miniscule) expression of creation, as is every other life. That you should resist using your training (or other advantages) to harm other lives. Accepting these truths, renew your aikido training enthusiastically. Do not be misled into a shallow, merely utilitarian view of practice. Allow your training to help you develop all the "Big aikido" character traits that will support your health and safety and otherwise enrich your life and the other lives that you encounter along your way.

> When autumn came
> My eyes clearly
> Could not see it, yet
> In the sound of the wind
> I felt it.
> — *Fujiwara no Toshiyuki*

---

[299] It shares some similarities with "drilling" in BJJ.

[300] Find your spot for *Kouyou.* http://kouyou.nihon-kankou.or.jp/, www.japan-guide.com/e/e2014_where.html

Living in Hombu Dojo

内弟子, 外弟子, ノタ弟子

(*Uchideshi, sotodeshi, notadeshi*)

One student who helped me a lot when I arrived in Japan had lived in Hombu Dojo. Another friend, arriving a few years later, did too. So you think you want to live in Hombu Dojo?[301] My first teacher (if you don't count my brief start in 1977, and I don't) liked the tale of the Chinese gentleman who was fond of dragons. The Chinese gent was so fond of them that he had dragons embroidered on his clothing, dragons on his dishes and tableware, paintings of dragons, sculptures of dragons, stained-glass windows of dragons, doilies with dragons, vases and carvings of dragons. He was so smitten, he even rooted for the *Chunichi* Dragons.[302] He knew virtually everything one could possibly hope to know about dragons. He just loved them, though he'd never actually met one. Well, the local lizard heard about this fanatic and flew in for a visit. When the enormous, razor-toothed, fire-breathing beast poked his head in through the front door, the man took one look at the real thing and leaped out the window, fleeing in terror.[303] Reality can exceed your imagination. Be careful what

---

[301] Given my age, circumstances, objectives, living arrangements, financial independence and prior years as a "*deshi*," I never gave it any thought other than, "Huh; if I were twenty-four maybe that would've been interesting." As it was, I had the best of all worlds.

[302] Nagoya's Chunichi Dragons of Japanese baseball's Central League. http://dragons.jp/index.html

[303] My first teacher agreed with my reckoning that the Asian dragon "myths" or rather human dragon myths (remember St. George and the Dragon) were probably rooted in some element of fact, some ancient human experience. You've all seen Komodo dragons on telly, no? Massive monitor-like lizards with razor teeth and saliva filled with virulent strains of bacteria. If you manage to escape after a bite, the septicemia will soon drop you, and then the reptile will feed. I can't remember which loopy-risk-taking-nutter-nature-presenter it was, but one of them was laying on top of a Komodo dragon they had captured and tagged. He and his crew were holding down the dragon before releasing it and he remarked that it was the single strongest critter he had ever come in contact with, even over a Salty. I figure those beasts, or their ancient cousins, used to live on the mainland, hence the dragon tales. http://animal.discovery.com/reptiles/komodo-dragon/ Then again, maybe it's a simple embellishment concerning large snakes—add some legs, wings and fire—since the English word "dragon" is derived from the Greek word drákōn (δράκων) referring to a water-snake of enormous size. The Drakon Ismenios was the gigantic serpent guardian of a sacred spring near Thebes; the Drakon Kholkikos was the guardian of The Golden Fleece; Drakon Maionios was a huge serpent in the land of Lydia that Heracles slew. Perhaps ancient constrictors were particularly

you ask for. It may come knocking.

Some people dream of living in Hombu Dojo as a trainee. Unlike Smaug's cousin flying down for a visit, it is actually possible to live in the dojo, though highly improbable.[304] It's equally improbable that most of you would survive it were you admitted. While it may not be quite as terrifying as a mighty dragon, it's not the romantic vision some *aikidoka* believe it to be. It may sound cool, but from all I've seen, heard and experienced, it's extraordinarily demanding. It's very cold; it's very hot. There's no hot water for showers, you're sharing bunk space and there's little or no privacy. You're practicing every day, many times a day. Plus, for *deshi* and some *kenshusei*, there's office work, uniform cleaning, teaching, taking *ukemi* for teachers outside the dojo, supporting dojo events, etc. etc. Of course, comfort's not the point. Extending limits, gaining skill, building strength, deepening endurance and forging character is.

As most *aikidoka* are well aware, a typical *deshi* (弟子, でし, disciple) or *kenshusei* (研修生, けんしゅうせい, trainee) program is unrelenting. It's intended to challenge you—intensively—so that you develop physically, technically, mentally, intellectually and spiritually. Training is ongoing— 24/7/365—and is not limited merely to scheduled classes that other students attend. It's a serious-minded old-school form of apprenticeship where the needs of the teacher and the dojo are put well ahead of the apprentice's personal needs. Depending on the dojo, training may include: aikido (*taijutsu* and weapons) perhaps *iaido*, *zazen* and some form of *misogi*. Customarily, there is daily *samu* (作務, さむ): cleaning, repairing, washing, gardening, etc.[305] Attending seminars and intensive training sessions may be required.

If you are new to aikido (or Japanese martial arts), a *deshi* is a young pupil, disciple, adherent, apprentice, student-helper all rolled into one. An *uchideshi* is a house disciple. You live there; you are on-call perpetually, and it implies a particularly close relationship with the teacher: eating together,

---

gargantuan. Either way, something about big reptiles resonates in the human psyche.

[304] You'll need a letter from a very high-ranking teacher at the minimum, and even then, who knows? Better still if you can speak Japanese, though that may be sightly less of an issue than it used to be.

[305] *Samu* is a word used to refer to work in a Zen temple and is a means of contributing materially to the collective effort of developing the mind, polishing the soul and cultivating a sense of humility, respect and gratefulness.

caring for him or her, etc. A *sotodeshi*, outside disciple, is someone who goes through the same or similar training regime but does not live in the dojo and may or may not be as close to the teacher. *Kenshusei* is another, perhaps broader, word for a dedicated trainee who aspires to deeper training, usually on the path to becoming an instructor. Actually, I believe the term used at Hombu Dojo for those living in the dojo, who are on their way to becoming professional teachers on the Hombu payroll, is *sumikomi-deshi* (住み込み 弟子), which means live-in disciple, rather than *uchideshi*. A friend of mine translated for a foreign journalist interviewing *shihan* at Hombu Dojo about *uchideshi* and two Hombu Dojo *shihan* said that there are no more "*uchideshi*," at least in the original literal sense of the word. Live-in students are not living with the teacher and caring for the teacher like a family member anymore. And, I believe the term used at Hombu Dojo for those not living in the dojo, who are on their way to becoming professional teachers on the Hombu payroll, is actually *kayoi-deshi* (住み 込み 弟子), which means commuting disciple. For example, I have heard that at least one current *shihan* had chosen to be a *kayoi-deshi* rather than a *sumikomi*. From what I saw at Hombu Dojo, *kenshusei* is used for some Japanese who live in short-term, e.g., before they are invited to join (or not) the *shinobu* (導部, しどうぶ, leadership) and become *deshi*. And all the foreigners I know who lived in were dubbed *kenshusei*.

It's a very real commitment in an increasingly superficial world. Does the process produce results? In my experience, remarkably so. When I moved to Japan start of '97, a number of the current sixth *dan* teachers were *sumikomi* or had just moved out of the dojo, and I had met many of them in 1994. All had advanced dramatically. One friend, a foreigner, had moved out of the dojo after a successful year and a half as *kenshusei*. He is an interesting case study. I had practiced with him in 1994 when he had moved in a few months previously and I thought, "Geez, this guy is strong." (He is gifted physically and works hard.) When I returned to Japan and we trained together, after his year and half in the dojo, my immediate thought was, "Oh, you must be joking. I'm supposed to get thrown like that for an hour?" I saw this same transformation over and over again with *deshi* and *kenshusei*. Life was hard in the dojo—a daily grind. It was extremely difficult for them, receiving a real pounding taking *ukemi* all day long. Accompanying teachers to teach outside the dojo or when they go out in the evening can be further exhausting. They could easily get run down, and many lost a considerable amount of weight. But it's supposed to be tough, and after they moved out? Good Lord; they just got phenomenally strong. It's as if the body was able to heal-up and catch up with the training—"grow into themselves"—like finally filling out one of your father's suits as you are growing up.

The path should be difficult. Most definitely. Teaching is difficult; teaching an "art" is all the more difficult and a massive responsibility. Not just anyone can do it, and a good *kenshusei* program should have its occasional casualties. While I was in Japan, two *deshi* dropped out and one *kenshusei* didn't make the cut, either. One *deshi* became a TCM practitioner, and the other one a wedding planner. Both were very talented. Very. It was disappointing to see them go. One friend and frequent practice partner took the first step as *kenshusei* in pursuit of being admitted as *sumikomideshi* but didn't make it. Who knows why? The guy was enthusiastic and had excellent *ukemi*. Years later, another friend entered as *kenshusei* while I was living there, but he lasted for about seven or eight months of his year-long term. It was very demanding physically, and the daily routine just ground him down to the point that he became ill and had to have an operation. It was a valiant effort, though, by a very determined person.

While I have heard of Western students back in the day of O-Sensei being referred to as *deshi*, who knows whether this was accurate or not. Hombu Dojo, as far as I know, has never had a formal *deshi* or *kenshuei* program for foreign students.[306] As I said, from time to time foreign students are admitted for a period of time (often short) as a kind of *kenshusei*, but it seems a rather opaque and ad hoc system. It's certainly not the kind of thing that you walk up to the front desk and ask for. Like so many things in Japan, it's relationship based. From what I have gathered, your teacher needs to have the clout to arrange it for you. If the opportunity lands in your lap, seize it and survive it, because it is a unique experience. It's not for everyone, though. A foreign friend of mine has been a long-

---

[306] I've heard chatter in the foreigner community over the years that Hombu dojo should have a formal *kenshusei* program for foreign students, but it's the family's art and the locals' culture, their dojo, their institution, they can do as they please. Such a system might be useful though. Like it or not competition begets effort which begets excellence. Competition for admission would probably be fierce and that might help produce good skilful instructors who would be very loyal to Hombu dojo. Frankly, it's good to see Japanese protect their culture.

time student of a formidable aikido teacher. My friend went to Japan in the 1980s to train for a few weeks, and when he arrived at Hombu Dojo, he found a letter waiting for him from his teacher (now living on another continent) instructing him to live in the dojo during his stay. Remarkably, my friend explained to the *deshi* that he preferred his hotel because he was extremely tired (or whatever). When I heard this, I was not surprised but I was shocked. I cannot say that I blame him, particularly when the *deshi* back then probably included Hori sensei, Shibata sensei, Yokota sensei and Miyamoto sensei. A hospital ward might have been in order over a hotel. But when he told me my initial reaction was "What!?" With reflection, however, I respected him for knowing his limits and being honest with himself and his teacher about it. Still, it was a once-in-a-lifetime opportunity and seems a Godfather-like "offer you can't refuse." I couldn't help but wonder how the polite refusal shaped his teacher's perceptions and their relationship going forward, even if my friend has skills and is a gem of a guy.

When I left L.A. for Tokyo, I had no desire to try to live in the dojo. I knew that my teacher would never want me to go to Japan, let alone write me the kind of letter of support needed to receive permission to live-in the dojo as one of the periodic *kenshusei*.[307] Frankly, my *kenshusei* years were behind me. And, like my friend in the '80s, I wanted my independence and privacy (after the years of commitments to my home dojo).[308] I was heading "into the woods" for a bit of solitude, not to bunk with a bunch of other dudes years younger than me.[309] "Sad, he can't play with kids his own age, eh?" But I could (and did) create my own rigorous personal training regimen.

Tokyo is a special place. Your training can easily include a myriad of physical, mental or spiritual disciplines and can evolve over the years as your needs grow and change. *Sado*, *newaza*, a gym, Pilates, *zazen*, umpteen

---

[307] Even if he would do it, I was well aware that accepting this kind of support from my teacher would only deepen the *giri* between us, and it was time for me to move on.

[308] Some might've said, I should "play with children my own age."

[309] The senior *deshi* stays downstairs at the end of the entry hall in the room to the right. And there are a couple of rooms on the fourth floor. One behind the dojo. Two or three to a room. I've heard they sleep where they like: room, second floor, or even outside as a friend did when the mosquitoes were less oppressive than the heat inside.

types of yoga, *iaido, kobudo, tempukai, ichikukai,* even *shugendō* ... literally whatever you can conceive of and handle, you can pretty much do.[310] [311] For me, it was aikido three to five times a day, six days a week, daily *suburi,* taking *ukemi* for my former *kenshusei* pal when he was teaching, a particular physical fitness regimen, swimming, *zazen* and study. I didn't have anyone pressuring me (a teacher or other *deshi*). It was all down to me. No excuses. For me, it was enough to try replicate the training schedule of a *kenshusei* as much as I could. Better to grasp the sweet fruit that's in reach than fret over bigger pickings on higher, inaccessible branches. But make no mistake, I was merely a dedicated student. Nothing special.

Why is it people strive to feel special? Maybe they get the vibe via consumerism; buying a slick watch, a hot car or sharp clothes. Or through diet, "I'm a vegan because it's so self-righteous." Or physique. Or intellect. Or partying. "I've never missed a Burning Man festival, dude!" Aikido is not immune. It's difficult to suppress a smile when you meet some enthusiastic *aikidoka* and ask him who his teacher is, and he proudly names some big teacher, but then you discover where the student actually lives and remember where the famous teacher actually resides and realize they are miles, even continents apart. In many cases, I cannot help but think, "Oh, you are so-and-so *shihan's* fan, but not really his student." More often than not, they are a student of a student of a significant teacher, part of that significant teacher's organization and not actually a direct daily student. Of course, if you say out loud that "the Emperor has no clothes," some people take severe umbrage. If so, the appropriate reply is "Aikido is *budo* not a カルト (*ka-ru-to,* cult)."

It's like some guy who tells me he is so-and-so's *deshi.* "Oh really? Great. Where do you live?" "Oh not in the same city, eh?" "Did you ever complete her *deshi* or *kenshusei* program?" "Uh, no? Couple of months living there, eh? Well that's good." "Never went back? Oh, that's too bad." "But you see him once a year for two, three or maybe even four weeks at seminars? I see." I am left thinking, objectively, you're a fan; a

---

[310] I used to see one of the young *shihan* at a gym in Shinjuku where he would run on the tread-mill routinely. Impressively, I must say. I was there for strength training of various sorts and swimming, not conventional weightlifting for sculpting muscles.

[311] *Shugendo* (修験道, しゅげんどう) is a sect of Japanese mountain asceticism-shamanism, an eso-teric form of Buddhism infused with Shinto elements.

fan of this amazing teacher, but ... his student? As a long-time Hombu Dojo student astutely summarized over drinks after the wedding party of Doshu's son: "In aikido, there are three kinds of *deshi*: *Uchi-deshi* (live-in disciples), *Soto-deshi* (live outside disciples) and *Nota-deshi* (ノタ弟子, Not a *deshi* at all but acts like he is one)."

To me, this kind of tenuous (if not fantasized) relationship is a sort of discipleship by long-distance course—a "ロングディスタンス弟子 (*rongu de-i-su-tansu deshi*, long-distance disciple). While the heart may be in the right place, the body clearly hasn't been ... or at least not often enough. With high-speed travel and mass communication, it's even easier nowadays to be a long-distance *deshi*. Imagine; if He had access to the Internet; why have just 12 disciples? JC could've had a gazillion friends on Facebook! "Were you there for the resurrection?" "No dude; I only made the wedding in Canna but caught the Easter rising on YouTube on my iPhone. Oh, man, that was so fuzzy and so fake." In reality, for many things in life you really have to <u>be</u> there to receive the full benefits of the experience.

Why is it even worth mentioning? Because too often in the aikido world all you need is a few loaves of bread, a knife and a couple of jars of mustard to make sandwiches out of all the baloney people pass out. I am all for ridding the art of these kinds of affectations (if not outright charades) that only add to the challenges in getting people to take aikido seriously.[312] In a world that is (or at least seems) increasingly contrived or superficial, I thoroughly believe in the quiet private pursuit of *honmono* (本物, ほんもの, genuine articles; "real" things and people). This doesn't mean to go through life a judgmental, smug, snide cynic. On the contrary, seek truth quietly and joyfully, turning away from phonies when you recognize them. In aikido, if we are to pursue truth on the *tatami*, in our practice and our technique, we have to start by being honest with and about ourselves. Even so, long-distance disciples are good for the art in one sense at least because such a student usually becomes very enthusiastic and does make her best effort to spend some time with whichever superb teacher she wants to emulate. However, it's bad for the art when people don't accept the experience for what it really is and act as if they

---

[312] Yes; I realize that this is my own delusion. Martial arts is traditionally full of eccentrics (nut-jobs).

are somehow special based on this positive but realistically very limited interaction. I'll say it again, aikido training should help us see things as they really are, not prop up our existing delusions or create new ones.

Whenever you meet a student (or teacher), of anything, always check their lineage.[313] Who was their teacher? Who did they train with on a daily basis? How long? How closely? Of course, don't assume that just because someone walked under the *magusa* (目草, まぐさ, lintel; lintel beam) into the *genkan* (玄関, げんかん, entrance way; foyer), stepped on the tatami and completed some *kenshusei* or *deshi* program that they're any good. They completed it. That's an accomplishment; no doubt. They are (presumably) better than they would have been had they not completed it. But that's about all it means. They still have to have talent. They still have to have been diligent students and developed their talent.[314] Have they continued to train, study and push themselves after they completed the program? If they are teaching now, the bottom line is not only what do they have to teach you (what skills and knowledge have they actually acquired), but can they transmit it (or enough of it) to you? Are they willing to transmit it to you? Or can you steal enough of it even if it's being hidden? I was a *deshi* for nearly six years—daily, directly.[315] What did I learn? What limitations did it have? What else do I need to learn? How well can I teach? I don't know. I'm finding out daily. Where I feel I am left wanting, I try to find a way to strengthen the weakness.

Right or wrong, fair or not, my skepticism extends to people in aikido who are noisily public about their pursuit of additional training beyond daily aikido *keiko*. Maybe it's my problem. Maybe I have just met one too many foreigners in Japan who, finding themselves just another ripple in the sea of the dojo's general membership, seemed desperate to feel "special" like back home at their dojo. Yeah; too often it seems people are searching for a way to feel special. "I am doing aikido AND this super special ancient ninja breathing method you

---

[313] More on this in the chapter on the People's Republic of China.

[314] And unfortunately the talent pool in aikido seems increasingly thin.

[315] In our dojo, being a *deshi* meant 7 days a week attending all aikido, weapons, Iaido, intensive courses, administrative work, samu (作務) (particularly caring for the garden at the entrance), study sessions and community service, e.g.10-12 demonstrations a year, and all that went along with those events. (Oh yeah, and Jedhi Mind Tricks and temperamental outbursts.) Since my first teacher was a legitimately ordained Soto Zen priest, he felt that requiring *zazen* might be seen as promoting religion by some (rightly or wrongly) so students were not required to participate in *zazen*. It was something I pursued myself, regardless of my religious convictions. From '91 through '96, there were just three *deshi*.

have never heard of and couldn't possibly ever endure long enough to learn, cuz I am just so frickin' special." Please don't misunderstand. Training legitimately in other arts or disciplines is interesting and useful. I've done it. I do it. I have found it rejuvenating to be a complete beginner in "BJJ" and judo— *shoshin ni modoru*.[316] No responsibilities. No presumptions of knowledge. Just practice. The additional training need not necessarily be another martial art but could be other forms of movement training, mental discipline or spiritual practice. Hell, real-life experiences are often the best forging experience because they are real, not contrived to approximate a potential reality. If you do "cross-train," do it because you love it or you believe it will be good for your development as a person or martial arts student.

The fact is that whether you are an *uchi-deshi, soto-deshi, nota-deshi* or nothing special at all, you can study aikido and live every day of your life with dedication, diligence, perseverance and passion. You can strive to make the most of the gifts you have been graced with from birth, develop other skills and face joyfully and bravely whatever daily life sends your way. What is in a word? *Kenshusei!* 研修生： 研 (polish; study of; sharpen) plus 修 (discipline; conduct oneself well; study; master) and 生 (life; genuine; birth). This is something anyone, regardless of time, title, talent or teacher, can and should strive for in pursuing a life well lived … as if creating a work of art. You don't need admission or other permission. You can start now. By yourself. For yourself. And if you choose to do so, your choice, effort and development along the Way will benefit others in turn.

---

[316] Of course, anyone can be inclined to talk excitedly about the new things he is learning.

"A Man's a Man. . ."
(and so's a Woman)

男は男だ（女も）
(*Otoko ha otoko da (onna mo)*)

After moving to China in 2005, I was surprised to learn that Scotland's famed national poet Robert Burns, the "Bard of Ayrshire" (1759 – 1796), had been much loved by the communist Chinese for, among other things, his celebration of the common man.[317] The Chinese do know poetry (shī, 诗) and but for the "burning of the books " (and burying of scholars) by that loopy and ruthless unifier of the three kingdoms Qín Shǐhuáng (秦始皇), the first emperor of "China," there might be anthologies even pre-dating the Shījīng (诗经) of the Spring and Autumn Period (770-476 BC). Burns was endorsed by no less than Shihuang's kindred spirit the great ("helmsman" or "puppet master," depending on one's perspective) Máo Zédōng (毛泽东) himself and a Mandarin translation of "My Heart's in the Highlands" apparently became a popular resistance song during the Japanese occupation mid-20th century.[318] The Japanese in turn borrowed the tune for Burn's nostalgic *Auld Lang Syne* (Scots which translates loosely as "old time's sake" or "days gone by") sung at New Year in the West for their own "Glow of a Firefly" (蛍の光, *Hotaru no hikari*) wherein the indefatigable Japanese student resorts to the glow of a firefly in order to continue his studies when no other light is available.

I wonder what Burns would've thought of aikido, particularly that practice can be a great social equalizer among people. My first year in Tokyo, I helped a friend teach aikido at various places around town and one of my favorites (and least favorites because it had those awful "puzzle mats" that fit together like a jigsaw) was the rather exclusive and posh American Club in Kamiyacho. It is situated right next door to the Russian embassy, which shows that Japanese officials are not entirely humorless.

---

317 See www.robertburns.org.
318 Read it at www.bbc.co.uk/arts/robertburns/works/my_hearts_in_the_highlands/.

At the club, highly paid expat business executives (American and otherwise) would sign up to study various martial arts, including aikido. It was really interesting to watch these "movers and shakers" struggle with having to be beginners at something. None of their position, none of their power at work, nor their social class, nor education, nor money was of any help to them. They were just plain beginners, and that was unsettling for many of them.

At Hombu Dojo, along with a variety of ages, genders, races and nationalities on the mat, another remarkable characteristic was the healthy mix of socioeconomic classes—in training and when out socializing after practice. In the U.S., apart from sporting events, the armed services and maybe some places of religious worship, this sort of interaction seldom if ever occurs. (Okay; at Tesco or Costco, too; you got me.) My first year in Tokyo, I was welcomed into a gang of *aikidoka* who were solid working-class guys. When they first heard I was a lawyer, surely eyes rolled, but in actuality we got on well enough. They started saying "dude" like a Californian and I picked "...., eh" like a Canadian. I laughed years later when one confided to me, "Dude, when you first got here, we would have a conversation with you over coffee back at the flat and when you'd leave, we'd scramble for the dictionary to look up words, eh." Hilarious, but not intentional on my part. We are all products of our training and experiences, and I had just come out of nearly nine years in the crucible that is the U.S. mega-law firm, particularly litigation. I'd forgotten rule one in communication, "Who's your audience?"

Honestly, I don't think much about these kinds of distinctions between people. I guess I was raised that way. My father was a Presbyterian minister and theologian (who would become president of Princeton Theological Seminary) and the son of a machinist (the only one of twelve children not born in Scotland). My mother was a schoolteacher and the daughter of hardworking German and Swiss immigrants. It's the Northeast of the U.S. or parts of the "High-South" where some measure of the English class system was transplanted and remains to a degree, but I was born and raised in California, when the California state schools were top-flight and private schools were for Catholic kids or troubled youths who didn't behave in state school. I was taught and really do believe what Burns wrote: *"The rank is but the guinea's [English pound] stamp, The Man's the gowd [gold] for a' that."* A person cannot be given a price; a person's character is the true gold. That's a key aspect of how I try to consider every person I meet, being ever mindful, too, that this life before me is the culmination of countless other lives, across the vastness of time, a living manifestation of creation and, in my personal view, a profound expression of the Creator.[319]

When my blue-collar buddies learned more about my family background and work history, any misguided perception of a gap in class was bridged. As I said, my paternal grandfather, the last of twelve children and the only one not born in Scotland, was a machinist. My maternal grandmother, the daughter of a famous German glassware manufacturer, worked on and then managed the shop floor of a book-binding business in Los Angeles after her family was ruined by WWI and she immigrated to the U.S. My mother and father instilled in all three of their children the value of hard work and the worth of all people. I had my first job at twelve years old, a newspaper delivery route (by bicycle), then another one for a better company, then worked as a "bagger" at a drugstore (putting shoppers' items in bags, collecting shopping carts in the parking lot, stocking shelves, etc.), then a valet parking attendant (best car I ever parked was a Rolls Royce, biggest tip $100), drove a Coca-Cola delivery truck at nineteen years old, as a summer job after my first year at university, and then worked as a driver/lumper (unloading the cans, bottles and kegs) on a Budweiser beer delivery truck—driving up and down the San Francisco Peninsula. I visited literally every mom-n-pop shop, supermarket, discount store, restaurant, convenience store, bar, hotel, you name it ... from Palo Alto to Brisbane.

The egalitarian, class-leveling aspect of aikido practice stands in clear contrast to the inherently elitist nature of martial arts and the hierarchy of a traditional dojo. Yes; martial arts are fundamentally elitist and not egalitarian. Not everyone can do them. Not everyone, even if they can practice regularly, can do them well. Martial arts were initially about defeating an opponent in a life-and-death physical confrontation. "Two men

---

[319] Easier said than done; there's always some guy who makes you think "what in creation was He thinking?" As the old joke goes: early twentieth century American humorist Will Rogers said, "I never met a man I didn't like." Will Rogers never met Richard Nixon.

enter; one man leaves!"[320] Survival in that context is based on skills which are the by-product of God-given abilities and your training to develop those abilities. Not everyone is blessed with the same physical, mental or spiritual capabilities. You can train and improve what you have received from the good Lord but all things being equal, or sufficiently approaching equal, someone who is a bit more "blessed" will defeat her less gifted adversary most if not all of the time. Strategy can compensate to a certain degree (but I consider strategy a part of martial arts training) and, of course, serendipity can cause unusual outcomes.

Socioeconomic class is but one of a myriad of human hierarchies and aikido, despite welcoming all on the mat for practice, is not immune. For example, when I moved to Japan, I hid not only my background (education and class) at the dojo but also my age. I kept my age private because I knew the moment I told anyone that would be the end of my taking *ukemi* in class. Age—thanks to Confucius—would have dictated it; it's a massive issue in East Asia. Fortunately for me, I was rather well preserved due to a combination of my parents' genes and daily long-term effort in diet and exercise. For all anyone knew or could tell, I was seven to ten years younger than I was. This was important for maximizing my learning at Hombu. I had hated looking young when I was younger, e.g., being asked for I.D. when buying alcohol in my late twenties, having to bring fake glasses with me to court appearances to look older, etc. but once I got older, it wasn't so bad.

Of course, there are historical, cultural and legitimate teaching/training reasons for hierarchy in the dojo. Japanese martial arts developed over the centuries in a social, political and religious environment shaped by indigenous Shinto, Confucianism borrowed from China (but adapted for Japanese), Buddhism from Korea via China via India (but adapted for Japanese), homegrown Japanese feudalism and militaristic authoritarian rule. To some degree, this structure has powered their excellence in their arts but it can also detract from the preservation and development if, for example, they drift too far away from rewarding only genuine excellence when it comes to promotion and teaching certification. One of the innovative and laudable aspects of Confucianism was the meritocratic imperial

---

[320] See Mel Gibson in Mad Max Thunderdome www.youtube.com/watch?v=pmRAiUPdRjk&feature=related.

examination system (from approx.165 BC) whereby anyone who passed the test could become a government officer, a position of tremendous wealth and honor. Your social class was not determinative of advancement. Japan, however, according to scholars, never fully embraced this approach, relying more on "blood" and class, which better suited feudalism.

I am not critiquing or advocating change in traditional Japanese martial arts training. The hierarchy, the structure (including the etiquette) serve valid purposes. Among other things, it helps build and maintain the proper atmosphere for serious (and sometimes dangerous) training. We are alert, we sit up straight, we don't talk, we try to pay attention acutely. We want to hear the teacher, not distract other students, develop (and learn to maintain) a heightened sense of awareness and focus, which helps avoid needless injuries and sharpens our powers of perception, including our instincts. There are plenty of places where you can chat or fool around. There are few places where you are expected to leave the outside world behind and dedicate yourself a hundred percent to serious physical, mental and "spiritual" training. After all, a goal of aikido training (at least in my experience) is to cultivate a particular state of being that reflects, among other things: alertness (*zanshin*, 残心, ざんしん), steadiness (*fudōshin*, 不動心, ふどうしん), freshness or openness (*shoshin*, 初心, しょしん), clarity (*mushin*, 無心, むしん) and even right-mindedness (*shounen*, 正念, しょうねん) and this requires a particular context and method.

Another goal of aikido training is to develop respect for all things (*rei*, 礼). The transmission of meaningful knowledge from one human being to another is not a trivial thing. From the Founder, we receive the gift of aikido. From the sensei, we receive knowledge acquired through countless hours of difficult practice and self sacrifice. From each other, we receive the opportunity to learn by borrowing each other as *uke*. So with small gestures, a bow, a "thank you," a "please," we show respect to each other and help avoid or ease misunderstandings or disagreements that may arise during training. It is not a bow of subservience. Rather it is a bow of mutual respect and service. Sorry to break the news to folks, but not every act of service is subservience.

An Australian friend really struggled at times with the hierarchy in aikido and in Japan in general. When we went out with a teacher after class, the evening was about the teacher, not any one of us students. He struggled with the deference to rank, the expectation of consideration towards others, having to be a bit reserved in action and speech and so on. Learning and accepting these constraints was one of the compelling attractions of East Asian martial arts for me. You could always tell when a foreigner had lived a bit too long in Japan, never fully accepting the cultural realities. He or she became increasingly and demonstrably irritated by all sorts of actual or perceived slights, injustices or irritating behaviors of the locals. My usual thought was, it's Japan, not Coventry or Kansas or Chinaman's Knob (seriously, in New South Wales, Australia). If you want home, go home. Don't expect other people (in their homeland) to bend to your sense of fairness or justice. If it's that irksome, leave.

Of course, I, too, experienced my own frustrations—prepare yourself for it—but I strove to remember that I was a guest and should behave as a good guest even when their ways were not my ways. As for aikido, I have never gotten too fussed by dichotomies between the purposes or benefits of training and the form or context, with its hierarchies, that was created to pursue those objectives. Aikido practice is grounded in a traditional cultural form that in its lengthy experience provides the proper structure for meaningful practice and yet, despite the order and structure, it has the ability to help us transcend human divisions of class, race, ethnicity, age, gender and so on. In no small part, it's O-Sensei's proscription against competition that helps free aikido to be more than a cool and clever way to knock people down in which we openly compete against each other for submission. This is another aspect of his genius and evidence of his reported hope that his new *budo* would prove a unifying force for humanity and not a dividing one. Certainly, not only Burns, but all of us should find that pleasing.

> Then let us pray that come it may,
> (As come it will for a' that,)
> That Sense and Worth, o'er a' the earth,
> Shall bear the gree, an' a' that.
> For a' that, an' a' that,

It's coming yet for a' that,
That Man to Man, the world o'er,
Shall brothers be for a' that.

A Man's a Man for a' That
Robert Burns, 1795[321]

---

[321] See www.robertburns.org/works/496.shtml.

A Man's a Man for a' That
Robert Burns, 1795

Is there for honest Poverty
That hings his head, an' a' that;
The coward slave-we pass him by,
We dare be poor for a' that!
For a' that, an' a' that.
Our toils obscure an' a' that,
The rank is but the guinea's stamp,
The Man's the gowd for a' that.

What though on hamely fare we dine,
Wear hoddin grey, an' a that;
Gie fools their silks, and knaves their wine;
A Man's a Man for a' that:
For a' that, and a' that,
Their tinsel show, an' a' that;
The honest man, tho' e'er sae poor,
Is king o' men for a' that.

Ye see yon birkie, ca'd a lord,
Wha struts, an' stares, an' a' that;
Tho' hundreds worship at his word,
He's but a coof for a' that:
For a' that, an' a' that,
His ribband, star, an' a' that:
The man o' independent mind
He looks an' laughs at a' that.

A prince can mak a belted knight,
A marquis, duke, an' a' that;
But an honest man's abon his might,
Gude faith, he maunna fa' that!

For a' that, an' a' that,
Their dignities an' a' that;
The pith o' sense, an' pride o' worth,
Are higher rank than a' that.

Then let us pray that come it may,
(As come it will for a' that,)
That Sense and Worth, o'er a' the earth,
Shall bear the gree, an' a' that.
For a' that, an' a' that,
It's coming yet for a' that,
That Man to Man, the world o'er,
Shall brothers be for a' that.

As a patriot, Burns may write in Scots, but his work expresses universally human themes.[322]

First, he says that we look down on poverty and all toil for gold ("the guinea's stamp") and miss that character, not wealth, is not the measure of person.

Second, Burns says that one may eat simple food ("hamely fare") and wear common clothes ("hoddin grey") but appearances, like tinsel, are just show. The honest man, though poor, is the real king of men.

Third, he says you see that cocky young man (birkie) over there? The lord? Folks may worship him, but he's an idiot, and any independent thinker looks and laughs.

Fourth, royalty can hand out titles at will, but good sense and self-respect are worth more.

Fifth, and finally, Burns prays that Sense and Worth shall become prized by all mankind and that the day will come when people around the world (Man to Man, the world o'er) will be brothers (and sisters).

---

[322] Scots dictionaries online. www.scots-online.org/index.asp and www.dsl.ac.uk

Finding your Way

方向音痴
(*Houkouonchi*)

兵法 は 術 に 非ず，して道 なり
Heihou wa jutsu ni arazu, shite michi nari
—Martial arts is a Way, not a technique

When my wife was in intensive care in Tokyo June to July 2003, my mother-in-law and I stayed close to the hospital rather than across town at our flat adjacent to Hombu Dojo.[323] You had to take one of the smaller train lines near Gotanda to get to the hospital. Every day, every single trip, during those hellish months my jangmonim (mother-in-law, in Korean) would walk off the train car at the station and turn the wrong way—walking away from the stairs that lead to the only exit. I welcomed the daily moment of mirth, a healthy distraction in the midst of that soul-wrenching ordeal, smiling reflexively as I realized where my wife's sense(less) of direction had come from. My jangmonim. Most of us know someone like that. If you show him where the bathroom is in your house and close the door on him, he might need a road map, rescue dog, three Sherpa, sat-nav and a trail of breadcrumbs to find his way out ... in a week.[324] [325]

The Japanese have an interesting expression for the "directionally challenged." *Houkouonchi* (方向 音痴， ほうこうおんち), which is a combination of "direction, orientation, bearing, or way" and "tone-deafness, amusia or, if you prefer, having no ear for music."[326] Most of you probably

---

[323] It's a long incredible story that many think should be the subject of another book.

[324] Jangmonim (jahng-mo-neem) is actually a Seoul University graduate, the top university in Korea. And she did it at a time when getting an education in East Asia wasn't so easy for women.

[325] Actually, smartphones are a Godsend for Tokyo because addresses alone won't usually get you where you want to go. Back in the day, people used to fax maps with directions to their office (that's a facsimile machine, kiddos) to each other. Then email. And now it's smartphones.

[326] Be careful how you use it. As with many expressions in Japanese, context usually determines whether or not it's appropriate or an insult. Said to or about a friend in a teasing way, it's okay. Said to or about someone you don't really know very well could be considered rude.

aren't churchgoers, but an old high school mate of mine was and he couldn't carry a tune in a bag. He would belt out those Protestant hymns with passion and commitment: "Im-mortal! In-vis-ible! God Only Wise!"[327] But, bless the Lord oh my soul, was my pal ever tone deaf. Completely lost. Standing on either side of him (or in front), it was all I could do to keep a straight face and stay on song. Nothing quite like suppressed laughter, particularly at fourteen years old and in church or some other socially inappropriate place.

If you aren't thoughtful about your training at Hombu Dojo, it's easy as a visiting student to lose your way, if not The Way. What I mean is that it's a big place with many different teachers and many different students from many different countries. It's not your home dojo. You're anonymous initially. Later, you still won't be under the intense daily scrutiny that exists with some teachers in the more intimate context of their personal smaller dojos. Also, the foreign students and many of the locals as well all started aikido elsewhere. It's not like home where typically everyone (or nearly) on the mat has or is studying under one person. At Hombu Dojo, which Way do you go? What path do you follow? If you start your training there, maybe it's different, but if you started elsewhere, particularly only for a brief period, you need to think seriously about how you plan to develop your aikido. "Failing to plan is planning to fail" as the trite truism goes.

Before I moved to Japan, my view of aikido was more limited or perhaps narrowminded. It had begun broadening, following my visits to Japan in '92 and '94. Of course, prior to that, I had attended seminars by various *shihan*, but my perspective would expand notably while training at Hombu Dojo. At the dojo, there are differences, sometimes substantial, between the different teachers' expression of aikido. It was true then; it was true before I got there; it remains true now. I say "expression" because ultimately that is what it is. Yes; there is "The Way" and one needs to be mindful in training not to turn "The Way" into "My Way" for convenience or other shallow personal predilection. Why? Because you won't develop as fast or as well. However, ultimately the technique you are learning is being expressed through your body, with your talent and abilities, both the innate ones you cultivate and the new ones you may develop over time. The qualities and imperfections of the wood limit the skill of even the greatest carpenter. You may want to run as fast as Usain Bolt,

---

[327] Hum along or belt it out. www.youtube.com/watch?v=-I_VwA4d44g&feature=related

but unless you've got "it" in you, it's not happenin'. No matter how hard you work. With hard work, one can achieve many, but not all, dreams. Hard work aligned with one's gifts, one's talents holds far more promise. You may wish to follow this or that teacher because you "like" his or her "style," but your body may be very different from that teacher.[328] Your temperament may be very different. Not surprising then if your aikido ends up looking, well, very different. Even so, sometimes studying what does not necessarily "suit you" can be beneficial for your development and, ultimately, achieving your own highest expression of the art.

Many of you will be familiar with the concepts *Shu, Ha, Ri* that are considered traditionally the natural process of learning Japanese martial arts: master form, break form, transcend form.

> *Shu* (守, シュ, "protect," "defend," "obey"): follow traditional wisdom; learn fundamentals.
>
> *Ha* (破, ハ, "rend," break," "destroy"): break from tradition, consider exceptions, search for new ways.
>
> *Ri* (離, リ, "detach," "separate," "digress"): transcend technique, moves become natural.[329]

Okay, but if you move to Japan and train at Hombu Dojo, whose form do you follow?

The answer will be different for different people, depending on where you are in your aikido journey, who your teachers have been so far and whether or not you already have some relationship with a Hombu *shihan* at the time you arrive.[330] When I arrived in Japan, I had already been promoted to *san dan*.[331]

---

[328] Hopefully, you've put more thought into your choice than simply a matter of "style," as if you are selecting a chocolate from a box searching for the one that gives you the most pleasure.

[329] The first step is realizing (and accepting) where you are in your training. It must be wonderful to reach that final stage and "break the form," but you'd best really be there. Try too soon, and you'll stunt your understanding and development.

[330] Many people who move to Japan to train at Hombu Dojo come with existing relationships with *shihan* who visit their home country or via their home teacher's relationship with someone. It is different for different people. My story is simply about what worked for me given my experiences leading up to 1997.

[331] Huh? Then why in 2000 was I taking a *sandan* examination at Hombu Dojo? Long story. *De mortuis nihil nisi bonum.* You could say it set me back four years, if one cares about those

I had spent nearly ten years with a single highly skilled sixth *dan* teacher who had studied with Kanai sensei in Boston, Doshu Ueshiba Kishomaru as *kenshusei* in 1969 and spent seven or eight years with a remarkable *shihan* in San Diego before a parting of the ways. A classmate of his from University of Southern California days in the late 1960s, a very sober-minded scientist, once told me that he saw my teacher pin a collegiate wrestler at U.S.C. After watching aikido practice, the wrestler had scoffed "the stuff doesn't work" and challenged him. The grappler shot for a single leg takedown, which was countered by *ikkyo ura* (一教裏，イキョウうら). *Tenkan* (転換，てんかん). Standard *ikkyo osaewaza* (押さえ技，おさえわざ, holding down, pinning or immobilizing technique). An apocryphal tale or not, my first teacher's lineage and training were exceptional and his intellect and knowledge extraordinary. There aren't many Harvard-educated martial artists.[332] I certainly hadn't come close to learning all that he had to offer, but I had stolen a fair bit, the time was right to move on and I was eager to learn more in Japan.[333] I was grateful for a solid foundation upon which to build something more meaningful still—if I found and followed another good path leading upwards.

At Hombu Dojo, I tried to be as agnostic as possible regarding who I would learn from, though I had my preferences on arrival. But even my preferences weren't built on some flimsy personal feeling of "Oh, I like that" or "Oh, I don't like that." It's not like standing at a salad bar gazing through the glass sneeze-guard at the fruit and veg and thinking, "My, my,

---

things, but Hombu Dojo was very good to me and in the end it was a blessing. From that experience—and my accepting things without complaint and handling the exam—I truly became and remain a Hombu Dojo student. In my view, rank inflation in aikido is epidemic. Three-year *shodan*? Nine-year *sandan*? *Yondan* one summer. *Godan* the next. Practicing a few times a week? Or in some remote location? Really? Really, really?

[332] Frankly, it's believable if you have seen photos or videos of my first teacher when he was very fit, and given how little Westerners knew about East Asian martial arts back in the 1960s. Plus, the guy who told me is highly credible.

[333] About my second or third year at my first dojo there was a mini-revolt (after the arrival of a *yudansha* from somewhere else) and a number of senior students, including my teacher's only *deshi*, left to form their own dojo. People are free to come and go, and it wasn't my business really, but I thought the manner in which they left was a bit disrespectful. Regardless, one couldn't help but chuckle after hearing the name of their dojo, City Aikido, since in Japanese writing it was シティーあいきどう, which sounds like Shitty Aikido. For me, it created a great opportunity. So many seniors were gone. My direct contact with the teacher, as *uke* and otherwise, increased twenty-fold. My teacher became extraordinarily motivated to teach again. The whole feeling in the dojo changed nearly "overnight" and for the better. He made a video series. He wrote a book. And he took on three *deshi*, two Japanese Americans and a token whitey: me.

the pineapple looks good. Oh look; beet root! I'll have some of that with the spinach, too." I wasn't at Disneyland going, "Oh! Oh! Space Mountain! And then Frontierland!" It's training, not entertainment, and I genuinely tried to reflect on what was lacking in my training. What did I really need, in order to improve? Who could I receive it from?[334]

The Japanese say to return to a beginner's mind. *Shoshin ni modoru* (初心に戻る、しょしん にもどる). The beginner's mind has limitless possibilities, while the expert's has few. Well, I most certainly wasn't an expert (then or now), so that was easy. I've seen this kind of mistake from other martial arts students that I've met over the years. Too often, people think they know something before they really know it, or they know it a bit, but there is still much more to learn. Better to ever approach study with an open, humble mind. "Cut off your head and train." Answers are revealed through practice. Understanding acquired through actual experience rather than explanation is often deeper understanding. Balance the acceptance of doctrinal teaching with your search for firsthand understanding that's not dependent on any authority or system.

> Instructors can only impart a fraction of the teaching. It is through your own devoted practice that the mysteries of the Art of Peace are brought to life.
>
> —*Ueshiba Morihei*

All the teachers at Hombu Dojo have expertise. If you are receptive, there is always something worthwhile to learn. But you can't attend all the classes, unless you are independently wealthy and have no other commitments. And, even if you could, it might leave you very confused. So you have to make choices. How do you find your Way? For me, there was a recipe and a dash of serendipity. In Japan, I realized how overly planned my life had been before, including my training regimen. Wake-eat-work-eat-work-dojo-home-eat-sleep-repeat. What I ate, when I ate, when I slept, how long I slept, where and when I exercised and so on. Controlled. Rigid. My adventure abroad reminded me that spontaneity begets liveliness and receptiveness and adaptability to shifting circumstances. Life is filled with an assortment of

---

[334] The short answers were "a lot more practice" and "anyone senior and qualified."

"curveballs," "sliders," "knucklers" and "chin-music" that comes at you despite "best-laid plans."[335] How do you respond when you have no control? When you slip-slide outside your "comfort zone"? As with *ukemi*, you need to be alert, nimble, flexible, responsive and adaptable (and to persevere).

I was fortunate to receive some good local advice and introductions to teachers, plus some remembered me from my past visits or their visits to the U.S. Frankly, whatever I received from a teacher I wanted to earn by my effort and attitude; I did not want to receive special treatment just because we shared a relationship with some third party or he happened to like me or I happened (not) to speak Japanese well. The most important thing was to show up and train sincerely and energetically. As a general principal in determining my training regimen that first year, I asked myself repeatedly, what do I think I need to progress? For the record, I asked silently—in my mind. It's generally okay to talk to yourself, so long as you don't answer back. Next I asked, what does this teacher or that teacher have that could be beneficial to my development? Sometimes you can watch a teacher one time and see it. "Wow! That's it!" Other times, you only realize it after many practices.

One thing was for certain in Japan. When I attended a teacher's class, I didn't just bow in and do my usual practice my way. I've seen so many people commit this sin.[336] They have learned a technique a certain way and they never deviate from that regardless of what a teacher is actually teaching in the class. They KNOW it already. For me, I chose to try to copy and learn whatever the teacher was teaching. To do it, his way—at least for that hour. Training is the only way to learn, and it will reveal many, if not all, secrets. Plus it's rather rude to go to another teacher's practice and just reject what they are teaching without even trying. How

---

[335] Hitting a baseball has to be one of the most difficult things in all sport. Michael Jordan couldn't do it well enough. John Elway couldn't. Danny Ainge couldn't. (Google them.) A "curveball" curves in towards you, if you bat right-handed as most people do. A "slider" breaks the other way. It looks like a "strike," like you can hit it but it slides away from you. A "knuckleball" floats and flutters so slowly and unpredictably you haven't a chance to hit it. "Chin music" is thrown "high and tight," meaning nearly at your head, just under your chin, to encourage you to step back from home plate when you're batting. If you are worried about being hit by the ball, you can't very well hit the ball. As a batter, you just don't know what's coming your way and have to quickly adjust for whatever does.

[336] I've even seen a few students step out of the men's changing room and sit on the mat, realize that there is a substitute teacher and then leave the mat immediately. Do not do that!

can I possibly know? Without experience? Why go to the class? Moreover, learning to watch and copy (accurately) is an essential martial arts skill. You are training your eye to discern movement, which is vital to self-defense outside the dojo. Taking *ukemi* for a teacher cultivates this skill as well. You are learning to look and really see (and otherwise sense). Placed in the context of genuine application, is my opponent bigger? Stronger? Faster? Right or left handed? Have weaknesses? And so on. This method of watching and copying to gain understanding, contributes to your developing this martial skill.

Some classes I chose to attend because the teachers had been closest to "the refiner's fire," O-Sensei. I wasn't at the dojo of just one *shihan* who had studied with O-Sensei. There were five or six or more. And even of different generations! Attending Doshu Kishomaru Ueshiba's class was the base, the stock of the soup. Sure it was review. Sure it was repetitive. Isn't that the point? *Repetitio est mater studiorum:* repetition is the mother of studies! How else is movement committed to muscle memory? An iPhone app? As for the other senior teachers, I attended their classes and just tried to snatch whatever pearls I could by watching closely and, if the opportunity arose, taking *ukemi* for them, practicing with their senior students or with young Hombu teachers who were attending. These people studied directly with O-Sensei, some were the *senpai* of Hombu *shihan* residing outside of Japan. How extraordinary to experience that? One step removed from O-Sensei. One generation earlier. Regarding the younger teachers at that time, there were two influences and one in particular. One was cat-quick, his aikido like a sword duel ... over in a flash. Blink and you miss it. The other was built low to the ground, his aikido like water—seldom insisting, ever flowing and surging, flooding and overwhelming whatever course was available.

Above all, I wanted aikido that developed power from my feet, legs and hips, not merely in my arms and chest like I had seen in so many Westerners, particularly North Americans.[337] Some of these "No-Ams" have huge forearms from doing countless *suburi* but their feet move like stones and their power

---

[337] This was one of the biggest differences I noticed between practice in Japan and in the U.S. (and since I left Japan and have trained in the EU and China). The power of Japanese aikidoka was typically in their legs and hips, not in their chests and forearms.

is in their chests, shoulders and arms.[338] Watching their *taijutsu*, the succinctly descriptive phrase "*Ude-bakkari*" immediately comes to mind.[339] "Franken-aiki," moving like the mad doctor's monster, arms extended rigidly: "Arrgggggghhhhhh." Watching them makes me want to alert the villagers, light torches and scare off the monster. So, some took the high road, but I took the low road. I chose the "low path" (aikido in the legs and hips), from a teacher of shorter stature, despite the fact that it would be very difficult for me—physically and otherwise. Our physiques were different, our backgrounds were different and so on. But, he had a quality that I wanted and I would spend eight years in Japan (and afterward) grasping for it. *Ad augusta per angusta*—to high places by narrow roads![340]

Life in Tokyo reminded me what my legs were for despite having been very active in Los Angeles: aikido, running on the beach or in the mountains and so on, but that was planned exercise, not a constant fact of life. In Tokyo, I walked ... everywhere. To the market and back. To the dojo and back. To Shinjuku and back. Down the street to the subway station. Down the stairs into the subway station. Up the stairs out (yes, sometimes I cheated with the escalator). I had tatami in my flat, so I sat on the ground a lot. Sit down, stand up. Every day. All day. This changes your body.

Also, consider your training partners.[341] Who are your training with?[342] Why? How should I train with this person as opposed to that person, so that we both can best learn? That year, sometimes my partner was just whoever happened to be sitting next to me. Other times practice was an hour of bad road getting bumped and bounced by some *senpai*. For awhile, I took the advice of a French senior student who advised that I train with women often to improve my *ukemi* and give up using my strength. I spent a lot of time being pummeled by an absurdly strong

---

[338] As most aikidoka know, suburi (素振り, すぶり) means practice-swinging, e.g., a sword, bat, tennis racket, etc.

[339] Merely by your arms. U-de (腕, うで) meaning arm and ba-ka-ri (ばかり, 許り) only or merely or nothing but. The characters can have other meanings but, in this case, "nothing but your arms."

[340] I hope I get there.

[341] Of course you can train with anyone and learn from everyone.

[342] In some teacher's classes, you train with the same person for the entire class. In other teacher's classes, you change partners periodically.

friend of mine who practices with a ferocity and physicality that few students, if any, can match or even withstand for an hour.[343] Practice with him was usually an hour of being unable to move the wholly centered and unmovable and then my moving like hell to keep my wrist, arm or other bodily bits from being busted.[344] The upside was that practicing with other people became a "walk in the park". The downside was ulnar nerve damage in my left arm, probably a compression injury from too many *shihonage,* although it may have been a crush injury from not tapping (quickly enough) to nerve and joint lock when practicing with Kuribayashi sensei in Endo sensei's class. Either way, my *ukemi* needed improvement.

Lastly, I often sought to train with people I didn't know or didn't know very well. There's an unpredictability to it that often involves a measure of caution and consideration that's absent with more familiar training partners. In Yokota sensei's old three p.m. class, I remember getting a nice "accidental" *gi* burn across my face (looked like a sunlamp accident) while doing *suwariwaza kokyo-ho* with a thick-set Japanese fellow in his mid-thirties (who became a very dear friend), who, I learned years later, had started aikido at Hombu Dojo at about six or seven years old, with Koichi Tohei teaching the children's class. Generally, I used the same method in training that I use these days in *newaza* practice. Sometimes surf the small waves, the shore break. Practice with partners with whom you can do as you please in practice, i.e., "make things work," use as little strength as possible and experiment. Or, surf shoulder to head-high breakers. Practice with a more evenly matched partner. Some days, it's *Big Wednesday* and you surf perilously overheard swells.[345] Paddle out into put-the-fear-of-

---

[343] Some people used to gripe that this guy "used power." Wrong; he was a diligent student and quite technical but also had God-given strength and a sturdy build that is simply uncommon in aikido.

[344] To get a further sense of it, grab a copy of Norman Maclean's "*A River Runs Through It.*" Sit down by the fire, put your boots up and read his additional short story "*Logging and Pimping and 'Your Pal Jim.*"
http://books.google.co.uk/books?id=5GL2_ctw58gC&pg=PA105&lpg=PA105&dq=norman+mac-lean+%22your+pal+jim%22&source=bl&ots=Ao61KNBPPD&sig=5zat37ZN21xep-oqTeR4UeuTEcc&hl=en&ei=rgKETvTyD4bF8QOXteQJ&sa=X&oi=book_result&ct=re-sult&resnum=10&ved=0CFgQ6AEwCQ#v=onepage&q=norman%20mac-lean%20%22your%20pal%20jim%22&f=false

[345] "When it comes to making surf movies, Hollywood sucks. ... but in Big Wednesday ... Hollywood got it right." See www.surfline.com/surfing-a-to-z/big-wednesday-history_759/ and www.youtube.com/watch?feature=player_embedded&v=ADDJwqqQbv8.

God- into-atheists kind of surf. Find a partner whose skill is such that you feel fortunate to survive the hour. Push yourself. Break routines. Challenge your conceptions. Recognize and admit your misconceptions. Identify your weaknesses. Work on them. Polish yourself daily.

During practice, I resisted the dualistic delusion of: "won/lost," depending upon whether or not I was able to put my partner down. I resisted letting my practice decline into some kind of bogus exercise in self-validation: "It worked; I feel great! It didn't work; I feel bad." One senior friend at that time told me, "To learn aikido, you have to lose."

He's right in several ways. My "failures" during training taught me a great deal. And, in taking *ukemi*, one relents to survive, learn and develop. Instead of focusing on the outcome, I tried to examine an entire movement seeking to find and fix a particular area of weakness in my practice, a specific problem with a particular technique or some affectation I had unwittingly added to the essentials of the technique.[346] For example, these days, in my Brazilian Jiujitsu training, during "rolling" (*newaza randori*), I don't just mindlessly focus on winning each five- or six-minute bout, but instead usually (without telling my opponent) allow myself to get into specific situations and then try to fight my way out (not always successfully), often working on the applicable defense or escape we've been taught in that class. Why not actually learn the art? Aikido *keiko* is different, but you can use similar approaches to vary practice and improve particular things in your technique: pace, timing, spacing, softness and so on. At Hombu Dojo in particular, a training journal (electronic or otherwise) can be a very useful study aid.[347] You may be taking classes from various *shihan,* and every so often they reveal some secret that you may never see again. Having written all these suggestions, remember that you can over think things, and fundamentally you learn aikido by feel, not thought.

One possibility you may want to consider, particularly if you have not yet received your *shodan,* is participating in the *Aikido Gakko.*

---

[346] Since leaving Japan, I have had the opportunity to learn the weapons of a *shihan* of extraordinary skill but for some time remained reluctant to copy anything other than the very source himself or his truly close students. Yes; I said before that one's aikido is an individual's expression of the art. True, but I had best be sure that I have not injected needless bits of my personality or my misinterpretations into what's truly essential.

[347] If you do, don't bring it into class. Write it down immediately afterward in the locker room.

Aikido Gakko (合気道学校、あいきどうがっこう) consists of a year-long course for Beginners Academy (up to fourth *kyu*), Intermediate Academy (third *kyu* to second *kyu*) and Advanced Academy (first *kyu* or above) that are separate from the daily Open and Beginner classes on the third and second floors. The *Aikido Gakko* courses are separated into two semesters: one fall (from October to February) and one spring (from April to August) and each lasts approximately five months.[348] Each course is led by specific *shihan* for the entire course. A course consists of small-group lessons, held twice a week in the evening for ninety minutes, in the much smaller fourth floor dojo. With the more intimate setting, longer classes and year-long course, there is more opportunity (in theory at least) for teachers and fellow students to observe your aikido and for you to forge relationships. Space is limited, applications must be filed with the office (check on dates), you are notified by mail whether or not you have been accepted and, if you are accepted, you must pay the additional fee of 52,500 yen for Beginners and 63,000 for Intermediate or Advanced courses. You are not required to have completed the Beginners Course in order to take the Intermediate Course or Intermediate Course to enroll in the Advanced Course. Each student receives a textbook, a certificate of completion of the course and will be promoted if he or she completes an examination successfully. I never joined, but some friends did, and they thoroughly enjoyed it.

Ultimately (and obviously), it is your choice, your path, and your Way, but I encourage you to use your time wisely when you visit. A lot depends on why you are studying aikido, I suppose, and where you are on that path. For me, I was exploring whether or not I wanted to become a professional teacher, and I considered it a serious question. Not everyone can teach, or at least teach well. Sure. Anyone can teach whatever bit they know (great or small), but to become a truly qualified teacher, of an art, this is a very difficult path of significant responsibility. Face it; some of us are simply *musai* (無才、むさい) lacking talent or ability. We can still enjoy and otherwise benefit from aikido, but we shouldn't be professional teachers. Anyone who aspires to become a professional teacher had best be

---

[348] Actually, the first semester starts in April, but I am writing about autumn so October gets the nod here. Check the Hombu Dojo website for official information about the program. www.aikikai.or.jp/eng/index.htm

brutally honest with himself about this truth—for him or herself and the sake of us all—because aikido is already shackled with enough mediocrity leading classes. Ask yourself: "Do I really have what it takes?" Physically, mentally, spiritually? "Am I being or have I been trained by a qualified teacher?" More than once a year or one month a year?

To me, these days, one should not only train in the traditional manner under a highly qualified teacher and learn by experience and "feel," but higher education and other forms of training should be undertaken as well.[349] Consistent with the *gaku* of the venerable Japanese formula: *gaku jutsu do(u)* (学術道, がくじゅつどう, study, technique, way), a good teacher's search for knowledge and understanding should be lifelong. So much more is readily available today thanks (or not) to technology. Where to begin, after or in addition to the obviously indispensable firm grounding in traditional aikido training and basic technique? Japanese language proficiency? Aikido history? Human anatomy? Kinesiology? Zen? Shinto? Psychology? Neurology? *Misogi*? Other forms of movement? Other martial arts? Conditioning and strength training? An ever incrementally expanding physical, mental and spiritual development towards mastery? *Ad infinitum*? "No one would ever teach then," said one fellow student who was discussing this with me. Maybe that would be a good thing, in some cases. I am all for raising the bar for us all. Additional book knowledge and experience is excellent, but in the end, aikido is transmitted by feel, not thought. By deeds not words. Still, that's not an excuse for any aspiring or actual teacher not to study. Don't listen to me. Find your own Way! Maybe you'll excel and enjoy yourself thoroughly at Hombu Dojo by relying on nothing more than well-worn SOPM: Seat Of the Pants Method.[350] For me, it made sense to think deeply about how to maximize the quality of my training time in Japan. I didn't expect to be there for a lifetime. *Ichi-go ichi-e* (一期一会) meaning literally "one time, one meeting" but could be translated as "for this time only" or "never again." Each day, each class, each hour and each minute, never again. My

---

[349] *Kodo* (古道, "ancient ways") are important to preserve; no doubt, but if you close your mind to the possibility of improvement or innovation, then your art may become a dusty museum piece.

[350] www.merriam-webster.com/dictionary/seat-of-the-pants

sabbatical year instilled a new appreciation and acceptance of life's transience (*mujō*, 無常, むじょう).

It wasn't an easy final four months of the year, except that the weather had less of an impact on practice. I was accustomed to living in Japan now, so I could focus even more intently on aikido. I pushed and pushed and pushed myself in training, deflecting intruding thoughts of melancholy over the year ending and perhaps my adventure with it. Things end. Life ends.

> I cried over beautiful things knowing no beautiful thing lasts.
> The field of cornflower yellow is a scarf at the neck of the
> copper sunburned woman, the mother of the year, the taker
> of seeds. The northwest wind comes and the yellow is torn
> full of holes, new beautiful things come in the first spit of
> snow on the northwest wind, and the old things go,
> not one lasts.
> —*Autumn Movement, by Carl Sandburg*

Bundle of laughs, ol' Carl. "Hi everyone I'd like to introduce Carl!" [Three hours of poetry later]. "O.K., let's all hold hands and jump off the bridge." In fairness to Carl, his verse is sunshiney compared to some Samurai death poems, often composed on the eve of battle:

> Like a rotten log
> half buried in the ground -
> my life, which has not flowered,
> comes to this sad end.
> —*Minamoto Yorimasa (1104-1180)*

I've had Minamoto-*san's* very thought (and pain) the morning after eating the worm on a bad-judgment-with-tequila-night in university. Yes; life is short and sad. Fragile and fleeting. In 2002, I stood inside a Buddhist temple in Vietnam gazing at the thousands of photographs of the departed posted on one wall ... an unending chain of human temporal struggle, decline and disappearance.[351] (And that was just one wall in one temple in one populous city in Southeast Asia.) Life is also exquisite and exhilarating. Sweet and sumptuous. And, one can learn to value people, natural beauty and life's experiences specifically because it will all pass away, just as we will.

Autumn is a season of great beauty and change, actually they all are, but with fall there's a weightier awareness of it because you realize that the year is heading to its end in the cold grip of winter and, in the Northern hemisphere at least, the shortening days and lengthening nights, the colorful falling leaves, the Harvest Moon are all powerful natural reminders that things are passing, slipping, fading away. The year is waning and you begin reflecting back on all you've done and all that you have yet to do. "OMG! It's October already?" Fall reminds us of our mortality; winter awaits us all. For me, the response is to live every day, every moment to the fullest, to the last breath and final fall. Rather than fret over the sand, as it runs out of the hourglass, choose to savor each precious unique grain as it passes. Better to make the best of what you have during the time you have rather than fretting over the inevitable end.

> Had I not known
> that I was dead
> already
> I would have mourned
> my loss of life.
> —Ota Dokan (1432-1486)

When I say that I pushed myself in practice that fall, I mean it. Why hold back? Plenty of time to rest when I'm dead. Plus, you don't necessarily need to climb to the top of a sacred mountain and stand under a secret waterfall chanting in a loincloth to purify yourself. You don't necessarily need to sit in a cave meditating on special thoughts or shouting

---

[351] I happen to be a Christian—a loaded word that means umpteen different things to umpteen different people—but even if one believes in an afterlife (and turns out to be correct) and prefers to make a joyful noise to the Lord instead of drowning in sadness or sneering in cynicism, we all go through the same stages of life, including the pain of birth and uncertainty of death at the end. No one knows what lies beyond. One may believe, but no one (living) knows.

special slogans. "Your own devoted practice." Your daily martial arts practice, the foundation of your training, can be your *misogi* and the fiery forge of your mind, body and spirit. It was easier to stomp on the gas pedal in fall because I was familiar with my surroundings plus I had worked hard earlier and survived my feet-first-blind-leap into intensive daily practice those first few months in Japan. Yeah; I had survived but it wasn't the cleverest approach and I don't recommend it. I've seen many people arrive at Hombu Dojo convinced that they are going to train hard only to end up injured, sick, burnt-out or all three. Maybe when they arrived they weren't as fit as they believed. Maybe they chose the wrong partners too often and got beaten up a bit. Maybe their knees blew up from the hard tatami and daily *suwariwaza*. Maybe the pace of life in Tokyo wore them out. Maybe they get hooked on the nightlife. Or they spent most of their time teaching English or otherwise working. There's any number of reasons and combinations of those reasons. I saw most, if not all of them, that first year in the stream of students who came and went at the dojo.

The smarter (saner) approach when you arrive is to build slowly, systematically. From all I've read (and practiced), Nakamura Tempu is one of the more fascinating people who've influenced aikido practice —a martial artist and ultra-nationalist super spy-soldier of the Japan/China and Japan/Russia wars at the the turn of the nineteenth century, turned tuberculosis patient, turned Western medical student, turned self-healer and creator of a "Japanese Yoga"—*Shin Shin Tōitsu-dō* (心身統一道,　しんしんとういつどう) Mind Body Unification Way—and pacifist.[352] Teaching his particular blend of specific meditation practices, psychological exercises, stretching and other health-promoting movements,

---

[352] Nakamura Tempu Sensei was born, Nakamura Saburo, in 1876 in Tokyo (present day Oji, Kitaku, Tokyo). His father, a Kyushu native, was a notable official in a government ministry so Nakamura sensei was able to study English from boyhood. After completing his formal education in Fukuoka, including studying judo and *kenjutsu*, he joined an ultra-nationalist organization (玄洋社, *Gen'yosha*, Dark/Black Ocean Society) working for a military intelligence officer of the Imperial Army, whereby he studied Mandarin intensively and later engaged in covert missions in China prior to the Sino-Japanese War. In 1902, age twenty-six, he became an intelligence agent of the General Staff Office, so when war started with Russia in 1904 he was again a covert operative deeply engaged in the fighting. A year later, he returned home as just one of nine survivors from his military unit of 130. His new career as a business executive was cut short quickly the next year when he was diagnosed with an aggressive (often fatal in that day) case of tuberculosis. Treatment in Japan failed so he sought answers by studying medicine, religion, philosophy and psychology. His studies lead him to America for medical

a number of prominent aikido teachers over the years joined the *Tempu-kai* and to that extent, at least, Nakamura sensei's teachings have influenced some in aikido. Elements of his health system appear in the warmup of certain teachers, for example. His system of "yoga" is grounded on four rather sensible fundamental principles:

1. Use the mind in a positive mind (negative thought is of no use).
2. Train the mind to concentrate fully.
3. Use the body naturally (obey the laws of nature).
4. Train the body gradually, systematically and continuously.

That's probably the best advice you'll ever get on how to approach aikido *keiko* or anything else productively.

However, it wasn't just familiarity and fitness that allowed me to work hard; autumn inspired me as well. Traditional Japanese culture recognizes, accepts and admires the momentary but often profound beauty that appears amidst the inescapable deathwardness of life, precisely because of the impermanence of beauty, of life.[353] The Japanese word *sabishii* (寂しい、 さびしい) expresses a sense of loneliness or lonesomeness as a present state of being or over some

---

treatment, where he recovered (ostensibly), so he enrolled at Columbia University to study Western medicine. After graduation he continued his studies focusing on the role of the mind in health, traveling to London, Paris and Germany to meet with a variety of scientists, luminaries, psychiatrists and progressive thinkers. Unfortunately, his disease relapsed so he decided to to return to Japan. He traveled home by ship and in Egypt met an Indian yogi by the name of Kaliapa. He returned with him to the Himalayas (the village of Gorkhe at the foot of the third peak of sacred Mount Kanchenjunga) to study Kaliapa's yoga (some mix of Raja Yoga and Karma Yoga) for over two years. His tuberculosis disappeared. He returned to Japan, bringing his yoga (and other studies)-inspired meditation, exercises and philosophy. He became a prominent businessman but in 1919, at forty-three years old, abandoned his social status and fortune to teach *Shin-shin-toitsu-do* full time, becoming a very famous and respected teacher in Japan to both its elite and its ordinary citizens. Nakamura Sensei died on December 1, 1968 at the age of ninety-two. The *Tempu Kaikan* (Tempu Society Hall) is on the grounds of *Gokokuji* temple in Tokyo. (For more see www.tempukai.or.jp.)

[353] I say traditional Japanese culture because I have read of concerns by some Japanese intellectuals that modern Japanese are losing this sensibility. Their overstimulating modern urban existence, their twenty-year battering of bad economic news, their dwindling involvement in traditional Japanese art forms are all (purportedly) contributing to the decline. For me, the tightly packed urban existence, the frenetic pace make the small, slow and subtle all the more stark, arresting and then calming. Indeed the amount of wealth destruction since the Japanese economic bubble is staggering, but Japan is a helluva lot better off than so many other places on the planet that I can't help wonder whether much of the hand-wringing is more the product of a state of mind than a state of fact. The bursting of the bubble itself—the layoffs, the lost affluence, the decline—can be viewed as modern *mono no aware*.

person or thing passed. You may hear the word on a night out relaxing and drinking with Japanese. "*Ah, sabishii!*" one may say in gentle sad recognition or reminiscence of someone or something. You may also hear *natsukashii* (懐か しい, なつかしい) which connotes a kind of dearness or longing or nos- talgia over something, someone or some time that's missed. *Sabishii* probably has an element of *shinmiri* (しんみり, solemnity, seriousness or sadness) that *natsukashii* lacks. In the eighteenth century, a Japanese academic actually coined a phrase for this aesthetic sensibility so intrinsic to Japanese culture—*mono no aware* (物の哀れ, もののあわれ).[354]   It's a combination of the Japanese word *mono*, meaning "thing or things," and *aware* meaning pity; sorrow; grief; misery; compassion; pathos; alack; alas. *Mono no aware* could be translated liter- ally as "the pathos (or poignancy) of things" and connotes a heightened aes- thetic awareness and appreciation of the fleeting nature of beauty and a gentle sadness over its passing.

The *Heike Monogatari* (*The Tale of the Heike Clan*) begins with:
> The sound of the Gion *shoja* bells echo the imperma- nence of all things; the color of the *sola* flowers reveals the truth that the prosperous must decline. The proud do not endure, they are like a dream on a spring night; the mighty fall at last, they are as dust before the wind.

The wistful feeling could arise in response to an inanimate object, a living thing, another person or a particular sense, like hearing the *Gion shoja* bells. Flowers and cherry blossoms in particular are the archetypal *mono no aware*

---

[354] *Mono no aware* was identified in the works of eighteenth century literary and linguistic scholar Norinaga Motoori (1730-1801) as an imperative of Japanese thought and artistic expression. *Norinaga* sensei was a member of a nationalist movement (*Kokugakushu*) that sought to distill indigenous Japanese culture from its foreign influences (principally Chinese at the time). In its day, the movement was highly influential on artists and intellectuals and even inspired a Shinto revival. They studied ancient Japanese texts, e.g., *Genji Monogatari* (*The Tale of Genji*), *Man'yôshû* (*Myriad Leaves*, the eighth century collection of Japanese poetry) and other works for intrinsically Japanese values. Norinaga sensei named an aesthetic ensconced in Japanese art, music, poetry and other thought. Ironically, the "foreign influence" Zen Buddhism prob- ably helped shape the notion of *mono no aware*. Buddhist notions that life is unsatisfactory, im- personal and impermanent found fertile ground in Japan, an island chain of limited resources under threat from natural forces: earthquakes, typhoons, volcanoes and tsunami, with a ruling warrior class who might have to forfeit their lives (or take the life of another) in an instant.

objects, blooming for days before withering and dying. Some writers describe it as the "the 'ahh-ness' of things" or the "oh" moment, but I can't hear the inflection which makes all the difference in interpreting the description. I suppose it's the kind of quiet sound one might unconsciously say aloud to oneself in calmly realizing something or a moment of poignancy.

I experienced periodic *mono no aware* moments in practice (and otherwise). In a morning class where Fujimaki san (now Fujimaki *shihan*) and I were practicing in the back right corner of the dojo (if facing the *tokonoma*), the clouds suddenly parted and the sun blazed through the back window onto the two of us. He stopped abruptly, as did I, gazing momentarily out the back window. A sunrise in the Land of the Rising Sun. Just as suddenly, the clouds closed. "Oh!" One evening practice, Matsuda sensei was demonstrating technique as the remnant of a spring storm was passing overhead; with the old wall-mounted steel fans and worn metal-framed sliding windows rattling with each gust of wind, faint thunder rumbled in the distance. Never again. It's not a term I've heard any Japanese ever use in daily conversation, but then again not many Westerners walk around saying Schadenfreude either.[355]

Come fall 1998 at Hombu Dojo, there would be other inescapable reminders of life's transience. Moving deeper into that autumn, Second Doshu Ueshiba Kishomaru became increasingly unwell. He had taught most of the morning classes and Friday evenings when I arrived in Japan, but his health would slowly fade. We are born, bloom and grow, then slide into entropy. Human decline may be an inescapable fact of life but that doesn't make it any less sad to witness or the eventual loss any less painful. I'll never forget his graceful movement, his calm but penetrating gaze, his presence, elegance and dignity as a man. He was in every sense the leader of The Way. Not only a man, but an era would be passing when the season finally turned.

> Green and vibrant it grew
> Golden and bright it turned
> Brown and brittle it fell
> An autumn gust and gone.

---

[355] Schadenfreude came to English from German. Schaden (harm) + Freude (joy) meaning the satisfaction or pleasure felt at someone else's misfortune.

A Party Before Parting

会者定離, 送別会
(*Eshajori, Soubetsukai*)

> Progress comes to those who train and train;
> reliance on secret techniques will get you nowhere.
> —*Morihei Ueshiba, O-Sensei*

Tenarai (手習い, てならい) is another interesting Japanese word. It means learning or study, but more literally "hand learning," and in particular writing practice with a brush, because in Japan (as in China) that's how *kanji* were studied—by drawing them over and over and over again. For some things, you just have to "get your hands dirty." Watching or explaining is no substitute. You have to do it (a lot) to understand. Traditionally, much of Japanese learning required actually using your hands in patient, intricate and delicate ways to master a particularly difficult skill, hence the generally recognized Japanese ability concerning minute, refined and subtle detail.[356]   Martial arts demand this type of learning. Quite literally "hands on."

However, many other martial arts are a bit easier to learn than aikido.[357] Push-pull. Punch-kick. Turn your fist into a rock. Turn your shin into steel. Who's faster? Who's stronger? I'm not putting those arts down; just stating fact. Aikido takes a long time to learn basics and longer still to develop "usable" skills, if that's what you're after.[358] In addition to the

---

[356]   Intricate Shinto rituals, imported fine arts and crafts from Korea and China (and the local expression and improvement of them) which were learned via master and apprentice relations (requiring the ability to watch and copy before ever considering innovation), a geographic and cultural environment cultivating a mindset that small incremental improvements may assure survival, the arrival and assimilation of Zen Buddhism and notions that mastery requires a harmonious melding of mind and body and the value and beauty of simplicity have all contributed towards a cultural obsession with reducing things to their artistic and functional essence. Even with   tedious daily tasks, there is a Way.

[357]   Many, not all.

[358]   The term "usable" must be grounded in context. Many martial arts practitioners or enthusiasts are misguided in believing that match fighting in a ring is the litmus test of the "effectiveness" of any martial art. They couldn't be more wrong. "Spontaneous fighting" (unknown,

process of body conditioning and basic patterns of movement present in any martial art, there are the particular subtleties of: *ma-ai, kuzusu, musubu, tenkan, irimi, kokyu-ryoku,* etc.[359] A student must learn to understand the expansion and extension of muscle (as a third way after pushing and pulling). Then there is conditioning yourself to relax, while remaining "extended," and to move around your opponent's power rather than conflicting with it (and either overpowering or failing to overpower him). Add to that learning to coordinate movement to breath, inhalation and exhalation, as a way of increasing power and stability. And then, years of committing all of that to "muscle memory," whereby you no longer need to think it to do it. It's spontaneously reflexive.[360] The difficulty of aikido is part of what keeps practice so interesting over many years. That and its goals of human development: developing your body (*tai-iku,* 体育), developing your spirit (*ki-iku,* 気育), developing your ethics (*toku-iku,* 徳育), developing your intellect (*chi-iku,* 知育) and developing common sense (*jyoshiki no kanyo,* 常識 の 涵養) to which I would add (if training in a traditional dojo) developing your intuition or instinct (*chyokan,* 直感, *or kan,* 勘). Like life, each day, step by step, your skill grows a bit, hopefully. But to get there, to gain the benefits (narrow or broad), you have to do it, a lot. *Tenarai.*

As mentioned, "eighty percent of success is showing up," and I'd

---

ungoverned, uncontrolled opponents and environment) and "match fighting" (two skilled, specifically trained, rules-governed opponents in a controlled environment) are very different, as mentioned and discussed elsewhere.

[359] For non-*aikidoka,* the list is: spacing/timing, unbalancing, connecting, turning, entering and breath power.

[360] O-Sensei made weapons training a fundamental part of his personal regimen. In my view, appropriate weapons practice is key, if you want to fully develop your Aiki. Aikido can be very beneficial to a practitioner purely as *taijutsu kata keiko* (body technique forms practice). No doubt. However, *jo* and *bokken* training are vital to *tanren* (鍛錬, たんれん, tempering; forging; hardening; disciplining). Despite the delusions of many, you are not learning sword-fighting in *bokken* training. (Go take *koryu kenjutsu.*) It's a tool for further forging your body, mind and spirit, including: developing stronger micro-muscle connections throughout your body, increasing hand strength, teaching that softness and flexibility enhances speed, understanding angles of attack, cultivating calmness in the face of danger, training your eye to pick up (see) fast movement (a *bokken* is much faster than a fist or foot), muscle extension and expansion, breath in connection with movement, footwork, spacing and timing, the use of the hands as a sword to blend/deflect strikes, the importance of controlling the center-line, gaining understanding of linear and spiraling movement. It helps train and reinforce the essence of movements in *taijutsu* (body techniques).

shown up at Hombu Dojo for my hands-on learning. It's not rocket science. Go often. When you go, arrive on time. Greet people when you arrive. Hand in your membership card. Are your dues paid? Take off your shoes, put them away on the left wall, remembering where. Walk up to the second floor changing room if you're a woman and the third if you're a man.[361] Plonk 100 yen into one of the lockers. Stash your clothes and things. Put on a washed and clean uniform (that's in good repair). Step through the curtain (or front door for the ladies) into the third floor dojo, sit *seiza* and bow towards the *shomen*. Go to the back left wall (when facing the back) and hang your key on the key rack (remembering your key number). If class hasn't started, sit *seiza* and wait or warmup.[362] Don't chit-chat, like some do.[363] Painfully pedantic enough? You're smart. You know the drill. Show up. Behave. Train vigorously and mindfully, giving to your partner sincere effort. Do that much and you'll thrive.

By December, I had improved dramatically … just by showing up. My year at Hombu Dojo offered things you cannot duplicate elsewhere. Keenly stating the obvious, there were extraordinary teachers—Second Doshu and the various *shihan* who had been trained by O-Sensei. Hombu Dojo provided many more experienced partners and an unmatchable diversity of training partners: the members (foreign and domestic), the countless visitors from other parts of Japan, the stream of visitors from abroad "coming to Mecca." Not having to work meant an extraordinary amount of time on the mat.[364] Plus, the pace of class was faster.[365] The mats harder. Life "on foot" in Tokyo tougher. The weather an extra hardship. And so on. So far, it had been every bit (and then some) the forging experience I had hoped for. I was buzzing from it – feeling healthier, stronger and more alive than ever. As planned (and hoped), I had shaved life close, to its essentials, living deeply, "sturdily and Spartan-like,"

---

[361] If you're unsure, flip a coin.

[362] Some teachers have a warmup at the start of their class. Some don't.

[363] There are plenty of places to chat outside. Go to a coffee shop or for a beer after class.

[364] There's nothing special about me; anyone could do it if they have the time and finances.

[365] There were exceptions and my statement is no disrespect to my first dojo or any other dojo I have visited before or since. People at my first dojo practiced earnestly and energetically. The teacher seldom if ever "talked" during class. However, a smaller space with twelve to twenty-two people (who are well acquainted with each other and their practice) could not match the greater dynamics of fifty, sixty, seventy people on the mat all excited to be practicing at the global HQ.

sucking "all the marrow out of life."[366] But my sabbatical year was into the homestretch, hard charging towards the finish line. Being mindful that "for everything there is a season, and a time for every matter under heaven" wasn't much consolation, even if, yes, everything has its natural spacing and timing.[367] I wanted more. Of everything.

I had come for intensive martial arts training, but there were so many other enriching aspects to life in Tokyo. There was the simplicity: walking, shopping and eating locally, and not missing a car (or insurance payments, fuel prices, parking fees or tickets) at all.[368] There were new friends at Hombu Dojo, not just from Japan but all four corners of the Earth: Argentinians and Nigerians, Japanese and Canadians, French and Singaporeans, Australians and Iraqis, Israelis and Kiwis and on. The best name ever was a Nigerian pal's: "Honey Jones." The best homeland story? A South African goes canoeing one day on the local river, and the wife opts to stay home at the last minute. Fast-forward to him paddling gently down the stream. CHOMP; a hippo bites the canoe in half, right where the Mrs. would've been.[369] I learned a lot that year. Apparently, every Israeli that ever visits Hombu Dojo is a former special forces operative; nobody's a potato-peeling private during their military service. (Uh-huh.) And Canadians really do finish sentences with "eh," run "organ-I-za-tions" and love their beer.[370] Usually this gathering of *gaijin* exuded a genuine, warm sense of community and consideration for its members, particularly in moments of crisis.[371] An American friend's apartment building, near the

---

[366] Henry David Thoreau in *Walden; or, Life in the Woods*, Chapter II *Where I Lived, and What I Lived For*. See www.barnesandnoble.com/w/walden-henry-david-tho-reau/1100200393?ean=9780807014257&itm=1&usri=henry%252bdavid%252bthoreau#MeetTheWriter or http://thoreau.library.ucsb.edu/.

[367] "For everything there is a season, and a time for every matter under heaven." Ecclesiastes, Chapter 3 Verse 1, English Standard Version (2001) of the Bible.

[368] This was true despite my being a car enthusiast. The superb BBC "petrol head" show Top Gear is a favorite. Being one of those three presenters has to be one of the best (most fun) jobs on earth. www.top-gear.com/uk/.

[369] This robust South African guy always had great stories, like the black mamba who curled up for a nap on a fellow sleeping soldier's head while his platoon was out in the bush on maneuvers. Great fun to practice with, too. Strong like Cape Buffalo.

[370] The hockey goes without saying.

[371] People are people, and I witnessed periodic acts of pettiness, intolerance and meanness; maybe some would allege I committed some. Years later, I would personally experience a very senior student behaving with small-minded shame in the midst of my wife's medical emergency. It was shocking (but not surprising) to see someone stoop so low to fulfill some perverse sense of revenge, even if seeking revenge and avoiding confrontation, discussion and

dojo, burned to the ground in 1997, and many of us banded together to help her, as did the locals. A student visiting with a tour from New York Aikikai became ill suddenly and had to be hospitalized. A number of us Hombu locals took on "bed watch" duties so the other touring students could enjoy their trip around Japan. Years later, during an emergency, my wife and I would receive extraordinary personal support from the dojo's teachers and students (both Japanese and foreign). It was a degree of support that's not easily if ever repayable. For me, Hombu Dojo proved remarkable in more ways than merely on the mats.

So the question that December was, what to do? What next? In life, knowing when to stop can be every bit as important as knowing when to start. Everything has its *ma-ai*, its spacing and timing. If you live in Tokyo, it's important for your well-being to know when to leave. Short restorative breaks are key to avoid being overwhelmed at some point. And, living overseas, it's important to know when to leave for home. The ten-year mark was a typical "sell-by date" for many foreigners. You could see them becoming increasingly bitter and short tempered. Having had to follow so many rules in Japan, they'd become rigid sticklers for rules and would get irritated by small things they used to tolerate (if they used to notice them at all): whether it's the crowded trains, the lemming-like mentality of the locals or "Sheeple" (as some *gaijin* end up calling them) or the ano-nymity and alienation of being "different" in a land of conformity.[372] Maybe some of the very things they used to find exciting or charming become annoying ... at a lower and lower flashpoint, with rising levels of accelerant. The trigger might be the relentless pace of Tokyo, the feigned manners, the suppressed feelings or the banal conversations. I've had "overripe" friends knock lit cigarettes out of the mouths of people while waiting on train or subway platforms (pointing to the "No Smoking" signs) and otherwise slip into a whole list of anti-social behaviors you couldn't have imagined them doing years before.[373] Other than their states of

---

resolution is "very Japanese." All this guy accomplished was to embarrass himself, sully his reputation in the community and reveal the hypocrisy in his years of *budo* training. Contemplated knocking his teeth in, but ... pitied him and quietly forgave him instead. Compassion isn't always easy, but forgiveness has been extended to me so many times, how can I do less?

[372] "Sheeple" are people who display passive, herd, sheep-like behavior.

[373] It's a no smoking area! I heard that one *shihan*, ages ago, saw someone smoking on his train car and walked over and put his hand over the smoker's mouth, pushing the cigarette inside and extinguishing it.

mind, things aren't really any different than when they arrived. Most of them realize it's their problem. Sometimes it pops out on the mat. Basically, someone needs a "timeout!"

So it's December, it's getting colder and, if you're from the West, some things in town start to look familiar for that time of year. For a country that expelled or executed ninety-nine percent of its *Kirishitan* (吉利支丹, キリシタン) population centuries ago, modern-day Japanese go in "with both *geta* on" for Christmas. Sure, it's heavy on the Santa and shopping and light on the "for unto us a child is born" bits, but my sense is that in addition to retailers seeking sales, the Japanese genuinely enjoy the festive spirit and iconic imagery of the season, be it secular or sacred.[374] [375] So whether you feel that "every idiot who goes about with 'Merry Christmas' on his lips, should be boiled with his own pudding, and buried with a stake of holly through his heart" or you "honour Christmas in [your] heart, and try to keep it all the year ... Past, the Present, and the Future," you will get a hefty serving of ho-ho-ho and hallelujah in Tokyo.[376] Whether it's the 900,000+ lights twinkling in the 150-plus *keyaki* trees lining über-fashionable Omotesando Boulevard or other illuminations around town: the fifteen-meter tall Christmas tree at the base of the Tokyo Tower, a Godzilla-shaped Christmas tree in a shopping mall, wandering singing Santa Clauses or the slightly disturbing Karaoke hit "*My Lover is Santa Claus*" (which sounds an awful lot like "my rubber is ..." when crooned by the locals), one thing is clear.[377] "Tis the season to be jolly." In Japan, Christmas Eve has somehow morphed into a romantic evening out for couples, and Christmas Day includes exchanging gifts and the inexplicable tradition of eating buckets of Kentucky Fried Chicken at home with the family. It's

---

[374] "Santa Claus is coming to town," says the The King at www.youtube.com/watch?v=OIF_rXj7mag. It may have been said many times, many ways, but ever sung better? ww.youtube.com/watch?v=l5s8h2d1RK8

[375] "For unto us a child is born, unto us a son is given: and the government shall be upon his shoulder: and his name shall be called Wonderful, Counsellor, The mighty God, The everlasting Father, The Prince of Peace." Isaiah 9:6 http://scripturetext.com/isaiah/9-6.htm. Set to music by Handel (www.youtube.com/watch?v=BHy78rXTwEA or www.youtube.com/watch?v=vn5Tjo_8llE) and foretelling the birth of the rebel Jesus. www.youtube.com/watch?v=PEC7d5jbAbo

[376] The quotation is from *A Christmas Carol* by Charles Dickens, first published by Chapman & Hall in December 1843. See www.stormfax.com/1dickens.htm.

[377] *Keyaki* (欅, ケヤキ) Japanese zelkova (*zelkova serrata*) are a species of elm-like tree.

KFC's biggest day of the year in Japan.[378] [379] Cakes are popular desserts on the twenty-fifth of December, and that tradition has birthed the rather cruel expression of referring to an unmarried woman who is twenty-six years or older *kurisumasu ke-ki* (クリスマスケーキ, Christmas Cake). After the twenty-fifth, nobody wants it.[380]

Despite the festive fare on offer in Tokyo, Christmas is particularly important in my family, so I flew back to the U.S. In late December '97 to join our celebration and hopefully gain perspective. But when I returned to Tokyo, what then? The same question would be waiting for me. Of course, I would have through the month of January to decide before my "sabbatical year" was complete.[381] And what of teaching aikido? I had arrived with questions. Had I found fulfilling answers? Would I be returning to Tokyo to say farewell? Well, if it was farewell, then I knew I would have a strong few months of training and a proper sendoff. The Japanese do that well: throw a party. Skeptical? The flawed impression that many Westerners (and even some "Easterners") seem to share about Japanese people is that they are very reserved, very self-controlled and not much fun. Context, context, context. It's all a matter of when and where and with who. Sure, generally speaking, Japanese can be remarkably (and admirably) composed and reserved, but when it's time to celebrate, they can cut loose with the best.[382] Still doubting, Thomas?

I've already mentioned Japanese *matsuri*. If you're unconvinced, here's one for you. Years after '97, I attended an unbelievable winter festival at Nozawa-onsen, a famous skiing and hotspring spot in Nagano ken.[383] Our snowboarding weekend coincided with the local fire festival or *Dousojin Matsuri* held every evening of January 15 since the mid-nineteenth century. It's a Shinto rite to secure a plentiful harvest, health and good fortune in the coming year by honoring *Dousojin*, a *kami* of fecundity and

---

[378] Lending credence to Stuart MacKenzie's conspiracy theory that the Colonel ("before he went tets up") puts an addictive chemical in his chicken that makes you crave it fortnightly? www.youtube.com/watch?v=TPMS6tGOACo

[379] If you think about it, though, the inexplicable becomes explicable. Most Japanese housing doesn't have an oven big enough for a turkey or a goose, so? Bucket o' chicken and all the fixin's is the closest available avian feast.

[380] After the twenty-fifth, she's past the expiration date and no longer marriage material. Thankfully, it's a bit dated now.

[381] Actually, so long as I had and I didn't mind spending money, I could stay and train as long as I liked.

[382] Right up there with Australians, the Irish, Koreans and Mexicans in my experience.

[383] See http://nozawakanko.jp/spot/dousozin.php or http://nozawakanko.jp/english/.

fertility (among other things).[384]   Simplifying the details of all the rituals and festivities, in the autumn of the preceding year, the twenty-five and forty-two-year-old men of the village hike the hills, deep into the forest, felling five tall sacred beech trees, trimming off the branches and joyously dragging the massive logs down the slopes through the snow to the village to build the *shaden* that is constructed annually for the ceremony.[385] Erected in an open lot adjacent to the village, the felled trees form the base and tall center poles of the wooden shrine. The ten-meter-high *shaden* has an unmistakable upright Y-shape with an evergreen branch roof that overhangs its thinner recessed wooden base. It bears resemblance to something familiar, something anatomically female, that I can't quite recall. Hmmmm.[386]   Several meters away, up a low gradual slope, stands a tall stalk of bundled dry sticks. It bears resemblance to something familiar, something anatomically male, that I can't quite recall. Hmmmm. Before the climactic event, a Shinto priest visits to perform a ritual endowing the shrine with a *kami*. Complimenting the shrine are several towering *tôrô standing and swaying near the front*. These elaborately decorated dedicatory red lanterns, sitting atop long thin poles and festooned with *kanji*-covered streamers dangling below, are donated by families in the village to celebrate the birth of first sons.

On the evening of the fifteenth, braving the elements, a crowd of locals and tourists begins gathering slightly uphill of the *shaden*. About seven p.m., *hanabi* (fireworks) are launched skyward to help open ceremonies. "BOOM!!! Crackle-crackle-crackle." "Oooooh." "BOOM!!! Crackle-crackle-crackle." "Aaaaah," go the exploding rockets and boisterous crowd in call and response. Sake is flowing liberally through the spectators (and copiously through the participants), thanks to the generous pouring by smiling local old men, some dressed in little more than a *happi*

---

[384] *Dousojin* can go by other names and is also a deity protecting travelers and children whose small stone sculptures can be seen along some Japanese roadsides. (道祖神, どうそじん). The word is comprised of *Dou*, 道, which you should recognize, meaning roadway; street; district; journey; course; moral or teachings; and *So* 祖 ancestor; pioneer; founder; and *Jin* 神 gods; mind or soul.

[385] A *shaden* (社殿, しゃでん) is a Shinto shrine.

[386] You can see the construction in a video on a Nozawa Onsen tourist site at http://nozawakanko.jp/english/event/ and a great shot of it going up in flames at www.youtube.com/watch?v=ShuTodHReOI.

coat and a headband. Some have a communal cup hanging from a string around their neck, in case you forgot yours, and if you're a foreigner, prepare for a bit of slurred "Engrish" practice while receiving your complimentary pour. The air is crisply cold, the sake refreshingly dry and the mood of the crowd crackly combustible. Men of the "unlucky" age of forty-two have clambered up the shrine and are now perched on top. Some are armed with meter-long evergreen branches. Like the *tôrô*, they sway back and forth (but in the *oji-san's* case, it's from rice wine lubrication), clapping, chanting and singing. The likewise unfortunately aged twenty-five-year-olds take up formation in front of the opening at the base of the *shaden*, pine branches gripped tightly, ready to defend it and their seniors upstairs.[387] From who? From what?

Soon, it's apparent. Up the slope in the snow, the tall, dry, stick stalk is ignited. From that bonfire, the villagers start lighting torches and, after some calm ceremonial attempts by young boys and their fathers to light the *shaden,* which are politely rebuffed by the defenders, an attack is launched in earnest. Now, I am not making this up. First one and then another screaming villager hurls himself down the path towards the the *shaden* trying to shove his flaming torch into the Y and set the shrine alight. The younger men defend the elders atop the tower by beating out the torches (and the attackers holding them) with the evergreen branches.[388] Sparks fly everywhere! Faces are smeared with soot. There's a concerted cry from the collective unconsciousness of mothers around the world of "Stop! You'll put your eye out!!" But, incredibly, the battle intensifies. More villagers. More torches. More shoving flaming sticks into the *shaden.* More oooh-ing and aaaah-ing from the crowd. More bashing of the attackers. The クレイジーゾーン (Ku-rei-zhee-Zon, Crazy Zone) in front of the *shaden* is now a frenzy of flying embers, flame, smoke, swinging torches and swatting pine branches. Like defenders of some medieval fortress wall, the elders are raining down abuse and sticks and cups of sake onto the attackers. Maybe it's the sake, but I swear I heard, "You

---

[387] By some cultural numerology, twenty-five and forty-two years old are believed to be unlucky ages for men, so they are chosen to build and defend the shrine.

[388] Why no women? Among other things, are not women far too sensible for this sort of completely mental behavior?

don't frighten us … you empty-headed animal food trough wipers!"[389] Nobody is holding back; it's all being left on the playing field, but somehow Japanese seem to still know how much is too far. I was watching and thinking that in the U.S. fistfights (or worse) would've broken out, but the local tribesmen played recklessly with fire without overstepping the rules of engagement.

About an hour after launching the assault, the attackers prevail. A resistant flicker appears on the shrine, then another; the flickers become flames and the flames burn to a blaze. The forty-two-year-olds descend (which is French for leaping or falling) onto the snow meters below. This pyromaniac's wet dream ends as the shrine is engulfed in roaring flames, completing the offering to the Gods. The *tôrô* are each tossed onto the raging pyre, and by now any fair-minded *kami* has to be pleased as hell and muttering, "Well done lads, well done. One good harvest coming right up." The intense heat forces the equally "well lit" spectators to move to safer ground, as the wind whips sparks and embers through the air. People count casualties and even those not in the Crazy Zone search each others' hair and clothes for signs of combustion.[390] It's been nearly two hours of absolute madness and mayhem—but unrestrained fun and a massive release. The power and energy of it has to be experienced to be believed. Why is it that the pagans always seem to have such a good time? As we crunched through the snow back to our inn, I remarked to my wife that in the U.S., everyone would be arrested and then sued. Or, shot first, then arrested and then sued.

Believe it; Japanese are experts at all sorts of "festive" occasions, including "slightly" more subdued parties, to mark all kinds of occasions. Back in '97, my sabbatical year was into December the season of "forget-the-year-parties" or *bōnenkai*.[391] *Bōnenkai* aren't held by everyone in Japan on a specific day but typically occur during the last two to four weeks of December. As the year winds down, the members of perhaps every conceivable kind of group in society gather together to celebrate by forgetting the troubles and hardships of

---

[389] See e.g., castle defenders at www.youtube.com/watch?v=QSo0duY7-9s&feature=fvwrel.

[390] The next day people went to the field to cook *mochi* (rice cakes) in the still smoldering embers of the *shaden*.

[391] 忘年会, ぼうねんかい, year-end party is comprised of 忘 (ぼう, *bou*) meaning in this case forget plus 年 (ねん, *nen*) year and 会 (かい, *kai*) meaning party (in this instance).

the passing year. Celebration as catharsis. So, it's *bōnenkai* season. Restaurants and *izakaya* are filled and especially boisterous. Taxis are scarcer at night, particularly if you are a male *gaijin*. Drinking casualties seem higher, as passed-out salarymen lay sprinkled on the sidewalks, in the stations and on trains, like a line of breadcrumbs leading homeward. A person living in Japan may be a member of several "groups," e.g., co-worker, aikidoka, classmate, hobbyist, club member, old friends, etc. and can look forward to a lighter wallet, expanding waistline and multiple hangovers from numerous *bōnenkai*.[392] To me, these parties are not only celebration as catharsis but serve to clearly demarcate past from future and help the group refocus on matters going forward—the tasks at hand. Many times, the same people who are meeting for a *bōnenkai* in December will be meeting in a few weeks for a *shinnenkai* in January to ring in the New Year. "But I just saw you!" "Oh, that's so last year."[393]

I wasn't working for a Japanese company, so I had been spared a *kamikinoukai* (上期納会, かみきのうかい) or first half (of the fiscal) year party and the six months following *noukai* (納会, のうかい) or final meeting of the year party. Two snoozefests; not one![394] If you "get" to attend one someday, expect some boozing and a meal and eventually the boss will make a lengthy speech that includes thanking everyone for their sincere efforts. The evening is often punctuated with a celebratory clap (*tejime*), waking everyone up and closing the event emphatically.[395] It can seem stiffly scripted (it often is), but these get-togethers do seem to nurture the spirit of the group positively, which is the fundamental point. I learned that year, too, that most parties in Japan, regardless of name, have a *nijikai* (二次会, にじかい) or second party, where

---

[392] Like many Japanese get-togethers, the bill tends to be split into equal shares for each attendee, so eat and drink up. Taxi drivers will often skip the *gaijin* flagging them down in hopes of nabbing salarymen too drunk or too late for a train home. Try not to take it personally. It's business.

[393] 新年会 (しんねんかい) New Year's party is comprised of 新 (シン, *shin*) plus 年 (ネン, *nen*) and (かい, *kai*) once again meaning party (in this instance). *Shinenkai* are social gatherings akin to *bonenkai* in terms of locations and attendees and shouldn't be confused with traditional, family O-shogatsu holidays (January 1-3).

[394] The objective is to have a more relaxed gathering for food, drink, celebration and discussion of company and casual topics plus to bond further; however in practice such events (and other things in Japan) can have the feeling of obligatory ceremony or role-play rather than the stated objective. I wouldn't loosen up too much if I were you.

[395] *Tejime* (手締め, てじめ) or *teuchi* (手打ち, てうち) is a Japanese custom of hand clapping, usually performed in a three-beat rhythm, to seal and signify the end of a special event. *Clap-clap-clap; clap-clap-clap; clap-clap-clap; clap!* www.youtube.com/watch?v=_cqH8EWgJ8

the diehards continue on into the night after the official festivities end. Such second helpings can last until you find yourself stumbling out into the early morning sunlight (the sun rises early in Tokyo) to the grating "caw-caw-caw" of a flock of sneering crows hopping about and picking over the sacks of garbage left out on the curb for a.m. collection.

So if January '98 was going to be my last month in Japan, at least I could look forward to a proper sendoff.[396] A farewell party is probably a universal cultural expression, but in Japan, as with so many things, it has a specific name, *soubetsukai*.[397] The *modus operandi* is familiar. Restaurant, *izakaya* or bar. Members of a group. Food and booze, chats and laughs, speeches and staggering home. In the case of a foreigner leaving Hombu Dojo for home, they are generally sincerely congenial events. However, people are people, so you'll get partygoers who will sincerely miss you, those who feign that they will sincerely miss you (at which the Japanese are champions) and those who are there for the beer.[398] For Japanese, leaving a group isn't an easy thing (though it's becoming easier), particularly an employment relationship. I learned years later that in such instances, as the evening progresses and the drinks flow at a *soubetsukai*, feelings both positive and negative may surface. Particularly if the person is leaving a company voluntarily and is going to arguably better employment, there may be some jealousy. It may come out at the party. Remember; in Japan, little hints and comments that you as a foreigner don't think much of can be the tip of an iceberg of emotion. Japanese rarely talk about what they really think or feel, so put enough alcohol in them and raw emotions can erupt … even with aikido people. I've seen a teacher throw a bottle at a student before, people punch each other (or nearly) and so on. Usually, it's all forgotten (or re-repressed) the next day. If you are receiving the farewell, you'll have to give a *sayonara* speech, during

---

[396] Please don't misunderstand. I don't condone reckless conspicuous consumption. I've seen alcohol ruin people both in Japan and elsewhere. Use your head.

[397] 送別会, そうべつかい, farewell party is comprised of 送 (ソウ, sou) to escort or send plus 別 (ベツ, betsu) separate; branch off; diverge and 会 (カイ) meeting; meet; party; association; interview; join.

[398] In terms of feigning affection or praise, the Japanese best even public-school educated Englishmen and High-South Americans; just. "Why Miss Maddie I do declare that is the most extraordinary Sunday hat I have eva seen!" (I'm amazed anyone would be seen alive wearing it.) Japanese are masters of the seemingly complimentary or neutral statement that is neither: "Oh, *Wi-ree-ya-mu san* (ウイリアム, William) your Japanese is amazing" (meaning it sucks).

which you may get some good-natured laughing and heckling while you thank everyone and apologize for leaving them. Remember to duck if you glimpse a Sapporo bottle flying your way!

In fairness, most such celebrations are not so unrestrained, particularly if organized by a notable company or organization. In 1998, I attended a particularly well-mannered, meaningful and slightly poignant party in Tokyo. It was November and held at a hotel near Hombu Dojo in a spacious ballroom with golden beige wallpaper and two ornate, overly lit crystal chandeliers. Even if you've never been in that room, you've been in its nondescript double in some hotel somewhere. What was special about the event wasn't the place but the person—the guest of honor—and the people hosting the party. It had been organized for Doshu Ueshiba Kishomaru by the "old guard" of The Morning Class. Due to his honored status, Doshu was usually surrounded by attendants whenever he went out. Public appearances were typically very formal, but not on that evening at that event. Some of the partygoers had known each other for forty, fifty years, maybe more, so there was a noticeable warmth to the festivities as old friends met yet again, joyfully eating, drinking and speaking with their teacher—the leader of the Way. Doshu's health had not been good, and looking back now it does seem a farewell of sorts or, more accurately, a respectful, warm and deeply appreciative final group "thank you." A mindful observer would recognize the unmistakable *mono no aware* moment.

A female foreign student at Hombu, who always seemed to know what was happening at the dojo, had invited me to go with her. Anyone could go, and it was very well attended, but I was shocked that my friend and I were the only foreign students to attend.[399] Two. There was a fee, of course, but consider who the party was for? And the timing? Sometimes, we foreigners deserve to be labeled "strange." Days later, I saw Ueshiba Moriteru sensei (current Doshu) at the dojo, and he stopped and thanked me profusely for attending. As usual, in speaking with Doshu, I idiotically stumbled over my words in reply: "It was nothing; of course; it was a <u>very</u> important event."[400]

---

[399] My big white head is "hiding" in the back of the group photo.

[400] Perhaps it was the language. I've never been able to figure out why I usually became tongue-tied around Doshu. As a former trial lawyer and son of a preacher, I've never feared speaking

As it turned out, not much more than a month later, while I was a universe away, once again wrapping up the Christmas festivities with four generations of family in Princeton, I received the terribly sad (but not surprising) news that Doshu, Ueshiba Kishomaru, had passed away on January 4, 1999. Wow. Doshu, leader of the Way, gone. O-Sensei's son. I'll repeat that: "O-Sensei's son"—because some people fail (or refuse) to recognize the significance, mentioning it like it's some meaningless factoid, "He had a cat."[401] He was O-Sensei's son. His third son albeit, but the son who followed in his father's footsteps, the son who he designated to lead the Way. I've heard and read a lot of conjecture over the years about Hombu Dojo and Aikikai. Some people have "issues" it seems, like Hombu's not teaching "O-Sensei's aikido" and so on. However, I repeat; Second Doshu was O-Sensei's son. Never underestimate the significance of that relationship, particularly in a culture so acutely attuned to the recognition and respect of relationships. It's for time-tested reasons that people say "blood is thicker than water."

I don't get too fussed when I read or hear opinions concerning Aikikai or Hombu Dojo. In my culture at least, people have a right to speak their mind. Right or wrong. However, as a lawyer, I always read (or listen to) anything with an eye (or ear) for bias.[402]   Does the author/speaker have an "agenda?" Is (s)he truly impartial?   I wonder, how has this person's relationship with Hombu Dojo been over the years? Any past disagreements? Any lingering resentments? Any personal objectives? To me, it's completely rational that students of O-Sensei received different things in their training with him at different times of his life. It doesn't follow, however, that this person or that time period is better or tougher or more original or any of the other various contentions that people toss about. I'm ever mindful that O-Sensei (or someone else very astute who attributed it to him) reportedly said, "Instructors can impart only a fraction

---

up. I'd been admitted to practice law and appeared numerous times in U.S. federal court, and there are few things more dangerous than a U.S. district court judge. They are appointed "for life" and can fine you heavily (or throw you in jail) for any number of errors in their courtrooms. "What's the difference between God and a federal district court judge?" "God doesn't think he's a federal district court judge."

[401] It's rhetorical; I don't know whether or not he had a cat.

[402] It's wise generally to listen to what people have to say, whether you accept it or not. Nothing anyone says about aikido is "holy writ" of some kind. In the end, you must find your own way, while rendering "Caesar what is Caesar's."

of the teaching. It is through your own devoted practice that the mysteries of aikido are brought to life." Politics, outside the political arena, aren't to my liking, so I let organizations do their thing and learn whatever I can from whomever I can.

Hombu Dojo has no equal, in many ways, being distinct from dojos run by a single *shihan,* for example. It's not as much a solo as it is a choir.[403] It's also a very big place. As the membership has grown over the years, has the teaching been aimed to reach the broadest audience possible?[404] When training there, I'm mindful that although the mat is filled, there are probably as many different personal training objectives as there are students on the mat.[405] For some, aikido is a martial art first and foremost, if not solely. For others, it's a method of using martial arts *kata keiko* to achieve broader purposes befitting modern society: developing the body, mind and spirit positively. For others, it's both. People are seeking different things from their practice, which is true of the global aikido community. At Hombu (as anywhere), I adjust my practice according to the level of my partner so we can both train productively. *Aite no chikara awasu.*[406]

Remember that many of the teachers on the Hombu staff have dojos or other outside locations where they teach regularly in addition to their classes at Hombu Dojo. From all I've seen (which is hardly conclusive), Hombu Dojo seems fairly accommodating to its teaching staff when it comes to the curriculum in their classes (at least for senior teachers) but it's a Japanese organization (a group effort) under the supervision of a clear hierarchy. It might be fair, then, to think of a teacher's personal dojo

---

[403] Every choir has its conductor and section leads.

[404] Has aikido changed as it's been popularized and globalized? Is this the case with all martial arts? I've noticed a similar development with BJJ since first training in 1996 in Los Angeles at the old Rickson Gracie Academy.

[405] Maybe three times as many, since so many are confused.

[406] *Aite no chikara awasu* (相手の力合わす, あいてのちからあわす). First comes 相手 (*aite*) meaning: (1) companion; partner; company; (2) other party; addressee; (3) opponent. Add the possessive article の (*no*). Then comes 力 (*chikara*) meaning (1) force; strength; might; vigor; energy; (2) capability; ability; proficiency; capacity; faculty; (3) efficacy; effect; (4) effort; endeavors; exertions; (5) power; authority; influence; good offices; agency. Finally comes the verb 合わせる (*awaseru*) of 合わす (*awasu*) meaning to match (rhythm, speed, etc.); (2) to join together; to unite; to combine; to add up; (3) to face; to be opposite (someone); (4) to compare; to check with; (5) to cause to meet (e.g., an unpleasant fate); (6) to place together; to connect; to overlap; (7) to mix; to combine; (8) to put blade to blade; to fight. So one could interpret (or misinterpret) O-Sensei's purported statement in numerous ways, but without question, one interpretation would be to adjust your power for your partner (so you can train well together).

as a type of laboratory or "Skunk Works" where he's free to teach what and how he likes, including weapons, or otherwise experiment.[407] If you want to study deeply with a particular *shihan* from Hombu Dojo, you might try to attend practice at his personal dojo or visit other places outside of Hombu Dojo where he teaches. By all means, be an enthusiastic dedicated student but not a ストーカー (*su-tou-kaa*, stalker).

As for regular practice at Hombu Dojo, you can gripe or take advantage of what's there. In my experience, training offered tremendous advantages: the unremitting emphasis on basics, the regularity of *suwari-waza*, the diversity of teachers and numerous training partners. Practice could be as challenging as I wanted to make it: by attending particular practices, by selecting certain partners, by setting a pace with *ukemi* (getting back up rapidly), by studying what I should study rather than what I wanted to study, by practicing on days when I didn't really feel like it, etc. Most of these are things you can do in your home dojo, but the scale and other qualities of Hombu Dojo multiply the possibilities and benefits. In the end, if you go, you'll experience Hombu Dojo for yourself, but what you experience and how you experience it will depend to a great degree on your effort and attitude, which is the case with so many things in life. There's no one intimidating you to pay attention, cajoling you to learn or pandering to you to stay. What you make of the opportunity is up to you. You have to take initiative and responsibility for your own study.

One simple drill I used, without telling my partner, was to tinker with *ma-ai* throughout the class, working from a distance that was intentionally too close to easily avoid a strike. I'd struggle to move quicker and quicker and quicker until I could avoid the strike or almost.[408] Adjusting back to a proper *ma-ai*, the attack seemed slower now. I would intentionally break

---

[407] "Skunk Works" became the nickname of aircraft designer Lockheed Martin's Advanced Development Programs (ADP), which created famous aircraft, such as the U-2, the SR-71 Blackbird, the F-117 Nighthawk, and the F-22 Raptor. The term has become widely used in business, particularly technical fields, for any specialized R&D group within a larger organization who, liberated from bureaucracy and management constraints, are free to develop innovative projects. The alias was borrowed from the name of the Kentucky backwoods factor—Skonk Works—in the satirical, hillbilly comic strip Li'l Abner by American cartoonist Al Capp, who brewed a bootleg drink Kickapoo Joy Juice from secret ingredients including dead skonks (skunks). http://lil-abner.com/dogpatch-and-dogpatch-u-s-a/

[408] Do this and you're going to get hit, so accept it and set your ego aside.

the timing of my practice as well. Aikido practice can become too met-ronomic and as a result more artificial because you can anticipate the at-tack better because, consciously or not, you have memorized the timing. Likewise, if my training partner was considerably smaller, I would try to be as quick and light as I could be. If my partner was bigger, I would work on *kuzushi*, trying to use as little strength as possible, scrutinizing each throw (by me or my partner) for points to polish, trying not to get caught in the dualistic trap of: "fell down = I won" and "didn't fall down = I lost."[409] I was ever challenging myself by trying to make practice uncomfortable or unpredictable. Yes; sometimes, unavoidably, there's such a mismatch in physique, experience and skill that, as *nage*, practice may feel like throwing tissue for an hour.[410] Still, I'd try to overcome neg-ative or destructive impulses and search for something positive, e.g., work on my *ukemi*. Anyone can moan and complain.

Returning to the life (and death) of 2nd Doshu, what do you think the son of O-Sensei received from his father? Nothing? O-Sensei gave his son less than he gave to others? Doshu just developed Hombu Dojo without consulting his father? Without trying to please his father?[411] I'm mindful, too, that creating controversy helps attract an audience and sell things, e.g., website memberships, e-zines, books, DVDs, etc. Not judgin'; just sayin'. Remember. This was O-Sensei's son. Doshu was also very well educated, intelligent and shrewd.[412] He was instrumental in skillfully shaping the basic curriculum at Hombu Dojo, training generations of in-structors, spreading aikido locally and globally, writing histories and tech-nical books of aikido and otherwise serving in so many ways the art cre-ated by his father and, in turn, its worldwide community of teachers and

---

[409] Perhaps *kuzushi* is the wrong word in the case of aikido, as it implies an aggressive destruction rather than harmonious movement that imbalances the *uke* (koo-zoo-shee, 崩す、くずす、(1) to destroy; to demolish; to pull down; to tear down; to level; (2) to disturb; to put into disor-der; to throw off balance; to make shaky...).

[410] Or, you're on the wrong end of the equation and are getting clubbed like a fur seal for sixty minutes.

[411] It's not a matter of who is the most physically talented? Or mentally gifted? Or who has the most attractive personality? You know that the greatest practitioners (in anything) aren't nec-essarily the best teachers. Some have a gift for expressing the art, others for transmitting it and some both.

[412] He graduated from one of Japan's top universities, Waseda University, in 1946 with a degree in economics.

students.[413] Practice today is built on the foundation of the toil, struggles and success of so many past technical, pedagogical and organizational greats, and Doshu's skill, among other things, helped hold it all together. But now, Doshu was gone. Another watershed in aikido. Yet another reminder of life's impermanence. *Eshajori* (会者定離, えしゃじょう り), "we meet only to part."[414]

Too often, for my liking anyway, it seems that *aikidoka* or maybe even martial artists in general don't feel they are being taught unless they are being wowed, scared, lectured or entertained. Doshu's teaching was so fundamental. Unshakably so. It was clear and precise, unadorned with personality to attract followers. Yet, attending his class you felt you were being permitted to participate in something very special. There was a seriousness but a liveliness to his classes. Practices were vigorous. How could you give less, considering who he was? How could you miss it, considering that he was up to teach at 06:30, on into his seventies? Good health or poor. I remember him one morning in 1994 standing over me, calmly watching as I was getting smeared by a particularly powerful *deshi*. Behind his calm, steady gaze I could see a flicker of concern but not alarm. He let us find our own way through practice. He didn't leap in judging our interaction as somehow overly rough or abusive. I reckoned the mats needed cleaning in that spot, and using me to wipe them was alright. Why waste a perfectly good rag?

So post-New Year 1999, I arrived back in Japan just after the

---

[413] In 1942, as he was relocating to Iwama, O-Sensei appointed Ueshiba Kishomaru head of the Kobukan Dojo in Shinjuku, Tokyo. Notably, Doshu was a student at Waseda University at the time, so he was young, yet O-Sensei entrusted him with his dojo. Doshu helped the dojo survive the war, including the fire bombings of Tokyo and deprivation that followed defeat. Following the war, he shuttled between *Iwama* and Tokyo working, studying and teaching. He oversaw the establishment of the Aikikai Foundation (財団法人合気会, *Zaidan Hōjin Aikikai*), the organization of aikido dojos in cities, towns, companies and universities all over Japan, the dispatch of *shihan* to teach around the world and the construction of the new headquarters in 1967 on the site of the Kobukan dojo. He guided the Aikikai through the regrettable departure of Tohei Koichi sensei in 1974 and on and on. He became a very poised and dignified figurehead for aikido during the post O-Sensei era and a "giant" in his own right.

[414] How do you say goodbye? I became acutely aware of this question when my own father died 5 November 2011, while I was in the midst of writing this chapter. The first affirmative step is to appreciate people and interact positively before they are gone. Whether you say it by deeds, words or both, leave nothing unsaid. Another is to honor their life by remembering them with affection and gratitude and living yours well. If your experience with them was bad, forgive them and live well despite.

otsuya held at Hombu Dojo on January sixth and the funeral ceremony, also at the dojo, on the next day.[415]   A multitude of people from all over the world attended the ceremonies, including the much larger public memorial held on January seventeenth at the Aoyama Funeral Hall in Tokyo.   It was a clear, cold and breezy day.   Attendance was overflowing, in the thousands.   It was a who's-who of the aikido world.   Gazing around at all the mourners, each neatly attired in the appropriately somber black of a Japanese funeral, you could see un-mistakably that aikido is an international family without separation by border, race, ethnicity, religion or creed.   Held in a large white tent, mourners entered from one end.   At the other end stood the *kamiza,* with a large photo of Doshu surrounded tastefully with floral ar-rangements.   A priest chanted, a brief biography was presented, and then the mourners queued to approach the alter, bow in respect, make a ceremonial offering of a fresh sprig of *sakaki,* then turn right and file past the seated family members to express condolences before exiting the tent.[416]   It was a beautifully simple and deeply moving commemoration of the second leader of aikido, the son of O-Sensei.

In the weeks following the funeral, the local aikido community was filled with deep sadness; understandably.   In the midst of it, I couldn't help but feel for Ueshiba Moriteru, who would become Third Doshu.[417] The death of a parent is a sad and surreal shock and all the more so if that parent is a public figure.   My father was famous in his field.   He was a Presbyterian minister, holding B.A., M. Div. and Ph.D. degrees (plus honorary ones from around the world), who became the Fifth President of Princeton Theological Seminary, perhaps the premiere theological in-stitution in America.[418]   I never felt the slightest pressure to follow him

---

[415]   An *Otsuya* (お通夜, おつや) is an all-night vigil over the body of the deceased, a Japanese wake, you could say.

[416]   *Sakaki* (*Cleyera japonica*) is a low-spreading, flowering evergreen tree (more a bush) found in warm areas of Japan and utilized in Shintō to demarcate or decorate sacred spaces. While the etymology is not entirely clear, the word *sakaki* is written 榊 by combining the character for the word "wood; tree" - 木 (*ki*) - with the character for *"spirit; god"* - 神 (*kami*). "Festooned ... with jewel beads, a mirror, and cloth" the *sakaki* was used to draw the sun goddess Amaterasu out of the heavenly rock cave, according to the *Kojiki.*

[417]   This can't have been easy in many ways, considering that many of the teachers and students remember him from childhood.

[418]   "Dr. Thomas W. Gillespie" was a great man but even better father. See www.ptsem.edu/in-dex.aspx?id=8539 or www.nytimes.com/2004/05/30/nyregion/in-person-changes-at-the-

but understood well what it means to have a father that is doing something important in the eyes of a public who revere him. For those who do follow in a father's footsteps, suddenly, instead of supporting that public figure … you're him. It cannot have been easy for Third Doshu, the grandson of O-Sensei, the son of Second Doshu. "Uneasy lies the head that wears the crown," though certainly Third Doshu wears it well.[419]

So by now, you know that I didn't leave Japan after one year.

> "I went to the woods because I wished to live deliberately, to confront only the essential facts of life, and see if I could not learn what it had to teach, and not, when I came to die, discover that I had not lived. I did not wish to live what was not life, living is so dear; nor did I wish to practice resignation, unless it was quite necessary. I wanted to live deep and suck out all the marrow of life, to live so sturdily and Spartan-like as to put to rout all that was not life, to cut a broad swath and shave close, to drive life into a corner, and reduce it to its lowest terms, and, if it proved to be mean, why then to get the whole and genuine meanness of it, and publish its meanness to the world; or if it were sublime, to know it by experience, and be able to give a true account of it in my next excursion.
> —Henry David Thoreau *in Walden; or, "Life in the Woods - Where I Lived, and What I Lived For"*

No; my sabbatical year didn't end in January 1998. I returned to Tokyo from the year-end holiday break in the U.S. determined to keep living right there in "the woods" among the rocks, trees, shrubs and critters, albeit eventually less Spartan-like.[420] I had tasted the local waters, drank as much as my belly (and bank account) could bear but thirsted for more. I kept training full-time into

---

other-princeton.html?pagewanted=all&src=pm.

[419] "Canst thou, O partial sleep, give thy repose; To the wet sea-boy in an hour so rude, And in the calmest and most stillest night, With all appliances and means to boot, Deny it to a king? Then happy low, lie down! Uneasy lies the head that wears a crown." So laments King Henry IV after wresting the crown from his cousin (who he had executed) Richard II. See William Shakespeare's Henry IV, Part 2, Act 3, scene 1. In the case of aikido, it was a less dramatic natural succession.

[420] This "extra time" more than made up for the unavoidable absences for visa runs during '97.

April, when I finally returned to work. There's a lot of economic opportunity in Japan. In business, it's sometimes because foreigners are more entrepreneurial than the locals and will take risks that the locals usually will not.[421] Over the years in Tokyo, I met a number of foreigners who arrived penniless or came as English teachers (near penniless) and in a few years were working for large foreign companies or running their own companies, including a guy who built a neat little empire teaching aikido at foreign locales, e.g., international schools, embassies and such. So, if you really want to stay in Tokyo and train, you'll find gainful employment. With the Internet and smartphones, it's exponentially easier than it was in 1997 and, in 1997, it was exponentially easier than five or ten or fifteen years earlier.

In the end, I went back to working as a lawyer. I had missed the intellectual challenge more than I'd expected plus I needed to pay some bills. But I returned to work with renewed vigor, perspective, understanding and appreciation of what's important in life, including a satisfying vocation. I took the job offer (out of three) that paid the most money. Unfortunately, I drew the short straw in the office and ended up working for the two old *oji-san*, one of whom was the much-rumored *sekuhara oyaji*.[422] Not of me, of the female staff, if the rumors were true. I do remember having a conversation with him when a chubby little secretary waddled past us. To the slow count of ten, his XXX-ray vision fixated on her rear-end. I was watching him in disbelief, thinking "Hello! Yo! Pervy-sensei. The conversation's over here, Pops!" Did he see my eyes roll in addition to hearing my "cough-cough-cough" trying to snap him out of his ero-trance? Did I care? It was my first experience in a Japanese office, and there seemed to be a lot of staying late and pretending to be busy, i.e., *sabisu zangyo* or "service-overtime" as it is called in Japanese. But, bills got paid. I would soon move on to a wonderful local firm where I could pursue the type of practice I wanted— both legal practice and aikido practice. I cut a deal with the gentlemanly senior lawyer over my hours, pay and *service-overtime*, otherwise they never would've been able to hire someone with my years of experience, and I would've been driven mental. I

---

[421] It's the reverse of my experience in China, where the locals are willing to take risks (with materials, quality or accounting) that the foreigners usually won't.

[422] *Sekuhara* (セクハラ) is a Japanese phonetic pronunciation of sexual harassment, which is then combined with the pejorative *oyaji* (親父, おやじ) meaning old man, in this instance.

put my heart into the work, though, and, in the end, turned a typical for Tokyo *"gaijin*-monkey-boy" job into a real Of Counsel position.[423] I would become the first foreign lawyer in the firm's 100-plus year history to negotiate a fee-splitting agreement with them on new business I brought in to the firm. I can hear my father in heaven, "Even a blind squirrel finds an acorn once in awhile, kid."

But what of aikido? Of teaching? My journey? Had it all been worth it? I'd arrived with questions. Did I find answers? Wasn't that the point? In fact, there were a lot of "reasons" to leave Los Angeles for Tokyo. I'd moved for intensive training and to discover whether or not I really wanted to teach aikido professionally. I'd moved on the cusp of "globalization," which proved positive professionally. I'd moved for adventure, because you get one life (as far as anyone knows for certain) and you'd better live it to the fullest, daily. I'd moved to simplify my life and test myself in numerous ways. And it had all been worth it. Unequivocally, unreservedly and otherwise emphatically, YES!

I'd learned that the point wasn't to GET something. The point was to experience everything on the way towards achieving what I initially aspired to "get." Of course, experience is a great teacher, and the year's experiences had taught countless lessons, both foreseen and unforeseen, well beyond my initial aspirations. The journey of an experience has a way of refining or redefining objectives. It was in some ways the most extraordinary year of my life, I could say. But I prefer to say that it was a big step in reminding me that every minute of every day is extraordinary, every breath of life. "Not even a million dollars can buy back a minute of your life." As the year closed, becoming a professional teacher seemed more remote than ever, requiring far more study (from a very early age), combined with considerable talent and a willingness and dedication to sacrifice oneself, including settling in one place for a long time.[424] It seemed more than I was willing to do or perhaps even capable of doing, and in any case

---

[423] *Gaijin*-monkey-boy was a term used back then by some foreign lawyers to describe a typical local law firm job for a foreign lawyer. The local firm leads out "the foreigner" for visiting clients to see; "Look, we have a foreigner," then they toss a banana into his cubicle, so he runs back inside to check the English of their documents.

[424] It also requires financial independence in my view. If you try to make a living from teaching aikido, without outside support, you are doomed to failure. You may become commercially successful but to do so you usually have to water down the art so much it becomes meaningless.

my journey wasn't finished. I had climbed as high as I had imagined—over a year of singularly dedicated practice—and found there was still a long way to the top. Anyway, an important decision shouldn't be based on some arbitrary date. I would just keep training. Who knew what life would bring me?

Making the difficult choice to go to Japan, planning to stay and live, adapting when the plan falters or fails (as all plans do), persevering despite numerous challenges; anyone can do this. Anyone with a dream and the determination to forsake whatever it takes to pursue the dream in earnest. "If you can conceive it, you can achieve it." I've read something like that online or in some self-help book somewhere. Bullshit! This isn't that type of book and I don't believe in the mythology of total control over your life. You can conceive of playing in the National Football League or the Premiere League, but unless you have the talent before starting down the path of working very hard, succeed in capturing the right timing and receive a measure of good fortune along the way, all the conceiving in the world won't achieve what you initially conceived, although you may find yourself blessed in other ways never originally conceived.[425] What you can control for certain is your attitude and your effort in facing the circumstances that actually arise from your choices and from events outside your control. That, you can conceive and achieve! You never know what life will throw at you. How you respond is your life-long challenge, and studying aikido can help you mightily in responding well.

As it happened, I wouldn't leave Japan for about eight years. Not until my wife was the victim of medical negligence in Tokyo and came within minutes or even seconds of dying in the ambulance on the way to the Intensive Care Unit at a large hospital.[426] People who know the story say I should write a book about that. Perhaps. It has been an incredibly difficult experience and the support of so many people, including students and teachers at Hombu Dojo, helped us to survive the ordeal. I know now, with a certainty, that you cannot control everything in your life but, among other things, you can work to forge a strong, enduring spirit to

---

[425] If I'm Jewish, gay, a gypsy or a trouble-making Christian in Germany in the 1930's, I don't end up in a concentration camp because I just wasn't positive enough? There's no "Secret." I'm there because some bad people did some bad shit and I couldn't stop them from doing it to me.

[426] Remember I was a defense lawyer, not a plaintiff's lawyer, so I don't make such an accusation lightly.

better live your life.

> But, nevertheless, the generation that carried on the war
> has been set apart by its experience. Through our great
> good fortune, in our youth our hearts were touched with
> fire. It was given to us to learn at the outset that life is a
> profound and passionate thing. While we are permitted
> to scorn nothing but indifference, and do not pretend to
> undervalue the worldly rewards of ambition, we have
> seen with our own eyes, beyond and above the gold fields,
> the snowy heights of honor, and it is for us to bear the
> report to those who come after us. But, above all, we have
> learned that whether a man accepts from Fortune her
> spade, and will look downward and dig, or from Aspira-
> tion her axe and cord, and will scale the ice, the one and
> only success which it is his to command is to bring to his
> work a mighty heart.[427]
>
> — Jurist, Oliver Wendell Holmes, Jr
> *U.S. Memorial Day, May 30, 1884*

I'm not suggesting that Hombu Dojo is the only or best place to train (I haven't been everywhere), but it's a very special place. I've been to a lot of places and seen a lot of teachers and students come through the doors of Hombu (from all over the world) and not once have I ever thought "Gee, I wish I had trained there instead."[428] What I can say with the conviction of personal experience is that it's a place where we can all train together and collectively support and sustain the art that we love. Go to Hombu Dojo. Visit. Live there. Train. "Bring [to your work] a mighty heart." Train with the locals. Train with the *deshi*. Train with the university students who visit regularly. Train with every other foreigner aikido *otaku* living in Japan. Train with all the visitors

---

[427] "In Our Youth Our Hearts Were Touched With Fire," an address delivered by the famed American jurist and Civil War (War Between the States) veteran Oliver Wendell Holmes, Jr. (March 8, 1841 – March 6, 1935) for Memorial Day, May 30, 1884, in New Hampshire, before John Sedgwick Post No. 4, Grand Army of the Republic. http://people.virginia.edu/~mmd5f/memorial.htm Massachusetts-born and Harvard-educated, Holmes later served as an Associate Justice of the Supreme Court of the United States (1902 to 1932) becoming one of the most cited and influential justices in American jurisprudence.

[428] Maybe I thought of training some place in addition to but never instead of; not once.

from all over the world. Aikido needs a center, a global point of focus, and Hombu Dojo fulfills this role admirably, gracefully, bringing so many disparate groups and dojos together under one roof. The art and each of its students will be better served if practitioners agree where they can (and cooperate) and agree that reasonable minds can differ where they disagree. Outside the center, people can go their own ways. Inside the center, set aside differences and practice together sincerely. "As iron sharpens iron, so one [person] sharpens another."[429]

The last practice before New Year is December twenty-fifth. You are expected to have taken your uniform home by the end of this practice at the latest, if you hang it in the drying room on the fifth floor, because the next day students come to participate in the dojo cleaning from 09:00. On December thirty-first, from 23:30-24:30, there is *Etsunengeiko* (越年稽古, えつねんけいこ, New Year's Eve Practice) to "ring out" the old year. The circle is complete, and with the first practice of the first week of January, the cycle begins anew.

---

[429] Proverbs 27:17 New International Version of the Bible.

Epilogue

"It's not the beginning but the continuing
of the same to the end."

— *Sir Francis Drake, sixteenth century English seafarer, explorer*

Aikido Keiko in an MMA World

稽古それとも格闘技
(*Keiko soritomo kakutougi*)

> An unfortunate thing about this world is that the good
> habits are much easier to give up than the bad ones.
> —W. Somerset Maugham

"Sensei; *konichiha*. Are you busy?" asked my fellow *deshi* politely, after dashing up the polished dark-stained wooden stairs to our teacher's living quarters and pausing at the entrance to the "office," which doubled as his kitchen and dining room. Sensei's residence was actually in the dojo, a hand-crafted dojo built in the style of a sixteenth-century samurai mansion and filled with Japanese antiques. Constructed in a secluded single-story brick warehouse, turned into artist lofts, it was an architectural marvel. His residence consisted of three rooms suspended miraculously above the back third of the mat area. A wooden staircase against the left wall led up to a first-floor landing and entrance to his living quarters. Two adjacent short wooden staircases connected that room to two more rooms, each with handcrafted woodwork, white walls and hardwood floors: one an airy bedroom-library and the other a storage room some twenty-plus feet above the training area. That dojo was an extraordinary space, which had a remarkable way of calming, even humbling, people who entered it. They quickly recognized that they were seeing something exceptional. Located just across the river from East L.A. (where some of the best students came from), three "cholos" dropped by to watch one night.[430] They entered rather loudly, then ... not a sound from them for the next hour plus. Another night, a well-known character actor in action films, a former football (gridiron) player, showed up with his friend to have a look, having heard or read about the place. I answered the door. Peering around me from the outside, glimpsing everyone

---

[430] "Cholo" is an ethnic slur of Latin American origin, which, in one modern usage, has been used to describe So-Cal "lowrider" gang youth. See the Urban Dictionary. www.urbandictionary.com/define.php?term=cholo.

with swords practicing *iaido*, they quickly became apologetic and quietly opted to return some other time.

"I have a minute," said my teacher without looking up from his computer or losing a keystroke of speed-typing. The *deshi* removed the bag slung over his shoulder, quickly stowing it in the men's changing room at the top of the stairs. Still clutching a videotape in one hand, he walked over to sensei's desk. "You have to see this," he said. My fellow *deshi* had done a bit of judo before and was very excited about whatever was on the tape. As my teacher continued typing, he nodded towards the video player on the shelf above his large dark oak desk. The student fed in the tape and pressed play. The screen flickered to life with "*Gracie in Action*" the promotional tape of "Gracie Jiujitsu" that was floating around martial arts schools in L.A. in the early '90s. The video ran for minutes without my teacher even stopping to look up in acknowledgment. As he finally did, he calmly folded his arms across his chest and considered the display intently before saying, "Yeah; interesting. That's old judo *newaza*" and returning to his work even more intently.[431]

Basically Japanese Judo?[432] His immediate recognition and candid observation was all the more remarkable because this exchange occurred well before the Internet was a household tool. There were no YouTube postings of the 1951 fight in Rio de Janeiro between *Kodokan Judo* legend Kimura Masahiko and Helio Gracie.[433] You couldn't pull up Kimura sensei's

---

[431] Judo was founded by Kano Jigoro (1860-1938) who created a Western style competitive sport from *koryu jiujutsu* (old styles). The full name being *Kodokan Judo*, after the name of his dojo. Taking techniques from particular *koryu* (perhaps modifying some) and perhaps including some from Western wrestling, e.g., *kata-garuma* (fireman carry) and *morote-gari* (double-leg takedown), he created the modern martial art and sport of judo. The pedagogical intention included building a strong physique, resilient spirit and higher moral character, e.g., learning to respect but never fear your opponent, building confidence but also demanding humility, honing fighting capabilities but also controlling aggression. This agenda was consistent with the Japanese warrior tradition and Victorian notions that good men could become better men through sport. See www.kodokan.org/e_basic/history.html, www.kodokan.org.

[432] *Kodokan Judo* has always had a broader curriculum than the techniques allowed in its sporting competitions, e.g., the Olympics. Early *judoka* included *koryu jiujutsuka* who were attracted to Kano sensei's goal to "modernize" *jiujutsu* and create a Western-style sport. Dislocation necklocks are but a few examples of judo techniques banned under standard competitions that are still taught. http://judoinfo.com/kubiwaza.htm This article was written by *Kawaishi Mikunosuke* (1899-1969) and published in "*My Method of Judo*" in 1955 and clearly shows "*dou-jime*" or "*dou-osae*" or "the guard" of BJJ fame. Leg locks and *Goshinjutsu* (護身術、ごしんじゆつ, self-defense) are two more examples. Aikido is much the same; there is a core curriculum but then countless other techniques.

[433] Reportedly, many of Professor Helio Gracie's nineteen professional bouts lasted for hours.

biography in English on your computer to read his thoughts on the match with the Brazilian who he described as a *"judoka"* (柔道家, judo practitioner).[434] I had no idea that over the years the rules for judo matches had changed, although old ways of competition and match-banned techniques had been preserved.[435]   At that time, you couldn't readily see the *newaza* of famed *judoka* like: Mifune Kyuzo, Oda Tsunetane, Hirata Kanae or Mitsunosuke Kosaka.[436] You couldn't easily pull up video of later generations such as: Okano Isao, Okuda Yoshiro or Kashiwazaki Katsuhiko.[437] These people all have (or had) consummate *tachiwaza* to go with their expertise in *newaza*.

Back then, few had ever heard of, let alone read a biography of *judoka* Maeda Mitsuyo (1878-1941)—the father of "Brazilian Jiujitsu"—who was sent by the *Kodokan* overseas with others to promulgate judo and travelled to the United States, Central America, South America, Europe and the Caribbean.[438]

This one was over in thirteen minutes. See https://youtube.googleapis.com/v/v2wO3dHUYwQ%26autoplay=1. While some claim Professor Helio was grossly outweighed by 20+ kilos (50 lbs), Kimura sensei was 170cm and 83 to 85 kilos and his biography states that Helio Gracie was 180 cm and 80 kilos, which tracks what Brazilian George Mehdi (a student of both men) reportedly asserts about the contest using photographs of him and Kimura sensei to verify his claim.

[434] You can read "My Judo" by Kimura Masahiko http://judoinfo.com/kimura2.htm and see him here www.youtube.com/watch?v=lkDBflFtPIw. Interestingly, one of the four victories ever over Kimura sensei in a judo match belongs to Abbe Kenshiro, who brought aikido to the U.K.

[435] For an overview of the rules changes, see http://judoinfo.com/rules2.htm or the lecture given to the EJU Foundation Degree Course at Bath University by Syd Hoare, Eighth Dan August 2005. www.sydhoare.com/development.pdf. See, too, the Seven University tournament in Japan, *Nanatei-judo* or *Shitchitei-judo* (七帝柔道、ななていじゅうどう、しちていじゅうどう) http://ja.wikipedia.org/wiki/%E4%B8%83%E5%B8%9D%E6%9F%94%E9%81%93.

[436] Watch Mifune Kyuzo (1883-1965) in his seventies www.youtube.com/watch?v=QJ0v2rXdBaY; Oda Tsunetane (1892-1952) www.youtube.com/watch?v=T7tk8cQ1VJ8; Mitsunosuke Kosaka (1906-1998) www.youtube.com/watch?v=35ux1U5_sjE; Hirata Kanae (1922-1998) www.youtube.com/watch?v=xjidQQz1yjM.

[437] See Nobutaka Mizuguchi (1934) at www.youtube.com/watch?v=RIzqk6WIkT8; Okuda Yoshiro (1941) see him at www.youtube.com/watch?v=RlQe6hiDsN4 and his video series at www.budogu.com/ProductDetails.asp?ProductCode=MBdSPD-3507; Okano Isao (1944) see www.youtube.com/watch?v=1NJoBxfBkRo&feature=related and www.youtube.com/watch?v=vkfGAyBXsCY and www.amazon.co.uk/Vital-Judo-Techniques-Isao-Okano/dp/0870405179 ; Kashiwazaki Katsuhiko (1951) see www.youtube.com/watch?v=A3HuBZLMDqg&feature=related.

[438] I cannot attest to the scholarship but two biographies of Maeda Mitsuyo are: *The Lion's Dream Count Koma, Maeda Mitsuyo* (ライオンの夢―コンデ・前田光世伝, *Raion no Yume, Konde Koma, Maeda Mitsuyo*) by Kouyama Norio and published by *Shogakukan* (1997) and *The Toughest*

I hadn't heard that he attended Waseda University and had entered the *Kodokan* around 1897, and by the time he left Japan for New York City in November 16, 1904 he was a fourth-degree black belt.[439] [440] Rather than return to Japan, he continued his travels. Back then, I'd never read that during his overseas adventure, he apparently survived financially and honed his fighting application of judo in something like 100, 1,000 or some say 2,000 wrestling and no-holds barred matches using the ring name Count Koma.[441] Watching that video, I had no idea that he had arrived in Porto Alegre, Brazil on November 14, 1914. He and his troupe (including his *Kodokan kōhai* Satake Soishiro and other Japanese *judoka*) performed in Brazil's main cities, and by fall of 1915 they arrived in the northern coastal city of Belém in the state of Pará.[442] Their journey

---

Man Who Ever Lived by *Bunasawa Nori* and John Murray, published by Innovations, Inc.; Second edition (2007). Another is *Conde Koma, O Invencível Yondan da História*, in Portuguese, by Virgílio Stanlei, Atom Publishing (2002). Maeda sensei is also mentioned by the rather erudite John Stevens in his book *Three Budo Masters, Kodansha* International Ltd (1995).

[439] Maeda Mitsuyo was "just" a *Kodokan judoka*. There's no credible evidence that he ever studied (let alone obtained any license to teach) some *koryu jiujutsu*. Notably, *Maeda* sensei describes himself as a *judoka* in his own writing. People also speculate that his judo was different because perhaps he studied closely with Tomita Tsunejiro or Tanabe Mataemon or Yokoyama Sakujiro. A simpler, less speculative, answer suffices. He was a diligent and skilled student of the *Kodokan* of the day. Of course, it's logical that through his wrestling and match fighting he acquired other useful techniques or tactics. It's important to separate fact from fiction, however. From his writing, it's clear that Maeda sensei considered judo the ultimate form of self-defense. Read Maeda sensei's 1935 manual *Jiudo: Uma Arte de Cultura Physica Japoneza* (Judo: An Art of Japanese Physical Education).

[440] The fact that Maeda Mitsuyo was assigned to accompany the famous Tomita Tsunejiro to the U.S. shows that he was highly regarded at the *Kodokan*, but being strong wouldn't have been enough to be appointed for the task. He would have had to demonstrate more than physical skill at the dojo.

[441] Another apparent myth about Maeda is that he was expelled from the *Kodokan* for prize-fighting. While his supplemental income may have been frowned upon publicly by his seniors (or even delayed his promotions), he was never expelled. In fact, most teachers in Japan will say they don't want you to fight (unless you win). Answers are never so black and white in Japan. In 1912, Maeda sensei was promoted to fifth degree. In June 1929, having started helping the Japanese community in Brazil, he received sixth degree. Although he died before the news arrived, he was promoted to seventh degree on November 27, 1941. It's important to remember that in Japanese martial arts after *yondan*, promotions are often linked to commitment and contribution to an art in addition to skill.

[442] Maeda (or Satake, Okura, Shimizu or Laku) did not introduce judo to Brazil (or *jiujutsu* either), though he certainly played a key role in promoting it. Japan's rapid modernization and defeat of Russia was inspirational to the developing world, e.g., countries like Brazil. The Brazilian Navy hired *jiujitsuka* as consultants, e.g., Sada Miyako (perhaps as early as 1903). A *Kodokan judoka* with the family name Miura purportedly arrived with the first Japanese immigrants in 1908 and began teaching, as others may have. The *Japanese Community in Brazil, 1908-1940: Between Samurai and Carnival, Page 52*, by Stewart Lone (2001) published by Palgrave, ISBN 0-333-63686-4. If you are keen on the subject, other pieces to the puzzle of *"Kano Jiujutsu" in Brazil* include judoka *such as*: Okoshi Tatsuo (Eighth Dan, 1892-1965) who arrived in 1924. Takagi

followed the end of the first rubber boom, which had brought incredible wealth to Brazil, and the Amazon cities of Belém and Manaus transforming these boomtowns. However, like much of the world in 1914, they remained fairly wild places.[443] Maeda sensei and his compatriots gave a demonstration that included a no-holds bout between Satake sensei and a local massive Capoeraist, which, according to newspaper reports, the Japanese won easily.[444] During the time of his demonstrations, Maeda sensei opened his first dojo in Brazil in 1915 at the Teatro Moderno in Belém.

Maeda sensei may or may not have referred to the art he taught in Belém as *jiujutsu* rather than judo.[445] If he did, no one knows for certain why. At that time, perhaps judo was sometimes called *Kano jiujutsu* or even *Kodokan jiujutsu*? Outside of Japan, that seems less likely. More likely, some Westerners had heard of "jiujitsu" (an incorrect romanization of the *kanji*), didn't have a clue what judo was and wouldn't understand the nuance of the *kanji*. "Oh, it means ... um, it's a new kind of ... oh, forget it; it's jiu-jitsu." Perhaps he used *jiujutsu* to avoid embarrassing the *Kodokan* with his entertainment exhibitions and match fighting for money? Maybe he did use the older word when match fighting, but it's more doubtful that he would do so in his own dojo. Perhaps he used both. Perhaps, it's a

---

Saigo, who arrived in 1924; Omori Geo (1898-1939), who arrived in 1928 (and like Maeda fought in matches); Naito Katsutoshi (Seventh Dan, 1895-1969) who arrived in 1928; The Ono brothers, Yasuichi (Eighth Dan, 1910-200⁰⁾ and Naoichi (Sixth Dan) who arrived in 1929 (also reported match fighters); Tani Sobei (Sixth Dan, 1908-1969) who arrived in 1931; and Ogawa Ryuzo (Eighth Dan, 1883-1975) who arrived in 1934. There were others apparently, including Yano Takeo, Terazaki Tokuzo and Yoshida Kazuo.

[443] Rubber trees were only been found in the Amazon until a British adventurer smuggled saplings out in 1876 and planted them in Malaysia, Sri Lanka and tropical Africa, eventually enabling the British Empire to assume control of the world rubber market because their plantations were more productive, efficient and cost-effective than in Brazil.

[444] A popular myth is that *koryu jujutsu* dealt solely or principally with fighting while armed or in armor. This notion that everyone was traipsing around in armor in Japan therefore "Japanese jiujutsu" didn't have effective techniques for people without armor is nonsense. The *Judo-Higaku-sho* (Secret Records of Judo) states "grapple was in vogue since Eisho era" and the Eisho era was from 1504 to 1520. See page 20, *Canon of Judo*, K. Mifune, Seibundo Shinkosha Publishing (Tokyo) 1958. Realistically, particularly after the establishment of Tokugawa shogunate in 1603, samurai were in fact seldom in armor. *Jiujutsu* had always been for fighting (killing or subduing) period: armed or unarmed, armored or unarmored, whether standing (*tachiwaza*, 立ち技), seated (*suwariwaza*, 座技) or on the ground (*newaza*, 寝技), at close quarters (*hakuheijugi*, 白兵主義), against single or multiple attackers. This was the Japanese mentality. All contingencies must be addressed. Failure is not an option.

[445] The term judo was not new when Kano Jigoro named his school of *jiujutsu*. It had been used to describe the way of *jiujutsu* in various schools in the past.

later move by others to differentiate from *Kodokan Judo* for commercial or other reasons, e.g., rule changes in 1925. If you market a similar product, your product better have some differentiators, and it's not unheard of for people to use the term "*jutsu*" rather than "*do(u)*" to sound tougher or harder. However, referring to what was being taught in Brazil as jiujitsu in order to try to link it to some earlier *koryu jiujutsu* (古流柔術, old style (classical) *jiujutsu*) and therefore materially different in that respect from judo is spurious.[446]

At some point, while in Belém, Maeda sensei met Gastão Gracie. Accounts differ. Mr. Gracie was a grandson of George Gracie, a Scotsman from Low Carronhill, Morton, Dumfries who immigrated to Brazil in 1826 and settled in Rio de Janeiro.[447] According to some, Gastão had moved to Belém for economic opportunity and became a business partner in a local circus that, among other things, staged wrestling and boxing entertainment. Some time in 1916, having seen a demonstration by *Maeda*'s troupe, Gastão's eldest son Carlos joined the group of newbies at the *Maeda* dojo. After learning all of this, I've wondered if perhaps Maeda sensei's teaching at his first dojo in Brazil focused on *newaza*, given the fact that he left Japan before the 1925 rules changes for judo matches and given his wrestling and no-holds match fighting experiences. If so, his approach would be broadly consistent with the *Kodokan* and *newaza*-focused judo in the high-schools and universities in Japan, which was done in part because it was easier to get beginners to a basic level of competency in *newaza* than in *tachiwaza*.[448] However, if you know anything about Japanese culture and the method for teaching martial arts (and education in general), then you understand the inescapable focus on *kihon waza*— basics, fundamentals—over and over and over again. There's speculation, of course, but I've seen no evidence to conclude that Maeda sensei taught any differently from how he was taught (the *Kodokan* method as he learned

---

446 See, e.g., the next chapter, The Fable of *Fusen*.

447 Though he fails to cite his sources, a Brazilian academic describes Gastão as follows "Gracie, the scion of an upper-class Scottish-Brazilian family from Rio de Janeiro, was the son of a former slave owner, but he was also cosmopolitan, sophisticated and educated, and he had modern standards. He, like the Japanese fighters, had been attracted by the riches of the rubber boom in the Amazon." See a draft of the thesis of Jose Cairus, *The Gracie Clan and the Making of Brazilian Jiu Jitsu: National Identity, Performance and Culture, 1905-1993*.

448 This point is reiterated by *jiujutsu* pioneer in Britain, Tani Yukio of famous London's Budokwai, in his 1906 book *The Game of Jiujutsu*. See http://fliiby.com/file/834999/kfmlf05qvy.html.

it before he left Japan) or what he was taught in Japan. Following the methods of his prior teachers would be predictably Japanese. Too many Westerners view Maeda sensei through the prism of their own culture and era, which skews their viewpoint and perceptions.

I didn't know it while watching that video, but according to biographers, Maeda sensei was travelling from time to time while Carlos Gracie was a member of his dojo. Maybe there is a clear record somewhere identifying which colleagues (perhaps Saigo sensei) or senior students taught class while he was away. In any case, apparently, some time in 1921, Carlos Gracie moved back to Rio with his family. So for some period of time, between 1916 and 1921, he was a student in the *Maeda* dojo. Perhaps the specific facts are waiting out there in a newspaper or magazine article or in a visual or audio recording or even better there is some credible document or documents showing clearly how long Carlos Gracie was a member of Maeda sensei's dojo.[449] Why care? It would be fascinating to learn how many students were in classes typically, what surface they practiced on, if they wore *keiko-gi*, the ages and sexes of students, how often Carlos attended, how often Maeda sensei was there, who taught when he was not, how long were classes, how often per day and per week, how much did it cost, what was the curriculum and so on. Carlos Gracie lived to be 92, so you figure there was ample time to ask him.[450] The oral history is that, after the move to Rio, Carlos taught his brothers and they opened an academy in 1925.[451] Watching the video, I had no idea that I was being asked to believe that a foreign student of a turn of the century Japanese martial arts master, following three to five years of study as a fourteen to nineteen year old, had then taught his brothers, and that one, some or all of them

---

[449] Lineage is very important in all martial arts, including BJJ. It would be typically Japanese to maintain clear records and, according to Brazilian friends, typically Brazilian not to bother.

[450] I'm a history geek so hopefully it's out there somewhere and I get to read it someday.

[451] After returning to Rio, one wonders if then-nineteen-year-old Carlos was immediately teaching his brothers what he learned from *Maeda* sensei or if he was training under someone else in Rio as well.

had created a new art surpassing their teacher's judo.[452] [453]

Watching that video, you never learned either that Maeda sensei had many other students in Brazil (as did other Japanese immigrants), people like Jacyntho Ferro or Luis França.[454] How could I have known that a student of Professor Franca, Oswaldo Fadda became a prominent teacher in Rio and pitted his students against Helio Gracie's in a match in the 1950s? In 1954, Professor Fadda reportedly took his students to The Gracie Academy for a competition and won.[455] At the 2011 BJJ "Mundials" (world championship), a student from this other Maeda sensei lineage won both his own weight class and the open championship.[456] Watching that video back in the '90s, I had no idea that in addition to a Carlos and a Helio there was a George, a Gastao Jr. and a Osvaldo Gracie who all practiced what Carlos learned, also taught Gracie Jiujitsu and also

---

[452] You may want to find a copy of the increasingly difficult to find pamphlet *Judo: Antigo Jiu-jitsu* by Takeshita, Kwanichi, Brasil Editora, 1954, 95p, www.estantevirtual.com.br/millasebo/Kwanichi-Takeshita-Judo-80141157 or www.traca.com.br/livro/341334/judo-antigo-jiujitsu; or read the chapter "The Circle and the Octagon in Martial Arts in the Modern World," (page 67-68), by Thomas A. Green and Joseph R. Svinth, Greenwood Publishing Group, 2003 ISBN-10:0275981533; a letter written in 1960 by a U.S. *judoka* who visited the Gracie Academy while on a speaking tour in Brazil. www.bestjudo.com/article/1255/early-report-bjj-brazilian-jiu-jitsu; or *Jujutsu: The Evolving Art, Part 4 - Other Jujutsu Derivatives: Judo & Gracie Jujutsu*, by Tom Ross & Christopher Caile published at www.fightingarts.com/reading/article.php?id=150.

[453] To read a sober and scholarly article, cut and paste revistas.udesc.br/index.php/tempo/article/download/2315/1790 into your browser to download one by Brazilian academic Jose Cairus entitled "*Modernization, Nationalism and the Elite: the Genesis of Brazilian Jiu-jitsu, 1905-1920,*" which "analyzes the introduction, creolization, popularization and globalization of the martial art known as Brazilian jiu-jitsu, by examining the trajectory of the principal agents of these events, the Gracie family who reinvented the Japanese martial art by creating a complex, ritualistic hyper-masculinized lifestyle, forged from the clash between tradition and modernity embed in [the] violence [of] "made in Brazil." See his C.V. at www.yorku.ca/gradhist/students/cv/cairus.htm.

[454] Jacyntho Ferro, a wrestler, studied with Maeda sensei from 1915 to at least 1922 and who, according to articles in the newspaper Folha do Norte of August 4, 1920 and December 14, 1923, was "Count Koma's most complete student." A *judoka* named Omori Geo (1898–1938) had a dojo in Rio and in São Paulo. He fought Carlos Gracie twice (draws), Helio (draw) and defeated a massive capoeiraist that was reported in the *New York Times*. Omori sensei reportedly taught Carlos Pereira and Luiz Franca Filho (after he studied with Maeda Mitsuyo and Satake Saigo). Amateur researchers claim there were others, e.g., Venicius Ruas. Their students were and are all practicing an art objectively identical (or virtually so) to GJJ, or BJJ if you prefer.

[455] A student of Professor Fadda's, Deoclecio Paulo, teaches in the capital Brasilia. See www.deojiujitsu.com.br.

[456] Maeda Mitsuyo > [Omori Geo ?] > Luis Franca > Oswaldo Fadda > Monir Salomão > Julio Cesar Pereira > Rodolfo Vieira. See www.bloodyelbow.com/2011/6/9/2215070/2011-ibjjf-mundials-world-jiu-jitsu-championship-results-review and www.youtube.com/watch?v=ytFRICyuC2Y&feature=player_embedde.d.

fought Vale Tudo matches. Apparently, George had been a rather prominent combatant for the art.[457] Back then, I hadn't read about the likes of Kastriot "George" Mehdi, who started studying Gracie Jiujitsu with Professor Helio but left Brazil for Japan to study directly with Kimura sensei.[458]

Even back then, the notion that Brazilians put "leverage" into "Japanese" *jiujutsu* to make it distinct from judo seemed highly implausible, but at that time most people had never heard of let alone read books like Tani Yukio's 1906 English language classic *The Game of Jiujutsu*:

> "You are clad in (at least) a jacket, and standing facing an opponent wearing a similar garment (See Chapter XIII, on Apparatus). Your object is to maneuver him, without using your strength, until he is in such a position that he is helpless and must give in. Consider this phrase "without using strength." It is not exact, because some strength must be used; it means practically with as little strength as possible. If you use more strength than the weakest has at command then it is bad ju-jitsu.

> As a beginner you will find that you can overpower another beginner by using more strength than he does; but until you learn not to do so you are preventing yourself from learning to use more scientific methods. You must practice each particular throw or lock until you can do it "without using your strength." In general your first object will be to put your opponent on the ground; then you will continue the struggle there until one of you is compelled to give in.

---

[457] *Judoka* Ono Yasuichi, the older of the *Ono* brothers (*Yasuichi* and *Naoichi*) who immigrated to Brazil in 1929 and started teaching judo, had choked out George Gracie and fought two draws with Helio Gracie.

[458] Some claim that Mehdi sensei contributed significantly to BJJ by teaching in Brazil the judo *newaza* he learned during his five years in Japan with Kimura sensei. His students have reportedly included Rickson Gracie, Sylvio and Marcello Behring, Mario Sperry and many other BJJ players. He is purportedly also a black belt in aikido and Kendo. See http://brunocarmenis-judoblog.com/779/judo-trip-to-rio-de-janeiro-brazil-october-2010-%E2%80%93-part-3/ and www.oocities.org/global_training_report/mehdi.htm.

It is convenient, then, to divide up the game into Standing-work and Ground-work, and to begin learning a little of the first before attempting the other. There is in this way less burden on the beginner's memory. Bear in mind however that the division is arbitrary. In practice ground-work follows a throw instantaneously. When you throw you want to put the man to the ground against his will in such a way that you have an advantage in continuing the contest. It would be quite permissible for him to go to the ground voluntarily in such a way that he would gain the advantage in the next stage of the struggle. Being first to the ground is not of necessity a point against you."[459]

That book was published nine years before Maeda Mitsuyo even shows up in Brazil. When you know even a little bit about Japanese culture and its obsession with incremental progress towards perfection—in anything—by an economy of effort and movement and consider, too, how much smaller Japanese were back then (reportedly Kano Jigoro was 5 feet 4 inches tall and 60 kilos, Maeda Mitsyo was 5-6 and 154 lbs, Mifune Kyuzo was about 5-2 100 lbs) then the idea that judo was a power game that Brazilians received and turned into Arte Soave is all the more ludicrous. The original characters mean *the gentle art*; translating it into the more sensuous Portuguese may sound cool but it doesn't make it materially different.[460]

Why deny the judo origin? I still don't get it. I mean "our original teachers were really tough Japanese immigrants who taught an early form of judo and applied it to free fights. We've preserved, developed and

---

[459] *The Game of Jujitsu* - Yukio Tani & Gunji Koizumi 1906, page 17. See more on Yukio Tani at Beyond Victoriana, *Yukio Tani and Sadakazu Uyenishi: Bringing Jujitsu to the West* http://beyondvictoriana.com/2011/07/31/85-yukio-tani-and-sadakazu-uyenishi-bringing-jujitsu-to-the-west/ or *The Odyssey of Yukio Tani*, Graham Noble http://ejmas.com/jalt/jaltart_Noble_1000.htm.

[460] If Carlos Gracie was born in 1902 and started with Maeda sensei at fourteen, that's 1916. Tani sensei's book was written in 1906. Perhaps the advantages of groundwork weren't a creation of Maeda Mitsuyo but simply an obvious part of the experience of *jiujutsu*/judo training. See more on Tani Yukio at http://ejmas.com/jalt/jaltart_Noble_1000.htm

spread it."⁴⁶¹ Cool, no? Instead you read a bunch of desperate silliness on the Internet about "jiujitsu" coming from India or China or the Ancient Greeks.⁴⁶² Uh-huh. Sure it does. That's why the overwhelming majority of available and credible (and obvious) evidence is that it comes from and still exists in Japan, existing for centuries in highly organized systems which were then mined by Kano Jigoro to create a new *budo*, judo, from which various other sport fighting traditions have been derived, including BJJ. Back in 1995, I had no idea that a series of martial arts—none of which (other than BJJ) was represented in the initial UFCs—were derived directly from *Kodokan Judo*: BJJ, Judo-do, *Kawaishi-ryū jujutsu*, Russian Judo and sambo at least.⁴⁶³ Watching that video, I had no idea that there was *Kosen Judo* in Japan, which is *Kodokan Judo* with different rules for matches—standing to submission.⁴⁶⁴ Watching that video, I had no idea then that BJJ had actually lost or drawn in matches against *judoka* in Brazil (in addition to Kimura sensei) and BJJ had a homegrown rival, too. Some say Luta Livre (meaning "free fight" in Portuguese) is the Western progenitor of modern mixed martial arts. Derived from Western wrestling traditions (and perhaps no-gi judo), its fighters wore wrestling shorts, not *keiko-gi,* and it included striking and kicking.⁴⁶⁵ Incredibly, watching that

---

⁴⁶¹ Many BJJ friends actually say this.

⁴⁶² Yes; we can all see grappling figures on ancient pottery. Fighting is as old as humans. However, the concept of *jiu* or *yawa* (柔, ジュウ, やわ) yielding and softness as the core principle of fighting is a distinctly "Oriental" one. So, no; Edison's lightbulb wasn't built on what Neanderthals had done eons ago with burning sticks.

⁴⁶³ Amazingly, the founder of Russian sambo faced a Stalin firing squad rather than denounce his Japanese teacher, *Kano Jigoro*, the founder of his art. Now that's loyalty.

⁴⁶⁴ *Kosen* (高専, こうせん) is an abbreviation of *koutou-senmon-gakko* 高等専門学校 (こうとうせんもんがっこう) which literally means technical colleges. It's not another "style" of judo but refers to different rules for judo matches between Japanese university clubs. The fight goes to the ground and keeps going. See, e.g., www.youtube.com/watch?v=Wp1B-2LEMS4, www.youtube.com/watch?v=7nlBJTUWjHg and www.akamonjudo.com. Post-grad, you can find *newaza*-focused judo practice too, e.g., the Newaza Kenkyukai (Groundwork Academy, 寝技研究家会, けんきゅうかかい), http://komlock.cocolog-nifty.com/5669/2009/02/2001-8cc2.html or http://saitamanewaza.web.fc2.com. Maeda sensei left Japan in 1904. *Kosen* tournaments started in 1914. Judo rules for standard matches changed in 1925, promoting *tachiwaza* and limiting *newaza.*

⁴⁶⁵ Founded in the mid-twentieth century by a wrestler named Euclydes "Tatu" Hatem, it gained notoriety when Tatu defeated George Gracie by submission some time in the 1940s. The system was aggressive and later influenced by Roberto Leitao (reportedly a university professor of engineering who was experienced in both wrestling and judo). Professor Leitao contends that leverage and strength are both advantageous—whatever gets the job done. Some say the greatest Luta Livre fighter was Euclides Pereira, "The Blonde Devil" who bested legends like

video in 1995, who would've guessed that (along with the Internet) a Japanese submission wrestler (and phenomenal showman) named Sakuraba Kuzushi would explode BJJ's invincibility claims by defeating four Gracies in a row in mixed martial arts fights in Japan from 1999 through 2000.[466]

In short, some Brazilians learned judo from Maeda sensei (and other Japanese immigrants) and have built a very successful sporting culture around *newaza*-focused judo practice, competitions along the lines of old-style standing-to-submission rules and continued the long tradition of Maeda sensei and other judo pioneers of applying judo to wrestling and no-holds barred matches.[467] [468] Fundamentally, it's a tactical and training emphasis on judo *newaza*, which in addition to making you highly skilled at *newaza* (if you play clay court tennis your whole life—you're good at it, but it's still tennis) is brilliant from a business perspective. *Tachiwaza* terrifies most people. People don't want to learn *ukemi*. It hurts.[469] It's technically more difficult (and more useful against multiple attackers). *Newaza* is far easier to learn (though still very interesting and technical) and safer to practice. You can tap quickly.[470] There are no (few) throws—just *hikikomu* (引き込む, pulling your opponent down) or more typically starting on your knees and then you roll around. It's reminiscent of wrestling with your pals when

---

Carlson Gracie, Waldemar Santana (who had defeated Helio Gracie), Ivan Gomez, Zulu and others during his undefeated Vale Tudo career. However, it appears that overall the record of BJJ in matches against Luta Livre is quite good. Fascinatingly (true or not), some contend the hostility between the two systems was in part class-based. *Keiko-gi* being too expensive, poorer Brazilians joined Luta Livre.

[466] The explanation, by some, was that *Saku* had studied BJJ. Scouted? Probably, like any good sportsman would, but winning his fights with BJJ techniques? Research and the Internet would expose that his were not the first wins by wrestlers against BJJ. A subsequent convincing loss to U.S. wrestler Matt Hughes in MMA and a (some say) controversial one to judoka Yoshida Hidetoshi (later ruled a draw) took further luster off the gem for some people.

[467] Vale Tudo wasn't invented in Brazil, either. For an overview of inter-martial arts contests in the nineteenth and twentieth century, read the article *The Forgotten Golden Age of Mixed Martial Arts—Part IV: Ultimate Fighting of the Belle Époque* by John Nash, Oct 31, 2011 posted at www.bloodyelbow.com/2011/10/31/2521315/the-forgotten-golden-age-of-mixed-martial-arts-part-iv-ultimate.

[468] *Kawaishi Mikonosuke* has been quoted as saying, about his bringing judo to France, "Judo is like corn or rice, it must be adapted to its soil."

[469] Kano Jigoro (and his colleagues) devised rules that permitted nonlethal and less injury-producing *jiujutsu* competition. This probably contributed to the popularization of judo in Japan (where it could be taught as physical education in schools) and the rest of the world. BJJ takes it a step further in safety (customer friendliness) by offering a version of *jiujutsu* competition that avoids *tachiwaza* near entirely.

[470] "Tapping" the ground or your body or your partner with your foot or hand is a signal of submission and to stop immediately. Can't do that mid-throw.

you were a kid. So, most typical guys think it's lots of fun. Plus, it's usually done in a much more relaxed environment than a traditional dojo.

Of course, with different rules for matches, it has become a distinct competition format, though arguably indistinguishable technically in substantially material ways from its parent judo.[471] Maybe with more study and mat experience I'll have some epiphany, but for me, fundamentally it's x% of Maeda's (and others) judo (until I can time-travel and see him teach a class and fight Vale Tudo and it's clearly evident otherwise) plus whatever has been added over the years.[472] The guy trained for how many years? Back in the day. Had 100, 1,000, some say 2,000 match fights (in a *keikogi* and without) against *jujutsuka, judoka,* boxers, wrestlers, brawlers, etc. around the world (as did other *judoka*), and one student who studied with him for three to five years kept working on it and passed him up? One, some, or all of his brothers he taught did, too? Surpassed their incomparably qualified teacher?[473] If you have studied traditional martial arts for a long time, you realize it takes incredible skill and many years of supervised instruction and hard training to ever surpass your teacher ... if it ever happens. A skeptic bets that whatever *newaza* Maeda sensei was teaching in Brazil (and his judo overall) was much closer to modern BJJ than most people want to believe.[474]

Watching that video, I had no idea that the tale of Brazilian jiujitsu is closely linked to the modernization of Brazil in the early twentieth century

---

[471] Techniques may be the same but the rules differ, and the rules make the contest and the contest changes the focus of training. Typically, if you do one technique a lot more than another, you'll be better at it.

[472] It's evident that the "meat and potatoes" of judo *newaza* (*katamewaza, shimewaza*) form the core of BJJ and judo has apparently continued to pollinate BJJ over the years, e.g., the late additions of the Triangle Choke (*sankaku-jime*) and "Ezekiel" choke (*sode-garuma-jime*) to the BJJ curriculum as *judoka* have trained at BJJ academies and BJJ students have read books or cross-trained in judo.

[473] Do not take this observation negatively. Do not forget that these students (and others) became highly skilled in their own right.

[474] I mean if someone offered you a choice, you can go back in time and study with *Maeda* sensei or, say, Professor Helio, who would you choose?

and the search for Brazilian national identity.[475] [476] I've since learned that many Brazilians (being very patriotic, like anyone else) didn't want to adopt this foreign fighting system when it first arrived around 1900. The country already had a thriving "fight culture," involving systems like capoeira, wrestling and boxing. So is it surprising then that, in opting to learn from the culture of one of their immigrant peoples, Brazilians have nationalized it in a way? Once you understand that, you can understand the near desperation of some to say "Made in Brazil."[477] However, what seems undeniable to me is that Brazilians (led by the remarkable Gracie clan) have created a tremendous sporting culture and industry around *newaza*-focused judo—both a sporting version and one for no-holds match fighting.[478] Brazilians didn't invent soccer, either, but they're awfully good at it and have developed their own approach, their own expression of it. And credit the extraordinary Gracies and other Brazilians for realizing what they had and spreading it worldwide. Seems to me that Brazilians have plenty reason to be proud. Japanese, in turn, have reason to be proud, too, and flattered that the people who welcomed them as immigrants thought enough of Japanese culture to adopt it so wholeheartedly. Everybody wins.

Of course, my first teacher recognized the obvious; he was an Asian studies scholar and martial arts geek. He could read original texts in Japanese and Chinese. He lived in Japan in 1969. Of course, he knew what's what. All Joe-Six Pack knew about Japan was that "they started WWII" and you can't trust them anyway cuz they're "Ornamental." The ignorant public thought, "Wow, you mean I don't have to bow and do all that other Asian-mumbo-jumbo and can still kick butt?" Brazil? Samba, beaches and bikinis? The marketing game

---

[475] Brazil was the last country in the world to officially abolish the institutional enslavement of Africans. Mounting pressure from many other countries (particularly the British and their navy) for commercial and moral reasons, plus activities of local abolitionists (e.g., Sociedade Brasileira contra a Escravidao), finally led to the Regent of the Emperor (his daughter while he was conveniently away) to sign the "Golden Law" freeing slaves (without compensation) on May 13, 1888. See www.aaregistry.org/historic_events/view/brazil-abolishes-slavery.

[476] Read a draft of the dissertation by Jose Cairus: *"The Gracie Clan and the Making of Brazilian Jiu Jitsu: National Identity, Performance and Culture, 1905-1993."* http://lasa.international.pitt.edu/members/congress-papers/lasa2009/files/CairusJose.pdf

[477] And in a way, it is now: the ranking system, the competition rules, the tailored "bling" uniforms, the attitude, etc.

[478] Of course, a distinguishing feature of BJJ academies is "no-gi" grappling, and I leave to you whether or not this is part of the legacy of Maeda sensei (you can see photos of him in his wrestling tights), Gastao Gracie's work as a wrestling promoter, an innovation or a response to its wrestling-based local rival, Luta Livre, or something else.

was won. Suddenly everything traditional was suspect. They'd seen it on TV, it had to be true (even though the biggest fight BJJ ever had, they'd lost to Kimura Masahiko, a Japanese *judoka*). Every sneering cynic came out of the woodwork. "See I knew it was kung-fu bullshit; we don't need that fortune cookie nonsense."

"Um, it's Japanese, and they don't make fortune cookies."

"Whatever!"

Every guy who ever wanted to be a badass or a bully but didn't like the cultural restraint (or confusion) that came with East Asian culture (or was a straight-up racist) was signing up for "Brazilian" Jiujitsu and then MMA. "It's not judo, that's a Way, this is just technique I can use to kick someone's ass. It's not Japanese (who committed war crimes); it's Brazilian; that's cool." It was as if East Asians had to prove all over again that their culture mattered ... and it was their culture! I joke with Chinese friends that if *jiujutsu* was a Chinese art (spare me the legends that it is) there would be protests worldwide at every Brazilian embassy. Most Japanese, if they know anything about BJJ at all, couldn't seem to care less. If anything, they seem flattered. People in the West are copying them instead of the other way around.

Even had the Internet been available at that time and had I known all of the foregoing, without a doubt I would've been impressed by the Gracie's passion for what they had been taught, their commitment to developing and promoting it, their level of skill and their willingness to put it on the line in matches—win or lose.[479] By fall 1996, I was enrolled in Rickson Gracie's old academy off Sepulveda and Pico in West L.A., next to a lumberyard. Of course! *Newaza* is one very useful part of an overall approach to self-defense, and where was I going to find *newaza*-focused judo practice in L.A.?[480] From teachers of that high of a level of skill? Unfortunately, I

---

[479] Whatever Carlos Gracie was taught by Maeda sensei, he and his brothers developed their own expression of it and their system for teaching it. What they've done is extraordinary in many ways. Kano Jigoro took years to develop the curriculum for judo. BJJ has developed since the 1920s when Maeda sensei students started teaching on their own, and it's still developing. It doesn't have a central authority like the Kodokan standardizing and managing curriculum, which has advantages and disadvantages. For example, according to some people, Rolls Gracie (a son of Carlos Gracie who tragically he died in a hang-gliding accident in 1982) began influencing some practitioners due to his experiences cross-training in collegiate wrestling, judo and sambo. It makes sense to develop an alternative strategy to using defensive tactics to sap an opponent's energy and then submit him.

[480] In Brazil, that's possible apparently (even outside of George Mehdi's dojo), for example in Sao Paolo at the dojo of Sensei Rodarte Correa. www.judomessias.com.br/sensei-messias.htm

was only there "for a cup of coffee" before moving to Japan, but I thoroughly enjoyed it and still have my membership card. The instructor was a great guy. People trained hard. It was a very positive experience and because of that experience (and probably my positive experiences meeting Brazilians in Japan), years later, I would take it up again at another Gracie academy.[481]   I'm grateful for the experience and what I've learned.[482]

The martial arts world has moved miles down the road since that video. The Internet has made many martial arts practitioners better (and less) informed.[483] The martial arts world's gone "open source" with people mining and "modifying" from all sorts of traditions—Eastern and Western.[484] [485] Forms of Western wrestling have come back into vogue: Graeco-Roman, Freestyle, Catch-as-Catch-Can and so on. Ironically, the shoe is on the other foot as BJJ has been mined to create "new" arts like "American jiujitsu" and other "evolutionary" systems or "styles" of jiujitsu. The dismissal (by many) of all but the slightest "Orientalism," the abandonment of *kata* practice, the emphasis on *randori* and competition in a gymlike atmosphere has attracted more people to martial arts and additional physical talent (some very athletic people), which in turn raises the level of the skills and the particular art. The focus (with some exceptions) is firmly on the accumulation of a set of skills to the individual's satisfaction and not the transformation of the individual by travelling a lifelong

---

[481]   Sure; I could've continued to study *newaza* while in Japan, but in those places, people have real judo *tachiwaza* skills so it might have been tough for me; plus I was in Tokyo for aikido, and you can only pour so much beer in the glass.

[482]   Cross-training in BJJ and aikido is actually becoming more common. It's a surprisingly natural and understandably powerful combination. See, e.g., *Shudokan Aikido* Association Technical Advisor—*Yasuhiro Sakahara* at www.shudokanaikido.com/modules/news/article.php?storyid=3 or Roy Dean at www.roydeanacademy.com.

[483]   For example, trying to research the origins of judo when you don't speak, read, or write Japanese produces very shallow if not futile results.

[484]   This process has always occurred in martial arts. In fact, Japanese already had a word for "mixed martial arts" *sogo budo* (総合武道,そうごうぶどう) meaning "composite" or "comprehensive" martial art—a martial art into which various martial ways have been integrated. See, e.g., *Yoseikan Aikido*. Perhaps the incidence has risen due to the availability online of books and video, even though the only way you can learn a martial art is through experience – doing, not reading or watching. With some exceptions, much of it seems like innovation without reason and imitation without benefit.

[485]   If it hasn't happened already, will we soon have these "New Wave" martial arts systems offering training involving Pushing Hands? Touting mind/body connection? Or the importance of muscle extension? Remaining connected to your opponent? Claiming they discovered, reinvented or "evolved" it?

path of study and hardship towards mastery of an art and self.[486] This immediate, simplistic, utilitarian and (in some places) self-serving and self-aggrandizing approach suits the times, particularly "Generation Me" with its love of self and app-or-gadget-snap-solutions for problems.[487] "I want my skills and I want them now!" Mixed Martial Arts has grown into an increasingly well-paid professional sport, which has led to all kinds of cross-training by the best in the world and improvements in diet, strength and aspects of training. While it wouldn't surprise me if people back in Maeda sensei's day were a lot tougher mentally and spiritually (i.e., having an unrelenting spirit), I'm skeptical that they were as gifted physically as people today.[488]

And then there's aikido.[489]

"The way of harmony with the force of nature." It's laughable to think that using aikido against another trained fighter in a sport fighting match (格闘技, *kakutougi*, かくとうぎ) is a core purpose of O-Sensei's martial art. Likewise, it's absurd to contend that aikido training is "ineffective" or "useless" because it does not translate 100% to the UFC or some other form of ring fighting. On that issue, it's no different than any other martial art. Some technical aspects translate to the sport and some don't. But the idea of putting Ueshiba sensei's Way to such a use seems antithetical not because "aikido is love" but because it is *budo* and its practice is a deep form of *keiko* intended to accomplish much more than provide "budo-tainment."[490]

MMA is a sport. The purpose of MMA is to entertain a paying crowd of live (and visual-media) spectators and to otherwise generate income for the

---

[486] One develops his or own "game," like in basketball or other sports.

[487] Some psychologists contend that since the 1980s, narcissism is on the rise among young people in the U.S. while empathy, a personality trait indicative of an absence of narcissism, is on decline. See e.g. *Narcissism Is Alive and Well in America, Is narcissism in America an epidemic?* May 16, 2011 by Jim Taylor, Ph.D. in The Power of Prime www.psychologyto-day.com/blog/the-power-prime/201105/narcissism-is-alive-and-well-in-america and *A Generations Vanity Heard through Lyrics*, by John Tierney, April 25, 2011 www.ny-times.com/2011/04/26/science/26tier.html?src=tp#.

[488] While they may have, in fact, been better prepared, they lacked the purported pharmaceutical assistance available to people these days—HGH being the least traceable "booster," apparently.

[489] There are many better written commentaries on aikido, authored by better practitioners, than this one. Find them.

[490] *Keiko* (稽古, けいこ) can be translated as practice, training or study, but to Japanese it has a deeper cultural meaning as the *kanji* reveal: 稽 think or consider 古 old.

promoters and everyone below them in the pyramid. There are rules and other parameters to ensure violence, but only to a degree.[491]   You're in limited space—a cage or a ring. You're in a safe space—no obstacles, sharp or rough points, edges or surfaces. No hidden assailants. No weapons. There are rules, referees, rounds and corner-men. You're barefoot, stripped to the waist and wearing board-shorts (whether you are from Siberia or Sunset Beach) and your hands are in fingerless four-ounce gloves. To do the sport well (or well enough), one only has to have passable: far (some kicks), near (some strikes), close (some *nagewaza*/ *newaza*) range attack and defense skills. Add athletic ability, a strong chin and fighting spirit, and you might fare well.

If you're keen to compete in this sport professionally, have talent and are starting from scratch, then you need about two to three years of BJJ, judo or sambo, some Western wrestling practice, Muay Thai and boxing, lots of conditioning and strength training plus time in the ring. Within three to five years, you could be fighting. Why waste your time with years of studying an entire traditional martial art, especially one with a very steep learning curve? That's like learning an entire floor exercise for gymnastics when all you want to do is do a double flip dismount off the high bar. Except, it turns out that traditional martial artists have performed rather well in such contests in recent years, so there is renewed interest in them.[492] However, *kakutougi* is not the litmus test of the merits of aikido or any other martial art.[493] MMA is a sport and just because someone is good at winning these kinds of matches does not make them great at self-defense. And there is more to studying martial arts than hand-to-hand self-defense. Kendo is a martial art, but apart

---

[491]   For a list of fouls, see the Nevada State Athletic Commission rules, NAC 467.7962 which include: head butts, gouging, biting, hair pulling (sorry Kimo!), fishhooking, groin attacks, finger in orifice, small joint manipulation, striking the spine or back of head, striking downward using the point of the elbow, throat strikes or grabbing the trachea, clawing, pinching or twisting the flesh, grabbing the clavicle, kicking the head of a grounded opponent (can be interpreted as any part other than two feet on ground), kneeing the head of a grounded opponent, stomping a grounded opponent, kicking to the kidney with the heel, spiking an opponent to the canvas on the opponent's head or neck ... timidity, including, without limitation, avoiding contact with an opponent ... and so on. www.leg.state.nv.us/NAC/NAC-467.html

[492]   A list might include, among many others: Chuck Liddell, Georges St Pierre, Lyota Machida, Karo Parisyan, Yoshihiro Akiyama, Ronda Rousey, Fedor Emelianenko. Enjoy the off-the-cage knockdown by Tae Kwon Do star Andy Pettis.
www.youtube.com/watch?v=LH7oRb5Knjc

[493]   Yes; I saw the original UFCs. A cynic would contend that opponents were carefully selected, for a format very familiar to one art and designed to force close engagement, and that a grip on a ponytail rescued a potential early loss. The rules have since been further tweaked for spectacle.

from understanding lines of attack/deflection and that a *shinai* is waaaaay faster than a fist or foot (which trains your eye to discern quick movement), it has no specific relevance to MMA.[494]

Of course, if you really wanted to do it, there is no reason that aikido couldn't be the platform on which you then built an MMA game.[495] The footwork, timing, body conditioning (pliability, hardening your body to blows/shock, *ukemi*), balance, unbalancing, lines of attack, deflection and other fundamentals are all directly transferable.[496] It's merely a matter of training and study the *ma-ai* in the ring. Transferable too are things like escaping grips, escaping clinches, defending arm drags, and take-downs all by using aikido principles and movement. Technique transfers as well. Unlike judo, the execution of aikido technique is not reliant on gripping clothing.[497] On the contrary, while the art wonderfully addresses defense to clothing grabs, execution of technique relies on grasping the opponent's body, not his sleeve, collar or anything else.[498] Without much effort, there are about eight to ten very good techniques that transfer.[499] Frankly, I am surprised that it has not already been "mined." But here's the punchline … you <u>have</u> to do *keiko*. Just as it is. You have to study aikido to do them well. There is no way around it.[500]

Let's face all the facts. Most people, including some studying it, have little if any clue about aikido. Due to a lack of understanding (including

---

[494]   A *shinai* (竹刀) is the bamboo sword used in kendo. See the 2012 All Japan Championships at www.youtube.com/watch?v=i9PBJ.haYodY.

[495]   Rik Ellis, son of British judoka and U.K. aikido pioneer Henry Ellis is an aikidoka and MMA fighter. http://rik-ellis.blogspot.com

[496]   Aikido *keiko* demands you practice right and left sides equally, developing ambidexterity, which is not only good for your brain but very useful in studying other martial arts or any physical activity.

[497]   In some dojo, you are taught various *shimewaza* (chokes) from standing and kneeling.

[498]   You can grab clothing, if you like. Forget for the moment many of the techniques which when practiced by some seem to require the attacker to hold on for inordinate amounts of time, many of which I believe generally serve a larger pedagogical objective and would not be applicable in the context of a sport fight.

[499]   Sorry. No hints.

[500]   Preparing for matches in this sport by only training in aikido (or any one martial art) would be madness. No fan wants to see some elusive guy get chased around the ring for fifteen minutes. You are expected to win by knockout, submission or points. Point systems include: aggressiveness, ring control, strikes/kicks landed, etc. BJJ, judo and wrestling no more stand there and exchange blows than would an *aikidoka*, until he had the additional skills to do so. The initial answer in aikido is the same as in judo or BJJ. Maintain or close distance. You have to add striking and kicking skills and condition your legs to receive kicks. You would have to train for three five-minute rounds, wearing four-ounce fingerless gloves and so on.

a lack of experience with a truly qualified instructor), people foolishly dismiss it. In some respects, in some places, perhaps dismissal has become justified.

> Aikido is a "budo," a "martial way," and therefore inextricably rooted in "jujutsu" or "martial technique." Yet when I look at the aikido world today, I see very little "budo-ness" being expressed in technique, and I wonder if people haven't begun to forget these important roots. ... There are even some who claim that aikido has no need for things like striking and weapons techniques. In many settings these days, aikido is becoming little more than a kind of health exercise pursued by the elderly, and women and children."[501]

On behalf of all (or many) *aikidoka*, thank you Nishio sensei. This quote comes from a man who studied karate, judo, swordsmanship, was a direct student of the founder and dedicated his life to aikido. You know better? Make no mistake. Aikido is <u>not</u> a philosophy lesson. It is a *budo*, developed from samurai killing arts of *jiujutsu*, *sōjutsu* (槍術, spear technique) and *kenjutsu* (剣術, swordsmanship).

> At about the age of 14 or 15. First I learned *Tenshinyo-ryu jiujutsu* from Tozawa Tokusaburo Sensei, then *Kito-ryu*, *Yagyu Ryu*, *Aioi-ryu*, *Shinkage-ryu*, all of them *jiujutsu* forms. However, I thought there might be a true form of *budo* elsewhere. I tried *Hozoin-ryu Sojutsu* and *Kendo*.[502]

And then, of course, at thirty, O-Sensei had that fateful meeting with Takeda Sokaku in Hokkaido and Takeda sensei "opened [his] eyes" to budo with his *aiki-jiujutsu*. It was out of these various experiences with

---

[501]   Preface to *Yurusu Budo* by Nishio Shoji sensei. See http://blog.aikidojournal.com/2011/08/22/preface-to-yurusu-budo-by-shoji-nishio.

[502]   Interview by newspapermen of O-Sensei published in the Japanese-language text aikido by Ueshiba Kisshomaru published by Kowado (1957), pages 198-219. A presumably accurate translation has been republished at www.aikidofaq.com/interviews/interviews.html.

other arts, particularly *aiki-jiujutsu*, and his other life experiences that ai-kido was born. While the system has highly ethical and moral ideals about preserving rather than destroying life, reconciling conflict and contesting and fighting nothing, aikido IS *jiujutsu* and the understanding of and the realization of its various ideals is only achievable through long, vigorous and continuous training. "This is not mere theory, you must practice it," as O-Sensei is quoted.

And yet, intertwined with his *budo* are broader training objectives of *keiko*, as another direct student of O-Sensei rationally explains:

> At the core of the practice of aikido, more than anything else, is a continuous hard training and disciplining of one's body and mind in order to develop wisdom. In the event of a confrontation, beast-like behavior aimed solely at protecting oneself and injuring the opponent must be avoided at all costs. To develop the determination to re-solve a confrontational situation with omniscience and omnipotence (that is, using not merely technique but ap-plying the entirety of one's abilities and wisdom) is *bugokoro* (*budo*'s spirit/mind). One must realize that aikido is neither more or less than the expression and embodi-ment of this *bugokokoro*.

> *Yamatogokoro* is what aikido advocates.

> Because aikido includes the elements of *bugi* (combat techniques), it is inevitable that, at times, the aikido prac-titioner must face the possibility and the reality of con-frontational circumstances. If one seriously and contin-uously probes into the reality of coming face-to-face with an opponent in a show-down situation where one's very existence is at stake, that is, where one's survival means the opponent's defeat or vice versa, and if one were to fully and openly recognize the inter-relation between one-self and the opponent, it would lead one to discover the most logical and efficient fighting techniques.

It is nonetheless true, however paradoxical it may seem, that in pursuing the perfection of this principle, one will eventually arrive at a harmonious state, born from the insight that no matter how strong one is, one cannot continue to exist if one tries to fight against all existence. This is the "Way" (or process) to reach harmony as advocated by aikido.

One should bear in mind, however, while trying to understand or attain the principle of harmony, that without going through the internal transformational process that begins in the state of confrontation and only after working through a critical process eventually arrives at the state of non-confrontation, there can be no *budo*.[503] [504]

Some dismiss aikido precisely because they disdain its moral and ethical objectives and the restraint that this imposes upon practitioners. Really? "What's so funny 'bout peace, love an' understanding?"[505] Such antagonism is nothing new. People challenged O-Sensei over his "new" *budo*. [506] "When a true genius appears in the world, you may know him by this sign, that the dunces are all in confederacy against him."[507] They failed.

People don't understand or distrust the method of instruction, too. Aikido training is principally a form of *kata keiko* (型 稽古, かたけいこ, forms practice). Fools scoff at *kata keiko*. You've read on the Internet *kata* is useless. *Randori* (乱取り, らんどり, freestyle training) is useful.

---

[503] Preface of *Technical Aikido* by Mitsunari Kanai, Eighth Dan Aikikai. See www.aikidosphere.com/mk-e-remembering or www.youtube.com/watch?v=6IT6CnUBYtE.

[504] You may also find the answers in this interview of aikido Shihan Chiba Kazuo, first published in Terry O'Neill's Fighting Arts International (issue #70), of interest. See http://omlc.ogi.edu/aikido/talk/others/chiba.html.

[505] "(What's So Funny 'Bout) Peace, Love, and Understanding," 1970s song written by English musician Nick Lowe and made famous by Elvis Costello and the Attractions.

[506] "The greatest trick the devil ever pulled was convincing the world he didn't exist," Kevin Spacey as Kaiser Souze in the film *The Usual Suspects* (1995) www.imdb.com/title/tt0114814/.

[507] Irish cleric, satirist, essayist, poet and political writer Jonathan Swift (1667-1745) is best known for *Gulliver's Travels* (1726). He is perhaps the greatest satirical writer in the English language. www.online-literature.com/swift/

Koryu jiujutsu only had *kata keiko*. Judo instituted *randori* as part of its practice. Therefore, judo became supreme. Yeah; right.

First, *kata* or forms practice is a time-tested method for preserving techniques and transmitting basics in all kinds of arts—not just martial arts. Most people react negatively to the notion of form because they instinctively feel it's the opposite of freedom. But form is much more complex than most people realize. Within form, there is in fact a great deal of freedom, but freedom without form is just chaos. Study form, break form, transcend form.[508] This is the path of a martial arts journey towards mastery—not the short cut to utilitarian proficiency with a few winning techniques based primarily on innate ability. "Art begins in imitation and ends in innovation."[509] Tellingly, Japanese warriors trusted their lives to this kind of practice, so to dismiss it is ignorance, if not simply childish rebellion.

Second, not all *kata keiko* is the same. Some methods involve extended sequences of patterned movements done by an individual in order to instil basics and reveal principles (as a starting point for training).[510] Other methods involve two or more people and may concern one or more types of attack and one or more techniques in response and can involve choreographed movements.**[511]** The individually performed *kata keiko* of karate is not the same as the *kata keiko* of judo. The *kata keiko* of judo is not the same as the *kata keiko* of aikido. In fact, what I principally refer to in aikido as *kata keiko* is the core practice of *taijutsu—nage* and *uke*.[512]

---

[508] Once again: *shu* (守, しゆ, protect, obey) learning fundamentals, techniques, *ha* (破, は, detach, digress) finding exceptions to traditional wisdom, finding new ways, techniques, *ri* (離, り, leave, separate) transcending techniques, moves are natural.

[509] Mason Cooley (1927–July 25, 2002) was an American aphorist, a graduate of San Diego State University (B.A.) and the University of California, Berkeley (Ph.D.) who served as professor emeritus of English, speech and world literature at the College of Staten Island after serving as an assistant and then adjunct professor of English at Columbia University.

[510] Hitting focus mits is *kata*. Kicking a bag is *kata*. Learning three or five punch combinations in boxing is *kata*.

[511] Weapons practice involves a series of planned movements but each done with the right/real energy to it. And, the genuine risk of serious injury, so it's the only sensible way to practice.

[512] There is so much freedom within this form of practice that there is certainly room for discussion as to whether or not this is "*kata*" in the traditional sense. See the cogent comments of aikido sensei and judoka Nial Matthews, who I used to train with sometimes in Arikawa sensei's classes. www.aikiweb.com/forums/showthread.php?p=306300

It is a type of drilling, like practicing scales on the piano.[513] Boring, perhaps, but you master fundamentals of an entire art by committing its curriculum to muscle memory, conditioning your body, training your eye, honing your timing, etc. What's the name of that well-known BJJ book? *Drill to Win*? The author is 100% right, if winning (or even just improving) is your objective.[514]

Of course, the level of aikido practice depends on the level of *ukemi* (which is a vital part of the art). Corrupting the confrontational interaction between *uke* and *nage* and reducing it to a sort of playacting of martial arts is all too common and is not genuine aikido. For beginners, practice is and must be a bit contrived, as one person assists the other in initially learning (and slowly improving) particular movements. The *nage* executes the technique with a speed and energy that allows the *uke* to receive it safely and develop his *ukemi*. As *uke*, you offer *nage* just enough energy for your partner to train, learn and improve. The amount of energy you deliver in attack increases over time as your partner's ability to execute technique increases and your ability to receive technique improves. Pursued correctly, a dynamic form of *kata keiko* emerges that is anything but contrived or compromised.[515] A sincere attack is made, with the energy of genuine intent, to provide your partner a means to study. The recipient seeks actual *kuzushi*, unbalancing. From the moment of attack through the throw or pin, there is a connection, liveliness and spontaneity to the interaction between *nage* and *uke*. One is trying to execute the technique perfectly and the other trying to receive it perfectly as an alternative to being stiff and blocking or countering.[516] It's not *kata* (yet it is) and it's not quite *randori*. Beyond committing technique to muscle memory, it's a perpetual study of the instance

---

[513] It is also a means of body conditioning and serves other pedagogical purposes.

[514] *Drill to Win: 12 Months to Better Brazillian Jiu-Jitsu* by Andre Galvao and Kevin Howe, Victory Belt Publishing (15 April 2010), ISBN-10:0981504485, ISBN-13:978-0981504483.

[515] However, unless you are careful, a degenerate form of the art results. "One of the most basic, chronic, and perhaps inevitable problems in practicing aikido is that aikido training can be reduced to an easy going exercise based on excessive compromise between the practice partners (*nage* and *uke*). This problem arises because aikido practitioners often base their practice on sincere but ill-founded philosophies and theories. Examples of the many incorrect interpretations of aikido as applied to practice include emphasizing an idea of an "Aikido style" ambiance, expressing an "ideology" of aikido, and misconstruing the concept of "harmony."" *Technical Aikido* by *Kanai Mitsunari*, Eighth Dan, Shihan, Chief Instructor of New England Aikikai (1966-2004). Scroll down the page at www.aikiforum.com/viewtopic.php?p=11343.

[516] You don't have to do aikido for years to figure out how to be stiff and strong. You know that walking into the dojo.

of engagement, the timing, structures and energies involved and of dealing with an attack decisively to end the conflict. Drills can be employed for *henka-waza* (changes from one technique to another) and *kaishi-waza* (counters to technique). This type of training is anything but impractical. It's straight-up old-fashioned drilling.

Third, *randori* was nothing new to *jiujutsu* when judo came along.[517] *Kano Jigoro* admits that his *Kito-ryu jiujutsu* teacher used *randori* as a teaching method.[518] Aikido has it as well—as a teaching tool, not as a competition—but the rules (and techniques) allowed in each dojo may differ dramatically. Remember that when you say the word "aikido," it's like saying "the Pacific Ocean."[519] What spot in the sea are you talking about? It can make a big difference. From the main tree of aikido have sprung different branches, and some of those branches have in turn branched off.[520] Even within *Aikikai*, if you attend the All Japan *Embukai*, you'll see all kinds of differing expressions of the art.

Randori or not, *Koryu* arts practitioners didn't sit in the dojo doing some kind of useless effete forms practice that rendered them unable to "really fight." They left the dojo and really fought—without rules. You either won or lost, which could mean painfully, bloodily or even fatally. That's how you tested your training.[521] This reality-based method took different forms. There were fights between schools known as *taryu-jiai* and forms of duelling known as crossroads-throwing (*tsuji-nage*) for body arts and crossroads-cutting (*tsuji-kiri*, sword or weapons duels). There was also the practice of dojo-

---

517 "This *randori* was also utilized by other *jujutsu* disciplines but Kano's theory of *randori* was "safety," physical strength development and balanced development" as well as "enticing interest in the student." It is widely known that even as such, safety was especially prioritized and *"atemi* (hitting)" and "hand and toes and it joints" as well as "wrist and ankle" targeted "waza (techniques)" were excluded. If there were a no-rule bujutsu match, the loser would either be injured or in the worst case, even die. As such, a no-rule actual fighting would never be accepted in a physical educational structure." See http://judoinfo.com/randori1.htm. Quoted from and article. No idea what the reference to "it joints" means.

518 Perhaps Kano sensei's greatest genius was in adopting and modifying techniques into an art that could be used for hand-to-hand defense, as a sport, for education and a life philosophy.

519 Apart from Tomiki Aikido (and *Yoseikan Budo*), the martial art refrains from competitions so there are no rules that tend to standardize teaching.

520 People also make huge distinctions between Daito Ryu Aikijujutsu and aikido and its various offshoots (and there are clear technical ones) but whether one is more "martial" than the other can change from one dojo to the next.

521 Some people did this kind of thing in Japan when I lived there. *Hyakyagyou* (百鬼夜行, ひゃっきやぎょう) many monsters, spirits, etc. forming a line and walking through the night; creepy characters roaming about, presenting a most scandalous sight.

storming (*dojo-arashi*) or dojo-smashing (*dojo-yaburi*) or dojo-touring (*dojo-mawari*) where a practitioner would visit a dojo, challenge them and if victorious maybe take something of value for ransom.[522]   Particularly given the cultural and historical context, it's laughable to believe that *koryu jiujutsu* training was unrealistic.[523]

Fourth, in many systems of classical *jiujutsu,* some techniques are too dangerous to practice in a *randori* or match setting (short of an actual duel), e.g., many kinds of *atemi-waza.*[524] In aikido, consider *shihonage.* Done with intent, the recipient is looking at two, maybe three broken bones or joints and a concussion even if the recipient reacts in time to take *ukemi.* Kick his closest supporting leg out from under him (like *O-soto-gari* in judo) after you turn and start the cutting motion of the throw and his chances of surviving intact decrease substantially. The difficulty for any martial art is that once you start to "sportify" it, people focus on whatever they are good at that has the best chance of winning a match within whatever rules apply.

To make the leap of "leaving the form" and transcendence to a spontaneous expression in response to an attack, you must dedicate yourself intensely to first studying and mastering the form. It's not so different from learning to play a musical instrument or anything else that's difficult to master. It takes time and dedication. However, in my view, if you seek to develop the ability to use your aikido for actual self-defense, you must also gain a feel for the application of technique on people who do not move like aikido people.[525] The opportunity exists to some extent in everyday practice, and it's not a matter of "making" aikido work on a "fully resisting" opponent by forcing technique. Anyone who has studied aikido knows that if the *nage* has

---

[522] One *shihan* at Hombu Dojo was rumored to have joined the dojo after attempt to "storm" the dojo resulted in defeat. He was also rumored to have killed someone with *shihonage.* Who knows?! I certainly can't imagine him staying on because "aikido is love." That's for certain.

[523] If you make an excuse like "Oh that old stuff wasn't effective," then you can feel justified in not studying it. You can do as you please, rather than as they should.

[524] Even judo and BJJ have techniques that are banned from competition, e.g. *daki age* (or "slamming" people). See www.youtube.com/watch?v=5X0QHIJhihhQ.

[525] "In order for each of us to experience personally the 'core principles of the martial arts,' we must not stop at the mere, repetitive practice of *kata. Randori* and sparing help to lead us closer to both the core principles of the martial arts and the true power that they generate by letting us experience the techniques studied in *kata* as they were meant to be performed: against a smart, resisting, and aggressive opponent." *On Jujutsu and its Modernization* by *Tomiki Kenji.* See http://judoinfo.com/tomiki2.htm.

the pieces in the right place at the right time, resistance is futile if not injurious. Instead of forcing your will, contest nothing. Cultivate the ability to transition freely from technique to technique—like water—seizing whatever advantage arises. Cross-training is another way to expand your experience and polish your ability to spontaneously express the art.[526]

The difficulty of learning aikido is off-putting to some people.[527] When I started BJJ, it was apparent to me that most people in the white-belt class weren't doing *jiujutsu* at all. There was no *jiu,* no softness or yielding. But they thought they were! Returning to Beijing from London and continuing classes, I told a friend after training one night that the students had excellent jee-ro-shu (肌肉术) and he laughed. In Mandarin, *jiujutsu* (弱术) is ro-shu (in ro-manized characters) and muscle is *jee-ro* (肌肉) so put them together and pro-nounce it just right and you've got "muscle technique." No yielding to be found; just muscling. The interesting point was that students could fool themselves—from the first class—that they could do it a little bit (when ac-tually it's rather technical and takes considerable time and mental as well as physical changes). Likewise, if studying boxing or Muay Thai, okay. You watch; you get it; basically. Judo and its *tachiwaza?* Tougher puzzle; much more complicated, but at least you can occasionally muscle your opponent off-balance and down so you feel like you got a win. In aikido? You haven't a clue. For months. First, there is the stance, then the footwork and the posture and the strikes, and spacing and timing, and connection and exten-sion and breathing and *ukemi* ... each so complex and unfamiliar to true be-ginners.[528] Even as a first-degree blackbelt (*shodan*), you've barely scratched the surface. You only have the basic pattern for your training going forward. If you consider who O-Sensei's original students were, aikido looks like a post-graduate course in martial arts. Teaching it to newbies and expecting them to understand it quickly is like teaching first-graders Shakespeare hoping

---

[526] Don't be a dilettante. Set goals for experience or rank. Train hard. Simultaneously training in more than one art is difficult: at one point, I was doing aikido, judo and BJJ. In aikido it was easy for me to borrow knowledge from other arts but when in judo and BJJ classes, I focused on learning what they had to teach. While I have thrown people, gotten submissions, escaped positions and grasps, effected reversals, etc. using aikido technique or principles, that's not the point of being there, so I seldom try. I love being a beginner and enjoy learning something new.

[527] Actually, it's one of the things that keeps it interesting your whole life.

[528] There are occasional exceptions, e.g., other martial artists who aren't so full of what they know that they can't learn something new as a beginner.

they'll be wowed by the prose. However, at some point the process becomes more familiar, the endless stream of techniques less baffling and you realize that you're learning useful things, being challenged in numerous ways and love it.

Some people distrust the very "Japanese-ness" of aikido training, particularly the environment of a traditional dojo, as suspiciously "Oriental" and, therefore, impractical or otherwise irrelevant. It's true that a good dojo pursues time-tested methods of training—including lessons being obscure at times—and has many detailed rules of conduct and etiquette. The specific purpose of this type of "form" is to create an ideal context within which students can refine and discipline themselves— strengthening their bodies, sharpening their minds and forging their spirits through rigorous training in mastering the techniques of aikido. The concept of individual refinement in pursuit of self-understanding (enlightenment) is uniquely characteristic of many Far Eastern disciplines (though the notion of this kind of enlightenment comes from Buddhism, which originated in India). The journey <u>IS</u> the point, not merely physical skill. You can train a monkey technique.

Aikido is a *budo* and the manner in which it is practiced matters. Japanese martial arts came to be taught in a certain way in a particular atmosphere in order to develop technical proficiency and more, to broadly and deeply shape the individual—mind, body, spirit—in ways some of them directly "martial" but all certainly related to the dignity and responsibility of a "warrior." Aikido, in particular, has pedagogical objectives beyond just defeating an opponent (in a sport match or some potential confrontation that may never happen in a lifetime) including developing: your body (*tai-iku*, 体育), your spirit (*ki-iku*, 気育), your ethics (*toku-iku* 徳育), your intellect (*chi-iku*, 知育), your common sense (*jyoshiki no kanyo*, 常識の 涵養), your intuition or instinct (*chyokan*,直感 or *kan*, 勘), your ability to concentrate fully, your mindfulness (*zanshin*, 残心), your respect for all things (*rei*, 礼) and a calm, clear mental state (*mu-shin*, 無心).[529] Training

---

[529] *Samurai* sought through their training to develop a combat (and then daily) mental state known as *mushin* (無心, an English approximation is "no-mind"), which is an abbreviation of *mushin no shin* (無心の心), a Zen (禅) expression meaning mind of no mind ... that is, a mind not fixed or occupied by thought or emotion and thus open to everything. This mental state is free from thoughts of anger, fear or ego and from discursive thought and judgment, so a person is

in martial arts can be much more than just adding a collection of physical tricks to what you think you already know.[530] It can be transforming on many levels that will enhance your daily life and the lives of others.[531] Any martial art can be taught this way, but the mats would be emptier.

More fortune cookie nonsense? Well, from personal experience, I can tell you that traditional Japanese martial arts training sorted me out in many ways to the direct benefit of my personal and professional life and some of these training objectives are in fact linked directly to improving your chances of avoiding or prevailing in physical confrontations (in a sport or spontaneous survival situation). December 1996, Phoenix, Arizona, after working all day on a project for a global oil giant, three co-workers from a consulting firm and I headed out for dinner and relaxation courtesy of the client. Driving back to the hotel that evening, I spotted the Oscar Meyer Weinermobile (no joke) parked on the side of the road.[532] "We HAVE to take our picture in front of it!" I said, pointing to the giant sausage-auto. Pulling into an all-night gas station, just around the corner, to see if they sold disposable cameras (they did), my friend and I leapt out and walked to the cashier window, while the driver and other passenger sat in the car. We were parked perpendicular to the gas-pump islands, with our cars lights shining on the walk-up payment window. At the window, about eight to ten meters in front of the car, I stood to my friend's right. It was late; the place was empty.

The first alarm bell was the cashier window being protected by bulletproof glass and iron bars. As we stood there, while the clerk searched for a camera, I sensed something wasn't right. Hearing shuffling feet behind us, I glanced casually and saw three youths (fourteen to seventeen years old) lined shoulder-to-shoulder three or four feet behind us. In an instance, I saw that their car was parked fifteen or twenty meters away at the pump to our left, all four doors wide open, the engine running and

---

[530] free to act/react to an opponent without hesitation from disturbance of thought.

[530] These things are cultivated by the physical practice, the following of etiquette, the serious, almost sacred atmosphere and the cat-and-mouse-jedi-mind-trick guessing games between teacher and student (when called up to take *ukemi* or otherwise).

[531] This transformation can only be achieved through daily training and is genuine. *Scientists find how relaxed minds remember better*, Wed, Mar 24 2010, Reuters article by Kate Kelland. See www.reuters.com/assets/print?aid=USTRE62N4VJ20100324.

[532] *Hot Diggity Dog! The Weinermobile Turns 70*. Associated Press, Seattle Times http://community.seattletimes.nwsource.com/archive/?date=20060704&slug=wiener04.

the driver standing up looking about—<u>not</u> pumping gas. My friend noticed nothing and was fiddling with his watch while waiting for the clerk. Something felt very wrong, so I turned my head again, casually, to my left, glanced and saw that all three now had pulled blue bandannas up over their noses "gangsta style."[533] In a flash, I saw the one right behind us now had his right hand under his jacket like he was gripping a gun. His fat girlfriend to his left was glaring at us. The third one, the guy on the far right, had his back to us now and his head turning left and right, sweeping the area with his eyes like some kind of lookout. The driver was back in the car. Just three doors were open now. Instinctively, I continued to turn—looking down slightly as if I hadn't noticed a thing—and positioned myself just slightly behind and off the right arm of the kid with the gun. Not so close that I'd spook him to pull it. Close enough that I could grip his shoulder/neck with my left hand, grab his elbow or wrist with my right and prevent him from pulling it and put him down hard if he tried. The kid instantly lost confidence. You could see it in his stance; feel it. However, standing there for what seemed like forever, sensing the tension rebuilding and not wanting things to combust, I said with a laugh, "Come on Tony (to my friend); let's go" and started walking backwards very slowly towards the car, keeping my eyes on the youths. My friend appeared to be joining me, turning, looking behind for the first time but then sharply turning back and freezing at the window. "I gotta go get him," I said towards our car with a sigh. Retracing those steps, closing that distance (there's the danger; *ma-ai* is totally wrong now) I felt a bubble of fear but popped it. Moving quietly, quickly but being careful not to show any urgency. Approaching the shooter's right shoulder again, the cashier looks at them and says, "Hey! It's not cold enough to wear masks!" breaking the kids' concentration.

They look at the cashier, "What?"

My friend spun on his heels, racing back to the car, running by me, camera in hand. Backing away, I jumped in behind him, and off we sped.

Speaking days later with my teacher (who used to work with the Los Angeles Police Department) and some police officers in the dojo, they all said, "Yep; they were going to shoot you. What you did unbalanced them,

---

[533] I couldn't risk saying something aloud, because it might set things off.

but didn't provoke them. They aren't thinking rationally, in that moment, but are reacting like animals. Feeling threatened, at any point, will set them off. Sensing weakness in you will set them off." *Chyokan* (直感), *zanshin* (残心), *mu-shin* (無心), these "fortune cookie" skills, forged in the dojo, part of the gift of Japanese culture that I'd received, had saved my life and that of my friend. All those years of wondering what the hell my teacher wanted when I was taking *ukemi* (since little was ever explained), watching and trying to figure out what the hell he was teaching, that constant tension in the dojo, had paid off with interest. These were abilities I could develop in a doio, through *keiko,* but never would in a gym. Did we take the photo? Of course! I still have it. Giant hot-dog car in the background. And after taking it, we turned the corner and stopped at a red light. Who pulled up next to us but our four little friends, all flashing gang hand signs. Sitting on the left behind our driver and closest to the gangsta-mobile, I tell my friend, "Give me the camera." Holding the camera up to the window I point it at the kids, "Cheese!" FLASH!!! Their car tore off with a screech, running the red light.

So to people who think "aikido doesn't work," what does that mean? Whose aikido? Work where? When? In a ring fight? In a "spontaneous" or "survival" encounter? I've used it many times, so what's your point? Trained in the right way, it's an excellent foundation for developing personal safety skills, in fact. Elsewhere in your life? The things that make up your usual day? Your work? Your physical and mental health? You bet it works. Just because you may not care for aikido or think Onisaburō Deguchi wore a funny hat doesn't mean that aikido is meritless.[534] "Aikido doesn't work." Maybe that's your experience, but my aikido works just fine, thanks.

Aikido technique, like any *jiujutsu*, works on scientific principles of leverage, centrifugal and centripetal forces and exploiting fundamental weaknesses of the human musculoskeletal system and bipedal movement.[535] [536] Of

---

[534] As mentioned, the extraordinary and eccentric Deguchi san was O-Sensei's spiritual leader at one point in his life.

[535] See, e.g., *The Physics Of Forces In Aikido: Making The Weak Equal To The Strong,* Jearl Walker, Scientific American July 1980. www.fightingarts.com/reading/article.php?id=284.

[536] The art is described in metaphysical terms in some aspects because it is a product of its culture, era of development and the founder and these aspects have yet to be scientifically analysed. However, the application of science to traditional arts is expanding. See e.g., *Science of Yoga: The*

course, the throws, strikes, controls, locks and pins of aikido are mechanically sound, but the footwork (the motor behind the technique): evading, entering, retreating, turning, fading is extremely useful. Likewise, gas for the motor, *kokyu-ryoku* (呼吸力, breath-power)—muscle extension and expansion (as opposed to just pushing and pulling) and the execution of technique in coordination with inhalation and exhalation to increase stability and power—is another distinguishing and empowering aspect of this type of *jiujutsu*. It's an entirely foolish notion that post-1940 O-Sensei neutered *Aiki-jujutsu* to create the more effete aikido. In fact, he turbo-charged it.[537] To the extent there's a problem, it's with the way some people practice aikido. But what do I care? Let them do what they please, just don't lump all aikido together.[538]

So which is worthwhile? 稽古それとも格闘技 *keiko soretomo kakutogi*? Studying old ways or sports fighting? Either. Both if you want. Do you enjoy *kakutogi*? Do you think you get something valuable out of it? If so, then do it. Who cares what anyone else thinks? Do you enjoy aikido *keiko*? Does it benefit your life? If so, then do it. If not, find something that does. For me, *budo* is a great way to learn about myself, develop skills and understand principles of self-defense (and conflict in general) and to learn and otherwise benefit from a very unique and fascinating culture. If you approach your fighting with the mindset and methodology of *keiko,* you will improve and get benefits outside of sport-fighting skills. And, if you approach your *keiko* as if your physical well-being actually depends on it, your aikido will improve as well. Aikido practice can serve as a mirror that reveals our true nature, exposing both our positive and negative traits if we have the courage to look closely and accept ourselves as we really are. But aikido does not stop with these revelations. It offers a path, step by step, day by day, to strengthen ourselves, polishing our mind, body and spirit to move ever closer towards our highest potential. 兵法は術に非ず、して道なり (*Heihou wa jutsu ni arazu, shite michi nari*): Martial arts is a Way, not a technique. However,

---

Risks and Rewards, William J. Broad, Simon & Schuster (26 April 2012) ISBN-10: 1451641427, ISBN-13: 978-1451641424.

[537] Compare the basic stances as a starting point. This doesn't mean there isn't value in studying *Daito-ryu Aiki-jiujutsu.* Some of my friends at Hombu Dojo do, and were I in Japan, I would, too.

[538] Were one of these super athletes doing professional *kakutougi* to devote him or herself to aikido practice under a skilled teacher, the person would be monstrously strong and deadly.

this path must follow the most physically, mentally and spiritually challenging training experience that you can handle … or it is indeed just "playing at martial arts."

The Fable of *Fusen*

不遷流の寓言

(*Fusen-ryu no guugen*)

The story of the evolution of Japanese martial arts from *koryu bujutsu* (古流武術, classical martial art) to *gendai budo* (現代武道, modern martial way) is a fascinating tale, as is the spread of Japanese and other martial arts around the world beginning from about the turn of the nineteenth century right through the Korean "conflict" of the 1950s. It's a story well worth telling, filled with bigger-than-life characters like Kano Jigoro, Ueshiba Moriteru, Funakoshi Gichin and many others acting against the backdrop of a turbulent and transforming time in human history. Unfortunately, with the sportification and particularly the commercialization of martial arts, objectivity and scholarship seem severely lacking at times (with some exceptions). You would think that the Internet would help (given its origins in scientific research and academia) and it has but it does its share of harm, too, by providing a global platform for every kook, crank, eccentric or conspiracy-theorist who can get wired. But that's part of its charm, too. As American political satirist Jon Stewart purportedly said, "The seven marvels that best represent man's achievements over the last 2,000 years will be determined by Internet vote ... so look for Howard Stern's Private Parts to come in Number One."[539]

For example, in years of searching, I have not found one shred of credible evidence to support the notion that Brazilian jiujitsu is derived from any *koryu jiujutsu* and, therefore, qualitatively distinguishable (on that

---

[539] The source is the Internet, so reader beware. See www.brainyquote.com/quotes/quotes/j/jonstewart146078.html.

basis) from BJJ's patently obvious parent *Kodokan Judo.*[540] [541] The oft-re-peated story on the Internet changes, but generally goes something like: around 1900 the *koryu jiujutsu* school *Fusen-ryu* challenged the *Kodokan* to a match between the schools and *Fusen-ryu* trounced the *Kodokan* in all but one of the [fill in the number] matches by using its special *newaza.* This crushing defeat caused the *Kodokan* to enlist the *Fusen-ryu* master to teach them. Therefore, *Kodokan newaza* was based on *Fusen-ryu* (skills which the *Kodokan* purportedly lost due to the rule changes of its matches post-1925). This *"Fusen-ryu newaza"* was transmitted to Maeda Mitsuyo (by some unidentified person before Maeda sensei left for America in 1904) and, in turn, while in Brazil, Maeda sensei transmitted his *Fusen-ryu* infused judo (within three to five years) to, fourteen to nineteen-year-old judo beginner, Carlos Gracie. Therefore, BJJ is based on *Fusen-ryu*, which differentiates it technically from present day *Kodokan Judo.*

Until faced with credible substantiating evidence, this story remains (to me) exactly that—a story. Examine the little evidence that's available and it sounds like a cybergame of "Chinese whispers"; each retelling of the tale adding bytes of embellishment.[542] Personally, I stop short of say-

---

[540] Starting points on *koryu jiujutsu* could include: Rev. T. Lindsay and Kano Jigoro, "The Old Samurai Art of Fighting Without Weapons," Transactions of the Asiatic Society of Japan, XVI, Pt II, 202-217. Reprinted 1915; see http://judoinfo.com/kano6.htm; the 1912 or 1913 editions of Englishman E.J. Harrison's *The Fighting Spirit of Japan.* See www.koryu.com/store/fightingspirit.html for a reprint; *Koryu Bujutsu: Classical Warrior Traditions of Japan, volume 1*, Edited by Diane Skoss, see www.koryu.com/bookstore/koryu_bu-jutsu.html; and, *Classical Fighting Arts of Japan: A Complete Guide to Koryu Jujutsu (Bushido--The Way of the Warrior)* by Serge Mol, published by Kodansha USA, (2001), ISBN-10:4770026196, ISBN-13: 978-4770026194; *Classical Bujutsu: Classical Bujutsu v. 1 (The Martial Arts & Ways of Japan)*, by Donn F. Draeger, published by Weatherhill Inc.; 2Rev Ed edition (1998), ISBN-10: 0834802333, ISBN-13: 978-0834802339. See www.scribd.com/doc/486921/Donn-F-Drae-ger-Classical-Bujutsu.

[541] If you read Japanese or can find good English translations, find the 1716 comprehensive survey by Hinatsu Shigetaka entitled *A Short Biography of the Martial Arts of Our Country (Honcho Bugei Shoden).* See Monumenta Nipponica, Vol. 45, No. 3 (Autumn, 1990), pp. 261-284, Published by: Sophia Article Stable at www.jstor.org/stable/2384903; *Judo-Higaku-sho* (Important Records of Judo) the Kodokan has a copy in its library; *Dainippon Judo-shi* (大日本柔道史,Great Japan Judo History), Editor Maruyama Sanzō, Published by *Kodokan*, 1939; *Judo Dai-jiten,* (柔道大事典, *Encyclopedia of Judo*, Contributors: Yukimitsu Kano, Toshiro Daigo, Kawamura Teizo,Takeuchi Yoshinori, Nakamura Ryozo, Published by Atene Shobo, 1999, ISBN 4871522059, 9784871522052; *The Canon of Judo: Classic Teachings on Principles and Techniques*, written by Kyuzo Mifune, Francoise White, Translated by Francoise White, published by Kodansha International, republished 2004, ISBN 4770029799, 9784770029799.

[542] A few are written rather persuasively but there are usually no citations (or maybe one) as it

ing it's told in bad faith, but, as for people buying into it, American humorist Mark Twain noted astutely that "a lie can travel halfway 'round the world while the truth is still pulling its boots on."[543] Why is it that so many people, so often, so willingly deny the obvious in order to believe something fanciful?

The first problem with the story is that *Fusen-ryu* is still practiced today, and it's clearly not a *newaza*-focused system.[544] What happened? Where are its special ground techniques? They forgot them? Discarded them? A Japanese *koryu jiujutsu* system just "lost" or ditched part of its "core" curriculum? After its glorious wins over the Kodokan? These are Japanese people we are talking about; right? Tellingly, Fusen-ryu technique doesn't look anything like *Kodokan Judo newaza*, but BJJ *newaza* sure does.

The second problem with the story is that the majority of the *Kodokan katamewaza* (holds, locks and strangles) curriculum was formulated between 1884 and 1887, the *Katame no Kata* (Form of Control).[545] That's about ten to twenty years before the purported *Fusen ryu* dojo-vs-dojo throwdown.[546]

The third problem is that when people bother to cite a source for the purported matches, it's usually limited to a statement attributed to an eighth dan Japanese *judoka* that's printed in an article in a French judo magazine (circa 1952) and the article doesn't mention a school-

---

seems to have been "researched" by someone who doesn't speak, read or write Japanese.

[543] Ironically, Samuel Clemens' purported quote may be a derivative! The Yale Book of Quotations includes: "A lie will go round the world while truth is pulling its boots on." C. H. Spurgeon, *Gems from Spurgeon* (1859). A preceding version appears in *The Portland* (Maine) *Gazette*, Sept. 5, 1820: "Falsehood will fly from Maine to Georgia, while truth is pulling her boots on." Even earlier, Jonathan Swift wrote in *The Examiner*, Nov. 9, 1710: "Falsehood flies, and the truth comes limping after it."

[544] Apparently *Fusen-Ryu Jiujutsu* is still practiced today. See e.g. www.youtube.com/watch?v=aEFwYpXFxQA. And I cannot vouch for this narrative as it lacks citations of any kind (I've seen the site it references but at the time of printing it was no long online. http://tohkonryujujitsu.blogspot.jp/2011/03/fusen-ryu-jujitsu.html

[545] "*The Katame no Kata* ... is composed of three groups of grappling techniques each with five representative techniques." http://judoinfo.com/katakata.htm Emphasis added.

[546] In 1906, the *Dai Nippon Butokukai* met and added five more techniques to the Katame-no-kata, expanding it to fifteen. One addition that some directly attribute to Tanabe Mataemon is *Ashi-Garami*. See www.judo-educazione.it/video/kime-no-kata_stefano_en.html. The *kata* is comprised of just fifteen representative techniques of pins, chokes and locks. The *kata* teaches the theoretical basis for execution and escape. It is not a catalogue of every technique that might be taught.

versus-school challenge of any kind.[547]   According to it and another accessible source (a book by a Japanese sports writer dated 1972), the contests occurred between 1891 and 1900 and concerned a lone *jiujitsuka*, Tanabe Mataemon, a teacher of *Fusen-ryu* (and apparently at some point its leader) who fought some grappling matches against *Kodokan judoka* employing the strategy of sitting down, avoiding *tachiwaza* (and injury or loss by throw) and keeping the contests on the ground.[548] [549] Considering the two writings together, it appears there were three to five "matches": at least one (maybe two) against Tobari Takizaburo (reportedly third dan), which Tanabe won, and two (or maybe three) against Isogai Hajime, which were all draws.[550]   Both translations of the accounts state that Tanabe possessed incredible physical strength.[551]   Interestingly, one account states unequivocally that the *Kodokan* already had a resident *newaza* expert who trained Isogai for the match, Samura Kaichiro, the eldest son of Samura Seimon of *Takeuchi Santo Ryu Jujutsu*.[552]   Neither written account is contemporary and neither states the basis for the purported knowledge of the speaker. Is it first hand? From a third-party? Oral or documentary?

---

[547]   There are probably more, but one of the two best-known accounts (outside of Japan) for matches concerning *Fusen-ryu* and *Kodokan Judo* are the reported comments of Shimomura Kainan, Eighth *dan* in *Kodokan Judo* in the September 1952 edition of Henri Plée's *Revue Judo Kodokan*. What's notable is that Shimomura sensei says these matches convinced the *Kodokan* that you had better be good at both *tachiwaza and newaza* but that *"Mataemon Tanabe*, too, <u>unconsciously</u> contributed towards the perfecting of the judo of the *Kodokan."* (Emphais added.) It's unclear whether his comment concerning 'the origin of the celebrated 'ne-waza of the Kansai region'" concerns *Fusen-ryu* or what *Kodokan* developed from that point forward. See e.g. www.kanosociety.org/Bulletins/bulletin6.htm.

[548]   The second source cited sometimes is *Japanese Judo: Hidden Records* (秘録:日本柔道) by sportswriter Kudo Raisuke (工藤雷介) published 1972 by 東京スポーツ新聞社, pp. 66-68, 108-111.

[549]   The *Dainippon Judo-shi* briefly mentions Tanabe Mataemon and recounts the origin of *Fusen ryu jujutsu* by a *Zen* priest who was renowned for his extraordinary physical and mental strength (thanks to *zazen*). According to one translation of the book, Tanabe Torajiro later headed the system and then his son Tanabe Mataemon. Mataemon was born in 1869 in Okayama prefecture and started jiujutsu under his father at age nine. By 1890, now twenty-two, he moved to Tokyo and became a *jiujutsu* instructor for the Tokyo Metropolitan Police. In 1906, he became a judo teacher and in 1922 he stopped teaching but, in 1927, at the age of fifty-eight, was honored as a judo master by the *Butokukai*. See www.sydhoare.com/FUSEN.pdf. Tanabe is also mentioned by a former General Manager of the *Kodokan*, in his book *Fifty Years of Judo* (柔道五十年, 1955年, Oimatsu Shinichi).

[550]   Presuming the translation was correct and other authentication and credibility issues satisfied, the Shimomura document can be read that defeats came in practice and then in a match or in more than one match. So there were either one or two matches between Tanabe and Tobari. Either way, Tanabe bested him.

[551]   Without reading the Japanese, one won't know if "strong" means physical strength or skill.

[552]   Samura Kaichiro (1880-1964) joined the *Kodokan* in 1898 and received Tenth Dan in 1948.

There is probably more in the vaults of newspapers or libraries somewhere, but discovering and deciphering it it requires the time, effort and expertise of a true scholar with native level Japanese language skills and who is trained to read such texts critically.

The fourth problem is that Maeda Mitsuyo left Japan in 1904, so actually he missed out on twenty-one years of the the "*newaza* renaissance," purportedly inspired by the *Fusen-ryu* matches of 1900, which resulted in: the addition of five new techniques to *Katame no Kata* in 1906, the creation of *Kosen* rule scholastic tournaments in 1914, and the 1925 rules changes for adult matches.[553]

The fifth problem is, where is the evidence (not conjecture, evidence) that Maeda Mitsuyo studied another form of *jiujutsu* or under Tanabe sensei (or anyone else)? Without evidence, the inescapable presumption is that whatever *newaza* Maeda sensei learned before he left Japan in 1904 came from his studies at the *Kodokan*—of judo not *koryu jiujutsu*. If you have studied martial arts in Japan and understand the cultural context and method by which culture is preserved and transmitted in all arts, including *budo*, especially over 100 years ago, you instantly recognize the Western pop-culture interpretation of the historical interaction between *Kodokan Judo* and *Fusen-ryu* is a fable.[554]

Newaza may have been a personal interest of Tanabe Mataemon, but it does not appear to be a unique feature of *Fusen-ryu*. More soberly, it appears that Tanabe was simply an experienced, excellent and exceptionally strong *jiujutsuka* who tried a new strategy to beat the *Kodokan*. Sometimes it worked. Sometimes it didn't. He was good enough and the results impressive enough though that Kano sensei apparently asked him to join the *Kodokan*, which he did some time before 1906 because he appears in

---

[553] One of these additional five techniques, *Ashi Garami*, is attributed by some to Tanabe Mataemon.

[554] Another commonly referenced but thinly sourced story about the purported origins of *jiujutsu newaza* concerns the Osaka dojo of Handa Yatarou. Some contend it was a *Fusen-ryu* and others a *Tenshin shinryo ryu* school. It is where Tani Yukio was purportedly a student before coming to London (he was nineteen when he arrived). There's a: reference to a Handa Yatarou in the *Judo Daijiten* and in a 1904 "Health and Strength" magazine interview with Uyenishi Sadakuzu (*jiujutsuka* and challenge wrestler) plus a 1915 interview of Miyake Taro, printed in English in a U.S. newspaper, that refers to a *Handa dojo*. It's all a bit muddled and insufficiently researched. Like Tani Yukio, Uyenishi Sadakuzu (who arrived in the UK at age twenty) authored a book, the 1905 classic *The Text Book of Ju-Jitsu as Practised in Japan*. See www.scribd.com/doc/58511038/The-Text-Book-of-Ju-Jitsu-as-Practised-in-Japan-Sadakazu-Uyenishi-1905.

photos in the 1915 English translation of the 1906 book *Judo Kyohan* demonstrating some *newaza*.[555] However, aggrandizing and then linking these turn of the century events (or the persons involved in them) to BJJ is wildly imaginative (absent concrete substantiating evidence). The evidence is that there is no connection between BJJ and any *koryu jiujutsu* except through judo, which assembled its *katamewaza* curriculum from a variety of *koryu* sources not just Tanabe Mataemon's *Fusen-ryu*.[556] [557] A genuine reason to study in a BJJ academy is that they are readily accessible, offer "all *newaza* all the time" and have many talented and passionately dedicated instructors, so you'll have the opportunity to become skilled.

---

[555] *Judo Kyohan*, by Yokoyama Sakujiro and Oshima Eisuke, first published in 1915, republished by *Buyu Shoseki Shuppan* (2003), ISBN-10: 4901619055, ISBN-13: 978-4901619059.

[556] People speculate that other *koryu jiujutsu*, like *Jikishin-Ryu* and *Takeuchi Santo Ryu*, also contributed significantly to judo's *katamewaza*. If so, that shows that more than one *koryu jijutsu* practiced *newaza*. However, *Kano Jigoro is reported as saying that katamewaza came directly from Tenshin Shinyo Ryu.*

[557] The group of teachers assembled by Kano Jigoro to help build the Kodokan kata syllabus met at the Dai Nihon Butokukai in Kyoto in July 1906. A photograph depicts in the front row: Inazu Masamizu of *Miura ryu*, Eguchi Yazo of *Kyushin ryu*, Katayama Takayoshi of *Yoshin ryu*, Hoshino Kumon of *Shiten tyu*, Kano Jigoro of *Kodokan*, Totsuka Hidemi of *Totsuka-ha Yoshin ryu*, Sekiguchi Jushin of *Sekiguchi ryu*, Yano Koji of *Takeuchi ryu*, Hiratsuka Katsuta of *Yoshin ryu*. Back row left to right is: Aoyagi Kehei of *Sosuishi ryu*, Mogichi Tsumizu of *Sekiguchi Ryu*, Hikosaburo Ohshima of *Takeuchi Ryu*, Hoken Sato of *Kodokan*, Kotaro Imei of *Takeuchi Ryu*, Mataemon Tanabe of *Fusen-Ryu*, Shikataro Takano of *Takeuchi Ryu*, Hidekazu Nagaoka *of Kodokan*, Sakujiro Yokoyama of *Kodokan*, Hajime Isogai of *Kodokan*, Yoshiaki Yamashita of *Kodokan*.

Wrestling with Aikido?

合気道について悩んでいるか

(*Aikido ni tsuite nayandeiru ka*)

To hammer the nail home harder still, you have to do aikido to understand aikido.[558] You have to feel it from someone who really knows what they are doing. In an age increasingly reliant on visual-media and instant answers, plus a troubling bent towards nihilism, people watch aikido videos on the Internet or otherwise (too many of which depict marginally skilled people) and think "oh, that's so fake."[559]

But you only have to consider O-Sensei's life story and know who his initial students were, not to mention the reactions of people like Kano Jigoro to Ueshiba sensei's *budo*, to realize his martial art is for real.[560] As one BJJ professor said to me one day, "You know; one thing about O-Sensei, you don't find his contemporaries dismissing him.[561] If aikido is so useless, why did all these hardcore martial artists go study from

---

[558] Oh, if you do aikido, then this chapter may bore you blind. If not and you're an aikido skeptic, then you may be bored, but you were already blind, so not my bad.

[559] Truthfully, they don't even know what they are watching. It's not their fault. They are viewing it from another perspective, usually match-fighting.

[560] I read on the Internet a hilarious description that O-Sensei must've seemed like "The Ghost of Jiujustu Past" to Kano sensei. Here he thought he had corralled all the stallions for his new sportified jiujutsu, and whoops, along came Takeda sensei's student Ueshiba Moriteru resurrecting "*ki*," ingenious joint-locking and striking, weapons work, etc. And the stuff "worked."

[561] "I have some thoughts about *Kodokan-Judo*. Briefly speaking, there is a person named *Ueshiba* who practices dangerous joint techniques. ..." One certainly wouldn't expect prominent contemporary martial artists to describe O-Sensei's technique as "dangerous" if his *budo* was empty. See the article, by *Shishida Fumiaki*, of Waseda University and Tomiki Aikido, and his personal views on the (1925 to 1931) diaries of Admiral Takeshita Isamu. Shishida sensei attributes the preceding quoted remarks to *Kodokan* representative *Honda Chikatami* following the first national tournament in the presence of the Emperor in 1929, as reported in "*Showa Tenran Shiai*" *Dainihon-yubenkai-kodansha*, 1930, pp.722-723.
www.scribd.com/doc/52142383/Aikido-Aikido-Japanese-Imperial-Navy-Admiral-Isamu-Takeshita-1925-to-1931.

him?"[562] Over and over again, O-Sensei is challenged, he bests the challenger and the person becomes his student.[563] It's important to remember too that the *zeigest* (and likelihood of personal danger) of pre-WWII twentieth century Japan, with its not so distant *samurai* past, rising militarism and visions of regional empire, must have differed dramatically from the post-war eras of: defeat and deprivation, to miraculous economic recovery, to highly affluent and a gentler, safer society. O-Sensei became a sensation in Japan during these more dangerous times because his art offered demonstrable extraordinary skills, not just philosophical musings. He attracted students the way all martial artists have done: by besting other men, by convincing them with acts of skill and strength.[564] [565] Yes; yes; I know. "Who is the equal of O-Sensei?" "Are people even doing what O-Sensei did?" Who knows? Practice hard! Study! Find your own way! The question isn't whether or not aikido is a martial art. Of course it is. The question is whether and to what extent the way a particular dojo practices maintains its martial qualities.[566] In some cases, yes. In some cases, aspects. In some cases, not really. People can and will think and do as they please, but *aikidoka* are not all studying or expressing the art in a unified way that can be collectively and comprehensively dismissed. At least, not if you are over fourteen and have a brain.

In October 2, 1930, Kano Jigoro, the father of *Kodokan Judo*, visited O-Sensei's temporary dojo in Shimo-Ochiai of Mejiro-dai to see a demonstration, along with many other distinguished guests.[567] If you do aikido, you have read about Kano sensei saying something like "This is my ideal

---

[562] Judo *newaza* specialist Oda Tsunetane and O-Sensei were reportedly friends. http://judoinfo.com/oda.htm

[563] O-Sensei apparently dispatched *judoka* Abbe Kenshiro (the slayer of judo god Kimura Masahiko in a match) with ease and Abbe sensei then studied with him for ten years. See Morgan, K., & Ellis, H. (2006): *Kenshiro Abbe Sensei 1915–1985: A man with too many friends* (originally published in Martial Arts Illustrated, December 2006).

[564] He supposedly developed 147 counter-techniques against judo, "Tai Judo," according to the notes of his powerful patron (and student) Admiral Takeshita. Written between spring 1930 and winter 1931, the "*Kon*" is a 252-page diary of the Admiral's training under O-Sensei that organizes and classifies what he learned.

[565] And, don't dismiss the attraction of paradox of extraordinary physical skill combined with great spiritual depth.

[566] Add to that how, after mastering and polishing fundamentals, one explores or advances boundaries.

[567] Stevens, John. Abundant Peace. Shambala Publications, Inc., 1987. I have read elsewhere that Kano sensei was accompanied by two of his top instructors, Shuichi Nagaoka and Mifune Kyuzo. Quite an audience.

budo." I don't know what Japanese word was used for "ideal" and it's advisable to be slightly wary of compliments in Japan, but soon two of Kano sensei's good students Takeda Jiro and Mochizuki Minoru were studying with O-Sensei.[568]   Notably too, in 1956, when *Kodokan Judo* added its self-defense *kata* (*goshinjutsu*, 護身術), a close student of O-Sensei, Tomiki Kenji (*Kodokan Judo* and aikido Eighth Dan), served as a special technical adviser to the committee and authored an instructional book.[569]   In the preface to Tomiki sensei's book, the then-president of the *Kodokan*, Kano Risei, is quoted as saying that Kano sensei had not yet systematized the self-defense aspect of judo and doing so was clearly important to him because he sent students to study with Ueshiba sensei. Analyze aikido by the "scientific" elements employed by Kano Jigoro for constructing his judo and it stands up to scrutiny: *kuzushi* (崩し, くずし), *tsukuri* (作り, つくり), *kake* (掛け, かけ) or destabilization, construction (position yourself in the right place in relation to your partner), completion (execute the technique).[570]

In aikido, *kuzushi*, or "unbalancing" if you prefer, starts with *ma-ai*, which as some of you know already, includes the concepts of spacing and timing.   When confronted, you start by controlling the spacing and then catching the opponent's timing.   Broadly speaking, you should initially be just close enough that your opponent has to move her center in order to make contact with a hand, foot or weapon.   Not too close, but not so far that she thinks it's pointless to initiate.   Good practice involves the perpetual study of this critical initial interaction.   Aikido is not a sport, however.   There is no obligation to initiate or engage in conflict.   However, it's a mistake to think of aikido as purely defensive.

It's Merely Defensive!

Actually, aikido embodies *koubou-ichi* (攻防一致, こうぼういっち) the coincidence of offense and defense.   In fact, it surpasses it.   Indeed,

---

[568] Apparently there is a letter from Kano sensei to Ueshiba sensei dated October 28, 1930, expressing his thanks and committing the two students to study with O-Sensei.

[569] *Kodokan goshinjutsu*, Volume 87 of *Supôtsu shinsho*, by Tomiki Kenji, published by *Bêsubôru. Magajinsha*, 1958 ISBN458301113X, 9784583011134.

[570] While Kano sensei's analytical framework can be applied, the methods for achieving his three steps, while sharing some principles, have substantial differences. *Kuzushi* connotes an aggression absent from aikido philosophy.

in any martial art, they can be viewed as one, depending on circumstances and perspective, but aikido goes one step further by rejecting the dualism of friend and foe.

> "It is not a question of either 'sensen no sen' or 'sen no sen.' If I were to try to verbalize it I would say that you control your opponent without trying to control him. That is, the state of continuous victory. There isn't any question of winning over or losing to an opponent. In this sense, there is no opponent in aikido. Even if you have an opponent, he becomes a part of you, a partner you control only."[571]

Many of you will recognize O-Sensei's remarks and recall the three fundamental combat initiatives of traditional Japanese martial arts: *go no sen* (後の先), *sen no sen* (先の先), and *sen sen no sen* (先々の先). While the mindset of an *aikidoka* may not be prone to aggression and the art may strive to cultivate a sense of inner peace, any of the traditional timings can be employed to seize initiative when confrontation is unavoidable, until you are so gifted that you can move as naturally as O-Sensei. Act by moving to counter, *go no sen*. Act by moving simultaneously, *sen-no-sen*. Act by moving preemptively, *sen sen-no-sen*.[572] Aikido can employ a variety of initiatives and still be for "self-defense" rather than aggression.[573]

Go no sen—"after move"—is the timing many people reflexively associate with aikido. In response to an attack, you defend or counter. In martial arts generally, this could be a counter-punch, blocking, ducking, slipping or otherwise evading and countering. The opponent's movement presents an opening to respond. In aikido, this might be moving just off-line and outside of a linear striking attack and "entering" (quickly closing the distance) and executing a throw ("take-down"). But you cannot simply sit-back and allow the *uke* to control the type, timing and direction of

---

[571] Remarks from a purported interview of O-Sensei in 1957, which have been republished by *Aikido Journal*. See www.aikidojournal.com/article.php?articleID=600.

[572] 先 can be read as *sen* or *saki*. It's the same *sen* as in sensei. It can be read as former; previous; old or an opening move like in the strategy games of *go, shogi*, etc.

[573] Yes; if right-minded, there is no confrontation at all, regardless of timing.

attack. You cannot react in time if a skillful, careful opponent uses a variety of rapid attacks. *Sen no sen* (or *saki no saki*, if you prefer) seeks control by simultaneously "attacking" as your opponent is initiating.[574] Looking carefully at your opponent: stance, eyes, posture, hands, feet and so on, you read his intention and initiate before his attack is fully formed. You don't wait; you act. It's discerning your opponent's intention and acting. *Sen no sen* might be using an overhead strike (*shomenuchi*, like hitting someone over the head with a bottle) so your opponent raises an arm and hand to block, and as he does so, grasping his arm and putting him down. *Sen sen no sen* (before, before the opening move) requires still greater skill, an alchemy of acute perception with accurate intuition. Considered the ultimate in classical martial arts, you sense your opponent's intention and either present a posture that he perceives as unassailable or you initiate a point of engagement before he can initiate the move he has in mind. Literally one move ahead of her (at least).

Referring to aikido as *go no sen no budo* (defensive martial art) means that it should be used in self-defense. It does not mean that you refrain passively when confronted. Good aikido is anything but passive. In fact, it is neither passive nor aggressive. It has moved beyond this polarity and can be initiating without the intention of harm or destruction.

> A budo that is only a *"go no sen budo,"* or that is only a *"uke no budo"* is not really a *budo* at all. In Japanese *budo* history, there has never been an art designed to gain victory by being backed into a corner or by putting oneself under siege. In every case the essence is to strike out and decide the issue of victory or defeat in an active way. Thus in aikido we do not sit back and let our partner push us here and there, neither do we actually attack them. There is no winning, and there is no being defeated. We do away with the distinctions of attacker and attacked. Aikido movement brings the two into a single accord.[575]

---

[574] If there is a *go no sen* and *sen no sen*, then there must be a *sen*. Initiating the opening yourself.

[575] From *Aikido: Its Spirit and Technique* by *Doshu Ueshiba Kishomaru*, an essay based on a two hour address by Second Doshu in 1986 to the 12th General Meeting of the Japan Martial Arts Society. First published in The Aikido, vol. 23 no. 2 in 1986 and republished online at at www.aikidosphere.com/dkuespirittechnique.cfm.

Mechanics Not Magic

As I heard one Hombu *shihan* put it, all *bugi* (武技, ぶぎ, martial arts), including aikido, operate on physics and mechanics, principles or rather *bujutsu no housoku* (武術の法則, ぶじゅつのほうそく, martial arts laws/principles), to which I would add strategy and tactics, in an effort to turn a situation presenting a potential or actual physical confrontation to one's advantage. In the case of aikido, it uses spacing/timing (*ma-ai*), continuous movement and unique ways of generating and delivering power, e.g., without necessarily having to stop and set your feet in a fixed position, and enables the practitioner to return a measured response that is appropriate for the specific situation.

For example, by leading, turning, entering or retreating (straight back or obliquely), an *aikidoka* seeks to position himself to exploit an assailant's *shikaku* (死角, しかく, literally dead angle or corner, an opening or blindspot). This includes not only the *uke*'s weak balance point(s) (people are bipedal so there are four areas—two in front (diagonally, left and right) and two behind (diagonally, left and right)—where their balance is especially vulnerable, particularly after an arm or leg is extended to grasp or strike you) but includes particularly those positions in relation to the attacker where you cannot be hit or kicked with much force (or they cannot exert controlling pushing or pulling power if you are being grabbed). An example of this "safe place" would be moving closer, just outside of an attacker's "over-hand right" punch, for example, to a point just behind his right shoulder ("entering") and then executing a throw.[576] The initially unsettling and very challenging part for new students is the feeling of moving into the strike—towards danger—but slipping just past it.

Another example (again considering an overhand right strike) is retreating (fading back) in an arc behind you, by moving your lead foot to the rear as the attack comes towards you (a lead left foot becomes a back left foot). You evade the blow by maintaining a safe *ma-ai* and deflecting the attacking arm downwards—batting it down with your right (now your

---

[576] It is not a long-term refuge; one would normally not linger for more than seconds or a fraction of a second.

lead hand) or both hands to unsettle his posture—somewhat like *kiri-otoshi* in swordsmanship. From this position, depending on various factors (including the position of his right elbow, his center of gravity and whether or not he is stable enough to attack with his left hand or either foot), a variety of techniques are available. As you deflect the striking arm down, you might establish a connection to your assailant's arm at the elbow (pressing, sticking to him and passing his arm slightly past your center to your right), so that he cannot turn and strike with the left hand or lift a leg to kick (at all or with any force). From this position, you can step forward with your left leg, back in behind him, moving your body into his *shikaku*, striking him with the left hand (in the kidney, floating-rib, neck, temple, jaw, etc.) if you like and then complete closing the distance to "take his back." Alternatively, as you deflect the striking arm down, you grasp his arm with two hands. Turning your hip powerfully to the right, using these core muscles to overpower the arm, you turn your opponent's body, exposing his *shikaku*. And on and on.

In addition to exploiting *shikaku*—a fundamental structural weakness of bipedal movement—aikido employs various ingenious, fascinating methods, in unison, to control ("harmonize" if you prefer) *uke*:

- seizing on additional physiological weakness, e.g., joints: fingers, wrist, elbow, shoulder, foot, ankle, knee, neck, even the spine (according to circumstances);
- exposing the mechanical limitations of an opponent's arm strength. Reaching forward, grabbing you, *uke* can push or pull quite strongly but struggles to control *nage* from moving side-to-side, diagonally or rotationally;
- rather than merely using the muscles of the arm to push or pull, you can "push or pull" using the bones of the arms as rod or rope powered by the irresistible rotation of the hip/torso muscles plus centrifugal and centripetal forces;
- leading and "blending" with opponent strikes rather than conflicting (no "rock on rock"); intercepting them earlier or later in their trajectory before or after the maximum point of energy;
- contesting nothing; instead of just pushing or pulling when pushed or pulled, *aikidoka* turn when pushed, enter when pulled;

and,[577]

- using all kinds of deceptive, pin-point *atemi* (for distraction, de-stabilization, debilitation or destruction).

That's a short list. The deep technical nature of this particular system of *jiujutsu* is part of what makes it so interesting to study.

Adding to the common misconceptions about aikido by the average Internet armchair-expert are various misunderstandings about aikido fundamentals.

What's With the Stance?

Watch film of the Founder and, along with his enthusiasm, dynamism and uncanny timing, you can't help but notice his superb posture. It's perfect in every movement. The right posture (muscle, skeletal alignment) is fundamental to optimizing movement in any physical activity. *Kamae* (構え, かまえ) can be translated as stance but "posture" would probably be better. The *kanji* means "base." *Kamae* includes mental readiness as well as physical posture. Can you move swiftly and smoothly when attacked, without hesitation? This isn't philosophical musing. Posture affects directly the mechanics and physics of technique. It's simple math. You engin-nerds will remember The Force Equation. Newton's Second Law of Motion is often written as Force = Mass x Acceleration.[578] Posture affects Mass. Posture affects Acceleration. Therefore posture affects Force. Bend over at the waist, and your center of gravity rises from your hips to your chest. Move like that and you are essentially utilizing only half of your body mass in your technique. If you are too stiff and your hips are in the wrong position, you impair acceleration. Force is diminished, by either occurrence, or both.

Aikido was birthed from *koryu jiujutsu* and traditional weapons. Its stance is derived from these arts and in response to them in order to address equally, within a single stance, the possibility of unarmed, armed

---

[577] Those aren't the only two options.

[578] The rate of change of momentum, acceleration (a), of a body (m), is proportional to the resultant force (F) acting on the body in the same direction as the resultant force.. Acceleration equals force divided by mass or (F = ma). www.physicsclass-room.com/class/newtlaws/u2l3a.cfm

or even multiple opponents. Gone is the stance typical of some *jiu-jutsu*—shoulders presented squarely to the opponent.[579] *Aikidoka* never present a square target. As in Japanese swordsmanship, the right or the left foot is forward, the other behind. Were you to draw a straight line from the heel of the front foot towards the back foot, the line would intersect the back foot slightly forward of the heel but before the arch of the foot. The body forms a triangle towards an opponent. Your torso is turned slightly towards the back foot, *hanmi* (半身, はんみ, half-person), presenting a smaller target.[580] Front knee is bent slightly. Back leg straight. Weight/feeling is about 60-70% forward, so you can advance or retreat quickly. Arms/hands are extended forward. Place your arms and hands in front of you as if you holding a sword with two hands. If the right foot is forward, then the right hand is the lead (or most forward). Hands are open, fingers splayed—"energized" but not stiff. The back is ramrod straight (which aligns the hips and feet for maximum stability, acceleration and transmission of power), shoulders down (raising the shoulders stiffens, slows and structurally weakens the body), the chest "open" (promoting proper breathing, relaxation and helps influence the shoulders).

Aikido utilizes this stance for numerous reasons, including:

- the head, spinal column and hips are all in alignment on a vertical axis;
- the center of gravity is at the hip level;
- the hips are aligned towards your opponent in a way that maximizes your ability to receive attack (without becoming unbalanced) and return technique powerfully and stably but not necessarily in a fixed position.

Consequently, you can move freely, in any direction, without having to first shift your weight up or down and back over your hips, so that you can then move rapidly. There is no delay.

---

[579] You certainly can't crouch over at the waist like a wrestler might do ... to get punched, kicked, stabbed or clubbed in the face.

[580] It is a martial art not a fighting sport and presumes that opponents may be armed, even beyond their feet and hands.

What's With the Feet?

Aikido footwork is related to footwork in Japanese swordsmanship. Both feet remain in contact with the ground, and when moved, a sliding/shuffling foot movement is employed—*suri-ashi* (摺足; すりあし).[581] Your feet remain in continuous contact with the earth, improving balance and allowing you to move spontaneously, smoothly and swiftly without first having to shift your center up or down, backwards or forwards, which slows you down and leaves openings to be unbalanced. No Praying Monkey stances. No rhythmic bouncing (that your opponent can time). Just moving swiftly, but stably. It's difficult to master, but very useful.

What's With the Hands?

People get confused over the kinds of strikes that are principally used in aikido practice. "Those aren't real." On the contrary. First of all, *shomen-uchi* (smashing someone overhead, like a hammer; it can be done as a more linear strike with the knife-edge of the hand as well), *yokomen-uchi* (slashing obliquely) and *chudan-tsuki* (thrust to your center) are each fundamental weapons-based attacks: blade or stick or other cudgel.[582] Secondly, they are killing or crippling strikes: edge of the hand (knife-hand) to the eye socket, between the eyes or to collarbone, to the temple or carotid artery or into the solar-plexus. Third, they serve a pedagogical purpose because they are better for transmitting basic principles of angles of attack, controlling the center-line, deflecting and blending, entering, turning or retreating (or fading) and eliciting "bigger" movement from the student at the beginning.[583] Once you have mastered these basics, then dealing with more "conventional" attacks is simpler than most people think. It doesn't matter what the weapon is: foot, hand, head, stick, bottle, etc. It's always a matter of angles of attack and *ma-ai* (spacing and timing). If you want to get proficient defending against a particular type of attack, you have to develop drills and do focused *randori* to learn to deal with it. It's that straightforward.[584]

---

[581] It appears in sumo, *Noh* and other arts in Japan as well.

[582] Yes; I realize there are more sophisticated ways to hold a knife. Aikido's strikes are "step one" in understanding.

[583] Big movement is a starting point in developing *kokyu*. Over time, movement will naturally become more efficient and smaller. They also provide opportunity for *uke* to develop and condition his body.

[584] Of course, you cannot sit within range and exchange short-range blows with someone like a trained boxer, but that should be obvious. Be outside and safe or inside and safe.

What's With Your Breath?

People get confused about *ki* and breath in aikido, breath-power, *kokyu-ryoku*. In very simple terms, every person generally understands that they can use their muscles to push, pull and twist. However, your muscles can also "expand" and "extend" powerfully, particularly when done in coordination with inhalation.[585] In aikido, it concerns, in part, the coordinated movement—in proper alignment and timing—of the skeletal, muscular and (the inhalation and exhalation of) breath to add additional stability and power to aikido technique.[586] In a gross simplification, think of the shot-put. The athlete inhales, moves and explodes with a massive exhalation of air as he "puts" the shot.[587] This produces more force and a farther throw. It's a simple, somewhat crude example. There is more to it than this. For example, breath and muscle "extension" has a stabilizing effect that makes unbalancing or otherwise moving you much more difficult. *Kokyu-ryoku* is something that you can feel when trying aikido with a highly trained teacher but cannot possibly see when watching it, whether live or on video.

Kokyu is one aspect that distinguishes *Aiki* from other forms of *jiu-jutsu*.[588] It is an entirely new skill, difficult to understand and it takes considerable time to master the basics and ongoing development. Just going to a gym and studying something where you only have to "pull, push, twist" is easier and provides more immediate positive feedback or at least the delusion of it (because there is real art in that kind of body movement, too). Aikido involves learning how to squeeze every ounce of energy and power your body can muster, and this means you are often left wondering "how is that possible?" when you experience it from someone well-

---

[585] "Fundamentally, skeletal muscle can do three different things: it can shorten, stay the same length, and increase length. In nerd terms, these are called concentric muscle actions (the muscle shortens under load), isometric muscle actions (the muscle doesn't change length) and eccentric muscle actions (the muscle lengthens under load). ... In general, people are a bit stronger when they exhale (this is part of why boxers and martial artists exhale when they throw a punch or kick) and since it's harder to lift a weight than it is to lower it, it makes sense to synchronize the breathing with the difficulty of the movement." www.bodyrecomposition.com/training/breathing-during-weight-training.html

[586] There are other features as well. This is a simplification as I have not mentioned how this allows you to connect, manipulate and unbalance your opponent's center.

[587] The movement is not always "explosive" in speed. The point is proper breathing is part of the physics.

[588] Note I did not say all.

trained.[589]

What's With the Knees Down, Walking About and Moving Behavior?

People see *aikidoka* doing knee-walking, seated/kneeling practice, and go "what the hell"? Knee-walking, *shikkou* (膝行, しっこう), is for *suwariwaza* or seated or kneeling technique. In case you missed it earlier, back in the day you might be required to defend yourself while standing (*tachiwaza*), sitting (*suwariwaza*) or lying down (*newaza*). It's unlikely that the locals were doing much *suwariwaza* on the battlefield, which shows again that Japanese martial arts were not limited to when wearing armor for battle. These days, *suwariwaza* is a training tool for developing stronger standing technique. It quickly exposes weaknesses in leg strength, balance and so on. Developing strong *suwariwaza* is integral to developing your best aikido. When most foreign students first visit Hombu Dojo, the amount of *suwariwaza* practice, on those hard mats, reveals gaps in their training back home that leave their knees swollen and bruised in Japan.

What's With the Falling?

Too much aikido offered for viewing via the Internet isn't very good. Even if it's good, people unfamiliar with the realities of practice and demonstration may see it and think, "Oh, the other person is just falling down." Well, yes and no. Yes, when beginners are involved or the level of practice is low. Otherwise, no. Not at all.

As many readers are well aware, there are two fundamental roles in aikido training—*nage* (投げ) and *uke* (受け, うけ). In other words, there is the person doing the technique and the person receiving the technique. As mentioned, *ukemi* is the art of receiving the technique safely.[590] The word is formed using two characters: 受 upon which many words are formed relating to matters of "receiving" or "acceptance," and the *kanji*

---

[589] Read more: www.livestrong.com/article/94350-importance-breathing-lifting-weights/#ixzz1tLUq3A5G, www.livestrong.com/breathing-techniques, www.expertboxing.com/boxing-workouts/boxer-breathing-technique, www.getinthezone.org.uk/media/26342/wellcometrust_11-14_knowledge_card.pdf, http://combatsportpsychology.blogspot.co.uk/2009/07/power-of-breathing.html.

[590] Actually, the word has several meanings but in aikido it is used this way.

身 which can mean body or oneself. I used to joke with friends that many people thought *ukemi* was Japanese for "rest time" (until it was their turn to throw the other person) but developing good *ukemi* is integral for fully meaningful and safe practice, the conditioning of your body, developing your most effective aikido and for your overall personal development as a student. To learn aikido well, you have to "take" *ukemi*. You cannot catch the "feel" of technique without it. You cannot learn to protect yourself without it. Without it, you're only learning half the art.

Just grabbing and blocking your partner's movement from day one doesn't allow her to learn and commit the curriculum to muscle memory. Just grabbing and blocking doesn't develop the *uke,* either. You don't have to study aikido for thirty years to learn how to be stiff and strong. You have a pretty good idea about that the first day you walked into the dojo. Aikido *ukemi* takes a different path than simply stiffening to resist, block or counter the movement that *nage* wants to practice. *Uke* seeks to receive the technique fully and yet survive intact, which is exactly what you must do if a technique is applied so strongly or quickly that you cannot resist it—that or break. I remember applying *sankyo* (a wristlock) on a BJJ black-belt one day. I had been graciously invited to teach in his academy, as this teacher is very curious about Aikido being a completion-art for his various martial arts studies. Not very hard, really; maybe 40% power? He nearly jumped out of his *gi* and hit the ceiling. "You okay?" I asked sincerely; smiling.

"Yeah, but any harder and I'm shuttin' down the class," he said, laughing.[591] Take *ukemi* for a few years and your wrist becomes conditioned and you learn where to move to reduce the pressure (and how to counter).[592] *Ukemi* seeks to improve your ability to survive, escape and counter or retreat ... beyond merely employing your innate level of brute force.

A good *aikidoka* works to develop his *ukemi* until it has the feeling of bamboo ... strong but flexible and responsive, not stiff, not blocking until breaking or offering nothing in response, merely collapsing like a noodle. There should be a "springy," lively responsiveness or "stickiness," by con-

---

[591] This teacher has a particularly excellent sense of humor.
[592] It's like after practicing judo and BJJ for awhile, my neck became about two inches thicker from all the *shimewaza* (chokes).

necting your center to your partner's through the particular point of contact, e.g., hand to wrist or hand to shoulder, etc. You receive the technique and fall safely as your balance is taken and the throw or pin is executed. Not too soon (fake) and not too late (ouch). Through *ukemi*, you learn to read/feel/sense the movement of your opponent (and react), build a strong but flexible body, learn to receive (rather than block) a technique without suffering injury. *Ukemi* allows you to practice safely, by avoiding injury from falls, locks and pins, and in the long term by helping to dissipate force rather than receiving the full power of techniques into your joints and internal organs, repeatedly through your years of study.

Throughout, however, Aikido *keiko* must remain uncompromisingly grounded on genuine principles of physics, mechanics and human physiology, or it can deteriorate into a kind of pantomime martial arts practice.[593] It is true that its fundamental form of training permits men and women of varying ages, sizes and abilities to train together productively—although the depth, meaning and results of practice are limited by the degree of variance in size, skill, health and other factors between the two partners. And, establishing a general method of practice, as a baseline that enables a broad inclusiveness, does not prevent some partners from practicing in more challenging ways to develop and preserve martial techniques. The second is simply a subset of the first. Neither one is necessarily more legitimate than the other. Everyone can learn to play the piano. Not everyone can play at Carnegie Hall … well. However, in Aikido, too often it seems that those who simply aren't physically, mentally or spiritually capable of engaging in a more demanding practice disparage those who are and vice versa. Compromises or accommodations are made so that more people can practice safely and benefit from it; that's good. But people (*aikidoka* or otherwise) shouldn't play make-believe that they can really defend themselves, when they can't. Practitioners should recognize and accept reality. As my first teacher's Zen master remarked, "Live life as it really is." Failure to develop and move beyond the initial cooperation by the *uke* results in a corrupt form of practice that's mired in a kind of

---

[593] Pantomime, a British tradition, is a form of raucous musical-comedy theater, often enacting children's stories, that's traditionally performed at Christmas for family audiences. "Panto" involves overacting, song, dance, slapstick, general silliness, cross-dressing, audience shouting at actors, actors shouting back, topical humor, double entendre and the like. See e.g., www.historic-uk.com/CultureUK/Pantomime/

repetitive fake confrontation that's too dependent on the training partner and therefore limits real improvement. As a method of human development, it may have tremendous validity, but as martial arts training it's "fake" or perhaps more accurately "flawed." The sauce in the bowl that I'm dipping my tortilla chip in may have chopped tomatoes, cilantro, onions and lime juice … but without the chilies, it's hardly salsa.

What's With the Samurai Sticks?

Aikido is a weapons-based system (like *koryu jiujutsu*). I mean, it addresses the issue of armed assailants.[594] And it does so daily, because the fundamental striking attacks in practice are the same or similar motion to basic armed attacks. Both sword and staff were fundamental to O-Sensei's training and his creation and expression of aikido. However, did O-Sensei create weapons *kata* to be used systematically in aikido training? Not that I've seen or heard. What's absolutely uncanny are the connections, the fundamental principles of movement, between the weapons work and empty-handed techniques. They are also teaching tools by which fundamental principles of *taijutsu* become better understood.

It is particularly ingenious (and beautiful) that fundamental movements and even techniques of aikido's *taijutsu* (body art: throws, locks, pins, etc.) are directly applicable if the attacker is armed. If a system's answer to non-firearm weapon-attacks is "run," they probably have little or nothing to teach you and are trying to sell you on something else. Fools scoff at weapons training like it's some kind of American Civil War re-enactment, but they don't understand that its purpose and value goes well beyond defending against an armed attacker.[595] The staff (*jo*, 杖, じょう) and wooden sword (*bokken*, 木剣, ぼっけん or *boku-to*, 木刀, ぼくとう) help teach fundamentals of posture, hip movement, footwork (sliding feet, entering, turning, etc.) and hand movement (lines of attack and deflection). They improve your sense of spacing and timing and train your eyes to discern fast movement. The tip of these weapons is typically travelling

---

[594] Armed means any handheld weapon other than firearms at anything more than point-blank range. I reckon explosives are off the menu as well.

[595] I take note that my American Southerner brothers and sisters (of which my wife is one) say "There was nothing 'Civil' about the War Between the States" wherein more Americans died than all other American wars and "conflicts" combined.

much faster than a fist or foot. Weapons work helps further develop your legs and it strengthens your hands and fingers—by teaching you fundamentals about gripping and then just gripping a lot.[596] My grip strength helped me tremendously when I started judo and restarted BJJ in 2008. I remember grabbing the outside sleeve, near the triceps, of a big young kid in BJJ class and getting *gi* plus a hunk of arm. He came back in the next day, "What'djya do? Goblin-grip me?!!" he said rolling up his sleeve to show his black and blue arm. Weapons training increases the element of danger and the potential for serious physical harm, which is good for developing courage and a calm mind. They also provide a means for training solo. They've become a highly useful contemporary training tool with a link to a remarkable distant past—the battlefields of Japan.[597]

What's so Striking?

"All war is deception" and, nonviolent or not, aikido makes full use of it. Unique, well-placed and deceptive *atemi*, strikes, using the edge of the hand, fist, palm, back of the fist, fingers, the forearm (like a club) or the elbow have all been taught to me over the years by many different teachers.[598] Among other things, they serve to disrupt the *uke*'s posture (both physical and mental). In aikido, they tend to be directed towards vulnerable areas of the body: cheekbone, eyes, solar-plexus, collarbone, ribs, elbow joint, etc. and come from unusual angles of attack.[599] Often they can be delivered at multiple points along the path of any technique. However, to do them and strike with real intent and power you have to condition your hands, just as people do in karate or wushu. I used to train with a *makiwara* (巻藁, まきわら) or slap a phone book or tree or wall.[600]

---

[596] Most people grip principally with the thumb and index finger, but weapons, especially swordsmanship, requires you to grip with your focus and power in the small finger.

[597] But if you think you are learning some kind of battlefield system, you are kidding yourself. Go study a *koryu jiujutsu* system or swordsmanship.

[598] While most aikido schools don't teach you to kick or use your knees, aikido *tai-sabaki* certainly creates openings for using them effectively. Master a Muay Thai low kick, push kick and knee and you're probably good to go if those are skills you want, but it's not essential to learning aikido or improving its "effectiveness." That said, I have seen teachers deliver kicks, had my legs swept by a teacher using his leg in the manner of a kick and so on, so it's not like everyone doing aikido is blind to the prospect of using your feet and legs as a weapon. They simply aren't reliant upon it.

[599] You are not trying to out-point or knock-out a foe in a sports match.

[600] Even just ten times a day or every other day for each type of strike: closed fist, back-hand,

You don't have to do this kind of thing to enjoy and benefit from aikido training, but to protect yourself from injury if you do hit someone, you'd best realize you are liable to injure yourself if you don't do this kind of intensive training. In fact, I believe that you are better off not relying on *atemi* at all (even feints) in your daily training for a number of years, while recognizing all the openings for them, and then learning them. Using them too soon and too often can stunt the development of better aikido fundamentals. You can become too reliant on striking to unbalance *uke*.

What's with no Competition?

I wasn't there to hear it, but most report that O-Sensei didn't want competition as part of his *budo*.[601] He hoped it would be more than something destructive and competitive, that it would develop our better selves.[602] I'd be shocked if he ever thought of it as becoming a "sport." But just because there are no formal contests doesn't mean people are not striving to their utmost in practice.

First of all, there is competition in class. Everybody knows it. Typically it's along the lines of *uke* giving *nage* a particular attack, with the specific energy required (maybe even with all *uke*'s might) but *uke* cannot block *nage's* technique or when the roles are switched one can block the other. Other ways people compete is with the pace or power of their technique. I'm not condoning it. "Not judgin'; just sayin'." It's most often a veiled sort of competition and always of limited meaning because it doesn't allow free attack, retreat, defense or countering.

Second, I do believe that in many things in life, competition produces excellence because it taps our survival instincts and otherwise motivates people to give their utmost. Generally speaking, for better or worse, humans naturally fear losing and relish winning. Fear and ego can be two powerful motivators. In martial arts, however, an overemphasis on winning under some set of rules in a match alters technique or tactics or both, which is disadvantageous in a spontaneous survival fight. One example would be lying on your back and holding someone between your legs

---

blade hand, fingers, etc. is beneficial.

[601] At least not competing for victories over anything but yourself.

[602] Sport can do this sometimes as well, but it doesn't condition it. *Budo*, particularly aikido, can help mold you well beyond good "sportsmanship."

(when no vital points, small joints, weapons or other assailants are potentially in play) until he tires, so you can submit them by lock or choke. Another would be grappling competitions, where the very things that are necessary to be effective in the stand-up phase, e.g., tensing the body, shifting your posture forward, dropping your hips, widening your stance and leaning your head forward are all dangerous in a survival fight because they offer prime targets and impair free movement (other than "shooting" and sprawling). Sports budo competitions can also lead you to practicing what "works" for you in a particular match—rather than studying and learning and improving on a broader curriculum. It reminds me of a sumo player when I lived in Japan who was impossible to beat if he got his right hand on your belt. Everyone just ran away from his right hand.

Third, aikido is not and, in the main at least, should not become a competitive sport. However, aikido *keiko* can be as competitive as you want it to be if that's what you want. If you are willing to accept the injuries, then you can make *randori* highly contentious. The truth is that whether or not aikido is practiced in a "competitive" manner is principally a matter of personal belief and action on those perspectives. In fact, most *aikidoka* tolerate if not accept fully that different people can choose different methods of aikido practice. O-Sensei's *budo* can be enjoyed as a kind of moving meditation, means for understanding or cultivating "ki" (vital-energy) or otherwise improving health and building character.[603] However, if you want to experience and express it as a dynamic and effective martial art and develop skills for a spontaneous survival situation, then you need to find ways to check the reality of your technique—via competition or some other form of contention. On that much, the armchair-aikido-critics are right. To which my father would say, "Even a blind squirrel finds an acorn once in awhile.

---

[603] "Ha, ha ha; Ki! That's bullshit." *Ki* (or qì, chi, in Mandarin, gi in Korean), is life energy, a concept that exists in a number of cultural traditions. It's not some mysterious force you shoot out your fingertips like Darth Sidious. Look at a baby. Look at an old person. Look in the mirror when you're well rested. Look after a bender. There are perceptible differences in vitality. Life energy. Even in the West, we speak of people looking energetic or vibrant. Certain systems of physical movement and other training help sustain and cultivate this vitality.

Aikido in China?

三国時代
(*Sangokujidai*)

"There are people who make a profession out of selling the arts. They treat themselves as articles of merchandise and produce objects with a view to selling them ... Someone who might want to learn such a way with the goal of making money should keep in mind the saying, 'Strategy inadequately learned is the cause of serious wounds.'"
— Miyamoto Musashi, 1645 (*Gorin no Sho*)

So here I sit, on a surprisingly cool and clear sunny May day, in a Starbucks in the Northern Capital (北京) of the Middle Kingdom (中国) trying to pen this tome while my monkey-mind races around chattering about whether to keep my Beijing dojo in its current location, move it to a new one or keep it and open a second one, all in the midst of arranging and coordinating the Seventh Annual Aikikai Hombu Dojo seminar for Beijing in mid-June when my old friend, now *shihan*, will visit us for four days of instruction. Twenty, ten, hell, even five years ago? That sentence would've sounded even more mental than it does today. China?

Yep. "The People's Republic of" no less. The world's most populous country! (We think: better check India after reading this sentence.) The booming economy of the twenty-first century![604] Nine percent economic growth? Any less than seven percent and you probably can't keep the lid on the kettle, there would be so many unemployed. "Capitalism with Chinese Characteristics." But a lot happened out East before the former home of local sages Lǎozǐ, Kǒngzǐ, Mòzǐ and Mèng Zǐ opted for the dogma of an obscure German philosopher and then Scotsman, Adam

---

[604] A skeptic might say that, basically, in the twenty-first century, "China" is completing the adoption of twentieth century Western technology to go with it's slant on a nineteenth century Western-European political ideology.

Smith, Sinified.[605][606]   Dynasty! The Qin (221-206 BC), the Han (202 BC–AD 220), the Wei and Jin (AD 265–420), the Cao, Wei and Jin (265-420), the Wu Hu (AD 304–439), the Southern and the Northern (AD 420–589), the Sui (AD 589–618), the Tang (AD 618–907), the Five Dynasties and Ten Kingdoms (AD 907–960), the Song, the Liao, the Jin and the Western Xia (AD 960–1234), the Yuan (AD 1271–1368), the Ming (AD 1368–1644), the Qing (AD 1644–1911), the Republicans (AD 1912-1949) and the Communists (AD 1949 to forever and ever, amen).

There have been Great Walls and conquering northern invaders who became rulers like the Liao, Xia, Jurchen, Yuan (Mongols) and Manchu.[607] A myriad of warlords, the temples of Shaolin and Wu Dang Shan (the home of Tai Chi). Rebellion by the bushel, including: the Yellow Turban Rebellion, the An Shi Rebellion, the Taiping Rebellion, the Punti-Hakka Clan Wars, the Nien Rebellion, the Muslim Rebellion, the Panthay Rebellion and the Boxer Rebellion, two Opium Wars, the Wuchang Uprising, a Republican revolution, a Japanese invasion, a Marxist revolution, great leaps nowhere, little-red-book madness in a cultural revolution ending with the "Capitalist roaders" leading an economic explosion, as China completes its march into and through the late twentieth century on into the twenty-first.[608]

I can't vouch for other cities, but since 2005, in the capital, it's been perpetual construction, hutongs being knocked down for shopping malls, blocks of high-rise flats and more office space. It's dust and skies stained oolong brown and the pollution meter atop the U.S. Embassy tweeting a stream of dire health warnings. It's a taxi driver telling me the Volkswagen

---

[605] Lǎozi (老子, maybe sixth century BC) is the mythical or actual author of the *Tao Te Ching* and founder of philosophical Taoism. You'll know Kǒngzǐ (孔子; 551–479 BC) as Confucius. Mòzi (墨子; 470 BC – 391 BC) innovative thinker of the early Warring States period and opponent to Taoism and Confucianism, Mèngzǐ (孟子, 372 – 289 BC) who you may know as Mencius, the most famous Confucian after Confucius.

[606] Squeeze a local megalomaniac in between those two Euro imports.

[607] I once asked a friend's Chinese girlfriend, who was blathering on about the "evil Japanese," if China was China after the Mongolians conquered it. "Yes". Then hadn't China tried to invade Japan twice (13th century) but failed? She blinked at me in stunned silence. The Yuan Dynasty! If you're going to beat your chest about "5,000" years of history, then you get all the baggage that goes with it.

[608] Chairman Mao described reactionary forces within (e.g., Deng Xiaoping) and without as "capitalist roaders" (走资派); zǒuzīpài who advance or relent to bourgeois forces pushing the Revolution towards capitalism.

I am riding in is a "Chinese car." It's Germans and Koreans (and the rest
of the planet) on the make. It's people making left-hand turns from the
right-hand lane or driving backwards on the expressway for a missed off-
ramp. It's two ten-year-olds standing in the middle of the expressway
trying to toss business cards onto the windshields of passing motorists
since traffic flow has slowed to a near standstill because two kids are standing in the middle of the expressway trying to toss business cards onto the
windscreens of passing motorists. Did I mention dust?

It's large gray tricycles, diàndòng sānlúnchē (电动三轮车), welded together from bits-n-bobs and odd-n-ends of various metals with myriad past
lives, powered by pedals and a jerry-rigged electric motor. They "stop" with
a stick-shift-like cable hand-lever brake welded to the central frame-tube.
Fitted above the back wheels is a long, broad weather-worn wooden board
for carrying loads. These trike-carts are usually teetering to the brink, toting
deliveries of who knows what to Lord knows where, going the wrong way
down the street.[609] Crossing the street? Forget waiting for the light to
change. Go local and take your chances.[610] While you're watching for the
cars, buses and trucks, it's the bikes, trikes and scooters that'll kill you as you
are looking right at oncoming traffic and they barrel in from your left. It's
a horse-drawn cart, laden with bricks, heading to a surviving hutong for
repairs. It's a high-flyer flying by in his Fǎlālì (Ferrari) while behind the
swanky street billboard for Rolex an out-of-towner drops his drawers for a
nick-o-time download. You're more likely to see a red Bǎomǎ (BMW) than
a little red book. Actually, the color of choice (in cars at least) is black and
an Àodí A8 (Audi) is the select badge of bureaucrats and bigshots. It's the
Chinese love affair with the car horn: "LA-BA, LA-BA."

It's crackling dry summer heat and booming late afternoon thunderstorms. It's a businessman on the street babbling into his iPhone as a
blind albino clad in rags plays the èrhú plaintively for a few coins tossed in
his tin cup.[611] It's bitter winter cold and mega-volt static electricity. Vistas
of the mountains towards Mongolia on biannual clear days. It's a flat,

---

[609] Bicycles of Beijing gives a sense of it – but a tidier sense: http://pdxacu.com/bicycles-of-
china/
[610] There's strict liability against drivers who collide with any other smaller vehicle or a pedestrian.
[611] The èrhú is a slender two-stringed instrument that looks like an emaciated banjo and is played
with a bow like a cello.

logically arrayed, city choked with cars. L.A. without the beach. Did I mention dust? The yellow sands of the Gobi desert seek relentlessly to claim the city. It's lots of good food: dumplings, noodles and every provincial cuisine you can conceive of (done with an abundance of oil) at reasonable prices.

It's lots of inquisitive, pleasant, interesting and straightforward local people … and more from the countryside. "You're fat." "How much money do you make? How much is your rent?" It's old folks stereotypically doing tai chi in the local park in the early hours. It's spoiled little emperor and empress toddlers with tottering grannies in tow trying to keep them in check. It's visible signs of gendercide, leaving too many men for too few women. It's daily showings on CCTV of "The Monkey King," cheesy variety shows featuring ostrich-tall willowy young ladies in flowing gauze gowns doing chorus-line dance numbers from the '50s while waxen-faced singers in military uniforms warble for the Motherland, daily dramas of evil little Tojos being defeated by noble communist patriots, the official "news" in English, daily NBA basketball, badminton and, of course, ping pong. It's an incomplete grasp of mobile-phone technology. To the good people of China! Brothers and sisters! There's no such thing as "Shout-Mode." Screaming into your phone doesn't mean the caller hears you any better. We "get" to hear you better.

It's massive improvements to housing and transport, leading up to and since the 2008 Beijing Olympics. It's millions upon millions of people—descendants of the long suffering masses—being lifted out of poverty by making things on the cheap for the developed world or laboring on domestic housing, resource extraction or infrastructure projects. In other words, it's a mad fantastic adventure. I'm living smack dab in the middle of epochal history in the making—like the British industrial revolution, Manifest Destiny or the Meiji Restoration. How the hell did I end up here?

Funny you should ask. Life has a way of happening between plans. My wife and I were loving life in Japan. I was still studying aikido fanatically. She was studying *sumie* and *shamisen*.[612] I was working at a fine Tokyo

---

[612] *Sumie* (墨絵, すみえ) is the art of ink painting. See http://musashi-miyamoto.net/musashi-artiste.htm. *Shamisen* is (三味線, しゃみせん) is a sort of three string Japanese banjo. Listen to the Yoshida Brothers. www.domomusicgroup.com/yoshidabrothers/

law firm that offered: good people, interesting work, financial opportunity and ample life outside the office. My wife was settling in working as a voiceover artist, working two days a week, plus auditions, and making a bundle from NHK TV and radio and other gigs.[613] She'd been an announcer at World Cup matches and the honey-sweet voice on subway trains announcing: "The next station is …" We went snowboarding in winter, surfing in summer and traveled whenever we felt the urge—both in Japan and regionally. Life was so good; perfect. I'd followed the dream, the dream had turned into reality: a new land, with a pot of gold and, even better, a beautiful princess at the end of the rainbow.

But in 2004, I had to leave abruptly due to my wife's sudden illness, misdiagnosis and near death from medical negligence in Tokyo. She is considerably younger than me, so how ironic. Fret about marrying someone older because he might die before you do and then you become mortally ill. It's a long story which, if I give into friends' cajoling, will be the subject of another book. In brief, when you tell people you live in Tokyo, they look at you like, "Wow. Tomorrowland!" Well, a lot of things are very modern and innovative, but many are not. Medicine was one area of concern. Compared to the Third World, care was excellent, of course. Compared to the First World, access to care was admirable if not enviable. However, the quality of care is (or was), in my now all-too-considerable experience, substandard for the then-second-largest economy in the world.[614] If you go to train in Japan, plan accordingly. Have insurance. Have an exit strategy. Don't just assume that things have changed.

As you may have heard, Japan can be very insular, change often comes slowly (when it comes at all) and the practice of Western medicine seems to be one profession that has suffered for it: training, nursing, drugs, equipment could all be substandard in comparison to the developed West. In East Asia, the commonly perceived centers of excellence are Singapore, Hong Kong and more recently Seoul. As the most Confucian country in East Asia, Koreans are obsessed with attending the best schools possible

---

[613] "Toyota! Drive your dreams!", said the television add voiced by a woman from New Zealand who was rumored to be making 7-figures doing various voiceover work in Japan.

[614] In 2012, Americans, in many respects, have zero standing to criticize anyone's healthcare system. Can we do it well? Best. Can we deliver it efficiently and fairly to all? Hardly. It was the best of times; it was the worst of times.

in their homeland: Seoul National, Yonsei, Korea University, etc. Graduates then seem equally driven to study in the U.S. or E.U. at the most prestigious institution possible before returning home to work. Professions in Korea benefit tremendously from this highly competitive pursuit of excellence abroad. Japan lags. Crisis of confidence? Fear of things foreign? Perhaps both. Maybe things have changed. Notably, the one doctor in Japan who turned things around had trained at Imperial College in London after completing his medical studies in Japan.

In short, my wife had been carelessly misdiagnosed by Dr. Fujii of the Tokyo Medical Surgical clinic.[615] Having felt unwell for at least six months, she visited for blood work, and he failed to do a basic screening test for autoimmune conditions (given her age, race, gender and complaints, this was an obvious consideration). Two weeks later, she was back for the follow-up on a Tuesday, still unwell, and he admitted he'd forgotten the tests. By Friday, the tests had been completed. The results were positive for an autoimmune condition. But Fujii failed to report the results to us, even though I had phoned and visited on Thursday to pick up meds, faxed and phoned Friday stating, "Are you sure this is chronic fatigue or flu? She's incredibly ill," and phoned again on Saturday and again Sunday, each time describing my wife's seriously deteriorating condition: high temperature, hiccuping, vomiting and serious weakness.[616] We were repeatedly advised that all was fine, but nobody at the clinic checked the report.

Returning to his clinic Monday morning, my Mrs. now barely able to stand, the receiving physician was shocked. "How long have you been like this?!!" I told him, "days". Fujii arrived about 30 minutes later. Funny thing about aikido training, you develop the ability to read body language quite well. Fujii was panic stricken. Despite best efforts to suppress it, his body and speech revealed all. He knew he'd screwed up; badly. Next? My wife was passed about like a hot potato: by Fujii to a rheumatology clinic and by its specialist Dr. Kawaguchi and Fujii to a tiny neighborhood hospital miles from both clinics and our home. "Very sorry; our hospitals are all full." Fujii and Dr. Kawaguchi were trying to distance themselves

---

[615] This clinic makes its money treating principally Westerners.
[616] Hiccuping, accompanied by a high temperature can be a symptom of meningitis, encephalitis or other serious illness involving the brain or brain-stem and requires emergency examination.

from the errors, an unclear diagnosis and an uncertain outcome. It was the small hospital or back home. Happy cheerful Dr. Kawaguchi, of the Joshidai Rheumatology Clinic, said so. Straight up. So, she spent that Monday night in the little local hospital. By Tuesday morning, she was dying of aspiration pneumonia, having lost her swallow from advancing nerve damage caused by the autoimmune condition that had been missed by Fujii, the specialist and the hospital.

Since Thursday, the physical symptoms of progressive nerve damage—my hiccuping and now drooling wife—had gone ignored or misdiagnosed, despite my pointing them out to each physician. "She's hiccuping constantly, vomiting and has a high fever" (signs of potential brain or brain-stem issues).

"Come pick up this prescription for antibiotics, so she doesn't inhale the vomit and get ill," said Fujii on Thursday.

"Is that some kind of nerve problem?"

"No, no; just dehydrated. Will get better with an IV," replied Kawaguchi the specialist on Monday.

"Is that some kind of nerve problem?" I asked the rheumatologist who visited the neighborhood hospital Monday evening. as we watched my wife continually use the wall suction tube like a straw to vacuum her pooling saliva. "No; she's just overproducing saliva." Ever wonder why a doctor says, "Open wide and say ahhhhh," as she sticks a tongue depressor in your mouth? Sometimes, the answer just is not complicated.

My Spidey-sense was tingling, as I left my wife in little Denen Chofu Chuo hospital and headed home late Monday night. Phoning first thing in the morning, I was relieved to hear that she was "fine". Then, ten minutes later, I received another phone call from the same nurse. In a panic stricken voice she said, I had to come to the hospital at once! "It's not good; dangerous; she has to go to a big hospital immediately." I phoned my wife's close Japanese friend, a graduate of U.C.L.A., to come to help with translation, phoned the agent at NHK, phoned our woman pastor at the Tokyo Union Church and I sprinted out the door to the subway. In forty minutes, I arrived and sprinted up the stairs into the hospital and to her room, not knowing what I would find. She was lying in bed, still using the wall-mounted suction unit. I felt her arms and legs—icy cold. It was clear (even from my limited lifeguard training as a youth) that she was going into shock.

Her friends had beaten me there, so at least she hadn't been alone; just scared. I had them stay and speak with her calmly, assuring her that all would be well, while I dashed to the nurses' station. I found the young female doctor in charge of her case frantically calling "big" hospitals, trying get her admitted. Begging, basically. No one wanted the problem. Finally, a hospital in Yokohama said yes. *Yokohama?* I thought. *Yokohama?!! That's forty minutes away if the road's empty!* My instincts (*kan*, 勘) screamed don't do it!![617]

"No! Closer! Faster! Now!" I slammed my fist into the table saying, "SHE'S FUCKING DYING!!!" A senior doctor, an eye specialist, who I had befriended the night before, quickly grabbed the phone from the young doctor and called his colleague at Showa University Hospital, a respected institution just ten minutes away, that had an expert chest unit.[618] They accepted her immediately.

Rushing by ambulance to Showa and then into its emergency Intensive Care Unit, there seemed just the slightest sliver of hope as they kicked me out of ICU. Doctors reappeared hours later with a horrifying chest X-ray, saying "She's going to die, but we will do our best." Her dear Japanese co-worker and the pastor began sobbing uncontrollably. Me? I was shocked, but failed to miss the irony. *And she worried I'd die first?* For three days, I waited in the hospital, pacing the floors, sleeping in a small tatami room upstairs, praying to my Maker and waiting for "the call" to come to her bedside as she was passing away. Her family flew in from Seoul and the U.S. within forty-eight hours. My parents (my father still acting president of a major graduate school) flew in within seventy-two hours. The call never came; she didn't die.

During the initial few days, I'd faxed the pages of blood work (that Fujii, the rheumatology clinic and small hospital had done) to my brother-in-law in the U.S., a board certified rheumatologist, and

---

[617] I later realized they were trying to get her out of their hospital and into an ambulance so she would die in transit and no one would have to accept responsibility. "Welcome to Japan!"

[618] Of course, I had phoned Fujii and he first said, "Well; I'm not responsible now." I nearly leapt through the hand-phone and killed him in replying that, "You are the initial treating physician. You missed this diagnosis. I hold you personally accountable." He promised he would help find a hospital. I never heard from him again except to receive a bill from the Tokyo Medical Service Clinic for the visit that Monday.

he diagnosed it correctly over the telephone—autoimmune condition, just as Fujii had suspected but failed to follow-up thoroughly. I told the Japanese doctors, but they didn't believe me. If only my brother-in-law would come to Japan! I mean, my father, seventy-two at the time, still a serving graduate school president, was at her bedside within seventy-two hours from Princeton, New Jersey. Surely an expert in the family would help? Fully? Selflessly? Apparently not.[619] [620]

After a month of dodging various "kill-shots" in ICU, she was moved to a single room.[621] The ordeal didn't end there. Nearly three months later, she was just becoming stable and strong enough to be evacuated West. Taking your time in making steel, electronics, autos? Incremental improvement towards perfection? Okay; that works well in manufacturing. In emergency medicine? Nope.[622]

Simultaneously, I'd been battling the insurance carrier for an evacuation and even flew in my own air-medicine expert—an Australian (of German and Japanese decent) fluent in Japanese—to evaluate my wife, work with the Japanese, write reports for me for the insurer and prepare her for the hoped-for flight out. Fortunately, when we got married, I'd increased our insurance coverage, buying the best available from the best carrier selling to expats in Tokyo. After all, my wife is her mother and father's

---

[619] Too bad I couldn't get him to come to Tokyo, as the Japanese doctors asked and our foreign medical advisor in Australia advised. Begged him to come. Offered a business-class ticket. Crisis reveals character. We learned acutely and painfully who were our real family and friends. Some say, "people do their best." I say, we can and all should do better. I start by working on improving myself.

[620] He preferred to phone in his help; for that at least I am grateful. Many dear family friends did help to their utmost. I was able to assemble a shadow medical team in the U.S. who I could phone and ask questions. I got advice on insurance coverage from lawyer friends. Too many people to name came to our aid. Bless them all.

[621] She'd survived a serious infection and a fall out of bed onto the ICU floor, cutting her chin. Two weeks in ICU, they'd administered a sleeping pill (the day before she was to be moved into a private room) and this caused a brain insult that knocked her between sleep and coma. Miraculously, she survived it all.

[622] A condition that I would later see controlled within one or two days in London during a relapse, took a month-plus to subdue in Japan due to inaction and insufficient action. The Japanese became so nervous and cautious about her situation that they nearly stabilized her into the grave. Rather than use the typical U.S. approach to a serious attack of this illness, which they eventually resorted to and which suppressed it, they tried to cure her in tiny steps, which didn't work. It only succeeded in keeping her bedridden, weakening her further, exposing her to infection and failing to halt the nerve damage being done. It took about forty days for her to get the drug treatment she had needed. She responded immediately.

little girl, my treasure and my responsibility. However, insurers are insurers. Takes three people to run an insurance company. One to sell the policies, one to collect the premiums and one to deny the claims. However, by controlling the information to the insurance carrier (they didn't speak, read or write Japanese), just maybe I could get my wife evacuated.

Throughout the ordeal, the Hombu Dojo aikido community (from Doshu on down) had been incredibly supportive (as were other friends from NHK, my law firm, Tokyo Union Church and so on.) They all knew my wife. I'm not so likable, but my wife? *"Akarui, sugoku cha-ru-meengu"* (bright, cheerful, extremely charming). Everybody loves her and people were rather distressed to see someone so vibrant and alive stricken so harshly. Once she was out of ICU and in her own room, my *Aiki*-pal from Canada organized different Hombu students to bed-sit each night, watching her, while I slept on a futon, leaping up for any crisis, of which there were many.[623] I'd tried to do it myself for the first week. If I'd maintained that pace, we'd have had two people in the hospital, so my *Aiki*-friends were a Godsend. It was truly extraordinary. Who better to endure a grinding task of that kind? We can never possibly repay all the many kindnesses extended to us during her hospitalization and afterward. All you can do is say "thank you" and do likewise for other people (in ways large and small) whenever the opportunity arises. Pass on the goodwill.

After battling with the insurance carrier (in New Zealand) and underwriter (in London) for several months, I won.[624] Because our insurance policy was via the famous Lloyds of London, she'd be flown to the National Hospital for Neurology and Neurosurgery in London—a center of neurological medicine and research of the highest reputation.[625] Yes, fellow Yanks. Even our doctors go there to study. After six and a half more

---

[623] After all the cock-ups by doctors, I trusted no one.

[624] If I weren't a former trial lawyer who had second-chaired a massive environmental insurance claims negotiation with Lloyds of London for a global oil conglomerate, in other words I could read a policy, my wife would've been left in Japan in some hospital corner drooling into a cup.

[625] I'd reflexively argued to go to UCLA (my university), with some success with the carrier, but the UCLA neurologist recommended the UK specialty center, and there was the issue of what would happen in the U.S. once coverage ran out and what I would do (hop on a plane) if the carrier and I had further disagreements. If we lived in London, I could go knock on their door.

months in hospital, the removal of her trachea tube (so she could eat again at last; they'd thought she might never be able to), eight or nine more months of helping her rehabilitate and she was stable enough for me to consider full-time work. I kept from worrying to death or otherwise going mental by finding a nearby dojo that was founded many years ago by a superb Hombu Dojo *shihan*. The *shihan* hadn't lived in the U.K. for a long time, so it was run by two *godan* who had studied with him in the U.K. years ago and a *sandan* who'd spent a few months studying with him in California, all under the oversight of another longtime student who no longer trained or taught. I was grateful for the opportunity to practice regularly.

My martial arts training had proved vital throughout the crisis, from having the intuition to know whether or not to agree to ship her to Yokohama, to having the physical, mental and spiritual endurance to preserve day-after-day of her month in ICU—seeing her two times a day for an hour each time—countless tubes, wheezing respirators, bacterial infections, drug-induced brain insults, a fall out of bed and so on. There was my building a shadow medical team in the West to consult. Decisions to do this. Decisions to do that. Decisions not to do this or that. Then came three months in the single room, more infections, increasingly intensive (and risky) drug therapies to beat the condition into retreat. It was a physical, mental and emotional grind (and I had the easy bit compared to my Mrs.). If aikido teaches you nothing else, it teaches you never to give up. It's a means of cultivating what my Brit friends might call "sheer-bloody-mindedness." More than ever, I needed a strong mind, body and spirit. Another life was at stake. If she saw me falter, she might, too.

People join special dojos to undertake all kinds of intensive physical or mental training. Great, but this shit was real. Every day; forging you. Or incinerating you. I mean, if I made the wrong call (in a foreign country and another language) when they were pushing me to let them offload her to Yokohama, my wife, someone's child, is dead. It's that simple. I wasn't chanting and ringing a bell or sitting meditating in some hall or climbing some mountain where if I felt like it I could stand up and walk out or turn round and hike back down. This was life. Actual. Happening. Like it or not. There is no other way but forward and through it; and, once through it, you are changed forever.

Some of you might be screaming, "medical malpractice!" You'd be right, even though I am no fan of the "plaintiffs' bar." Fast forward a year later and I was looking for a lawyer in Tokyo to handle her case, no easy feat in Japan with its notorious xenophobia and regrettable history with Koreans.[626] It took some strategic thinking, some connections and my, perhaps unfair, maneuver of wheeling my wife into the key meeting with the prospective lawyer. It was a meeting in Tokyo where he thought only I'd be there and where he probably planned to say, "very sorry; cannot." However, he'd seen her "head shots" for her media work and when faced with the "after shot" (seeing her face to face post-illness in his office), the top medical malpractice lawyer in Japan took our case.

It is incredibly difficult to sue anyone in Japan, especially for professional negligence. From what I know, they won't take the case unless it's airtight and even then you might lose, especially as a foreigner, particularly one of Korean descent. So, even after an independent medical expert confirmed a finding of negligence, we decided not to pursue it further, despite horrific damages to my wife and the inexcusable conduct of the initial care-provider (the Tokyo Medical Surgical Clinic, Dr. Fujii) and everyone else in the "hot potato" chain. We did not want the final care provider— Showa University Hospital—to be blamed at all (despite errors in treatment according to the expert) and we just couldn't trust the Japanese legal system to get it right in the end. Do all that work? Live life looking backwards? Spend all that money? (There are no contingency fee cases.) Invest all that time? Do it all well and you might win, but the math still might work out like $1+1 = -2.5$. As a fellow foreign lawyer astutely observed, "Japanese law is German law translated into Japanese by a Frenchman." And I would add, then applied by Japanese elites who often lack life experience. In the States or the U.K., my wife would've been a multimillionaire and rightfully so. She nearly died, suffered terribly and was left with deficits that prevented her from working in her field ... all because someone was careless and lazy. Very un-Japanese behavior, in fact. How ironic. Living in probably the least lazy and careless place on the planet, we got sideswiped by a lazy and careless doctor. "Stuff" happens.

So there I was, having undertaken my quest to Tokyo only to end up

---

[626] We had three reasons to pursue a claim. Justice. Protect others from future harm. Compensation. Her illness wiped us out financially; completely.

in London under very unusual and unfortunate circumstances. So? So, we did what you do in *keiko*. Get out or get going. Step by step; together, like our climb up Fuji-san, we endured and persevered—minute by minute, hour by hour, day by day, never forgetting to savor life's sweetness even in the midst of crushing challenges. Never failing to be thankful for what we still had.

First was the matter of maximizing her recovery. My experiences in studying and teaching martial arts were handy once again. Build her physical strength. Restore her confidence. There were numerous challenges to overcome. Spring 2004 post-discharge, she couldn't walk down the street alone and, even if assisted, not without my having to kneel down on one knee every 300 meters to let her sit on my other knee to rest. Eventually, we would have to go to Japan to meet the lawyer, so we built up to it. Slowly. First trip post-discharge was by train to Scotland, Glasgow, to see my parents who were visiting. Coping well, we took the Eurostar to Paris for our anniversary. Next we flew to Barcelona for an aikido seminar with a favorite teacher from Japan who is very fond of my Mrs. Then we went intercontinental—to the U.S., Princeton, for the new year holiday. By March 2005, we were back in Japan visiting friends, saying thank-yous, practicing at Hombu Dojo, meeting the lawyer. Triumphant. Out of the abyss, certainly, but plenty of sheer rock cliff, straight up, to climb.[627]

Returning to London, I was introduced by a friend to a guy from Bank of China who wanted to form an advisory business regarding China and London's capital markets. I said, "Hmmmm. Interesting. Make the business model China and its two biggest regional foreign direct investment partners, Korea and Japan, and I'll do it." That way, we were distinct from every other person from London running around China with their hair on fire chasing China deals. So began Tiger Capital Partners.[628] One day I was jobless: senior lawyer, sick wife, no clients, and the next I was doing international business from London, the home of the first globalized institution, the Royal Navy![629] And, I would get to Japan regularly! Not

---

[627] But for the support of our parents and some dear friends, we'd have never made it.
[628] www.tigercapitalpartners.com
[629] See *To Rule the Waves* by Arthur Herman.
http://books.google.co.uk/books/about/To_Rule_the_Waves.html?id=dF2W7BAo4x0C&redir_esc=y

much comfort compared to our losses, but it's better to live life looking forward than backward.

By May, I was touching down in China for the first time, flying into Shanghai from Incheon, South Korea. Walking off the gangway, past a uniformed guard standing at attention, I suppressed a Cold-War slur by my id. Passing smoothly through immigration, picking up my bag and clearing customs, I walked into the arrivals room and saw my name on a handheld sign waved by some local leaning over the arrivals railing. "Mr. William." A U.K. law firm had invited me to visit and booked me an incredible suite at the Shangri-la Hotel, quite the uncomfortable contrast of circumstances to the invalid beggar out front. I switched on the TV, tuned in the BBC and started unpacking my things when suddenly the screen went black. "What the heck?" I pressed the on-off switch; nothing. Other channels worked? What the hell happened? "Ahhhhh," it dawned on me, "the Dear Leaders don't want me to see that report on The Beeb that contained the T-word." Tibet. Welcome to China! Enjoy the news, as "harmonized" by Uncle Chen!

After a few days of local business, I hopped a China Eastern flight to Beijing to meet one of my business partners (a Glaswegian that both English and Chinese speakers struggled to understand regardless of tongue) and a potential first client he was introducing. From all the nightmare stories I'd heard, from friends who were old China-hands, e.g., pilots practicing touchdowns and takeoffs with a planeload of passengers, I wondered what I was in for. Their tales were from ages past, however, or their stories were just that: stories. Things had advanced substantially. The stewardesses were still rude, clueless or both, but at least they couldn't beat me arm wrestling like on most U.S. airlines (or Lufthansa). Still, with all the fakery in Chinese business, one can't help but wonder nervously about aircraft maintenance and authenticity of parts in The "Center" Kingdom as you board a plane.

In Beijing, we inked our first client, a P.R.C. Chinese who had become a Canadian and later proved to be a colossal crook.[630] I wouldn't have to read the book *Mr. China*, I would live it for two years. I headed back to the hotel in Central Business District in east Beijing. Like many itinerant

---

[630] Americans can't get too self righteous. We have Bernie Madoff.

aikidoka, I'd packed my *keiko-gi* and *hakama*. Using the Internet (or watchful Uncle Chang's version of it), I found a dojo way up at the northwest corner of town at Beijing University—Bei-Da—a university club. Aikido in China. Wow. You'd naively expect that everyone in China would be in silk pajamas doing Tai Chi Chuan or Shaolin Boxing (and some are), but apparently, despite the best efforts of the worst of the Japanese Imperial Army and the daily reminders on CCTV, some young Chinese agree with many in the rest of the world that "samurai stuff" is pretty cool.[631] Plus O-Sensei's golden path of peace, perfecting the ancient warrior's route, has undeniably universal appeal.

I didn't speak much Chinese at the time, so I had the hotel concierge pen the characters for gymnasium, 体育馆 (tǐyùguǎn, body + educate + public building). Wandering 'round a bit, I found the building and with a bit of "international charades" found the third-floor gymnasium where students were setting up mats at the far end of an indoor synthetic athletics track. It was separated from the adjacent badminton courts by ceiling to floor, deep-green nylon-cord netting that shielded runners from stray shuttlecocks. There were about twenty students setting up for the class being led by a former university student. Along with him, there were a couple of other *shodan*, and yes, they were all a bit surprised (and frightened) to see me. I joined other latecomers in finding a spot by the wall and changing publicly into *keiko-gi*, bashful or not. Once changed, I helped set up the "mats." The mats were an unusual collection of several-centimeters-thick, square-meter pieces of heavy black rubber that had the consistency of a worn-out auto-tire. These black squares were arranged on the ground to form a larger square practice area and then a green carpet-like sheet, like the fake putting greens of miniature-golf courses, was laid out over the "tires" to hold them all in place. Innovative.[632] After Hombu Dojo, mats anywhere usually seem unduly soft, but this stuff didn't absorb much energy when you landed, "thud," though I'd expected even worse. Even so, I was so keen to practice that the class was really enjoyable. Well organized. Teacher and students were enthusiastic and sincere, even if rather new to aikido. What can you expect of a university club? It was amazing to see

---

[631] I've heard many Chinese tell me "*hakama* is cool." One dojo features one prominently on the front page of its website. Hopefully, the interest in aikido is more than a fashion statement.
[632] You see this kind of innovation and "making the best of it" often in China.

aikido taking root some place new on the Earth.   I mean, aikido only came to Beijing in what?   2002?   After class, I learned from some Japanese students (studying overseas) and other club members that the dojo was under the guidance of Suganuma sensei in Kyushu (as was another adjacent university where I would practice later).   Man, oh, man; if he were in town, happy days.   I'd be in his class every day!   But alas, no.   Annually; maybe biannually.

Realistically, even ten years hence, aikido in Beijing remains in its Three Kingdoms era—*Sangokujidai*.   "ROTK," *The Romance of the Three Kingdoms*, is a fifteenth-century Ming Dynasty epic historical novel by Luo Guanzhong set in the Three Kingdoms period (roughly 220 AD to 280 AD).[633]   Sort of an *Iliad* of China, it's a creative mix of history, legend and fiction, with hundreds of characters, in several volumes, with something like 120 chapters and nearly a million words.   Considered by many as one of the four great novels of classical Chinese literature, it still influences contemporary Chinese.   It chronicles 100 years of the Byzantine schemes, power struggles, plots and betrayals, battles and other conflicts between feudal lords, retainers and officials after bits of the failed Eastern Han Chinese Empire (25 AD-220 AD) aligned into the competing three kingdoms (三國) of Wei (魏), Shu (蜀) and Wu (吳).   To the north, Wei. To the southwest, Shu.   To the southeast, Wu.[634]   Each vying openly and treacherously for hegemony, it has been called one of the bloodiest periods of Chinese history, and that's saying something.   The book begins with the prophetic: "It is a general truism of this world that anything long divided will surely unite, and anything long united will surely divide."

Aikido in China, Beijing at least, remains divided into various "kingdoms."[635]   First, there are three or four protectorates of various Hombu

---

[633]   The fundamental historical records on the era are *Records of the Three Kingdoms* by Chen Shou and the antecedent annotations of Chen's writings by Pei Songzhi (372–451).

[634]   "Three Kingdoms" is a misnomer, since each state had an emperor (not a king) who claimed rightful succession to the Han. 3K is just one part of nearly 370 years where the Middle Kingdom was a collection of disunited kingdoms following the decline of the Han Empire. Academics contest how early 3K starts, but basically it's the period from the foundation of Wei in 220 AD to the conquest of Wu by the Jin Dynasty in 280.

[635]   As of June 2012, there was no local person above *sandan* and it's a wonder how—training here—anyone has really achieved the rank of *sandan*. *Aikikai* requires a teacher be at least *yondan* in order to independently manage a dojo, hence all but one *Aikikai* dojo in Beijing are managed from abroad by someone else.

Dojo *shihan*. Each has a dojo (or more) as part of his organization (or otherwise oversees it remotely). Daily teaching is left to the locals, none of whom (that I've met, seen or heard of, anyway) have spent any significant amount of "hands-on time" with the particular *shihan*, e.g., completing a *kenshusei* or *deshi* program of meaningful length. Lots of "*notadeshi.*" Second, there are a few non-*Aikikai* dojo. They are not from the usual *Aikikai* offshoots but rather "independent states" or "Autonomous Regions" if you prefer that are doing some semblance of an aikido class. There are all types. There are "certificate mills." 500 RMB for a *kyu*-test and a fake certificate?[636] 6000 RMB to register your *shodan*?[637] 2700 RMB for membership with a guarantee to test for black belt in twelve months? "Package deals"—2600 RMB —to leap from *nidan* to *shodan* in one exam? It's all under the tutelage of Hewlitt-Packard *shihan* and his faithful *deshi* Adobe Photoshop who spit out your certificate when the "exam" is over.[638] A local *aikidoka* I met explained, "Chinese people know it's fake. They want an easy practice and easy tests, so they don't lose face by failing, and an easy way to get *shodan* from Japan."

When your goal is personal entertainment or to impress others, who needs reality if the perception of reality accomplishes the goal?

In China, quite often it seems, it's all about obtaining a certificate or letter with the official red stamp on it. I remember reading the fascinating book by Jung Chang, *Wild Swans*, about three generations of women in China during the turbulent 1930s through the Maoist terrors. The writer's mother manages to get some official letter from Deng Xiao Ping or something and later this proves vital for safe passage in China, as if showing it to some official was some kind of force field or magical protective totem. I thought, in the U.S.A.? You show your official letter to a cop or trooper who means you ill will and, *shred-shred-shred*, "What letter?"

Here in China? Everybody goes "Oh no! A certificate! Look! It has a red stamp!!! Ooooohhhhhhh."

A typical student would be soft-spoken, well-mannered, college educated (where she or he may have first been exposed to aikido), has a decent

---

[636] Right now, 6.15 RMB = 1 USD. 80 RMB = 1000 JPY. Hombu Dojo charges 1000 JPY to take a *kyu* test.
[637] It cost just 880 RMB to register a successful *shodan* applicant.
[638] It's not a China issue per se; there are "McDojo." all over the world.

job and is just as likely to be female as male.[639]   More likely than not, she or he is there because aikido is "fun." The fundamental purpose of practice is lost on many because it's seldom, if ever, been shown or otherwise explained or, if it is, understood and adopted. They're not stupid; just not well informed. [640]

A typical local "teacher" might be some guy in his late thirties or forties. Out of shape, smokes, and never practiced much to begin with or not very hard when he did or not at all or often with anyone of any consequence. He holds practice at his "dojo" (mats in a health-club somewhere) two or maybe three times a week. [641]   He's probably fast tracked his way shodan to sandan.[642]   Some locals have delusions of becoming some kind of kingpin of aikido in Beijing or across China. Promoting people like this swiftly and beyond their abilities, frankly, is bad for aikido in China.[643] China has enough challenges with fake stuff: baby formula, eggs, cooking oil, beer, cigarettes, wine, clothes, DVDs, medicine and airplane parts; hell; they even have fake Apple stores.[644] Must aikido join the list?

For foreign teachers wanting to teach here, there are cautionary tales. There's a local story of two people of Chinese descent, I forget which country, opening a dojo in China and using a local student as a "strawman" local citizen to "own" the business vehicle.   Fast forward and the local guy claims he really owns it (including whatever cash was invested), expelling the two foreigners. Presto! Now he's the professional aikido teacher. Yep. I don't know whether to believe it or not but I've seen this kind of maneuver in business here, more than once. A City of London finance guy told me there was a Chinese company that listed on the London Stock

---

[639] Mao Zedong famously encouraged women's roles outside of the home with his "women hold up half the sky."

[640] There are some exceptions, probably, and I cannot speak for other cities in China.

[641] So far, that may sound like a lot of teachers in a lot of places in a lot of martial arts.

[642] Can you really achieve sandan or yondan practicing three times a week in a dojo in some remote place in the aikido world? Under a teacher who visits once a year for a weekend? Or a teacher you see maybe for a week in his home country? Really? Really, really? I'm skeptical, which is a polite way of saying no f-ing way.

[643] But hasn't rank inflation become endemic to aikido worldwide? To many martial arts? I saw a guy in the West, of negligible skill, go from *sandan* to *yondan* in 2004 and by 2012 he was *ryokudan*. All the while, he was merely teaching in a small dojo.

[644] My Chinese friends, students and clients absolutely detest this situation, in the same way that certain things about America might drive me mad at times.

Exchange and it turned out that the CEO didn't even exist![645] As a China-born client in Beijing remarked recently, "William, people here think that if they can fool you, it's not them who are bad; it's you who is stupid."

On the other hand, I've met people who are very sincere and helpful. One local instructor is a particularly good fellow who has loaned us everything from mats to a black belt when I was asked to film something for a CCTV sports show (my belt had become frayed and gray, not black enough for the producer's liking). Pudgy as a grain-silo mouse, he probably couldn't survive being hit by a french fry in a foodfight, but he's sincere in his love of aikido and fundamentally a good person in my experience. He knows his aikido basics, too. Whether his character is a product of his aikido training or just his inherent good nature, I don't know. However, I'll take him as a friend over some "tough guy" martial artist any day.

Some dojo here can be described fairly as Cine-Plex dojo. "Cine-Plex"—a combination of cinema and complex—where the latest movies are shown. In Beijing, in aikido, this means whichever Western teacher happens to wander through town (and I mean teacher in the broadest sense, you might have a *nidan* from some place) is given billing for a special class at the Cine-Plex. "Now Playing; Gustaf sensei!" Afterward, up go the photos on the dojo website. "See how important we are; we have many foreign visitors!" Some marketing value? Some entertainment value? But are they learning? Not really. People here, like people in many places outside of Japan, do not understand well the difference between training and entertainment.[646] My first teacher spoke endlessly about not confusing the two. Real seminars from real teachers can serve as a useful break from your training routine, allow you to practice with people you do not know, and great teachers can inspire you. Maybe you'll even find one to really go study from.

---

[645] Or consider the case of Sino-Forest, whose collapse triggered mass alarm over Chinese companies listed on Western exchanges. A forestry management company and one-time darling of the Toronto Stock Exchange with a market capitalization near $6 billion, its value tumbled after a research firm labeled it an "established institutional fraud." A series of accusations from analysts and investigators quickly followed alleging the company had used a string of affiliated companies and chain of bank accounts to inflate revenues by circulating cash. Deceitful documentation was allegedly used to exaggerate the size and value of timber assets and holdings. Sino-Forest filed for bankruptcy protection in March 2012. Executives are facing regulatory charges and The Royal Canadian Mounted Police are conducting a criminal investigation.

[646] They aren't bad people; they just don't understand the difference because they haven't been taught.

Aikido in China means the annual Hombu Dojo seminar at the end of spring. Since 2005 at least, Hombu Dojo has dispatched a teacher to Beijing for a weekend of instruction.[647] In 2005, Mori shihan, who was a *deshi* when I moved to Japan, came to China. Great to see him. The mat was packed. Fantastic to really practice! However, after a bit I noticed that two locals (wearing *hakama*) were strutting around the seminar giving instructions to students, rather than practicing like the rest of us. How odd. I learned later that these two jokers were purported judo black belts who had given themselves aikido black belts and taught from books. They later claimed direct affiliation with an extraordinarily skilled *shihan* from another country, proudly displaying a massive photo of him at each practice, but this too wasn't quite true, if not patently false. Probably my favorite thing about that dojo was their female member who wore her white belt on the outside of her *hakama*. "Looks cool!" It's not a matter of fashion. It's like wearing your baseball glove on your head and using your cap to catch the ball. Novel, but wrong.

So these two guys are strutting around the seminar, as if they're teaching. I was practicing with a large Frenchman. *Morote-tori tenkan kokyu-ho.*[648] We were training rather vigorously, it was hot, my new French friend became a bit tired, so (being eager to stay fit) I just took his *ukemi* over-and-over again. One of the two *judoka* turned *aikidoka* took a break from supervising and bowed in to our practice. I took his *ukemi*. Then he grabbed me and tried to "clamp-down" on my arm so … inhale, exhale, "WHAM!!" He looked up at me from the floor with this dumbfounded look on his face. Again, "WHAM," a touch more mustard. The look of disbelief turned to fright. I told him, "Grab hard." Same result; bigger noise. He quickly bowed out and walked on. Unbeknownst to me, these two knuckleheads had been bullying the other *aikidoka* in Beijing for several years (or that was the street story) and I had just vanquished one of the "Beijing bullies" to the great satisfaction of all locals in attendance. I had noticed they seemed to be unusually interested in my practice. Folks, if you train in some backwoods point on the planet, you can only progress

---

[647]   They prudently skipped Beijing in 2008 during the run-up to the Olympics and heightened tension in town.

[648]   Your partner grasps your wrist/arm firmly with two hands, like grabbing a baseball or cricket bat.

so far. Even so, too often, a lone frog at the bottom of a well thinks it rules the sea.

Of course, some teachers actually discourage their students from attending this annual seminar for fear of losing students to other teachers. (Sound familiar?) There are examinations on the last day, but who needs those when you are charging four or five times as much at your own dojo and don't register any promotions in Japan until *shodan*?[649] Another local guy, for the past two years, has asked Hombu Dojo if he can have private examinations at his school, as if he is someone special. Maybe he likes to hear the word "No." Xiào pín, bù. Laugh at the poor, not the prostitute. Meaning the whore not the poor has money. So if you have no shame, no bottom line, then asking and doing anything is pretty much fair game, as one disgusted Chinese-Canadian friend lamented to me about his former homeland.

Like anywhere else, there are cultural barriers to learning. Paralleling "the rise of China" is a virulent nationalism, chauvinism and egoism among some young people, particularly some young men.[650] [651] Of course, aikido, given its geographic origin and spiritual message, does not attract too many of this ilk. It's perhaps no more challenging than the rising Web-fed narcissism and egotism of too many Western teens and young adults. Perhaps the biggest challenge of teaching in China is the notion of face (面子, miànzi). A German I met, who was working for Volkswagen in Beijing, remarked to me one day, "The first step to improvement in anything is to recognize and admit that something is wrong. If you are so concerned about face, you cannot improve. Opportunities for improvement are killed by the culture." Too harsh? Perhaps, but the notion of face in the P.R.C. does seem even more sensitive, from what I've observed and experienced (among men at least), than in Korea or Japan. Different. In aikido, in particular, you have to lose to learn. Fail. Do the technique thousands of times, inching ever closer to "right." Receive the technique; fail; be thrown; fall down. Stand up. Do it again.

---

[649] Why deliver people something real? Just take their money. That's the thinking.
[650] This kind of behavior is nothing new to the world. You can find the same kind of people in just about any country.
[651] It's not limited to men, as I learned when pushing my one-year-old in her pram onto an elevator only to have a young woman rush in front of us, bumping the baby-buggy, just to make sure she boarded first. Admonishing her, she replied, "This is China!"

Without it, you cannot improve.

Aikido in China is described by an American friend, a twelve-year China vet, *judoka* from famous Jimmy Pedro's dojo and fellow BJJ'er, as teaching the most precise martial art on the planet in one of the least precise countries on the planet. He jokes (unfairly), if cutting corners was an Olympic event, "Another win by China!!!" as the announcer boomed at an international judo competition that he and I attended here.[652] So, as surefire Golds for China, there would be the new sport of "Fudging-it" plus games Americans prefer to do drunk at picnics: ping-pong and badminton. Hard to argue that "beer pong" wouldn't be a more interesting Olympic sport for television.[653]

There is an endearing sincerity from many students here but modest proficiency and scarce talent in aikido.[654] Hopefully, this will improve with time.[655] There's the usual lack of reality when it comes to the actual application of technique. Youku.com is the Chinese YouTube copycat. There's a painfully tragic video of a big chubby fellow from a local certif-icate-mill (who had been posting online how he has the "real aikido") get-ting his backside kicked (and everywhere else) in some kind of standup mixed-martial arts contest. There's another of some hopeless guy in a *hakama* getting whupped by some MMA brawler at an outdoor demon-stration at a shopping mall.[656]

Aikido in China is inviting a friend from North America in 2007, who is about 130 kilos, former Tokyo bar bouncer, to come over and help me teach at a dojo that I was assisting. (It was under the guidance of a Hombu *shihan* living outside of Japan.) "Grizzly Bear," as Masuda sensei dubbed him in Tokyo, walked into the dojo the first time dressed for class and I could hear the Chinese gasping and whispering, "What's he need aikido for?" And yet, a few minutes later, in practice, I am watching some slight local *yudansha* trying to muscle his technique on my bear of a man friend. Ikkyo

---

652 Apart from the big chicks, there weren't many wins.
653 See www.beerpong.com/wsobp/official-rules-of-the-world-series-of-beer-pong; World Series of Beer Pong in Las Vegas www.youtube.com/watch?v=JOYduGqZSRc; and "The Center of the Beer Pong Universe" http://www.bpong.com
654 There are plenty of physically talented people, but they are doing other physical activities or nothing at all.
655 You don't have to be talented to study aikido, but it's helpful for developing skilled teachers.
656 Several foreign martial arts friends have been asked to fight in kickboxing or MMA events and "take a dive" against a Chinese fighter. Smartly, they declined.

looked like a stork hanging from a grizzly's fore paw. Fortunately, the grizzly's only response was, "Silly bird."

Aikido in China is opening my own dojo in 2008. Yeah; really. After all my blunt observations, I genuinely care about the place, the people and sharing aikido here. Still, if someone had told me years ago, "Yes, young William, you will travel to the Orient some day, study martial arts in one Asian country and teach it in another."

"Yeah, whatever wise-man."

How did it ever happen? Well, fast-forward to landing in Beijing in 2005. First, I was practicing with one of the Japanese *shihan*'s university groups. Really nice group of young people. Then, after bouncing the bully at the first Hombu Dojo seminar, I was asked by a local teacher to help another *shihan*'s dojo.[657] Happy to help. Another really nice group of people. I'd teach, but just jump into class because I need exercise and frankly much prefer being a student. However, a different guy than the local teacher "ran" the dojo. That little fellow kept getting into squabbles with the local landlord and changing the dojo location like a seasonal migration.

Shortly before their next exodus, I had joined a local BJJ/Muay Thai school run on the BJJ side by an American who turned out to be very enthusiastic about aikido and O-Sensei. When I joined, I didn't say a word about aikido or doing other martial arts. (I enjoyed being an anonymous white belt.) They noticed, though. I could sit *seiza*, tie my belt, pay attention in class, take *ukemi* and had, in their words, an exceptionally strong grip. So eventually, the cat came out of the bag. "Come on, what did you study before?" I was asked to start a class. Said I'd think about it, but when the itinerant aikido dojo moved again, I began teaching aikido at the BJJ/MT school. Both BJJ instructors joined in. It was enjoyable and edifying teaching people with physical ability and prior martial arts training.

Soon, however, the BJJ and MT teachers were asked to join a large new martial arts center. I followed. Then the place it was located, the Cable 8 Creative Center, an old factory converted to an arts, cultural and

---

657 Of course, I told them to ask their *shihan* for permission first.

small business center, was targeted for redevelopment. The local authorities would soon be knocking down the building. Getting out was wise, as the lingering tenants were chased out by hired thugs armed with pipes and bats, according to reports. The school moved to an even bigger venue next to Workers Stadium. It had a boxing ring, MMA cage, punching bags, weights and a separate room with tatami mats for grappling arts. It had great potential, but access was a challenge whenever the stadium held events. The rent was exorbitant and the build wasn't right. If you are going to spend all that money, design and build it well. Intelligent use of space? Showers that drain? Toilets that work? A dojo where you aren't hearing pounding house music from the Muay Thai fitness class? Rushing to complete something and missing key details is all too prevalent. I knew the new mega-gym was doomed soon after walking in the door, since I work with venture businesses (and do martial arts). The high rent, lack of cost control, poor service, lack of cleanliness and so on doomed it. Plus, they had rushed and opened another mega-gym in Shanghai, which struggled too. A year in and I began warning my students, so we started looking for a new space of our own.

If we could avoid sharing space and all the problems that can include, a move would be worthwhile. However, finding a place in booming Beijing would be a real challenge. Rents are sky high. Property bubble. One advantage of aikido students is that they are often highly educated, intelligent and successful and ... in China, *guānxi* (relationship) counts for everything. We were lucky that one student lived in a posh residential tower that has a gym, dance room and a third activity room that had been occupied by a defunct exercise business of some kind. I rented the third space at a reasonable rent and started building a traditional dojo in Beijing.

I have ZERO desire to become some aikido warlord in China. First, I'm not Chinese. Second, my aspirations are modest. The hope is to help plant the seed of a dojo that is connected with the local Japanese community and which will grow and produce Chinese students who can grow it further under the care of Hombu Dojo. Chinese people deserve good aikido, just like they deserve all the other benefits of the globalized world that everyone else enjoys.[658] This dojo would not be a new "kingdom"

---

[658] They can join us too in innovating to make the worthwhile benefits sustainable and available to all humankind.

but a neutral state.

The MMA center? Closed. It was rumored to have been signing up new students for the annual membership fee right up to the day before it shut its doors. "Welcome to China!" as cynical expats say. It rematerialized months later in a new, potentially scalable location—several rooms on the second floor of a high-rise office complex. The owner still wanted aikido (and other martial arts) back but the BJJ teacher was resisting sharing prime mat times. We couldn't speak face-to-face, since I was in London, so I decided "no aikido until I return to Beijing." I explained to the owner what I thought was wrong with his business and explained a simple five-point plan to fix it. He responded by asking me to work with him. Well, it sounded good, but it's China, and Chinese entrepreneurs are a particularly "special" version of that breed of mercurial business person. Despite appreciating the risks, I accepted the engagement for several reasons. First, the gym owed my students services. Second, I genuinely thought we could help by implementing a new scalable concept and interim management, which would give them a chance to raise money. I conceived and developed a unifying thematic gym design based on Chinese culture and martial arts to broaden the activities and market appeal beyond a "tough-guy gym."[659] The founder had realized the hard way that MMA wasn't a scalable moneymaker here. Most Chinese view BJJ as two men having sex with their clothes on. Third, I could get the much-coveted yearlong Z-visa out of it. Fourth, I could seize the Holy Grail, i.e., as a corporate officer I was permitted by the owner to use the red stamp of the sports/cultural business and a copy of its business license, enabling me to sign a contract with a location for the Hombu Dojo seminar. Eureka![660]

If you had told me years ago that on 4 June 2012, I would be sitting on a fading-yellow wooden-slat bench in the late afternoon shade of a poplar tree, in the courtyard of a pale-pink, dusty tower-block housing development in Beijing, on a pleasantly dry hot day, editing my book about my martial arts experience in Japan, before I go to teach class in my new dojo, I would've thought your butter and jam had come off the bun.

---

[659] A former student of mine was a professor at the China Academy of Fine Arts so I involved one of its graduates on completing the design.
[660] I was still waiting for our own certificate to arrive.

There go two little toddlers stumbling about in their toilet-training trousers with the open crotch, ready for street relief. Two guys playing Chinese chess have their t-shirts rolled up, exposing their bellies but covering their chests like some kind of "man-ssiere" or "bro."[661]   Over there; two grannies are squabbling over seating rights, nearly coming to cane blows. They sound like two old cats howling with mashed potatoes in their mouths. There goes another dog that looks like the creatures I used to see in the Cali-Mexico border town Tiajuana. Weird dog, giant rat or Chupacabra?[662] A quiet loner sits cross-legged atop the public ping-pong table, as if he's meditating deeply.   People are popping in and out of the mom-and-pop shop behind me. Pretty sure the tea and water I just bought there are real. A tired-looking, overly pliable plastic bottle and a cap that twists off a bit too easily are usual tip-offs to fakes. That and the occasional scent of gasoline.   A young mom and baby on a glittering electric bike glide in through the rusty gate street-side. Teen girls in shorts too short for this or any previous generation. People all enjoying the cool shade of the trees. A girl sits side-saddle on her bo-friend's white Honda scooter as he whips out the gate, engine humming and silly sing-songy techno-horn sounding "be-be-be-bweep!"   Oh whoops, his "Běntián" scooter (Honda in Mandarin). Chinese words are used for Japanese names and for anything else as well. Basketball in Japan is ba-su-ke-tu-ba-ru. Here? It's lánqiú. Of course. Chinese words for basket and ball.   Sinofied U.S. city names, sounded out with characters, are generally unrecognizable unless you are lucky enough to have lived in Luòshānjī (Los Angeles) or Lúndūn (London).

It's just two weeks till the Aikikai Hombu Dojo delegation comes from Tokyo for the 2012 spring seminar. The "delegation" consists of my friend of nearly twenty years who is now a *shihan*. Does that make it easier or harder? Harder and easier. Planning for this event has been a serious challenge. First, I returned to London last October (for a few months break from China) and then life delivered a series of body-blows

---

[661]   Presumably many of you missed the U.S. comedy T.V. show *Seinfeld* and its wacky next-door neighbor New Yorker Kramer who invented a brassiere for men that he dubbed the "man-ssiere" or "bro" (instead of bra).

[662]   El Chupacabra—the goat sucker—is a legendary creature purported to inhabit parts of the Americas. See, e.g., www.cuerochupacabra.com/

that turned three months into six months. My father died suddenly in November. Work got wobblier and wobblier into the new year. We applied for Brit citizenship (dual), so we were stranded for a bit. Failure is never an option, so we would return to China. Of course, while I was away, dojo attendance dwindled to single digits even though I had a very experienced *sandan* from New York and Hong Kong covering classes. Locals are funny that way. I return and there were ten to fifteen students on the mat. Practice is not yet about learning fundamentals, which they could learn from many people in the dojo, or maintaining a consistent practice. It's about having the head teacher there to entertain you. Otherwise, why bother going? However, there are 1.3 billion people here (plus or minus). And just when you think you have the stereotype cast in stone, someone shows up to blow it to smithereens. My students are really lovely people. I have one student in particular who is extraordinarily diligent, considerate, responsible, intelligent, well-mannered and so on. Startlingly, so. Of course, he comes from a good family, that has a bit of money, and he is well-educated (becoming an attorney), so maybe that's the difference maker? Although I've known enough rich educated people from all over the world who are complete shits. Maybe he just makes the effort to be good?

Anyway, his dedication was indispensable to surviving the move from the MMA club, securing the new location and the initial planning of the Hombu seminar. Finding a seminar location was a massive challenge. We looked and looked and looked. Two problems. One a place. Two, as mentioned, the right license to sign the contract. Of course, we returned immediately to the place where it has been held most often. The Chinese women's judo team trains there and I have a friend on the team. Oddly, they were unwelcoming. Not everyone in Beijing was pleased that we were asked to handle the seminar and some behind-the-scenes interference wouldn't surprise in the Warring States Period of aikido. However, Hombu Dojo was absolutely right to return to rotating the event between dojo. The broad objective is improving aikido in Beijing, not building the prestige of any one dojo.[663] And, my personal objective was to improve

---

[663] My dojo is neutral ground and I'm a Hombu Dojo student, so it makes sense, freeing local people to just enjoy the event on equal terms.

inter-dojo cooperation and jointly host the event.[664] As a starter, in 2011, I'd hosted two "Friendship Practices" at my dojo, inviting other local instructors to come for a joint practice and teach a class. First two dojo, then three dojo came.[665]

Still, we weren't at that level of cooperation yet, so my dojo had lots to do. We persisted with our search and eventually found a place, a sports school where the Chinese Taekwondo team practices, which was nearly perfect. Among other things, it had a nice hotel on the premises and the lakeside area of Houhai was adjacent with plenty of places to eat and local color.[666] Felled three birds with one stone. Still, there were the registration and other forms (in two languages), the restaurants for each meal, the volunteers, the transportation, bottled water (it's hot in June), medical care, building a *shomen*, a gift for participants, a gift for the teacher and on and on. Then I lost my right-hand student to a family emergency. What could I say? "Go take care of your family. You're not allowed to help or attend," is what I said. It was that serious and he'd already helped enough. His absence was a severe blow, but there were teaching and learning opportunities in it. Wonderfully, my other students: Chinese, Japanese, Russian, Spanish, French, all rose to the challenge and lent a stronger hand. In fact, thanks to one student's ingenuity and effort, in particular, we were able to receive the financial support of the Japan Foundation and the endorsement of the Japanese Embassy as well. Both firsts.

But how to improve the event? The 2011 seminar had just three or four hours of aikido over two days. On paper, there were six hours each day: 14:00 to 17:00 on Saturday and the same on Sunday but, apart from ceremonies of state and the Olympics, timeliness is often a challenge here. At past Hombu seminars, organizers might arrive late with the teacher, perhaps very sincerely taking him on some local site-seeing adventure (that he'd perhaps rather miss since he's come to teach). Doing "big" things to impress people is very important here, but the impact of that approach on this seminar has been to reduce practice time. Moreover, the

---

664 One challenge is the locals view the event as a potential money-maker, so services are sacrificed in pursuit of profit.

665 We moved, so I discontinued the events, but a local teacher began organizing some. Unfortunately, only a few dojo go.

666 Beijing traffic is murderous so this arrangement was key. The only travel would be from and to the airport by driver.

location and weather are usually too hot for most people, which slows the pace or further reduces class time. There are also exams for the last hour and half to two hours on Sunday. Maybe there were three classes in total? 2012 had to be different. Trying to encourage some interaction between dojo and local teachers, I established an Instructors Course on Friday night—two hours. Each dojo could bring four people (the teacher and three top students). We could train together and help each other improve, but the spirit of such a special course was lost on some of the locals. [667] Rather than seeing it as a means to unite people, they searched for some advantage to stand out. "Advantage and leverage" are two necessities to surviving in business (or anything) in China.[668] One group phoned and asked, since they had "four" dojo (they practice in different locations on different days of the week), could they bring sixteen students on Friday night? Eh? I just smiled and politely said "no," knowing that in China, appearances count tremendously. Biggest! Most! Original! They wanted to look big to the *shihan* and to their neighbors.

Saturday, the course would be 13:00-18:00, which I knew could end up being at least three and hopefully four hours of genuine training. As a courtesy to visitors, we booked extra time in the room, before and after the training, so the event wouldn't feel rushed (an extra expense). Sunday would be 10:00-12:00 and 13:30-16:30.[669] Examinations would be after lunch on Sunday. Of course, knowing human nature and the local spin on it, the registration rules required that if you wanted to test on Sunday you had to participate in both the Saturday afternoon and Sunday morning sessions, absent specific permission from the organizer. The overriding objective was to act as good hosts for the benefit of Hombu Dojo, everyone attending the event and for the development of aikido in China. In the view of some, it had been run as a money-making enterprise by past organizers.

I'm not going to bore you further by stepping through the timeline.

---

[667] Most understood and showed a good spirit.

[668] Advantage: the other party must need something from you or they won't do as you say. Leverage: you must have some means of compelling the other party's behavior or they won't do as you say.

[669] Incredibly, before printing this book, I saw a post by a dojo on Weibo (China twitter/facebook copycat) that "a seminar is not exercise. There will be plenty of rest between sessions." Lounge chair anyone? Oh, and bring me a refreshing fruity drink with a little parasol in it please.

Miraculously, against heavy odds and perhaps the machinations of oppos-
ing "kingdoms," the event went well. There were nearly eight hours of
aikido. It even started and stopped on time. Of course, there were moments of local color. My driver of five years (whom I used periodically
for airport runs), was a no-show when we were going to pick up sensei.
Telephoned him. No answer. Had seen him the day before and reminded
him. Day before that, my wife had seen him and had reminded him. I
saw him two days before that and had reminded him. Saw him three days
before that and had reminded him. "No problem!" Problem. He probably got offered more money doing something else. Back-up driver? No
answer either. I quickly reduced the welcome committee to: me, my wife
(who sensei knows) our toddler and sent the students in a separate cab to
the school with some remaining supplies. Naturally then, my cab driver
went the wrong way on the expressway. We had to go aaaaalllll the way
into town, miles, before we could finally turn around, backtrack and head
to the airport. Accident? Accidentally on purpose? Zero chance that I
paid him the extra fee he'd tried to trick us into incurring. We made the
airport run in the nick-o'-time.

As an organizer of an event like this here, it can often feel like herding cats.
Broadly speaking, people from different cultures display differing demeanour.
[670] How do you get 100 Canadians out of a swimming pool? "Will you all
please get out of the pool!" How do you get 100 Scots? "Will you all please …?"
"Fack off!"[671] I post forms on our website as PDFs, so that we can receive
hard-copy of registrations and exam applications and we don't have to print
them all. Naturally, everyone asks for Word documents, so they can fill them
in, send us soft copy and have us print them all. Friday night, a group of four
from a certificate-mill tried attending just the Instructors Course. Huh? Sending just four students, when their dojo brags online that it is "the biggest" in
Beijing? This was comically rude. I'd suspected some knucklehead would try
this and a typically local evasive email reply to me earlier in the week, regarding
how many students from their dojo would attend (or wouldn't), had tipped me
off. I replied—twice—and told them they couldn't attend just the Instructors
Course. No reply. A student of mine then went to the gym where they practice,

---

[670] Heck; in countries like China or the U.S. people's broad customary behavior can differ regionally.
Some Chinese say to me it differs city to city.

[671] Actually, trick questions: both places are too cold for pools.

met with the chief instructor and told him point-blank that the Instructors Course was an extra benefit for dojo that fully supported the event. He relayed my polite but clear message, "If you aren't sending your students to the main seminar, you cannot participate Friday night. Sorry."

The reply by the teacher was, "Oh, thank you. We are discussing it tonight." As an American friend of Chinese descent explained to me years ago, in China, "Yes" means maybe; we will be negotiating continually even after we sign the contract. "Maybe" means no. And "No" means I am figuring out whether and, if so, how to kill you. In fact, according to a student from that group, who later joined my dojo, this dojo hadn't even announced the Hombu Dojo seminar to their students. According to another ex-student, the businessman who runs it dare not actually practice at the seminar (he's that ill-trained) and he is worried that students will quit and join other dojo if they attend. So, Friday night? As I'd predicted, four of their students waltz in. "Sorry; you cannot attend. We explained the rules to you very clearly. Three times. Twice in writing. Once face to face." The key point was sincerity.[672] You could not participate in the special event without fully supporting the main event. So, "a little travelling music, maestro!!" They waltzed out. Straight online to smear me from the safety of their computer screens. Ouch.[673]

About thirty-five well-behaved people participated on Friday and it was a good first night. I'd doubted if I could convince some of them to step on the same mat but they did. I even got them all to help wash the mats together before we started (and afterward). Unprecedented, not only because the filthy black water in the buckets said it was probably the first time those mats had ever been cleaned. Disappointingly though, once the training was over, people reverted to form. Only a handful, mostly my students and other foreigners, joined in taking sensei out for food and drink. "Rode the ride, got the t-shirt, let's head home."

Saturday, over 100 people showed up. As the organizer, my opening remarks encouraged everyone to practice well, not to compete with each other and to practice with people from other dojos. Of course, most of them just practiced with students from their own dojo and did whatever

---

[672] I didn't need their fees. We'd received independent financial support for the event.
[673] It wasn't the first time (or the last) I'd been smeared in Chinese chat rooms. The first time, I felt so accepted. One of the tribe!

practice they know from home, not bothering to try to emulate what the teacher was actually showing. Truthfully, three days of aikido was too much for most people. For three days, I couldn't figure out why the prime space in the center of the mat in front of the *shomen* was always so empty of participants. Then a local student explained. "Sensei, everyone practices near the edge of the mat so they can take a break without being noticed and losing face." Really? Okay then.

Sunday's attendance was smaller but it too went smoothly, including the examinations. People here, perhaps like people elsewhere, are absolutely traumatized about failing. Frankly, many should have failed, even some of my own (who I'd let test just for the experience of being under pressure) but the *shihan* was gracious, passed them all and reminded them to correct their errors in daily practice. This makes all the sense in the world in Japan and perhaps some other places, but here? Now? The likely internal dialogue of the average examinee while the *shihan* admonished them was, "I got the certificate! I got the certificate!"

Thankfully, the seminar ended without major incidents or serious injuries, apart from some treatment for exhaustion, which was a wonder since most people (domestic or foreign) didn't seem to be moving fast enough to be tired. The medical assistance and bottled water proved handy. The classic bit about the free water was the out-of-towners (non-Beijingers) hoarding three and four bottles rather than just the two per-person per-day we'd advised.[674] In the end, the event was a miraculous success. No doubt there were mistakes by the organizer. There is room for improvement in coming years, but considering what we'd been up against just sixty days prior, I was very pleased and extremely proud of my students—foreign and domestic. I still remain hopeful that subsequent events can be hosted cooperatively, by the various dojo in Beijing.[675]

Isn't that one of the attractive aspects of China? The potential? So many people? So much development to do? One of the great ancient cultures of the world modernizing? So don't misinterpret my remarks.

---

[674] Read a bit of Chinese history and you may appreciate the mentality.

[675] I say the same thing every year about the local Hombu Dojo seminar. If you want me to organize, I'll do it. If you want me to organize with someone else, I'll do it. If you want me merely to attend, I'll do it. I support it to support it. Not for "face". Not for money. Not for any gain. Supporting your home dojo is just what you do. What is important is what is good for Aikido in Beijing, for the development of Chinese students and the local community.

It's much more interesting reading observations of the unusual rather than some whitewashed politically sensitive phony account. I truly enjoy the adventure of China, learning about its ancient culture and getting to know "The Chinese People" of today. "The Chinese People." That's a misleading phrase, frankly, because it suggests a kind of dull, borg-like uniformity of look, thought and action that belies the individuality of the people I meet. Heck, people from different regions of "China" sometimes can't even understand each other. The language can differ considerably. I was speaking last week with a middle-aged lady in Beijing. After overcoming her "Oh my God; the white monkey can talk" reaction when I spoke to her, she exclaimed "Wow. I understand your Chinese much better than all those country people from Sichuan and Yunan. Wish they'd leave Beijing."

Despite the discord and all my tales, you shouldn't look down on aikido in China. After just ten years, is it much different from aikido in countless other countries where it has been grafted onto a very different local culture?[676] Unqualified teachers. Promoting students to make money. Promoting students to build dojo empires. Competing factions. Even so, aikido in China has all the potential in the world, if it develops properly. Trained teachers, genuine practice, uncompromising adherence to standards and principles are each vital, even if achieved in just a few spots on the map. Or, will aikido careen wildly off the path, being compromised and otherwise sullied for some misguided agenda? Will it fall victim to chauvinist attack? "Originally from China!" bellows the TV ad for a martial arts program on CCTV 5. "Biggest! Most! First!" Such claims seem very important in the PRC, from what I've experienced. "Aikido comes from China, because Ueshiba Morihei studied Chinese martial arts in Manchuria!" Total nonsense but, believe me, it could happen.[677]

Whither China? Or rather, aikido in China? Who knows!? The world has a way of turning out differently than "experts" tell us it will. Otherwise, the experts would just lay their bets with brokers and retire with their winnings to massive yachts—shuttling between the Med and Caribbean—and wouldn't need to be "experts" any longer. Does it matter if aikido grows

---

[676] China and Japan may be close geographically and Japan may have borrowed (and modified) a lot of culture from the Tang dynasty (AD 618–907), but the two cultures couldn't be more different in many core ways.

[677] A cynical friend says, "they'll probably create a department in a government ministry to "research" and "prove" it.

in China? If you want to make money off aikido, yes. If you want to maintain it as an art form, probably not. The rest of the world is and has been doing just fine with aikido, without China, for many years. But there's no reason to exclude PRC people from this meaningful path of personal development; of course! However, including them doesn't mean patronizing them with easy examinations, rapid promotions or otherwise lax enforcement of standards and rules. That's insulting. Detrimental to them. Detrimental to aikido.

If Chinese people really want to become skilled *aikidoka*, then they need to do what it takes to earn it, just like everyone else has done. The lack of local teachers makes it all the more important that they go to Japan, live there, study Japanese, train at Hombu Dojo, learn and improve.[678] I don't mean just go for a visit or to take some examination there, which the Japanese, being ever gracious hosts and sensitive towards China and twentieth century history, will be highly likely to allow you to pass. Commit to really learning aikido. Sacrifice the time, sweat and blood it takes to do so.

Maybe the question is, what do Chinese aikido students want? Zhēn-de (真的) or jiǎ-de (假的)?[679] Real or fake? It's a daily question in China. Many Chinese I've met won't care about the quality. "Which way makes me money?" "Which gives me prestige?" That's the typical criteria, in order of importance. But some locals genuinely do care. They do understand. They want the real thing. In my experience, they are certainly just as capable as any other people on the planet of working hard and doing well, if given the real chance to do so.

One thing's for certain: China, aikido in China, will continue to be an adventure. You may be able to guide it or influence it, but you cannot control it. That's the thing about adventures. You don't quite know where all the bends and twists in the road lie ahead. That's exactly what makes the experience so real, so alive. Like aikido practice, too predictable and

---

[678] Some PRC Chinese will be shocked to learn that no, Japanese culture is not just some copy of Chinese culture (as they are taught in school). The English language has upwards of 2,000 French words, but nobody's ever going to confuse an Englishman with a Frenchman.

[679] Hear them pronounced on the MDBG Chinese/English dictionary at www.mdbg.net/chindict/chindict.php.

it's merely lifeless form. It's the unpredictability, the risk that's the spark of liveliness. And, how you respond to it makes your life. So the question remains. What do you want? Zhēn-de or jiǎ-de?

> Day after day we can't help growing older.
> Year after year spring can't help seeming younger.
> Come let's enjoy our winecup today,
> Not pity the flowers fallen!
> - 王維 (Wáng Wéi, AD 699-759)
> Tang Dynasty Poet and Painter

About the Author

William was born behind the Orange Curtain (Orange County) in Southern California but at age six trekked north to the Bay Area (NoCal) before returning to SoCal for college at U.C.L.A and later law school. He worked as a trial attorney and an emerging companies lawyer, before starting an advisory/investment business, Tiger Capital Partners, sourcing deals in East Asia (China, Japan and Korea) for London based and other investment houses. He currently resides in Beijing (with breaks in London, Tokyo and Seoul) with his beloved wife Angela and precious four year old daughter wee Isla. William is the founder and chief instructor of Beijing Aikikai, which is a not for profit dojo dedicated to bringing authentic Aikido practice to local people and developing Chinese teachers for the benefit of Aikido in China.

Printed in Great Britain
by Amazon